The Visual Object of Desire
in Late Medieval England

THE MIDDLE AGES SERIES

Ruth Mazo Karras, Series Editor

Edward Peters, Founding Editor

A complete list of books in the series
is available from the publisher.

The Visual Object of Desire
in Late Medieval England

Sarah Stanbury

PENN

UNIVERSITY OF PENNSYLVANIA PRESS

Philadelphia

Published by
University of Pennsylvania Press
Philadelphia, Pennsylvania 19104-4112

Printed in the United States of America on acid-free paper

10 9 8 7 6 5 4 3 2 1

A Cataloging-in-Publication record is available from the Library of Congress

ISBN-13: 978-0-8122-4038-2

ISBN-10: 0-8122-4038-3

For Bob

Contents

INTRODUCTION: PREMODERN FETISHES   I

FETISH, IDOL, ICON

1. KNIGHTON'S LOLLARDS, CAPGRAVE'S *KATHERINE*,
AND WALTER HILTON'S "MERK YMAGE"   33

2. THE DESPENSER RETABLE AND 1381   76

CHAUCER'S SACRAMENTAL POETIC

3. CHAUCER AND IMAGES   95

4. TRANSLATING GRISELDA   122

5. THE CLERGEON'S TONGUE   153

MOVING PICTURES

6. NICHOLAS LOVE'S *MIRROR:*
DEAD IMAGES AND THE LIFE OF CHRIST   172

7. ARTS OF SELF-PATRONAGE IN *THE
BOOK OF MARGERY KEMPE*   191

NOTES   219

WORKS CITED   259

INDEX   279

ACKNOWLEDGMENTS   291

Introduction

Premodern Fetishes

ONE OF THE MOST STARTLING SURVIVALS of English gothic architecture
is the Lady Chapel at Ely Cathedral. Begun in 1321 and completed in 1349,
the chapel is an undivided, open structure measuring 100 feet long by over
40 feet wide, the widest span of any English church, with vaulting soaring
to 60 feet (fig. 1). It seems, on first sight, cavernous.[1] The sense of empti-
ness may derive partly from the effect of light; except for tracery and lancet-
head remains assembled on the south wall, the five vertical windows on
each side contain clear glass, as do the great east and west windows. It also
may come from the absence of color. Walls, ceiling, and floor appear now
almost entirely as gray limestone and marble (fig. 2). Yet starkness comes

Figure 1. West façade. Lady Chapel, 1321–40s, Ely Cathedral. Photo: V. Raguin.

through most dramatically due to the absence of images. Even though a circuit of carved canopied niches runs around the walls beneath the windows, all of them are empty; and although some figures remain, as in the spandrels above, the heads of virtually all them have been cut off. All of the 147 extant statues of Mary and other saints had their heads knocked off in a purging inspired by Reformation iconoclasm—carried out, so one story goes, in the late 1530s by Thomas Cromwell's men, who rode through the chapel on horses, smashing the glass with their pikes and lopping off the heads of images with their swords, leaving the chapel a gallery of the headless (fig. 3).[2] To call the Lady Chapel a gothic survival is in fact a misnomer, since its architectural attitude today, a kind of grand simplicity, owes far more to Reformation image breakers than to the fourteenth-century craftsmen who designed its space and decorated its interior.

Reflecting in *The Idolatrous Eye* on the dramatic iconoclasm that transformed this space, Michael O'Connell also pictures Ely's chapel as a point of departure for, in his case, a study in tensions of the visual in early modern theater. What made its sculptures and its glass painting so abhorrent to sensibilities in the 1540s that they had to be defaced?[3] My first visit, in the mid-1990s, to this haunting survival made me wonder what was lost:

Figure 2. Interior. Lady Chapel, Ely Cathedral. Photo: V. Raguin.

What would the Ely Lady Chapel have looked like in the fourteenth and fifteenth centuries? Inference from contemporary iconography and from the surviving program indicates a particularly concerted, spare-no-expense effort for the spectacular effect.[4] Niches were filled with images of saints and bishops, while a narrative life and miracles of the Virgin circulated in the spandrels above. The carving, as Nicola Coldstream observes, was exceptional for its grace and detailing.[5] Color was used for vivid and dramatic effect. Surviving stained-glass fragments suggest that all the windows would have been fully glazed. The interior as a whole, which a nineteenth-century architectural historian described as "one of the grandest specimens of medieval architecture," was decorated in "figures of roses, lilies, and crosses, painted in prominent colours on a ground of whitewash."[6]

Little of this remains; and indeed, only a small percentage of the devotional material culture of pre-Reformation England as a whole is still extant today. Many of the objects we can see today exist in mutilated form, like the Seven Sacraments Font in Norwich Cathedral (fig. 4). Ely's Lady Chapel is a fascinating memorial in the history of the object, testimony to the vital linkages in late medieval and Reformation England of "art" with patronage, power, and ethical passions. The century and a half preceding the Royal Injunctions of September 1538, when parish officers were ordered to remove images from their churches, saw a dramatic efflorescence in devotional art of all kinds, not only in England but also across Europe.[7] Historians have amply documented this dramatic proliferation. Images of the saints offer just one example. Eamon Duffy, who has written extensively on the vitality of fifteenth-century lay worship, remarks on the "luxuriant flourishing of the devotion to the saints" as manifested in the long inventories of images and painted pictures that could be found in most fifteenth-century parishes.[8] As Richard Marks has recently noted, the flourishing of saints' images in the fifteenth century reflected a transformation in their cultic use from distanced iconic objects to personalized

Figure 3. Compound canopies, ground range. Lady Chapel, Ely Cathedral. Photo: S. Stanbury.

Figure 4. Seven Sacraments Font. Chapel of St. Luke, Norwich Cathedral.
Photo: V. Raguin.

intercessionary agents. Proliferating on chantry altars and on murals covering parish walls, saints' images transformed the nave, the single public space of the parish church, from unadorned aisle to gallery.[9] Saints, newly personalized, also came to face the parish congregation on painted screens separating the chancel from the nave. An early fifteenth-century innovation, screens painted with images of the saints and holy family multiplied in "dazzling array" throughout English parishes, as Paul Binski says.[10] Saints also appeared on painted wooden panels, a new portable kind of devotional object,[11] and as wood and alabaster carvings, either freestanding or in bas relief. In addition to images of saints, paintings and statues of Christ's life and Passion, of the Trinity, of bishops, and of lay and even clerical donors also proliferated throughout churches and cathedrals in late medieval England. As Michael Camille comments, late medieval Europe saw an "image-explosion" that profoundly altered the relationship between viewers and devotional objects: "Guy Debord's *Society of the Spectacle* did not suddenly come about in the twentieth century; its roots lay in the multiplication of image investment, in altars, statues, paintings, and windows that cluttered the medieval church."[12]

The chapters in this book, spanning the period from the 1380s to the mid-1400s, examine the dynamic image culture of late medieval England through the responses of its textual commentators. Through a reading of literary texts—and in one case, an altarpiece—I explore how the representation of devotional images in those texts engages with performances staged by what we might think of as the premier vehicle of the medieval media: the church, with its daily performances of sacred ritual in spaces visually illustrated with its founding narratives by statues in wood and alabaster, stained glass, embroidery, and panel and wall painting. As these writings and objects demonstrate, England in the late Middle Ages was keenly attuned to and even troubled by its "culture of the spectacle," whether spectacle took the form of a newly made queen as in Chaucer's *Clerk's Tale*, or of representation of Christ's life and death, as we see in Norwich Cathedral's Despenser Retable and in Nicholas Love's *Mirror of the Blessed Life of Jesus Christ*.

Although visual evidence of England's image culture has been largely destroyed or moved to museums, testimony to a world of powerfully animate devotional forms survives in the rhetoric of affective piety. The desire to see, expressed so insistently in late medieval religious lyrics and dream-vision poetry, might even have been voiced, in part, as a response to a culture of images and their strategic deployment in liturgical spectacle.

A striking and recurring feature of the representation of visual experience in late medieval England is the expression of desire—at times profoundly erotic, at other times deeply spiritual—such that we may describe the drive to *see* as one of the great passions and great myths structuring medieval representation. The desire to see fuels some of the most important prose and poetry of the late Middle Ages, shaping the language of desire in lyrics of the Passion, with their repeated calls to look on the suffering Christ; structuring the trajectories of desire in dream visions such as *Pearl*; offering a set of terms for meditation in the *Shewings* of Julian of Norwich; grounding the narrative of religious instruction in Love's *Mirror of the Blessed Life of Jesus Christ*; and offering defining metaphors for Chaucer's explorations of love, sanctity, and chivalric spectacle. In many texts the gaze itself, the very privilege of vision, is not only a solitary desire but a carefully orchestrated act mediated by others who tell the viewer how and what to see. The gaze, articulated by rich material displays of devotional images, even can emerge as a prize in a contest or a struggle to see—a vision contest. Seeing has the extraordinary and transformative power of witnessing: to look on the beloved, to look on the grail, to see the elevation of the host, to stand face to face with God.

Yet even when visual desire takes as its goal a purely mystical sight beyond the material world, the mechanics of vision link it with sensory experience and even material objects. As recent work on medieval visuality has shown, writings about vision and on optics in the Middle Ages often understand sight to be a property of physical contiguity. In looking we are connected physically to the object we see by the agency of species, or visual rays. Images, through their species, literally touch us, linking us physically with them in ways that underwrite the dramatic physicality of late medieval affective piety.[13] When we desire to feel Christ's pain as we look on his suffering body, our empathy is charged by a physical as well as emotional cathexis. And is this a desire for Christ the exemplar, or is it for Christ as image, come to life? At the moment of consecration and elevation during the Eucharist, the host becomes Christ's living flesh, a transformation that occurs at the moment when it is held up before the congregation. Affixing or transfixing the gaze, the inanimate object becomes a living body.[14] Discourses on images in the late Middle Ages repeatedly instruct us to use images only as devotional aids to get to the ideas beyond them; we are exhorted to worship the idea beyond the image and not the image itself. Images themselves seem to confuse this hermeneutic, however. What do we love, the thing or the idea behind the thing? The carving and color at Ely's Lady Chapel, in the fourteenth and fifteenth centuries fully comparable to the splendor of Paris's St. Chapelle, in many ways celebrate the pleasures of objects. The spectral lives of images in the popular imagination suggest that images crossed the lines between matter and spirit or the living and the dead. In the language of affective piety, object and exemplar often seem to fuse uncannily, as desires to see, touch, know the suffering Christ are articulated in relation to a body that often seems very like Passion scenes carved above the rood screen or on alabaster panels in a parish's side chapels.

Voicing the most direct responses to England's visual culture were Wycliffite attacks on devotional images, critiques that sparked a complex debate on the role of devotional objects in public life. In the late 1380s and 1390s, statements arguing both for and against the uses of images were emerging from both university and lay circles, chiefly but not exclusively in connection with the Lollard movement.[15] As studies by W. R. Jones and Margaret Aston have shown, Wyclif himself was moderate about abuses of images, writing in his "Treatise on the Decalogue," the *Tractatus de mandatis divinis* of 1375–76, that although images can be worshipped for deviant forms of pleasure, they can serve to rouse the faithful: "It is evident that images may be made both well and ill: well in order to rouse, assist and kindle the minds of the faithful to love God more devoutly; and ill when by reason of images there is deviation from the true faith, as when the image is worshipped with *latria* or *dulia*, or unduly delighted in for its beauty, costliness, or attachment to irrelevant circumstances."[16] Within Wycliffite writings, however, opposition to images was the chief distinguishing feature from the beginning of the movement until the end,[17] generating public response as early as 1383 when Thomas Brinton, bishop of Rochester, delivered an Easter sermon that included the statement that heretics "newly preach and assert that the cross of Christ and images should not be worshipped."[18] Arguments pro and con, defending the uses of images as visible texts for the laity and attacking carved images and pilgrimages as twin forms of idolatry, emerged as a topic of heated academic debate and public controversy in the last decade of the fourteenth century, according to Aston.[19] Wyclif's acknowledgment that images can serve as useful guides to Christians as well as his cautionary note about the possibility of abuse when we love the thing and not the form of devotion to which the object is directing us were to become the chief points in a growing public debate, which itself portended the mass destruction of devotional images in the iconoclasm of the sixteenth century.

Central to this debate, and implicit in Wyclif's own statements, is acknowledgment of a problematic interpretive line, hard to make out, where legitimate *use* of an image for spiritual ends shifts into possession, and worship before images slips into idolatry, worship of the thing itself rather than the abstraction to which the thing directs us. The debate about images took place not only across the lines of orthodoxy and heresy but also within orthodox circles as a central component of a reformist polemic, and consistently pointed to problems of interpreting "correct" or legitimate use. Just as Walter Hilton uses the "merk image" as a provocative metaphor for desire and disgust, as I argue in Chapter 1, writings on images by his contemporaries, both orthodox and Wycliffite, grants to them a mesmeric corporeality, disciplining the subject before the image with a moral rhetoric that in our own time might be reserved for sexual deviance.

A text that dramatizes, in dialogue form, the problems of distinguishing between rightful and idolatrous uses of images is *Dives and Pauper*, an anonymous treatise on the Ten Commandments that has been dated to the period 1405–10.[20] This text is important as one of the fullest surviving contributions to the debate on images from pre-Reformation England and also one that dramatizes, in its dialogue form, the social desires and public anxieties surrounding images in the church. In the First Precept or dialogue on graven images, Dives, who, according to Priscilla Heath Barnum, personifies the text's intended audience and represents the newly literate and worldly class, is advised and instructed on how to worship images by Pauper (the voice of orthodox rectitude) before the discussion shifts into a long analysis of astrology, human will, and God's authority.[21] Asking questions that doubtless the reader of the book would be expected to be able to answer correctly, Dives takes the part of a rube, a credulous but troubled literalist who has trouble distinguishing between objects and signs; for in fact the interpretation of signs forms the subtext of the First Precept. Much in the same way that the questions asked in Q-and-A articles in popular magazines will often seem obtuse, even embarrassingly so, and hence create a safe space for the airing of our most intimate fears, the anxious ordinariness of Dives (who is us) makes us willing to listen to the smart Pauper (not us, but one who occupies the moral high ground). Worried about the proper responses to images in a world in which images are proliferating, Dives shows himself a conformist concerned with doing the right thing in a changing world: to what extent should he be like everybody else and do as other "men doon"? "And þow meen doon makyn þese dayis ymages gret plente bothin in cherche and out of cherche, and alle meen, as me thynkyзt, wurshepyn ymagys, and it is wol hard to me but that I doo in þat as alle meen doon, & ȝyf Y wurshepe hem me thynkyȝt I doo ydolatrye and aȝens Godys lawe."[22] To Dives's question about how to respond to images, "how shulde I rede in þe book of peynture and of ymagerye?," Pauper, who defends their uses, offers a line that doubtless had the familiarity of a catechism by the early 1400s, "worship God and not the image": "wurshepe hym abouyn alle thyngge, nought þe ymage, nought þe stok, stoon ne tree, but hym þat deyid on þe tree for þi synne . . . so pat þu knele, ȝyf þu wylt, aforn þe ymage nought to þe ymage."[23] This dialogue, introducing the commentary on the Commandments that comprises the text, clearly points to public or lay doubts about the relationship between ordinary members of a church community (Dives) and the material and ritual structure of the church, for Dives repeatedly expresses concerns that other members of the congregation and even the clergy, during the performance of the Mass, seem to be worshipping images themselves rather than using them as signs for God. Even though Dives voices concerns central to the Lollards, saying early on, "Qherof seruyn þese ymagys? I wolde þey weryn brent euerychon," even implying here that images are like heretics, appropriate for burning, the dialogue form allows his voice safe play.[24] Through Pauper's answer, the text can expound an orthodox defense of images while also voicing concerns that traverse a cross section of positions. Dives's wish that images be burned even voices a social reality that would have lent his question and wish a particularly dramatic frisson in the years following the 1401 edict, "De heretico comburendo," licensing the burning of heretics. Speaking from the position of a Lollard who wants all images to be burned, he also points to the fate of Lollards who make that very claim.

The distinctions between images and idols, implied in the dialogue between Dives and Pauper, receives a particularly clear illustration in a miniature from a manuscript of Lydgate's *Pilgrimage of the Life of Man*.[25] Both the Lydgate text and the accompanying illustration expressly highlight the link between idols and human manufacture and articulate as well how worship of the sculpted idol should be separated from "right worship" of images of the saints. In a colored drawing from a Lydgate manuscript (1430–50) Dame Idolatry, partially concealed by the supporting timber, shows Pilgrim an idol, an "ymage . . . crownyd lyk a kyng"[26] (fig. 5). A man kneels in front of this idol in a posture of worship, and on the floor are scattered chisels and other tools that expressly identify this idol as an object of human construction. As Idolatry (undermining her own position) explains, the man is the carpenter who has made the idol, forging with his two hands, "hys handys tweyne," an object that will not help him at all:

> The same selue carpenter
> Dyde a-forn hys bysy peyne
> To forge hym, wyth hys handys tweyne
> And make hym ffyrst off swych entaylle
> And wot he may nothyng avaylle
> To helpe hym, whan that al lys do. (20934–39)

In marked contrast to this picture of the idol as a made object, the next image in the manuscript illustrates the orthodox positioning of the self before devotional pictures (fig. 6). Men kneel before a raised altar on which a crucifix is flanked by six saints and apostles, Katherine to the far left and Margaret on the right. Pilgrim voices the standard defense: Worship the idea behind the form, "the holy seyntes / off whom they beryn the lyknesse," and not the form itself:

Figure 5. Pilgrim and Dame Idolatry observe a carpenter with tools kneeling before enthroned idol. Lydgate, *Pilgrimage of the Life of Man*, BL MS Cott. Tib. AVII, fol. 65v, 1430–50. © British Library Board. All rights reserved.

Ffor, sothly, we nothyng laboure
The ymages to honoure,
Stook nor ston, nor that men peyntes;
But we honoure the holy seyntes
Off whom they beryn the lyknesse. (20977–81)

The idol, in marked contrast, is dead "as ston or tre" (20927).[27]

The demarcation pictured in this manuscript between the idol who is as dead as stock and stone and the ordered, hieratic devotional tableau that should direct our attention beyond the images to their abstract exemplars is very neat—and perhaps even deceptively clear. In a recent analysis of these images, Michael Camille suggests that the illuminators might actually have been using the apparent contrast to equate them, showing image worship as another form of idolatry.[28] Most late medieval commentary on devotional images, either pro or con, recognizes that the line is often blurred: people believe, however mistakenly, that images themselves perform the miracles.

Figure 6. Altar with crucifix. Lydgate, *Pilgrimage of the Life of Man*, London, BL MS Cott. Tib. AVII, fol. 68, 1430–50. © British Library Board. All rights reserved.

Concerns about devotional art as voiced in reformist polemic may
also have been fueled by perceived inequities in visual privilege: who gets
closest to the object, who gets their name inscribed in the image. As I discuss below, widespread discussions that arose in reformist texts underscore
the close ties between images, visual regimes, and capital—the formative
desires linking the gaze and its objects. Painters of crucifixes, a Wycliffite
sermon writes, expend resources that should be used for the poor; they
also distort history and mislead the public will by visually transforming
stories of apostolic poverty to spectacles of luxury. The rich order up rich
images to mirror their "owne cursid lif," and images come to signify not the
ethics of sacrifice but the pleasures of the marketplace.[29] In their public
condemnation of devotional images, Lollard reformers—perhaps allud-
ing pointedly to a particular crucifix or image of a popular saint even as
they preached—were commenting broadly on the uses and abuses of public image-making in their time, targeting in their critiques not just images
but also the system of their production, circulation, and reception. In ways
that seem prophetic of postmodern studies of ideology formation, these
polemical texts are shrewdly attuned to the ways that a culture can imagine itself in its visual icons. They also seem fully aware of the powers of
spectacle, in turn, over the public will—of how images operate, in Žižek's
words, as the "sublime object[s] of ideology." Do we worship the idea
behind the object, or is it the beautiful object itself that we adore? How
do we position the self in relation to a devotional image and still heed the
second commandment forbidding worship of graven images? Less clearly
articulated but also central to what we might call the "image debate" were
social and economic anxieties: Where do we locate ourselves in a material
field in which images are proliferating, the technologies of production and
display are rapidly transforming, and the liquid capital for endowing and
even purchasing images is becoming increasingly (if unequally) available?
Voices from the image debate express anxieties about *objects*; images are
not only devotional signs but are also forms of circulating capital, part of
the culture of things.

This book contributes to a broader inquiry that has increasingly recognized the profound impact of these debates on contemporary aesthetics
and practices of representation. Art historians, especially Michael Camille,
have drawn our attention to the close discursive ties between devotional
images and idols in late medieval writings and representation.[30] Is our veneration of images and our pleasure in their traditional housing in the parish a form of idolatry, a corrupt worship of mammon? Kathleen Scott has

speculated that Lollardy may have had a decisive and impoverishing effect on English manuscript illumination from the 1390s on, as insular painters, responding to the censorship of Lollard doctrine, shied away from the techniques of naturalism that were flourishing in Continental work.[31] Scholars have only begun to address the effects of Lollardy, and its suppression, on literature in late medieval England, but as recent research has suggested, the impact was profound and wide-ranging, particularly as crystallized in Arundel's Constitutions of 1407–9, which made it heretical to read Wyclif's books and also new books on religious matters that had not received approval by a panel of theologians approved by the archbishop.[32] David Aers, Lynn Staley, and Nicholas Watson have contributed important reassessments of Langland and of Julian of Norwich's mystical discourse, demonstrating the close connections between allegorical and mystical self-fashioning and broader political/theological debates.[33] Work by Watson as well as James Simpson has argued that acts of censorship that began in 1382 with the outlawing of writings by Wyclif and escalated in 1401 by the statute authorizing the burning of heretics had a profound, even impoverishing, impact on many forms of cultural production, though the extent of that impact is the subject of debate.[34] A centralized Lancastrian authority that consolidated its powers, in part, through the aggressive suppression of Lollardy decreased possibilities for social critique and dramatically narrowed the range of subjects and approaches available for vernacular writers.[35]

This book, taking as its primary focus literary and artistic productions from the last decades of the fourteenth and the first half of the fifteenth centuries, works to understand how writers deploy accounts of sight and images to articulate some of the ideological and material concerns of late medieval England, particularly as those anxieties were inflected by the image debate. English discourses on vision from these years are often disciplinary, couched not in the mantra of denial ("see no evil . . .") but rather enunciated through explicit instructions for *how* to see, as if seeing were a personal and social *habitus* or practice that one learns through individual and group discipline. Discourses on the gaze and its objects sometimes take the form of a contest or debate and in this form, I argue, respond to contemporary debates about images and emergent tensions of an increasingly material culture. The pressures fueling this vision contest can be traced to increasing contestation about the uses and control of social space, and chiefly the church and its treasures. In late medieval England a vision contest staged as well a debate about access to the spaces in which devotional images were housed—for example, the choir, the high altar, and the private chapels of local parishes and of major cathedrals, filled in pre-Reformation England with a brilliant array of devotional images in panel painting, sculpture, and stained glass, many of these objects gifts of prosperous lay patrons. Polemical writings that attempt to mark out the boundary between acceptable and idolatrous uses of images may thus also be voicing tensions about property and exchange, exacerbated particularly in a time of increased circulation of capital and the increased production and proliferation of manufactured goods—and among those goods, devotional images themselves. For saints, of course, are promissory, their uses transactional: One prays to a saint for something—for luck, fertility, the safety and well-being of loved ones, the speedy passage of one's own soul and the souls of others through purgatory. The saint's image is apotropaic to the body in a system of circulation, and the saint's own occupation of matter, taking on transactional properties of matter, is centrally at stake in the debate. Devotional images trouble reformers, I suggest, not only because they threaten a material intrusion in the devotional sphere but also because they signify the very market-based operations of the spiritual system itself.

It is this anxious discourse about images in public spaces and private worship that forms the backdrop to this book, which offers readings of important texts from the beginning of the image controversy in the 1380s until the middle of the fifteenth century. How do writers construct discourses on devotion within the terms of this debate, using devotional images to imagine or discipline the ethical lives of their readers? Devotional objects were social objects, bound to the community through ties of politics and patronage. As I argue below, in late medieval reformist polemic, devotional objects display many of the same uncanny ties to commodities and even sexuality that would be targeted in much later discussions, which invented the term "fetish" to label objects that we love too much or that circulate as forms of "abnormal traffic." Chapter 1 then examines several texts in which objects and female bodies interface as fetish forms: Knighton's commentary on Lollard destruction of an image of St. Katherine; Walter Hilton's uses of the "merk ymage" as a figure for idolatrous flesh; and John Capgrave's *St. Katherine*, which offers a rich commentary on the morphology and powers of iconic forms through the actions of the saint and also of her token, the wheel. An image metaphorically comes to life, I argue, in Henry Knighton's account of the burning of a Katherine statue and in Capgrave's *Life of St. Katherine*, a compelling and popular narrative that pictures the saint as an embodied devotional image in a struggle against idolatry, with her famous wheel as both fetish item and idol. Then taking a look at a devotional painting that demonstrates complex social and political links to the community, Chapter 2 examines the Despenser Retable, a large altarpiece given to Norwich Cathedral in the 1380s, and takes up a long-standing scholarly hypothesis that the altarpiece was given to Norwich Cathedral as a thank-you gift for the suppression of the 1381 rebellion. Outlining Despenser's role in the suppression of the revolt, this chapter reads the panels themselves as a Passion text that should be understood in the context of the painting's frame, blazoned by the coats of arms of important local families.

In the second section, "Chaucer's Sacramental Poetic," I consider Chaucer's responses to the image debate as well as his own figurations of ritual spectacle. In a kind of counter discourse to Hilton and Knighton, Chaucer's poems from the 1380s and 1390s take a decidedly skeptical approach to images and the systems of public credulity that they subtend. As I argue in Chapter 3, Chaucer may have responded to the image debate by a practical strategy of avoidance. In his poetry, even his most overtly devotional, such as the *Tale of St. Cecilia* or the *Prioress's Tale*, we find virtually no descriptions of popular devotional forms, such as the Trinity, the crucifix, the saints, or scenes from the life of Christ and the holy family. Although Chaucer describes "images" with precise detail, evincing a keen interest in objects of representation, he restricts ekphrasis, the description of a work of art, entirely to images that would have been classed as pagan idols—and hence safely outside the contested discourse. Nevertheless, the phobic account of relics in the *Pardoner's Tale* and the drama of a devotional daisy in the Prologue to the *Legend of Good Women*, both texts that echo language from Wycliffite sect vocabulary, suggest that Chaucer was well attuned to nuances of reformist discourse on devotional objects of all kinds, even if he engages with those debates only through irony or play. Chapters 4 and 5 take a close look not at images themselves but at sacramental spectacle and staged performance, or more exactly, at the uses of characters as devotional icons, in two of Chaucer's most troubling "religious" tales. Paired chapters on the *Clerk's Tale* and the *Prioress's Tale* examine Chaucer's representations of sacramental transformation in the context of his abiding interest in the relationship between the private will and public spectacle—the tensions between iconic bodies and uses people have for them.

Chapters in the third section, "Moving Pictures," explore texts in which Christ operates as a dynamic image, a figure articulated within reformist discourse on devotional icons and animated by a carefully orchestrated devotional gaze. The last chapters examine two well-known fifteenth-century texts, the *Mirror of the Blessed Life of Jesus Christ* and the *Book of Margery Kempe*. Both of these texts adopt explicitly orthodox positions against Lollardy, and both of them picture Christ as a living person, even one, as Kempe's text demonstrates, to whom we can speak. Through this animate Christ these texts offer a metacommentary on the vital life of images in the contemporary devotional world. In the *Mirror*, Nicholas Love engages with the image debate through a kind of conjuring, invoking the fifteenth-century parish with its displays of pictures through his spectral appeals to "imagination." The *Mirror* locates its reader/viewer before "live images," as opposed to the "dead images" condemned in reformist literature, staging a direct intervention in the image debate by orchestrating an ideal gaze and its objects. In her *Book*, Margery Kempe also imagines Christ as animate, engaged with her in compassionate dialogue not just as a spectral presence but also as a devotional image. Kempe seems to have been aware of uses of donor images, and in her *Book* works to connect herself to the material fabric of the churches that she names by imagining herself in the role of donor/patron, speaking to and kneeling before a Christ that may take pictorial form from the iconography of the indulgenced Man of Sorrows.

As these readings collectively show, writers found multiple ways of responding to England's image culture and image debate. All of the texts discussed in this book seem to recognize, however, that devotional images are complexly tied to the performance of power; images work as agents in the service of systems of authority—though as we see in the chapter on Margery Kempe, ordinary, lay women could find ways to lay claim to them. Vehemently condemned from some quarters, passionately defended from others, devotional images in late fourteenth- and fifteenth-century England work as touchstones for many social and economic hot topics; witness, for example, Chaucer's brilliant satire in the *Pardoner's Tale*, where the selling of false relics, old bones and rags, gives a dramatic illustration of corrupt ecclesiastical practices. The Pardoner's relics do not just give us a commentary on the selling of indulgences but also engage with the contemporary discourse on devotional images in general, a conversation with increasingly high stakes in positioning its participants on issues of orthodoxy and dissent.

The uses of devotional images and sacramental display, whether addressed polemically or imaginatively, as in the texts discussed in this book, are questions with religious, economic, and social import. As the "image-explosion" dramatically changed the interiors of fourteenth- and fifteenth-century English churches, it also altered the relationships among lay patrons who donated or underwrote the images and the clergy who used them in the performance of the Mass. The image explosion linked the parish and the public in vital new alliances and conflicts, particularly as it fueled a debate that helped redefine the terms of orthodoxy and dissent. The texts discussed in this book show contemporary writers grappling with the ethics of the object, both its pleasures and its seductions. If the theatrical display of ritual objects in a text provokes sharp emotional responses from its reader or from its characters, those reactions bespeak as well a response to the image debate out there in the world. They also describe a relationship to the *habitus* of the image, the physical spaces and cultural performances by which images were graphically and often strategically displayed. Recent studies of English parish culture in the late Middle Ages have inspired a vigorous reappraisal of the connections between the material world of church life—the parish buildings and their rich collection of images, fabrics, glass, and plate—and the economic and social life of communities.[36] Discourses about images and spectacle in late medieval texts are in conversation both with the controversies sparked by reformist polemic and with things themselves, the devotional fetish objects that made up the material fabric of ritual life.

The Premodern Fetish

To speak of a fetish is to speak of an object that always carries an obsessional trace. As object, the fetish occupies a zone of illegitimacy, somewhere between excess and insubstantiality: too much, not enough. The fetishist's desire is both insatiable and inauthentic. Always in excess of the object of its fixation, it is fixed in things even as it announces their lack. If I fetishize shoes—or even houses, as Marjorie Garber's book *Sex and Real Estate* suggests is a possibility—shoes and houses stand in for other desires I might not choose to acknowledge or even know I have. As a label, "fetish" carries with it an outlaw pleasure. I do not announce or admit myself to be a fetishist—for fetishes are items of "abnormal traffic."[37] The fetish is generally the fixation of somebody else.

This gift of fetish fixations to others, whether those named are identified as primitives or sexual deviants, is closely bound up with the history of the term. Recent studies of the fetish, turning the spotlight onto the term as a speech act, have focused attention on its history as a discursive mark: what we talk about when we talk about the fetish. If I would prefer not to be called a fetishist, it is partially because the fetish implies a disavowal of spirit for matter, and hence the fetishist is, de facto, a cultural dupe, hankering for the material thing and unaware of the forces that drive his or her desire. As Sut Jhally, in a study of advertising and fetishism, puts it, "fetishism consists of seeing the meaning of things as an inherent part of their physical existence, when in fact that meaning is created by their integration into a *system* of meaning."[38] Even that statement implies the superior knowledge of the analyst who recognizes ("in fact") the truth that the fetishist himself cannot see. The fetishist who eroticizes the shoe is incapable of seeing the oedipal prehistory that binds him to the object— or even if he does, the shoe still carries its magical charge. Discourses of the fetish, on the other hand, bespeak distance and disenchantment. The fetishist says, "I know, but even so," while the fetishist's analyst or historian asserts, "I know."[39]

Fetishism is, and has always been, a discourse about objects and about false attachments, a label marking an Other whose difference is signed by excessive attachment to a material object, whether that object is religious, financial, or sexual. The term "fetish" first appeared in anthropological literature to describe the magical talismen of west Africans, and from its first uses has remained a pejorative label marking material enchantments. Recent studies of fetishes and fetishism are particularly indebted to the historical genealogies of William Pietz, who traces the term from Latin *facticium*, a made or constructed object, to *feitico*, a Portuguese term for an object related to witchcraft.[40] In their logs and accounts, fifteenth-century Portuguese traders to west Africa consistently use the term *feitiçaria*, witchcraft, in conjunction with *idolatria*, idolatry, to describe religious practices among the peoples they encounter. From this early term, which gained rapid and widespread currency, the word "fetish" emerged, though as it evolved in the eighteenth century, "fetish" came to carry with it a meaning radically transformed by post-Enlightenment attitudes toward the material world.[41] In 1757 Charles de Brosses coined the term "fetishism" (*fétichisme*) which was transferred by Marx in the 1840s to designate "commodity fetishism," the mystified religiosity of capital, and then in 1880 was applied for the first time to sexual perversions and obsessions—where much of the current usage of the term, post-Freud, still rests. The fetish, which came to be the common term for most forms of "primitive" worship, signified (as it still does) an object of perverse attachment, imagined wrongly to possess animate or at least surplus powers.

Discourses about devotional painting, crucifixes, and sculptures of the saints in late medieval England carry some of this disciplinary weight. In Lollard polemic devotional images are alleged to bear many of the perverse powers of attachment that later European ethnographers attributed to fetishes of primitives or that Marx would attribute to the fetish of capital, the "sensuous supersensuous thing."[42] Explicit in Lollard commentary is that people love devotional pictures and objects sensuously, wrongly reverencing inert matter. Less explicitly stated, but liberally implied, is that lovers of images also disavow the exchanges of capital that work to give them their appearance of agency. Inert things with a mystified aura, images conceal their social investments.

As we shall see through a closer look at reformist rhetoric in the late medieval image debate, devotional objects also embody multiple contradictions, the most direct and problematic of which can be traced to money, the dynamic agent that exposes the riddle of valuation. Even as material objects, images also seem invested with spiritual powers. Inert (dead) matter, they look like living people. Money, however, attaches new and incommensurate exchange values. Objects fabricated from simple raw materials (wood, stone, or metal), painted and even dressed-up statues of saints not only appear laden with false riches but in fact take on value as commodities through their transactional uses in an art and spirit market.

*   *   *

In Lollard discourse on images, the love of objects and belief in their powers recur as one of the most common refrains. An early fifteenth-century Wycliffite "Tretyse of Ymagis" speaks repeatedly of the false belief that images engender by leading people to trust in the object rather than in the idea. Addressing God, the treatise opens with the observation that people who believe that "ymagis han done þe werkis of grace and not ʒee"[43] err because of the false work of artists who represent God, Christ, and the Holy Ghost as living beings. Later the treatise expands on this circuit of credulity. Rather than sending their devotion to the saints or Christ in heaven, people turn instead to material crosses and statues, "þe swete rode of Bromholme" or "þe swete rode at þe norþe dore"—the cross at Bromholme, a priory in Norfolk possessing a fragment of the true cross or the famous rood at St. Paul's in London.[44] They even touch them, "sadly strokande and kyssand þese olde stones and stokkis, layying doun hore grete offryngis, and maken avowis riȝt þere to þes dede ymagis to come þe nexst ȝeer agayn."[45] This disciplinary polemic makes it clear that the performance of egregious devotional sensuality is a form of idolatry. Statues crafted from wood and alabaster are only base matter—stocks and stones.

An even more graphic picture of the fetishlike physicality of devotional objects is offered in the Twelve Conclusions of the Lollards, a manifesto that was posted in 1395 on the doors of Westminster Hall, where devotional objects are compared to the lips of Judas. In a memorable analogy, the eighth conclusion condemning pilgrimage, relics, and images claims that reverence for the cross and instruments of the Passion are forms of idolatry: "For if þe rode tre, naylis, and þe spere and þe coroune of God schulde ben so holiche worchipid, þanne were Iudas lippis, qwoso mythte hem gete, a wondir gret relyk."[46] Yoking devotional images with saints' relics[47] and brilliantly eliding the cross with graphic implements of torture and sanctified objects with a body part—Judas's lips—that presents Christianity's most graphic sign of betrayal, this stunning analogy also gives grotesque corporeal form to the objects of the Passion: They are like disembodied lips. They are, that is, things we also kiss, a kiss that is itself a betrayal. These are not only objects that we love or fear but also objects that we touch in an act of love. Like fetishes, these devotional things lure us, and seduce us, through their sensuous physicality.

In a discussion of the sacraments in medieval theater Sarah Beckwith also describes the work of sacramental signs as a touch with the lips: "They are like a kiss. For a kiss does not make love, but without it love cannot be made."[48] Visible signs of inward grace, the sacraments of the church operate at the threshold between visible and invisible, matter and spirit. As Hugh of St. Victor explains the agency of sacraments, "A sacrament is a corporeal or material element set before the senses without, representing by similitude and signifying by institution and containing by sanctification some invisible and spiritual grace."[49] Gatekeepers at the border between the visible and invisible, the sacraments bespeak an incarnational faith in which consecrated things, words, or acts can, like the sacramental kiss, activate spiritual grace. In late medieval England, the most direct and also the most controversial action of embodied spirit occurs, of course, with the Eucharist, the sacrament that most fully embodies the miracle of the incarnation—and the one article of faith that came most fully to distinguish the true believer from the Lollard heretic. Humbert of Romans in the thirteenth century succinctly articulates this crucial distinction among the sacraments: "in all other sacraments Christ's power is spiritual, but in this one—Christ exists corporeally; and this is the greater thing."[50]

If devotional images and relics can easily masquerade as Christ's essence, that crossover is also enabled by their participation in incarnate history. Images, of course, are theologically exempt from the incarnational grace that turns the wine and the wafer into God's body but participate nevertheless in some its actions. During the Byzantine controversies over images and idolatry in the eighth century, John of Damascus, the first writer to apply Augustine's distinctions between *latria*, the honor due to God alone, and *dulia*, the reverence for his creation, to the topic of devotional representation, argued that the fact of the incarnation justifies the use of secondary images of God: "I do not worship matter; I worship the Creator of matter who became matter for my sake, who willed to take his abode in matter; who worked out my salvation through matter. . . . Because of this I salute all remaining matter with reverence."[51] In his distinction between worship and reverence, John also selects matter—both flesh and, by extension, devotional images—as worthy of reverence. John's writings elaborate on the position of Germanus I, patriarch of Constantinople at the beginning of the controversy: To reject icons is to disavow the incarnation.[52]

In fourteenth- and fifteenth-century defenses of images, the Byzantine arguments are often brought into play. In *The Testimony of William Thorpe* (1407), Archbishop Arundel draws on the analogy with the incarnation in his defense of devotional ornament in the church: "Siþ Crist bicam man it is leful [lawful] to haue ymagis to schewe his manhood."[53] A tract that is usually attributed to Walter Hilton, *De adoracione ymaginum*, also notes that the incarnation is the singular event endorsing the imaged world of Christian worship: "Even though the images of the church cannot represent to the eyes of onlookers any semblance of divine nature in themselves, nevertheless they can represent and signify the semblance of an assumed human nature, in which God brought about man's salvation."[54] Images enter into a signifying system through their participation in incarnational action even though, as Hilton is careful to point out, they can only represent. They are to be revered "as symbols, not as things."[55]

The incarnational miracle that authorizes the uses of images as signs for the laity also underpins their slippery masquerade as objects containing divine nature "in themselves." The trouble with images is not unlike the trouble with the Eucharist, at least in Lollard thought. The eucharistic wafer as well as images of the crucifix and of the saints are material objects, or even material fabrications or concoctions, that are wrongly believed to contain a supersensuous essence. When, in the early 1380s, a shrewd commentator on the public scene remarked, "there's a real brawl going on about the Eucharist right now" ("quia hodie circa eucharistiam est dissensio plus brigosa"),[56] he could easily have extended his comment to include images, which were troubled by some of the same problems of hybridity as the Eucharist. As Paul Strohm remarks in a study of political appropriations of transubstantiation in the early fifteenth century, "Denied, in the process of Lollard reasoning, is the possibility of easy transition between matter and spirit. Baldly put, this is why Lollards distrusted material images, like representations of Christ's cross, as objects of spiritual veneration in their own right."[57] Hence the worship of the crucifix can seem like reverence for Judas's lips. Like the kiss of Judas (and radically unlike the sacramental kiss) our attachment to image or relic connects us bodily to that bodily thing, promising us spiritual change but really tying us to matter in a purely material transaction. Things, like the lips of Judas, betray.

*   *   *

When the word "fetish" emerged in the eighteenth century as a term to designate a particular type of religious object, it took its meaning from a set of attitudes toward the spiritual and material world that had been distinctively shaped by both imperialism and capitalism, according to Wiliam Pietz. In tracing the history of the fetish from object of sorcery to the "value bearing material object" imagined by later European anthropologists and explorers, Pietz argues that the idea of the fetish could emerge only with the revaluation of commodities that had occurred during sixteenth- and seventeenth-century trading on the west coast of Africa. Fetishism, as first coined and understood in the eighteenth century, can be traced to specific and localized developments in the idea of goods, developments that are coterminous with modernity and indeed, even constitutive of postmedieval capitalism. Trading on the coast of Guinea, early Portuguese traders described their encounters with the problem of relative value, in which objects that they valued appeared to have little or no importance to the Guineans. In the account of the Gambians written in the 1450s, Cadamosto, one of the earliest merchants to West Africa, writes, "gold is much prized among them, in my opinion, more than by us, for they regard it as very precious; nevertheless they traded it cheaply, taking in exchange articles of little value in our eyes."[58] This new problematic of relative value was precursor, Pietz argues, to a later splitting in contingencies of value, in which "the truth of material objects came to be viewed in terms of technological and commodifiable use-value, whose 'reality' was proved by their silent 'translatability' across alien cultures. All other meanings and values attributed to material objects were understood to be the culture-specific delusions of peoples lacking 'reason'"—or the domain of the fetish.[59]A specific concoction of wood and feathers might give a fetish its potency on the west coast of Africa, but would have little value in the market squares of Lisbon or London—where wood and feathers bore very different commodity value as objects of construction or of fashion. In an argument extending Pietz's studies of the fetish to nineteenth-century imperialism, Anne McClintock comments that fetishes are "impassioned objects" that have been transferred among recipients in a trajectory that follows the history of European imperialism. The fetish is, at heart, a contradictory object and displaced "social contradiction," the material and symbolic ground for negotiating the mystery of value.[60] Soap, she argues, became such a fetish; a newly marketed commodity in nineteenth-century Europe, soap came to stand in for social divisions between clean and unclean, upper and lower class, white European and black African. An item with inherent spiritual essence (cleanliness being next to godliness), soap literally whitewashed these distinctions even as its marketing campaigns made it clear that soap, or cleanliness, marked the superiority of its "civilized" users.[61]

In the attacks on and defenses of devotional images in fourteenth- and fifteenth-century England, anxieties about contingent value and materiality were very much in the air; and Pietz's argument that the European idea of the fetish had its origins in the problematic of relative valuation as first encountered in fifteenth-century west African trade could also be brought home to include as well the traffic in images. In some Lollard critiques, images are troubling not only as material things to which people falsely attribute spiritual value but also as things that have market value. Attacks on devotional images often cite practices of decorating them with precious metals and gems and of using them to attract gifts of money to the church.[62] The "Tretyse of Ymagis" repeatedly returns to the marketability of glamour. People paint images "wiþ greet cost, and hangen myche silver and gold and precious cloþis and stones þeronne," and in dressing up statues with gold and silver they not only pervert the gospel message of apostolic poverty but also create a complex social and even market object. These richly decorated images offer a mirror to the mercantile self, short-circuiting spiritual exchange with a market trade, self for self; we value them (hung with silver and gold and precious cloths) because in them we can see ourselves in glamour mode: "But þus don false men þat lyuen now in þer lustis to colour with þer owne cursid lif by þis false peyntyngis; and herfore þei lyen on seyntis, turnyng þer lif to þe contrarie."[63] The impulse to picture the saints as rich, this passage says, comes from the worshipper who uses the image to justify his or her own worldly pursuits.

In addition to mirroring and hence justifying the finery of their worshippers, rich images also inspire more direct economic exchanges when they divert money from the poor into the pockets of priests and the coffers of the church. Painters of images use capital wrongly in their pigments and gold, and the products that result unequally attract rich gifts. Such images (statues and images tricked out in gold and silver) have been created by the clerks of antichrist "to robbe pore men boþe of feyþe and hope, of charite and of worldly godis, and to mayntene anticrist clerkis furþe in her pride, coueytise and lustis aȝenus Cristis lif and his apostelis."[64] The image becomes not a spiritual conduit but a commodity in a perverse exchange of real goods—gifts in the plate for the priests who collect them. A text that articulates these tensions with skillfully dramatized descriptive vitriol is the late fourteenth-century *Pierce the Plowman's Crede*, an alliterative verse satire influenced both by Langland and by Wycliffite writings. In this satire a friar, an example of the corruption of his order, promises the narrator that if he gives the order money, he will get his picture displayed in the form of a donor image in the middle of the west window, folded in the cope of St. Francis and presented to the Trinity.[65] Later in the text Peres the Plowman, the voice of Lollard rectitude, condemns distracting church imagery, tying it explicitly to the seductions of aristocratic display: "For though a man in her mynster a masse wolde heren, / His sight schal so be set on sundry werkes, / The penounes [pennons] and the pommels [ornamental knobs] and poyntes of scheldes [heraldic shields] / Withdrawen his devocion, and dusken his herte."[66] Voiced in this passage is a critique of images as exclusionary property. Images channel desires socially, "darkening the heart" with desires for heraldic self-representation, the satire suggests. Images also circulate a promise of life as a kind of mercantile exchange. If you can afford to pay for it, you will be portrayed with the saints in the west window. Along with your image your name will be written, "and, in remembraunce of the, yrade [read] ther forever"[67]—either read through the text inscribed or vocally read aloud when the chantry priest intones your name in his prayers for the souls of the departed. As the dialogue in the *Crede* illustrates with considerable dramatic force, painted windows depicting donors short-circuit desire by turning it back to the self, the real object of admiration. The temptation is either to become an image (in the west window) granted the illusion of permanence through our picture or our inscribed name, or to worship others as images through their heraldry. In various ways, these materialist critiques suggest, images sanctify the laity.

The critique of gold and silver, the spirit of the argument captured succinctly in a Wycliffite text stating there is no place for a Christ "naylid on þe crosse wiþ muche gold and siluer," was ubiquitous, as Margaret Aston has documented, and became increasingly strident when picked up as part of iconoclastic rhetoric in the Reformation.[68] Indeed, Lollard polemicists as well as orthodox defenders of images critique excesses and worry about the potential distractions of expensive display. *Dives and Pauper* attempts to delineate proper uses of images through the repeated injunction, "worship before the image and not to the image," a distinction that becomes ever more difficult to make in front of the seductions of lavishly decorated statuary.[69] Voicing concerns about devotional images that were widely voiced by both sides, Dives points out that they seem to operate as signifiers not in a spiritual but an economic system of exchange: "me thynky3t þat þe feet so shoyd in syluer shewyn þat þe loue and þe affeccioun of meen of holy cherche is mechil seth in gold and syluyr and erthely coueytise, and sueche ryche clothyngge of þe ymage is but a tollyng of more offryng and a tokene to þe lewyd peple qhere þey shullyn offryn and qhat."[70] A richly ornamented image lures people to give donations; as a "tollyng" and a "tokene," it is also a sign in a larger system of material, "erthely," exchange. Langland points to precisely this interrupted exchange in the B text of *Piers Plowman*, when Mede's confessor promises her, as a quid pro quo, that if she glazes the window and engraves her name as a donor, her soul will speed more quickly to heaven.[71] Langland's wry comment, developed more fully in the Lollard *Crede*, is directed not against veneration of images nor against abuses of images as prompts to the giving of gifts which would be put to better use by the poor; rather, it points to the wealth and passions for self-portraiture of the gentry or even merchant classes who donate images to the church and use visible records of their patronage as a means to gain public recognition.

Perhaps the most succinct marker of the liminal identity and motility of images in late medieval England is to be found in the anxious insistence that they are dead. The "Tretyse of Ymagis" reminds us of this repeatedly. People stroke and kiss old stones and stocks, promising to these "dede ymagis" to come again next year; ignorant people trust completely in these "deade ymagis" and love God and his commandments the less.[72] The term derives from the Book of Wisdom, which condemns idol worshippers for praying "to a thing that is dead (13.10 ff.) and for trusting in "lifeless idols" (14.29), and from a passage from Psalm 115: "They have mouths, but do not speak; / eyes, but do not see. / They have ears, but do not hear; / noses, but do not smell." The epithet is ubiquitous in Lollard polemic. In one passage from a treatise on the Decalogue, the phrase "dead images" is repeated five times:

For such dead images be lewed men's books to learn them how they should worship saints in heaven after whom these dead images are shaped. And also that when men behold these dead images [they] should have the sooner mind and the more mind of the saints that be living in heaven, and to make these holy saints their mean between God and them, and not the dead images, for they may not help themselves nor other men. And certis if men had any kindness to themselves or any belief in God, they should not regard or ascribe it to these dead images the miracles that God doth alone by his own power, and believe that the image doth it himself.[73]

This passage, which attempts to mark a clean break between the twin worlds of living spirit and dead matter, insists that the object is inert and agency is elsewhere—with the saints in heaven and not with the carved and painted image. Dead images are books ("lewed men's books") and reminders of the saints, which are our real intercessors. Dead images themselves cannot help us at all. If people had any faith or natural reason ("kindness") they would know this, and not credit images with powers belonging to God alone.

Yet the assertion of deadness protests, of course, too much. What is this fear that images will come to life? The very insistence on the deadness of images points to their potential vivacity—to their potential for animation. Many people, this passage implies, believe in the powers of the objects, crediting them with agency and even life in a system of intercessory exchange. In the insistence that images are inert matter, we can detect uneasiness about their role in an incarnational faith and even about their circulation as commodities. If we are tempted to endow images with life, it is because we want to pray to them in a cost/benefit exchange. This temptation to impute life to man-made objects is expressly condemned in the *Lanterne of Liȝt*, a Lollard text from about 1410, which says, "Þe peyntour makiþ an ymage forgid wiþ diuerse colours til it seme in foolis iȝen as a lyueli creature."[74] Fools impute life to dead or inert matter, granting agency to an object or picture that can only be a sign. Much like the fetish fixations of others, the image is a manufactured ("forgid") object of perverse attachment, a concoction of materials that wrongly appear to give it agency.

A belief that the image is a living being thus generates another sort of exchange among things. Attacks on rich images not only voice concerns about Church corruption, I would suggest, but may even be said to articulate tensions about images and art as new forms of capital and status. The insistence on marking images as "dead" stocks and stones, lifeless matter of little value, and the critique of their circulation in systems of patronage and luxury both voice concerns about the circulation of objects in a market economy. As images take on vivacity they claim gifts of money—and take on life as well as they come to look like living beings when people dress them up with clothes, gold and jewels. Indeed, the attachment to money is one of the most insistent refrains in the Lollard attack on images. In the *Lanterne of Liȝt*, the same fools who believe that painted images are living creatures are also the ones who offer to them, contributing to the riches of priests and the impoverishment of the folk[75]—though the object of the invective shifts to the priests who "beguile" people by suggesting that one image has more miracle-working power than another.

The problem of materiality, in which the very substance of the image invites further participation in the exchange of goods, seems to reflect a broader anxiety about the uses of devotional objects in an era in which they were dramatically proliferating. It may also be that the new monetization of the European economy[76] contributed to anti-image sentiments, as an increasingly active marketplace showcased devotional objects as commodities. When Dives says, "þow meen doon makyn þese dayis ymagys gret plente bothin in cherche and out of cherche," he seems to be voicing a response of the public response to production, or even overproduction; "these days," he says, images are showing up everywhere.[77] Reginald Pecock, writing in the middle of the fifteenth century, also recognized that proliferation of images could result in their devaluation, and argued that images of saints should "not be multiplied so wijde that at ech chirche, at ech chapel, at ech stretis eende, or at ech heggis ende in a cuntre be sett such an ymage, for certis thane tho ymmagis schulden be as foule or of litel reputacioun and schulde be undeinteose [unpleasing] for the grete plente of hem."[78] Fifteenth-century England witnessed massive building and reconstruction of its churches, supported largely by capital from international trade in wool; and along with the rebuilding of churches went a commensurable proliferation in private chapels and new demand for altarpieces and freestanding statues.[79] Just to mention the alabaster industry alone, over two thousand English alabaster panels and figures survived from the fourteenth century until the sixteenth, when all production was stopped in the Act of 1550 against superstitious books and images.[80] English alabaster images, popular items for trade to continental Europe, were produced in a thriving workshop industry in Nottinghamshire and were sold to churches as altarpieces as well as to private individuals as meditative images. Evidence from wills, inventories, and export lists indicates that in the fifteenth century the cost of alabasters dropped dramatically, due, according to Francis Cheetham, to competition among workshops and to the use of standardized models or patterns for the most popular images, such as the Trinity, crucifixion, or John the Baptist.[81] If two thousand alabasters survive, we can only guess at the thousands more that were destroyed.

This new market for images also appears to have also influenced the ways people used them—and bought them. Devotional images and objects served multiple functions at once, bridging the status symbol and the devotional aid: As Richard Marks puts it, "personal items of adornment, like the Clare Cross and the Middleham Jewel, were simultaneously status symbols, financial assets, fashion accessories, apotropaic reliquaries and devotional aids."[82] Eamon Duffy lists, from the parish church at Faversham in Kent, four images of the Virgin in addition to thirty-one images of saints— St. Agnes, All Saints, Anthony, Barbara, Christopher, Clement, Crispin and Crispinianus, Edmund, Erasmus, George, Giles, Gregory, James the Great, two of John, John the Baptist, Katherine, Leonard, Loy, Luke, Mary Magdalene, Margaret, Michael, Nicholas, Peter and Paul, Thomas the Apostle, Thomas Becket, Ronan, and Master John Schorne. These saints were engaged with the spiritual life of the community in ways that were also vitally commercial; as Duffy puts it, "The men and women of late medieval England were busy surrounding themselves with new or refurbished images of the holy dead, laying out large sums of money to provide lights, jewels and precious coverings to honour these images."[83]

The phrase, "to honour these images," points, however, to just the gap between object and self that collapses in many acts of donation, in the fifteenth century as much as in our own time; for in the process of honoring images, medieval gift-givers were also commemorating the self. As Joel Rosenthal notes in *The Purchase of Paradise*, a study of chantry bequests, virtually all acts of medieval philanthropy had "the purchase of prayers as their ultimate goal," suggesting that the medieval philanthropic gift was clearly understood to negotiate a commercial transaction, with prayers for the soul, one's own or someone else's, purchased as a form of afterlife insurance.[84] Taking a deeply suspicious and much more material look at gifts of money, jewels, or expensive clothes to devotional images, the Lollard "Tretyse of Ymagis" condemns the decoration of images of saints as grotesque projections of our own love of luxury. In this polemic the separation between self and object, body and soul, has fully collapsed; the gift to the image is a gift to the self.

*　*　*

Identifying longing and mystified value as common denominators of three different modern discourses of fetishism, Emily Apter comments that "fetishism records the trajectory of an idée fixe or noumen in search of its materialist twin (god to idol, alienated labor to luxury item, phallus to shoe fetish)."[85] It is precisely the tension between the longed-for place of spirit and the consolations of objects that is the central domain of the fetish—and also a key issue at stake in late medieval polemic against images for self-commemoration. The image lover's trajectory of desire fails to move from thing to spirit but does the reverse; the idée fixe searches out the saint's image and takes its solace there. The uses of images of saints for self-commemoration, and their use in ways that tag the transaction like a receipt, took increasingly explicit shape during the fifteenth century with the proliferation of donor images and personal inscriptions marking gifts. One form of this, for example, appears in the practice, first appearing around 1450, of signing the name of a donor or commemorative person below pictures of saints on rood screens, the wooden partitions that separated nave from chancel in English parish churches.[86] Rood-screen paintings on the parish church in Attleborough, Norfolk, illustrate this kind of visible claim. Panels on the north and south side of each screen are each marked with an inscription, *orate pro*, below the picture of the saint or the trinity. Although the names of recipients have been scratched out, perhaps during the Reformation in reaction against personal claims on salvation, "orate pro" or "pray for" would have been followed with the name of a patron. Facing the nave and hence property of the devotional community, the painting is signed as the special agent of one of that community's lay members.[87] As recent studies on the role of the laity in church ritual and maintenance indicate, the painting of screens was funded largely by corporate and lay endowments; and hence the inscriptions, when they appeared, most likely commemorate the donors who financed the projects.[88] In a study of rood screens in East Anglia, Eamon Duffy comments that the

rood screen "was a crucial focus of ritual activity and piety, of direct interest to every parishioner," and support for its construction, ornamentation,
and maintenance the product of "complex patterns of benefaction" involving many people, even if a single donor or married couple is named in
the inscription.[89] Practices of self-commemoration through names and
donor images painted and etched onto the fabric of the parish multiplied
throughout the fifteenth century. On her husband's death in 1470, Alice
Chester of All Saint's, Bristol, provided for the gilding of the altar of the
Virgin and of images of the Virgin, St. Katherine, and St. Margaret, and
donated as well "in carved work a tabernacle with a Trinity in the middle
over the image of Jesus, and also at her own cost had it gilded full wor-
shipfully." On her husband's hearse cloth she had her own name listed
with her husband's, the benefit of prayers redounding to both of them via
her generous gifts: "Orate pro animabus Henricus Chestre et Alicie uxoris
eius."[90] Perhaps the paramount survival of visual commemoration is the
parish in Long Melford where major donors in the Clopton family have
their names prominently displayed throughout the church, even etched in
a frieze along the outside walls.[91]

When Bill Brown, in *Things*, writes that "thing theory" seems like an
oxymoron, he is speaking, of course, of a post-Enlightenment idea of
materiality. How can inanimate objects have theories attached to them?
Things, he writes, seem to us "beyond the grid of intelligibility."[92] In late
medieval England, however, the debate on devotional images seems to
offer a particularly vital kind of "thing theory." Participating in an incarnational economy, inanimate objects could easily threaten to morph into
supersensuous things. That, for reformers, was the very problem. Several
contemporary chroniclers describe Lollards putting images to the flames.[93]
Wyclif himself writes, "Certes, these ymagis of hemselfe may do nouther
gode ne yvel to mennis soulis, but thai myghtten warme a mannes body in
colde, if thai were sette upon a fire."[94] In Wyclif's proposal, as perhaps in
accounts of image burning, we might detect not only a desire to destroy
them but also a desire to return them to their proper category. As "dead
stocks," things carved from pieces of wood, they are objects made for burning. Inscribed personalized prayers, "orate pro . . . ," articulate the problematic interchange among money, images, and spirit that fueled the image
debate even before practices of visible commemoration became widespread.
Similar practices of self-commemoration are targeted in the earlier *Piers
Plowman* and *Pierce the Plowman's Crede*, both of which expressly satirize
the purchase of donor images and inscriptions. The inscription *orate pro*

invites the congregation/viewer to pray *for* the person named in a dialectic with the saint as intercessor. In the view of the *Crede*, since the prayers are financially entailed, the endowment of the image should properly be understood as payment for services.

Devotional images, especially as they assumed a new status in the marketplace of the fifteenth century, erupt from their categories particularly energetically in their troubled links to capital. Where they seem most like later fetishes is articulated in the concerns that they violate natural boundaries delineating object, body, and spirit. Money is the sign that crystallizes this hybridity. When reformers claim we love rich images more than poor ones, they are saying we confuse two systems of valuation. When reformist discourse insist that images are dead stocks and stones, the term itself points toward domestic economics (or the market) as well as to incarnational transformation: images as stocks and stones are raw materials of little value; as stocks and stones they also remain inanimate things even if they take the shape of living beings. Devotional images in late medieval England may be said to occupy a psychosocial niche unaccounted for in Pietz's periodization, which locates the idea of the fetish in a world where faith and matter are split—or as he puts it, within "Protestant Christianity's iconoclastic repudiation of any material, earthly agency" connecting a believer to God.[95] The fetish becomes a stand-in for that traumatic severance as the material world is stripped of its essences. In Lollard polemic, likewise, the image operates as the "value bearing material object" that Pietz identifies as the uniquely modern and post-Enlightenment thing.[96] Images become, in the minds of image worshippers, far from passive signs, but active agents uncannily attached to spirit and to capital. Whereas idols, as so often featured in narrative lives of the saints, will sooner or later display their true nature as inert matter, dead and ineffective, images are more ambiguous. The trouble with images, according to the Lollards, is that they persistently display their own materiality, and frequently this involves ventriloquizing or performing vivacity through their attachment to commercial forms of valuation—gems, goods, money. Pietz's distinction between medieval and modern valuations of objects may draw rather too sharp a divide that overlooks the debate over images in pre-Reformation and Reformation Europe, a debate deeply invested in questions about their troubled valuation in systems of patronage and currency.[97] Like fetish historians (or analysts), Lollards parse the thing and its false noumen in a polemic against material culture and its social props, targeting systems of production that fabricate images, worshippers that use them for social status, and clergy that profit from their display. This polemic did not have the word "fetish" at its disposal to describe the crucifix and images of saints and the Trinity, which it labeled instead "dead stocks and stones," but even so, in naming images as the fixations of others, deluded by matter, who substitute *res* for *deus*, it anticipates traits of the fetish that would take shape in much later discourses.

I

Knighton's Lollards, Capgrave's *Katherine*, and Walter Hilton's "Merk Ymage"

THE MOST SENSATIONAL ACT of iconoclasm in pre-Reformation England is recorded in Henry Knighton's *Chronicle*, written in an Augustinian abbey in Leicester and covering the years 1337–96. In a long discussion of the Lollard heresy, Knighton tells the story of two "collatores principales," chief sustainers of heresy, William Smith and a chaplain Richard Waytestathe, who chopped up an image of St. Katherine and then burned it as fuel to make a cabbage stew.[1] In this account, which is told with Knighton's characteristic skill as a raconteur and with an eye to the lurid horrors of Lollard violations of decency, Knighton gives us information about character, motivation, and place: William Smith, "so called from his craft," was deformed in person and had taken on an extremist sectarian faith when he was spurned in love. Place is also carefully noted, an abandoned chapel "near the leper hospital outside Leicester,"[2] where the two lived and "had there a kind of academy of evil beliefs and opinions, in which heretical error was taught." In a corner of this chapel, one of the two Lollards finds an old statue, "carved and painted in honour of St. Catherine" ("in honore Sancte Katerine formatam et depictam"), and says to the other, "Aha . . . my dear chap, now God has sent us fuel to cook our cabbage and appease our hunger. This holy image will make a holy bonfire for us. By axe and fire she will undergo a new martyrdom, and perhaps through the cruelty of those new torments she will come at last to the kingdom of heaven" (297).[3]

Knighton's account says little to explain the choice of a Katherine image as object of desecration, beyond a kind of arbitrary or random chance, the image that happened to be there closest at hand. It is an old image, found in a corner of the chapel, as if to imply that the chapel has been so thoroughly reconfigured into a clubhouse of heresy, an "academy of evil beliefs" ("gingnasium malignorum dogmatum," 296), that its old gods have been pushed into its darkened corners. Nevertheless, elements of the story mime the *passio* of many of the most popular virgin martyrs, and particularly of St. Katherine herself. With not-so-subtle echoes Knighton fictionalizes his anecdote as a saint's life and romance in which historical, chronicled locals take the part of pagan persecutors, and an image, first decapitated, then burned, plays the part of a virgin martyr. These parallels suggest that the saint's image, fuel for a cabbage stew, also fuels, so to speak, the action of the story as a whole. The choice of saints would seem to be significant, perhaps for the two Lollards but far more likely for Knighton who constructs a narrative from an incident in the historical record.

In grabbing an image of St. Katherine to burn for their soup, the two Lollards choose one of the most popular saints in England, and indeed, in all of Europe. The Katherine legend, which first appeared in Greece in the tenth century, spread widely across Europe in the late Middle Ages.[4] In England, an early version was written in Anglo-Norman by the twelfth-century nun Clemence of Barking.[5] The first English version is the early thirteenth-century legend from the Katherine Group, a collection of texts written for nuns and female recluses.[6] Fourteenth-century versions are extant in the *South English Legendary*, in the Auchinleck MS, and in Richard Spaldyng's alliterative hymn to St. Katherine.[7] In the fifteenth century, Katherine becomes something of a celebrity saint and the subject of numerous lives, among them two versions in midcentury: Osbern Bokenham's *Legendys of Hooly Wummen*, a unique collection of lives of only female saints, and John Capgrave's stunningly long verse version—over twelve hundred stanzas (about eight thousand lines).[8] Images of St. Katherine, represented both as a single icon, the saint with her wheel emblem, or in narrative sequences depicting her life, were equally popular as subjects for representation. In surviving fourteenth-century English wall painting, St. Katherine of Alexandria ranks at the top in popularity, second only to St. Christopher.[9] In late gothic manuscript illumination, St. Katherine is one of the most frequently depicted saints, often appearing in constellation with Margaret and Mary Magdalene.[10] Katherine's popularity also spanned the household and the marketplace. The Florentine Cardinal Dominici, in his *Rule for the Management of Family Care* of 1403, advocates images of saints in the home for the education of children: "And so too little girls should be brought up in the sight of the eleven thousand virgins, discussing, fighting, and praying. I would like them to see Agnes with the fat lamb, Cecilia crowned with roses, Elizabeth with many roses, Catherine on the wheel."[11] The immense popularity of her cult in mid-fifteenth-century England is given a vivid public dimension by Reginald Pecock in his long treatise defending the uses of devotional images. Images and pilgrimages are "seeable rememoratiif signes" (209), Pecock says: "Whanne the dai of Seint Kateryn schal be come, marke who so wole in his mynde alle the bokis whiche ben in Londoun writun upon Seint Kateryn's lijf and passiouns, and y dare weel seie that thouȝ ther were x. thousind mo bokis writun in Londoun in thilk day of the same Seintis lijf and passioun, thei schulden not so moche turne the citee into mynde of the holi famose lijf of Seint Kateryn and of her dignitee in which sche now is, as dooth in ech ȝeer the going of peple in pilgrimage to the College of Seint Kateryn bisidis London."[12] Pecock tells us that images and pilgrimages are superior to books for inciting devotion; but in mustering his evidence he also attests to the wide popularity of Katherine in written texts.

The "lijf and passiouns" that people will know from all the books, as Pecock says, would comprise the story of her early life and mystical marriage to Christ and the somewhat separate story of her passion, which normally includes the dispute with Maxentius over worship of idols, her debate with the pagan philosophers, and the various stages of her torture and ultimate martyrdom. In the first part of the story, called the life or *vita*, King Costas of Alexandria has a daughter, Katherine, whom he raises with a superb education—even in some accounts building her a separate library and study of her own. In Capgrave's account, she is even called a "wondyr woman."[13] After the death of Costas, Katherine is under pressure to marry, and some accounts make much of the fragility of a land with no king, with Katherine's refusal to marry represented as a kind of stubborn selfishness. Katherine parries with a "deal" that she'll marry, but only a man who is rich, beautiful, brilliant—and also immortal. Later in a sequence that in some texts is represented as a dream vision and in others as an actual occurrence, she is taken into the desert where she meets Christ and the Virgin, and marries Christ in what is known, and often represented in art, as the mystical marriage.

The passion, or *passio*, takes off from this point, and is often told as a separate story. It is the *passio*, and not the *vita*, that is pictured in fourteenth-century English wall paintings. The *passio* begins with the dispute between Katherine and the Emperor Maxentius on the worship of idols. Katherine, queen of Alexandria, hears a commotion in the marketplace and emerges from her study to see what is going on. Maxentius, the emperor, has arrived in town and has proclaimed a festival, with an ordinance that everyone sacrifice to the gods. She accosts him, claiming that idols are false and contain false promises of immortality. He is taken with her brashness and her beauty and commands her to sacrifice to them. In most accounts he even offers to make an idol of her and set her up among the other gods. She refuses, in many versions, quite rudely. Maxentius then sends for fifty philosophers from far and wide to debate with her. In some texts this section is encapsulated briefly and in others, as in Capgrave, it comprises a long philosophical disputation. The philosophers are convinced by her arguments and convert to Christianity. Maxentius has them burned at the stake. Then follows a series of tortures. Katherine is scourged, put in prison, starved. Maxentius's wife and Porphyry, the head of his military guard, visit Katherine in prison, and they also convert. Maxentius then has his wife's breasts cut off, and executes both her and Porphyry. Katherine still refuses. Maxentius orders a huge wheel built, or as it is often described, four interconnecting wheels, with sharp knives that will cut Katherine to bits. This is set up in the market square, but before Katherine can be cut to pieces God sends a thunderbolt and the wheel shatters, its shards impaling and killing thousands. Then Katherine is beheaded, but at the moment of her martyrdom angels descend, Christ's voice speaks from heaven, her blood turns to milk, and angels transport her body to Mt. Sinai.

The questions I address in the first part of this chapter derive from the curious overlap between Knighton's story of a saint's image and contemporary stories of misogyny and idolatry as they circulate in the lives of the virgin martyrs, and particularly in the popular Katherine legends. A closer look at the parallels between Knighton's Lollard anecdote and the Katherine legend can offer insight into the craft of the chronicler and the *mouvance* of narrative paradigms among genres: Knighton, as romancer, sifts tropes from popular stories around a contemporary event, fictionalizing history, or more exactly historicizing a contemporary anecdote with resonances to "true" events from early Christian history. By interpolating stories of the virgin martyrs into an account of an act of image breaking, Knighton also gives us a fascinating commentary on the debate about objects of popular piety in England in the late fourteenth century. The chapter then examines the figure of the "merk ymage" in Walter Hilton's first book of the *Scale of Perfection*, a text written within a few years of Knighton's account and one in which an embodied image also plays an important dramatic as well as disciplinary role. Like Knighton, and also like Knighton an opponent of Lollardy, Hilton invests an image with female corporeal form, though "image" in this text serves a very different agenda. Using the metaphor of a dark (*merk*) image that the female recluse addressed in the text must identify within herself, Hilton adopts language nuanced by contemporary reformist discourse for use in a devotional romance. The *Scale of Perfection* was one of the most frequently read devotional texts of the fourteenth and fifteenth centuries, and at least some of that popularity might be due to its strategic topicality. Hilton uses "image" with subtle drama.

The chapter concludes with a consideration of saints' attributes, astonishingly material fetish forms, and also returns to the Katherine legend in a forward look at Capgrave's mid-fifteenth-century *Life of St. Katherine*, a narrative that brilliantly crafts a story about idols—among them the horrific wheel—to highlight the superior powers of incarnate bodies. How do Knighton, Hilton, and later Capgrave respond, in their treatment of feminized devotional images, to broader social concerns with the display and potency of devotional objects? The larger questions pursued in this chapter, framed through a discussion of texts that span the historical scope of this book, address the relationship between the image debate as it developed in late fourteenth- and fifteenth-century England and the circulation or entailment of images as objects and even as forms of property. Critiques of devotional images often target the seductions of material form; people take pleasure in objects rather than in the ideas that those objects are meant to represent. In these critiques, as I have noted, writers often comment on the luxury materials—gems, gold, lavish housings—used to make images, suggesting that images operate in a market economy rather than a spiritual one. A related materialist critique seems to have been fueled by popular practices of making named donations, signing images with the name of a benefactor or testator—the personalized claiming of saints as special or individualized intercessory agents. In the first book of *Scale*, the hints about a dark image and the final revelation of its identity consistently blur the lines between the flesh and an object of popular piety, and imbue the body with some of the inert torpor that attaches to devotional objects as fetish forms. Hilton's uses of the "merk ymage," as well as the fate of images in stories about St. Katherine, may be linked with tensions about the circulation of material goods, or what we might call the vivacity of objects. To what extent is the saint as spectacle or the flesh as image a fetish on display within visual structures of desire: the saint, we might say, in the marketplace? How, I would like to ask, was the drama of the image shaped by contemporary discourses about images as *goods*?

*   *   *

Knighton's account of the image breakers Smith and Waytestathe, overlaid on a story or stories of the virgin martyrs, voices anxieties about the afterlives of images: Is this saint's image bodily in any way, and what does it do for us? In Knighton's anecdote the destructibility of the saint's body, or image, is the key question at hand, and one that circulates in the context of a philosophic or quasi-philosophic discussion about the powers of the body/object to resist death. It is also the central "stake" in the Katherine *passio*. In many of the Katherine legends the subject of her famous debate with the fifty pagan philosophers is the immortality of the soul, Christianity's trump card over paganism. In virtually all of the Katherine legends, she engages in a spirited debate with the emperor over the worship of idols; and in most of them, Maxentius responds to her attack on his festival of idols by turning the tables and offering to have an image made of her. In multiple ways, as we shall see, the Katherine legend affirms the excesses of life that can reside within the human form as well as within the objects that represent that form. The body of the beautiful, learned, rich young woman as object for possession, and that body's cult image—troubling the market as contested property—are closely entwined.

Knighton dates his story of Smith and Waytestathe to 1382. As scholars have noted, Knighton's chronology is not always reliable, and the incident may have occurred later in the decade, even as late as 1389 when Archbishop Courtenay gave Smith the penance of walking barefoot and bareheaded in a Leicester procession, carrying an image of St. Katherine in his right hand.[14] The later date also seems consistent with the developing intensity in the public dialogue over images during the decade. In a wide variety of literate circles the appropriate uses of devotional images were debated, and with increasing tensions as the critique of images, or iconomachy, became identified with Lollardy.[15] As Nicholas Watson notes, the date may be a back formation; Knighton may have attached the incident to 1382, since 1382 was the year of condemnation of Wyclif's opinions in the Blackfriar's Council and "the ecclesiastical establishment's formal declaration of war against the new movement."[16]

In narrating a story in which two Lollards burn an image, Knighton builds a sensational story that seems clearly embedded within and contextualized by a public controversy. Scripting the story in mock-heroic mode, he details character, place, motivation, and dialogue in ways that resonate with the form of saints' lives, the two Lollards taking, in inverse form, the part of pagan idolators and torturers of the innocent. The appearance of a Katherine image in a story dramatizing a peculiar act of iconoclastic zealotry seems too coincidental to be random chance. Although the refusal to worship pagan idols is a common trope in saints' *vitae*, it is particularly dramatic in the Katherine *passio*. Katherine brings on her own martyrdom not only through her refusal to worship pagan idols when commanded, but also—rather like the two Lollards in Knighton's story—through her directed assault on images. Hearing a commotion in the marketplace, she chooses to leave her study verbally to assault Maxentius for leading people astray with the worship of the fiend, "fikel it is and al feyntise," as she says in the fourteenth-century Auchinleck manuscript version of the Katherine *passio*.[17] Her attack on the worship of idols sets her *passio* in motion, as Maxentius responds by sending to the fifty philosophers to debate doctrine with Katherine. It also figures in a certain ironic return as Maxentius, besotted, turns to Katherine after he has cast the philosophers in a fire for their failure to defeat her with logic and offers to make "an ymage" of her that will be worshipped by high and low:

> Þou schalt be worschiped as the quen,
> Boþe in bour and halle;
> And in þi name schal be wrou3t
> An ymage fair wiþ-alle,
> And in þi borwe it schal be sett,
> Hei3e and lowe to louten alle.
> Of alle þe nedes of þis lond
> To þe we schal conseyl calle. (lines 241–48)

The statue, furthermore, is just the beginning. He offers to have her image encrypted in a marble tomb to be worshipped as one of the gods:

> Hei3e and lowe worþschipe þe.
> Katerine, do as y þe bede!
> And 3ete we schal þe more do,
> 3if þou wilt wirche after mi red:
> A temple in þi worþschip make
> Of marble ston, when þou art ded;
> Among our godes þou schalt be sett
> In siluer and in gold rede. (lines 249–56)

While this response may be read as a strategic move to tempt Katherine with the very object of her vitriol, it also performs a commentary on the

seductions of images, drawing on visual cultic practice to discipline the reader. Maxentius's offer to have an image made of Katherine plays to a common tenet in the critique of idolatry, which is that worship of idols is tantamount to the worship of self. In the market square challenging the emperor or debating the philosophers, Katherine is spectacularly visible: she is the center of all lines of sight—like an image, in fact. The Katherine legend circulated in the fourteenth century and beyond in a culture saturated with Katherine images; yet in her discourse in the *passio* she disavows both the image and the cult. An early reader of the Auchinleck MS could well have in his or her mind's eye a favorite image of the saint, precisely what the soon-to-be martyr is at pains to disavow in the legend. Indeed, in the conclusion of the legend, in which six angels transport her body to a tomb on Mt. Sinai—a tomb notably made of marble (line 774)—she transforms into precisely the kind of cult object that Maxentius earlier proposed. The difference, of course, lies in affiliation to the right kind of family: To worship Katherine's image, one has to be a Christian, and hence worship not only Katherine but also Christ, her mystical husband. Where Maxentius also goes wrong lies in his promise of an image that is entailed by both sex (his infatuation) and money (silver and red gold on her tomb). In this text, a romance, we are invited to take the parts of both Katherine *and* Maxentius, resisting him but also desiring her, a hybrid mix of conflicting affiliations that works to discipline the self before the cult image on Sinai in the final lines.

In Knighton's story of Lollard desecration of a Katherine image, a subtext of love gone awry also circulates to define the question of response to images as an issue of desire. As he frames his incident of image breaking to connect the story of the two Lollards with the larger social epidemic of Lollard heretics, Knighton also transforms the story into an act of misogynist violence, unmanning Smith and Waytestathe as impotent Lollards while underwriting a defense of corporeal images. Much like Maxentius, the beauty-struck and enraged tyrant of the St. Katherine legend, Smith and Waytestathe take action not only against an image, but also against a certain resistant femininity. Knighton mobilizes the pleasures of romance— that is, love, sex, and violence—to transform a response to an image into a story about reactions to a body, crossing genres between romance and chronicle to blur as well the boundaries between object and flesh.

Knighton's account begins with a causal moment that attributes Smith's fanaticism to female rejection, a fervent asceticism embraced in reaction to the spurning of a marriage proposal: "Despicable and deformed in his person, he had once sought to marry a young woman, and when she spurned him he affected the outward forms of sanctity so extravagant that he despised all earthly desires, renounced the embraces of women forever" (293).[18] Later, when Smith and Waytestathe destroy the image, Knighton casts that act as one of misogynist violation. Although he makes no overt connection between the destruction of the image and the earlier jilting, the narrative offers a clear map of the psychic etiology. Preparing to chop off her head, as one holds the axe and the other holds the image, Smith and Waytestathe speak of the image as a "she," rather than a neutral "it," and conduct their experiment to find out if *she* is holy: "experiamur certe utrum hec uera sancta sit" (296). Furthermore, their curiosity about whether or not she will bleed once her head is chopped off evokes the martyrdom of St. Katherine, killed by decapitation. In an action that would seem to hearken to that evidentiary moment, Smith and Waytestathe not only burn the image for fuel, but first decapitate it to see what will happen: "for if her head should bleed when we strike it, then we shall worship her as a saint. On the other hand if no blood flows, she will make fire to cook our stew, and thus our hunger will be abated" (297).[19] While some particulars of the Katherine legend change from account to account, a constant of her story is the miracle of the transformation of her blood; as recorded in the Auchinleck St. Katherine, when her head is cut off, "but for þe blood þe mylk out ran."[20] In Knighton's story, decapitation is the occasion for a kind of culinary *reductio*. Like the legendary milk, the statue still affords nourishment—but in the form of cabbage soup.

Knighton never tells us whether or not the statue bleeds when its head is cut off but suggests instead that the use of the statue for cooking fuel performs instead an inverse transubstantiation, feeding a raft of ill-begotten disciples in a kind of first/last supper that lures them to heresy. Much of the story is told in a long piece of doggerel in Latin hexameters—the traditional form of the mock heroic—spliced with sexual and scatological innuendo.[21] The poem ends with a promise of the soup in the conditional: "'If blood flows when she is struck, let her be called true / But if not, per orders, let her be considered food for our fire' / the more quickly the miserable trash is cooked, the more their hunger will be satiated with the cabbage, and hunger flees from them quickly."[22] Knighton then resumes his chronicle to tell us of the consequences, which is that the trick converted the multitudes: "The numbers believing in those doctrines increased, and as it were bred and multiplied greatly, and they filled the land, and peopled it as though they were begotten in a single day" (298–99).[23]

Although Knighton recounts the anecdote within a vitriolic attack on Lollardy, Smith and Waytestathe as *collatores* are described only as *sceleri*, scoundrels. By the use of lively dialogue, a mock-heroic poem, and a detailed recounting that imagines the act in all its singularity, Knighton makes light of the menace of iconoclasm, presenting this event as both extremist and aberrant: Image burning is a dirty joke. Yet even if the account asserts that heretics have little power over images, it concurrently claims that images have power over heretics; and even more, it claims that the power of images is coterminus with a certain sexualized or feminized agency, either the social agency of women to jilt or the magical agency to survive violation. Knighton even splices his account of the desecration of the Katherine statue with an aside on Lollard iconomachs, or image haters, that makes a specific equation between the hatred of idols and the fear of female saints: "It was a characteristic of that sect of Lollards that they hated and inveighed against images, and preached that they were idols, and spurned them as a deceit, so that when one of them referred to St. Mary of Lincoln, or St. Mary of Walsingham, he would call them sorceresses [epialtes], that is, in the mother tongue: 'The witch of Lincoln, [Wiche of Lincolle]' and 'the witch of Walsingham [Wyche of Walsyngham]' and the like" (297).[24] This aside lends the local account of the two Leicester outlaws a larger resonance, explaining the actions of Smith and Waytestathe through the logic of sectarian fanaticism. In the 1380s, Knighton suggests, iconophobia was particular to certain groups within Lollardy rather than a defining characteristic of the movement as a whole. The aside also reverberates in surprisingly prophetic ways with much later Protestant iconoclastic dogma, which consistently invoked metaphors of female sexuality to justify the desecration of images. As Huston Diehl argues in a study of post-Reformation iconophobia, Protestant rhetoric consistently feminizes and sexualizes images of the saints. Diehl suggests that for the Protestants, religious images came to condense multiple forms of desire; phenomena came to stand in for pneuma, dead material images for forms of desire that were not dead, but outlawed.[25] Iconoclastic violence, she also claims, expressed a rage against the repression of bodily and imaginative pleasures: "Implicit in iconoclastic acts . . . is a profound recognition of the world's luminous beauty, the body's sensual pleasures, the imagination's splendid creations: the iconoclasts fear what they love, destroy what they desire." The rhetoric of violence against images, expressed both in acts of literal destruction of images and in fictive acts of murder on the Renaissance stage, became inseparable from a rhetoric of violence against women, a collapsed semiotic that yoked adoration of women with adoration of seductive and feminized images, and punished both.[26]

In suggesting that Smith's rage arises from a specific act of rejection in love, Knighton pictures a similar etiology, though his account suggests that this event was local and idiosyncratic. It was not yet part of a wide-spread iconoclastic fervor. Written 150 years before the systematic destruction of images in the Reformation, Knighton frames his story to suggest that not only were Smith's actions prompted by his rejection in love but also that Lollard response to images in general was fueled by a rage against women and a reflex to a renunciation of bodily pleasures. In the generalizing aside that punctuates the dialogue between Smith and Waytestathe as they prepare to chop the image, Knighton targets two important female cult images as the objects of Lollard hatred, and even translates Smith and Waytestathe's invective into the vernacular (the *materna lingua*, the mother tongue), as if fully to exploit the implications of local space usurped by the Witch of Lincoln, the Witch of Walsingham.[27] Later, in the midst of verse reprisal of the event (a poem that Knighton credits to another, "a certain rhymster"), the dialogue attributed to the Lollards even pointedly alludes to the pollution inhering in the female body and sexualizes the violation. Searching through an old chapel for cooking fuel, one of them finds an image of Katherine on an altar and quips that it has been decaying, with implications of putrification, like the virago Eve: "que putret ut Eua uirago" (298). The image, that is, is insentient matter; like the body, it is liable to decay. It is also specifically like a female body, the body of Eve, and a female body that has violated categorical definition and hence gone rotten even in life. Transgression is also suggested in the term "virago." While "virago" appears both in the Vulgate and in the Wycliffite Bible as a synonym for Eve, (Genesis 2:23), the context in Knighton's poem is far more suggestive of mannish excess, the "virago" Sultaness of Chaucer's *Man of Law's Tale*, "O Sowdanesse, roote of Iniquitee! / Virago, thou Semyrame the secounde!"[28] Their action on the image is a thinly veiled rape: "let us test whether this woman was / A true nurturer through our burning of her, or let us violate her; / If blood flows when she is struck, let her be called true" (298).[29]

* * *

As he casts the Lollard antipathy toward images as a kind of "gynophobic iconophobia," to borrow a term from Diehl,[30] Knighton thus seems at pains to English his terms and localize the discourse, as if in an effort to capture a *mentalité*. "Witch of Lincoln," "Witch of Walsingham" and "Virago Eve" all suggest the power of the image in a feminine incarnation to exceed inanimate form. Expressed in the invective is a belief, or rather a fear, that images are *not* just dead stocks and stones. This form of name-calling is also particularly resonant in a story about the destruction of an image of St. Katherine. In the Auchinleck Katherine, Maxentius says to his wife, after she has converted to Christianity, "Now y wot, þou art desceyved / þurch wichecraft of þat woman" (254, lines 524–25)—shortly before ordering that his wife's breasts be cut off. In this accusation, echoed in other versions of the Katherine legend,[31] such as John Capgrave's much later *Katherine*, when Katherine defends Christ and Mary against accusations of witchcraft from the king of Media, Katherine seems to take on the social role of Lollard, engaging in public preaching and facing accusations of witchcraft. As Karen Winstead points out in *Virgin Martyrs*, St. Katherine acts like the "sterotypical Lollard wife," particularly in Capgrave's mid-fifteenth-century reprisal, "deriding tradition and quoting scripture" as she preaches to Maxentius and the philosophers.[32] Also like a Lollard reformer, Katherine defines her platform through her condemnation of pagan idols as dead stocks and stones.

Yet in its broader contours, the legend of St. Katherine in its many retellings in the late Middle Ages in fact tells a story of sorcery, or at least Christian magic. While certain elements of the Katherine legend appear to ally the saint with the outlaw and the heretic—speaking out, challenging authority, and attacking the worship of idols—the legend also affirms a highly orthodox narrative of sanctity, in which the body of the saint in effect performs the role of sacred image, but one situated in the uneasy zone between object and person. In the excesses of her own *passio*, impermeable to death, and even in the substance of Katherine's debate with the philosophers, her life and discourse dramatize the very excesses of desire and female bodiliness that are evoked in Knighton's imagining of the Lollards' metaphor that describes the statue rotting like the virago Eve, "ut Eua Virago." In some versions of the *passio*, her discourse with the philosophers also affirms verbally that life can inhabit the human body in miraculous and excessive ways. While the nature of this exchange differs significantly from account to account, a common form of the debate in later versions represents Katherine in a defense of the Trinity and of incarnate form. In an early fifteenth-century prose *passio* that gives a particularly lengthy version of this debate, the pagan philosophers take her to task for believing in God's triune nature, a challenge that she meets through a skillful defense of plurality by congruity.[33] When a second philosopher challenges her to explain why the three persons of the Trinity are not each incarnate, Katherine answers through the analogy between the soul and reason, both of which operate together in the body (lines 737–52). When a third philosopher challenges her beliefs by denying the possibility of the Virgin birth, Katherine counters by pointing to the flowering of Aaron's rod as an indication of God's power to permit bodily miracles. What all of Katherine's rejoinders share, besides a skillful use of logic to outargue the logicians, is a focus on the ability of the divine body to express the miraculous and to defy singular and normative processes. Much as her own coming martyrdom will confirm the lasting vivacity of the saint's body, Katherine's philosophic defense of the incarnation and of the triune nature of God converts the philosophers through her picture of the miraculous ways that life inhabits and animates Christ's body. Christ's body and the saint's body are both wonder-working images whose efficacy is inseparable from bodily form.

Certainly it can be said that saints' lives in general enact this drama of excess. Along with a fantasy of resistance to tyranny and paganism, the saint's legend also dramatizes a fantasy of resistance to death. This dream of resistance to dying is without a doubt the darkest and sweetest longing voiced in the medieval lives of the saints. While death is a necessary precondition of sanctity, of course—and Katherine of course dies—the form of the *passio* conventionally casts that death as an incidental property of painless acts of torture. The saint rarely appears to suffer, but like Cecilia or Chaucer's Litel Clergeon, sings after his or her throat is cut. In *Afterlives of the Saints*, a study of the devolution between medieval hagiography and post-Reformation romance, Julia Lupton casts this resistance within the framework of originary lack and compensatory sacrifice, arguing that the "reliquary encryption" of the saint's body plays to psychic desires for wholeness; the saint in its idealized beauty and vivacity is the body as it wishes itself to be, and the saint in the shape of relic the circulating form of the Lacanian *corps morcelé*.[34] Katherine's heroic resistance to Maxentius gives us a story of survival against all odds, and a survival that carries with it considerable carnage to others: the death of the fifty philosophers, the death by mutilation of Maxentius's wife and of Porphyry after they have converted to Christianity, and the death of thousands when the Katherine wheel breaks into sharp pieces. Just before Maxentius cuts off Katherine's head, she is given a guarantee of life by angels who welcome her into heaven. As milk pours out instead of blood, even her body promises nurturance.

In the Katherine legends, the saint's own extraordinary corporeality affirms the miraculous efficacy of the wonder-working image, even as her critique of pagan idols attempts to stake out a clear line between the living and the dead. A central concern in Lollard critiques of the worship of images, and one that was also voiced in orthodox reformist opinion, centered on the failure of worshippers to distinguish between the form of the image and the idea behind the object. As W. R. Jones puts it, "the kindest thing that Lollards could say about images was that they were mere 'blynde stokys' and 'dede stonys,' possessed of no marvelous power and, therefore, incapable of the wonders attributed to them by popular credulity."[35] The saint in the saint's legend affirms a curious permeability, in which the forces of life clearly exceed mere corporeal form. Sanctity is this very promissory inseparability, in which the intensity of life that prompts her martyrdom is also the quality that guarantees her the status of the undead. She is neither blind nor dead.

Knighton's account, linking the destruction of a Katherine image with vitriol directed against "Eua uirago" and also local cult images of Mary of Walsingham and Mary of Lincoln, identifies the Lollard animus against images as a fear of excess, of the ability of objects to exert precisely the kind of power that the Katherine legend affirms as central to the martyr's body. The Katherine legend plays out a high-stakes drama of the life and death of images, in which Katherine affirms their essential vivacity as Maxentius attempts both literally and figuratively to sever life from bodily form. But the divide between person and image is unclear, of course, because the legend tells a story of a person becoming an image; and in the Katherine story, we are particularly conscious of this transaction as a young woman, wooed from multiple sides as a form of property, transforms into a cultic site, public property, in a sense, for all. Within Knighton's story of deviant fears of an object for its hints of life, we may detect as well, I suggest, an expression of anxieties about the pleasures of material goods—the afterlives of objects and the claims not only that images exert on the beholder, but also that beholders can exert on images. Knighton was writing his account at a time of dramatic growth in the production of devotional images, and also at a time of growing anxieties about the public display of expensively decorated devotional images, a critique voiced in sermons, secular texts, and anticlerical satire. As I have suggested, the critique of images, both Lollard and evangelical, was closely entwined with the attack on rich images. Implicit in this literature is a recognition that images not only claim their worshippers but also that pilgrims and devotees exact very particular claims on images, and that the contingencies of value circulating within and around devotional images are profoundly and complexly allied with wealth, and perhaps even rather specifically with class. Many of the critiques of images for their potential as commercial objects were voiced within orthodox circles as reformist opinion. Richard Fitzralph, archbishop of Armagh, in 1356 denounced those who worshipped the images of St. Mary of Lincoln and St. Mary of Walsingham—like Smith and Waytestathe—and in the same sermon condemned the keepers of shrines for creating miracles for their own benefit.[36] As Jones and Aston both note, Lollard polemic frequently targeted the expensive ornament of images for its promotion of "idolatry, clerical luxury, and aristocratic avarice,"[37] yoking money, class, and religion as entwined components of a pernicious fetishism. What connections can we draw between fears of the magical powers of images and tensions about patronage and lavish ornament of devotional objects? And what features of St. Katherine might make her a particularly likely target?

There is little in Knighton's account to suggest that this Katherine image is a rich image or that the seductions of the cult Marys are materialist in nature—to suggest, that is, that Smith and Waytestathe singled out this image because of its particular ornamentation or its status as cult property. Nevertheless, the narrative trajectory of the Katherine legend allows us to consider that this assault on a Katherine image in some ways articulates a refraction of the materialist critique. Intrinsic to both the saint's legend and the devotional image is excess or superfluity, matter that cannot be contained as matter and whose alloyed substance promises returns in the afterlife. Material possessions, whether in the form of an exquisitely carved image of St. Margaret standing on her dragon or of a household chair, are always totemic. Extensions (sometimes metastatic) of the body, possessions either stay fixed and close to the bone as tactile extensions of the body or else circulate in the world, sold, given or bequeathed, as bionic or cyber projections that carry transactional powers to resist pain and survive death—a transactional process particularly resonant for late medieval England, with its influx of capital and of material goods. The apparent fascination with death, often invoked when describing the fifteenth century, should perhaps be understood rather as resistance to death or even a fantasy of permanence, a redefinition of the rule of the body to append to the body the objects that it has claimed. Fifteenth-century testators speak of death in very familiar ways, and speak of it often, not from a terror of death but from a curious position of familiarity, and with transactional rhetoric: death can be bought off through the "purchase of paradise."[38] As Gail McMurray Gibson observes, the endowment of posthumous prayers and charities is the signature focus of fifteenth-century wills; and many wills involve gifts of objects (altar cloths, plate, candles, and so on) to the church.[39] These "gifts," however, should properly be thought of as bartering chips. If we follow Derrida's logic and agree that the gift is an endgame, its status as gift determined by its hypereconomy, as that which cannot be given back, then we should consider lay endowments not gifts at all but rather as commercial transactions, designed to be repaid.[40] Chantry endowments and gifts of objects to the parish fall into the category of the toll, payment to the gatekeeper to speed the way through purgatory. The self is no longer confined to the life of the body and the hereafter, but can also live on in objects that one gives as legacy. The rhetoric of morbidity in pre-Reformation England often takes the form of a quasi-legalistic negotiation with death that will change, if not the time of its coming, then the form of its claims. Death may not be optional, but it is negotiable.

While properties of miraculous survival may be said to be true generally of the Christian martyrs, Katherine is a particularly vivid example. Indeed, her philosophical defense of immanence blended with her potently linear narrative of survival might account in part for her extraordinary popularity in late medieval England, with its burgeoning circulation of capital and concomitant obsession with death and the beyond. Through her attack on idols and her contrasting defense of the Christian body to contain both body and spirit, immanence and permanence, Katherine celebrates body, and specifically a highly desirable female body, as a form of capital. At the same time, however paradoxically, the radical ethics of her story also lie in her demand of "originary freedom," in Foucault's terms; or to borrow a phrase from Judith Butler, she practices the "art of voluntary insubordination in the politics of truth."[41] She resists tyranny with a self-immolating act of will. Her own drama, caught between freedom and possession, insubordination and subordination as property on a marriage market, parallels some of the tensions about images circulating at large and played out in her own story. Who lays claim to her body—or her image?

The conventions for representing Katherine in late medieval images and even specific forms of patronage exploit this imbrication of matter with vivacity, even suggesting that it is the upper-classed body that triumphs over death. In an illustration from an Hours of the Virgin, c. 1400, St. Katherine, signed by her wheel, downward-turned sword, and the ring of her mystical marriage, stands in marked contrast to St. Margaret, commanding visual space in a curiously assertive mastery. Her right hand curls around the spiked wheel, while her sword appears to spear Margaret's dragon (fig. 7).

Figure 7. St. Katherine and St. Margaret. Oxford, Bodleian Library, MS Lat.
Liturg. F. 2. fol. 11v. Courtesy of Bodleian Library, University of Oxford.

In fifteenth-century manuscript illustration, Katherine is often notable for her elegance. As Karen Winstead shows in her generously illustrated book, in glass and in manuscript painting Katherine is often represented as a beautiful and fashionably dressed rich girl. Torturers and their instruments are displayed almost playfully, Maxentius as a squashed figure under Katherine's foot and the spiked wheel designed for her dismemberment as a prop or even almost a toy.[42] An illustration that incorporates Katherine into an aristocratic household with particular vividness appears in a fifteenth century Book of Hours, made for a lady in the diocese of Poitiers (fig. 8). In this miniature Katherine is in her study. Her identifying mark, the wheel, has almost taken on the status of what Panofsky calls a disguised symbol, just part of the furniture, suggesting a woman's spinning wheel more than an instrument of torture. The sword of her martyrdom, which often appears as a secondary identifying mark, supports the table like an extra leg, connecting the table with the wheel on the floor. On the table is a large book, Katherine's particular emblem as a philosopher and also a marker of learning that would make this image of particular appeal to a female patron.[43]

In a study of the Katherine cult, Katherine Lewis argues that while the saint was certainly popular with people across a wide range of social backgrounds, the appearance of her *vita* in household books of well-to-do families suggests that Katherine functioned as something of a model of conduct for the upwardly mobile, and that the Katherine cult "appears to have been bound to an identity of power and status."[44] The appeals or demands of class might also be read into a brief record in Walsingham's *Chronicon Angliae* of 1387, which tells how Sir John Montagu stripped the images, with the exception of St. Katherine, from the chapel at his manor and hid them away. St. Katherine was put in a bake house because "plures afficiebantur"—because many loved her.[45] Katherine's unique association with philosophical learning might have also contributed to a certain class-based appeal. While saints in late medieval English panel and wall painting are often represented as carrying books, Katherine's book has a direct association with the story of her unusual education and uses of philosophical argument to refute the sages. We can speculate that Knighton might have fictionalized Smith, "so called from his craft," as lashing out at a Katherine image in a directed assault on an image associated with the gentry—or with desires for gentrification. Katherine's widespread popularity among both men and women from a wide range of social classes, from queens to wheelwrights and wet nurses, suggests we should use caution, however, in

Figure 8. St. Katherine. Baltimore, Walters Gallery MS W. 222, fol. 30v. Courtesy Walters Art Museum, Baltimore.

drawing simple parallels between the class of individual patrons or iconoclasts and the class of their chosen saints.[46]

Knighton's narrative, however, scripts the motivation with broader
strokes to align Lollard iconoclasm with hatred of life itself. Knighton's
psychological portrait of an image breaker implies that Smith's action had
at its heart a rage against loss and that Smith's animus against specifically
female saints rose from the denial of certain pleasures. Renouncing meat,
wine, and women, living in a ruined chapel near a leper hospital, and burning a saint's image to make a peasant soup—the Lollards as Knighton tells
it inhabit the margins, somewhere between life and death. Katherine, to
the contrary, signifies life; saints' images in late medieval England bespeak
a highly materialist promise of life, the powers of the body to resist not
only pain but death and to do so through transactions that are often
remarkably commercial. The ties to capital that circulate around the narratives and cult images of Katherine are dramatized most strikingly in her
own *passio*; and even as she foregoes the world and denounces idols as
dead substances, Katherine herself becomes a far more dynamic form of
currency. Do objects have life? Lollard as well as conventional reformist
dogma argue no. Yet the cult image, annexed to and animated by capital,
makes a very different claim.

Hilton's "Merk Ymage"

Within a few years of Knighton's narrative of image breaking, Walter Hilton
wrote two tracts in which an image figures as an important structuring
metaphor: the *De ymagine peccati*, a letter from the early 1380s, in which
an image (as the title suggests) is a metaphor for an excursus on sin, and
the first book of the *Scale of Perfection*. Midway through *Scale of Perfection 1*, his devotional guide for an unnamed anchoress, Hilton introduces
a startling new conceit, one that will reappear and structure his discourse
almost to the end. Advising the anchoress to withdraw her thoughts from
all earthly things and bodily sensations, the narrator warns that it will
be difficult, "traveilous," because vain thoughts will pull downward from
her heart. You are seeking Jesus, the narrator says, but will find something
else. And what, he asks at the end of Chapter 52, will you find? The narrator caps his warnings on the importance of bodily discipline with a picture
of the inevitable cracks in self-control, the pressures and descent "down"
from the pure control of evacuated thought. What you will find, he finally

says, is a "merk ymage," a dark and painful image of our own soul, "whiche hath neither light of knowynge ne felynge of love ne likynge. This ymage yif thou biholde it wittirly, is al bilappid with blake stynkande clothis of synne, as pride, envie, ire, accidie, glotonye, and leccherie" (52.1495–98).[47] This "merk ymage," as he explains it, is both visual and physical, "bilapped" in its allegorical clothes of the seven deadly sins. It is to be seen and even touched.

In this section I would like to consider the bodily nature of this "merk ymage" in the first book of *Scale*. The representation of the image of sin as a thing, and even as a body, is nuanced by some of same horror and disgust that iconoclasts Smith and Waytestathe direct toward a wooden carving of St. Katherine. How does Hilton's image of an image engage with reformist concerns about devotional objects, and particularly with concerns about their material seductions? During his life and in the years following his death Hilton was one of the most widely read and influential of the fourteenth-century English writers in the mystical tradition. As attested by its forty-five extant manuscripts, *Scale 1* was a work of deep and enduring influence, a popular lay devotional text in England during the fifteenth century and, following its printing in 1494 by Wynkyn de Worde, in the sixteenth century as well.[48] Some of its popularity might be due to its rhetorical engagement with timely issues, among them the image debate. In yoking "dark" with "image," Hilton creates a new and unusual metaphor out of two terms that both had wide currency in the theological writings of his contemporaries. For instance, Pseudo-Dionysius, a foundational author for writers in the late medieval contemplative tradition, speaks of a "luminous darkness" that exists between us and God. "Luminous darkness" is adopted as a central term in the *Cloud of Unknowing*, a work that Hilton knew well and to which he responds in *Scale 2*.[49] "Image," at least as a metaphor for the likeness of God in us, was equally familiar. According to J. P. H. Clark, Hilton sees the rational soul as the *imago dei*, a reflection of the trinity governing the inferior body. Derived from Augustine's *De Trinitate*, the *imago dei* became a theological commonplace taken up, for example, by Bonaventure, Peter Lombard, Aquinas, Hugh of St. Victor, and Bernard. Although Hilton's uses of the *imago dei* are consistent with the "deliberately conservative Augustinianism which pervades his writing,"[50] less traceable to theological antecedents is Hilton's "imago peccati" or his "merk ymage" that occludes the *imago dei* in us. Clark speculates that doubtless Hilton "draws on some sources—probably close to him in time—which are yet to be traced."[51]

Those sources may indeed be close in time to Hilton. In using an
"ymage" as a sign for sin Hilton takes up a term of newly topical resonance,
importing some of the horror with which devotional images had been
invested in reformist writings but then using that horror to condemn not
objects of popular devotion themselves but rather sins of the body, or even
more broadly, the evils of self-love. In a recent study Nicholas Watson
has tracked the uses of the terms "image" and "idol" in Hilton's writings,
arguing that Hilton's rhetorical uses of these terms evolved in dialogue
with his contemporaries, among them Lollards as well as the anonymous
author of the *Cloud of Unknowing*.[52] While it has not been possible to date
either *Scale 1* or *2* with any certainty, both were written most likely between
the early 1380s and 1396, the year of Hilton's death.[53] The dark image,
figure for a self-love that moves not to God but back to the carnal body,
may even be said to embody some of the traits of devotional images that
are specifically condemned in reformist polemic, even though Hilton, a
conservative Augustinian in many respects, was a firm opponent of Lollard
doctrine.[54] Commenting that Hilton "belongs to the same thought-world
as the Lollard radicalism he opposed," Watson argues that Hilton uses the
shock value of images in ways similar to the Lollards.[55] In *Scale 1* the "merk
ymage" becomes a metaphor for a constellation of wrongs that include intellectual error as well as moral and bodily weakness. Hilton seems to use
the metaphor of the image to comment less on public uses of images than
on sin—even turning this important term from Wycliffite critique against
the Lollards themselves. In his uneasy response to material devotional
objects, Hilton may have been writing as a proponent of reclusive meditation or as an intellectual, skeptical about the theatrics of devotional excess
in the churches of his time. Most readers believe Hilton to be the author
of *De adoracione ymaginum* (*On the Worship of Images*), a tract defending
the uses of images in worship, although, as Watson notes, they are defended
only with "passionless correctness."[56] In Hilton's other Latin and vernacular writings, "images" refer either to pure negativity or "nought" or else to
idols of the self and are given a grotesque sensuality. As Watson concludes,
"Hilton, all said and done, did not like them very much."[57]

In *Scale 1*, however, Hilton imbues an image of an image with both
passion and sensuousness, giving the dark image, from its first appearance
in the middle of the text, a dramatic and attenuated form as the object in
a kind of quest-romance. The rhetoric of the "merk ymage" is ethically
charged, a fetish discourse about the love of an object attached to our
being. The "merk image" as well as the idol that it is finally revealed to

be both take particular shape in *Scale 1* through the feminizing of the reader and operate with a strategic metaphoric doubling to yoke sexuality, and especially female sexuality, not just with deviance but also heresy. Read in the manner of allegory, the text develops a conventional devotional program: In the search for Jesus, we will first be sidetracked and waylaid by Jesus' antitype, the covetous soul. In its dramatic development and local echoes, however, the first book of *Scale* is by no means conventional. Carefully attuned to a female audience and deploying an unusual metaphor that had become complexly freighted in the late fourteenth century with disciplinary echoes, *Scale 1* is goal directed, attentive to its audience, keyed to desires and fears. In the religious climate of late fourteenth-century England, "image" offers Hilton a metaphor that is brilliantly apt for a meditative program that takes both heterodoxy and bodily pleasure as its targets.

Hilton's "merk image," held out as an object or fear and fascination, is itself built of contradictions: the evacuated body or "nought"; an object we can hold in our hand; our own body, suddenly erupting with extra limbs and spliced for horror—rather like the growing amoeboid Blob in Irvin Yeaworth's 1958 horror film or like the monstrous spider in Ridley Scott's *Alien* films, outside in another place in space/time yet also in our own bodies, but after all, just a bug, a "nought." Desires for simple binaries, inside and outside, clean and unclean, often lend those desires that cross boundaries or threaten the borders the features of monsters, as work in postcolonial studies has shown.[58] These are the desires that Hilton's narrator tells the anchoress to wall out of her body and also of the anchorhold, the inorganic structure that stands in for and perfects the body's permeable borders: "thu schuldest knowe that the cause of thy bodili enclosynge is that thu myght the betere come to goosteli enclosynge; and as thi bodi is enclosid fro bodili conversacioun of men, right so that thyn hert myght be enclosid from fleisschli loves and dredis of alle ertheli thynges" (1.18–21). From the first chapter, enclosure is imagined through exclusion: heart, body, and cell are pictured through what they exclude.

"Merk" is an apt modifier for the image that crosses these boundaries. In the York *Creation and Fall*, God specifies "merkness" as a palpable darkness that can only be named through negatives: "In hell shall never mirkness be missing; / The mirkness, thus name I for night."[59] In *Scale 1*, the "merk" image comes to fill, in a sense, the gap opened or performed by the evacuation of bodiliness, presenting itself as a figure for the carnality from which the anchoress has been instructed to withdraw.[60] Adopting a rhetoric of suspicion toward the senses, all of which are to be evacuated, the text offers "merk ymage" as its figure for them in compacted form and ultimately as an object of disgust. And from the start this "merk ymage" is presented as mysterious: What is it and what is its form? Is it a thing, and if so what kind of thing? In asking these questions, Hilton also places them in the mouth of his imagined reader. As hints about this dark image intensify, questions about its nature and value also get sharpened through the parable of the woman who searches her house for a lost penny or drachma. Throughout, however, the nature of this image remains a paradox. It is both something and nothing, a "nought." That is, the image of sin in the self has substance as the error of fleshly desire; it is "nought" or negativity, in that sin, in an Augustinian sense, is the absence of the good; and it is "not" as the obverse of the "likeness" of Christ in which we should "array" ourselves (51). Perhaps its most striking feature is its indeterminacy as it shape-shifts between object and evacuated negativity, a thing or else "nought," a figure of absence.

Hilton's image, not black but "merk" or dark, containing the crepuscular quality of absence that turns its own materiality into an oxymoron, the thing that in its darkness would even be hard to see, comes from this border zone. In its hybrid status, thing and negativity, object and body, the dark image may refract concerns about the proper uses of religious sculptures and paintings circulating in the contemporary image debate, especially the refrain, echoed from all courts, urging us to worship not the image itself but the idea that the image represents. In *Scale 1* Hilton dramatizes this familiar commonplace of image worship, making capital of our displaced desire for stability invested in objects. Driving the ethical drama of *Scale 1* is the longing to see, know, and even touch this image, a quest that Hilton frames through hints that the image is a thing, however ominously or queerly charged. We long, that is, for things and for the revelation of things in their bodiliness and materiality. Only through discovery of the dark image (in ourselves) can we redirect the quest to the likeness of God.

Before that redirection, the dark image will need to be exposed for what it is. This false image in the self, "wel foule disfigured and forschapen with wrecchidnesse of alle thise synnes whiche I have spoken of," is an idol, a "mawmet" (84.2418–20). It is ugly to look on, and its limbs and members and body parts can each be identified as a particular kind of sin. We have looked it over, investigated it, and now see the whole thing: "Inveni idolum michi" ("I have found the idol of myself") (84.2417). In revealing that the dark image is in fact an idol, Hilton echoes a reformist critique of images as useless idols, worshipped wrongly for their imagined powers.

When Dives remarks that people who kneel and pray in front of images seem to be worshipping them, Pauper answers that if we pray to images themselves we practice idolatry and cannot be excused, for idolatry is a sin against reason and against nature.[61] For Wyclif all manufactured objects could potentially be idols: "Therefore the variety of apparel, buildings, utensils and other objects invented by pride constitutes the book or graven image of the devil, by which mammon or another is worshipped in the image. Therefore the whole Church, or a great part of it, is tainted by this idolatry, because the works of their hands are effectively more highly valued than God."[62] In his treatise on the Commandments Wyclif also warns against the body as a site of idolatry: "Whoever sins in deed, as when he inordinately loves the creature, offends against the first commandment by committing idolatry."[63] In *Scale*, the revelation that the image is an idol may be colored by similar anxieties: If we can locate an image in the self, we may also be close to a dark revelation about our own idolatrous nature. And that idolatrous nature, like Wyclif's love of "the creature," is essentially carnal. Hilton's achievement lies in part in his skillful interpolation of the language of popular ethical discourse, using the "merk ymage" as a figure in a vernacular meditative romance—or more exactly, a work of instruction that uses the language of seduction to achieve its own disciplinary ends.

Michael Camille's study of the imagery of idolatry can further shed light on the inherent eroticism of the figure of the image in *Scale 1*, particularly in the later chapters. As Camille demonstrates in *The Gothic Idol*, idols in medieval art are nearly always naked, and in fact offer offered the Middle Ages one of its few representations of the nude: "The rejection of the body in Christian art—an absolute reversal from the aesthetic standards of the ancient world—is one of the most crucial transformations in the history of Western art."[64] As a consequence of this renunciation, one of the few sites of licit representation of the body was the illicit—the idol, sign of the sins of Adam and Eve. The sexual deviance of idols is dramatized in these images as well as in medieval lives of the virgin martyrs, where a pagan emperor, usually a worshipper of idols, is also a devotee of the virgin's body; carnal worship is equivalent to carnal desire. In the many legends of St. Katherine, the saint whose image inflames the fires, so to speak, of Lollards Smith and Waytestathe, the *passio* explicitly interleaves eros and idolatry. The emperor's desire for Katherine and his plans to have an idol made in her image show that idolatry and lust are effectively the same.

Toward the end of *Scale 1*, when the "merk ymage" is described as a tactile thing, both images and idols seem to become carnal objects. In this text, as in Knighton's account of an assault on a statue of a virgin martyr, the carnal body is particularly lurid when it is female. When the image is finally revealed to be an idol, the anchoress is urged to "lifte up this image and loke wel al aboughte" (71.2041) and to "turne this image upsodoun and loke wel thereinne, and thou schal fynde two membris of envie and ire fastned therto" (64.1839–40). The gaze on the image in these passages seems astonishingly sexual. The "merk ymage" has morphed into a thing one can handle, like a small devotional object, and also, paradoxically, a body, dangling with members. It is both a body and an idol, imbued with an ambiguous materiality that clearly suggests that the carnal human body is itself an idol. She is looking at its underside—under its skirts. It has "members," a term whose primary meaning in Middle English is genitalia, either male or female.[65] In a later chapter the narrator comments even more specifically on the limbs of this "uggli ymage": The head is pride, its back is covetousness, its breast is envy, the arms are wrath, and its "members" are its sexual nature: "the membris of hit arn leccherie." He cites Paul, "yee schullen not gyve youre membres, speciali youre pruvé membres, to the armes of synne" (85.2446–49). In exposing these two members of the idol that is herself, the anchoress in a sense confronts her own carnal nature: She holds the pagan idol, and her body, in her hand.

Revealed at the end of a search that is rhetorically charged with longing and dread, the idol is thus overdetermined as an object of horror. Love of the self, especially our carnal self, that is, constitutes idolatry. Inflected by the image controversy, the idol represents an even more troubling discovery, for through it the narrator also suggests that we who have an idolatrous core might even be somehow associated with the discourses of idolatry, or even possibly be at risk for heresy ourselves. Images and idols carry a taint. Writing from the position of orthodoxy, Hilton invests an image with even greater horror than do the Lollards Smith and Waytestathe. It is just a short step, Lollard writings remind us, from prayers before devotional images of Christ and of the saints to prayers to those statues themselves, with all their material charms.

Capgrave's *Katherine* and the Wheel

The story of St. Katherine of Alexandria endures in a single symptom: the wheel. Most people today, if they know anything at all about St. Katherine, would probably mention only the wheel and would almost certainly describe it as the instrument of torture on which she was martyred. The wheel has even come to have a life of its own as an object entirely separate from the Katherine legend in the form of a popular fireworks display, the circular "katherine wheel." In pre-Reformation Europe, when narrative versions of the life and passion of St. Katherine enjoyed tremendous vogue, the wheel also frequently trumped the story in an iconic, highly material coalescence. In English and Continental manuscript illumination and stained glass, where the Katherine story only rarely appears in narrative form, the wheel is the saint's signifying mark, sometimes held in her hand in a gesture of mastery, sometimes haunting the background or floor.[66] As Pauper explains to Dives in *Dives and Pauper*, the wheel stands in for a causal and narrative sequence. Using Katherine's wheel as an example of devotional "ymagerye," a book of signs for the ignorant, Pauper explains that the wheel is a "special token" of the horrible wheels that Maxentius made to tear Katherine limb from limb but that were instead destroyed by an angel, "so they dedyn here noon harm."[67] Leaving her body miraculously untouched, as the Katherine legends say, the wheel nevertheless remains attached to Katherine's image in all virtually all visual representations, lodged between menace and triumph, a sign of torture or of survival. Like Lawrence's grill or Margaret's dragon, the wheel is the sign without which Katherine is unrecognizable.

The menacing materiality of the wheel is also a key factor of its function in the narrative lives of Katherine; and as I will argue in what follows, the wheel's materiality also marks it as an idol. An ineffectual object or thing, the wheel offers a dramatic foil for Katherine's incarnate vitality. Essential to the wheel in the Katherine legend is its manufacture. The wheel is not just brought in as an instrument of torture; it is constructed as a machine of techno-terror and in full public view. The narrative lives of Katherine are attentive to the production of the wheel and to the fear the construction inspires. In Capgrave's long verse *Life of St. Katherine* these features of production and construction are particularly marked. The manufacture of the wheel is the brainchild of Cursates, mayor of Alexandria and "puncher [punisher] of all cryme," who takes on the role of both "controllere and clerke," overseeing himself the work of carpenters and smiths, Robin and John, as the device is built close by, "right on the banke."[68] As a miracle of technology, the device also takes its peculiar form from its own self-propelling mechanism. As Cursates explains the device to the emperor Maxentius, it will work through four interlocking wheels. On the spokes of each wheel will be attached nails, sharp as a knife. Each of the four wheels will have angled saws fixed to the outside to connect them to one another, so the device as a whole will set in motion a whirling set of knives:

> Ech of hem be othir ful sotilly shall glyde;
> Summe shall com upward with her cours wide,
> Summe shal go downward, and thus shall thei rend
> All thing betwix hem and therof make an ende. (5.1285–88)

As an instrument of public punishment, the Katherine wheel represents a curious technological advance from wheels as they were used in spectacular punishments, almost exclusively for men, for particularly vivid crimes against community—robbery with murder or the murder of a spouse. Breaking on the wheel, a punishment used throughout Europe from the early Middle Ages into the eighteenth century, was a carefully engineered public spectacle that involved a highly ritualized and protracted mutilation of the body, followed by a lengthy display of both wheel and corpse.[69] The spectacle of the elevated body, displayed in format resonant of the crucifixion, is vividly conveyed in an illustration from the so-called *Book of Numquam*.[70] The condemned man, shaved and naked, is lashed to the raised wheel, his limbs broken and bleeding, as the executioner, holding fragments of the rope in his hand, displays his work to a group of spectators on the other side. Antonio de Beatis in 1517–18 describes the procedure: "The torture of the wheel consists in this: under the arms of the condemned man timbers are placed on the ground, and the executioner or a criminal breaks his arms with a wooden wheel, then breaks both his legs, and then with the same wheel breaks the man's back. Thus broken and shattered, the man is raised on the wheel and set atop a large beam upright in the ground—there the wretch is left breathing with difficulty."[71] A key component of this horrific spectacle is the agency of the executioner as a human manipulator of the community's most important tool, the wheel. The wheel is the instrument of breaking, but it is the executioner who literally does the labor of fracturing the body. The precise operation of the wheel is conveyed in a panel painting from 1480 from the Circle of the Master of the Martyrdom of the Apostles, *Saints Felix, Regula, and Exuperantius Broken on the Wheel*. Felix lies tied supine to a rack, gazing with horror on the wheel as it is about to be brought down again on his already broken body. In the background, Felix's sister Regula and their servant Exuperantius lie already broken and elevated, each tied to a wheel that is itself lashed to a sawed off tree trunk.[72]

The story of the wheel, which appears in some form in all narrative accounts of the Katherine *passio*, is no doubt to be imagined through the framework of this punitive social spectacle of breaking on the wheel.[73] The instrument in the Katherine narratives departs markedly in technological elaboration, however, for a particular horror of Cursates' wheel is that mutilation occurs from the whirling of the wheels themselves, with no apparent intervention by an executioner; and although someone must turn the wheel, no such agency is named in Capgrave, nor in other Katherine lives. In the *South English Legendary*, the wheels are self-propelled, "with ginne": "Four ʒweles of Iren he let fullen: with rasores, kene I-knowe, / And with ginne heom makede tuyrne a-boute."[74] In Capgrave, Katherine is brought forward and set between the wheels, and then all we are told of the agency behind the instrument's propulsion is that two wheels go downward and two slide upward (5.1308). The fear it is intended to inspire clearly lies in the multiplication of pain through internal mobilization. This particular form of spectacle, fear mobilized through the agency of a machine, meets with a dramatic reversal, or perhaps reprisal, for before the wheels can do their work, Katherine prays to God to destroy this "horribyll new torment" (5.1330) and an angel sends a thunderbolt, fracturing the wheel and setting in motion an incendiary holocaust, pieces of the burning wheel flying through the air, which leaves Katherine unharmed but four thousand of the pagan spectators dead. In a miniature from a fifteenth-century breviary, an angel carries out God's orders while Katherine turns away in prayer. In a kind of mechanical chaos, bodies collapse with the wheel (fig. 9). In this image, as in the narrative *passio*, technological propulsion is trumped by divine pyrotechnics. In a dramatic inversion, it is not the body that is broken by the wheel but the wheel itself that is exploded.

Although the wheel operates in the narrative as something of a grotesque curiosity, one that ultimately displays the emperor's weakness and Katherine's contrastive miraculous powers, it reinforces a larger commentary on objects and agency. The wheel in a sense appears as a technological construction of uncertain operation in a story that interrogates the status and powers of material things, particularly of idols. The story's central tension, the worship of idols, circulates in the narrative within a complex commentary on the location of agency—whether agency is to be found within the body, beyond the body in the powers of spirit, or within the image of the body, its constructed likeness. The Katherine story not only structures a saint's legend around the challenges of idolatry, it uses the framework of a saint's legend as a venue through which to rehearse issues about the uses of images. While the refusal of the saint to offer to pagan idols is a feature of many saint's lives, in the *passio* of St. Katherine the saint's refusal to offer not only signifies her special Christian status, but also sets the story in motion. The worship of idols in essence *is* the plot.

*   *   *

In John Capgrave's *Life of St Katherine*, written c. 1445, the commentary on the image debate is both modernized and localized through importation of terms from Lollard sect vocabulary. By the middle of the fifteenth century

Figure 9. An angel destroys the wheel. Breviary of St. Paul. Cambridge University Library, MS DD5-5, fol. 397r. Fifteenth century. By permission of the Syndics of Cambridge University Library.

the debate about images, as with other aspects of the Wycliffite heresy, had lost much of its public edge but was still an active topic of debate. Reginald Pecock's vernacular defense of orthodoxy, the *Repressor of Over Much Blaming of the Clergy* was written c. 1449, just a few years after Capgrave's *Katherine*. Defending visual images as crucial "seable rememoratijf signes" for simple folk, Pecock's treatise indicates the extent to which iconophobia remained an articulate presence.[75] In Capgrave's text, the question of images takes on spectral life through the image of the wheel, as we have seen, and also through the language and even persons of the central characters. Speaking out, challenging the emperor's use of images, engaging in public preaching, Katherine takes on a curiously Lollard-like position. Maxentius even calls her a "concyonatrix," a woman who harangues or makes speeches (5.960). The pagans, in a similar crossover, take the part of orthodox Christians; Maxentius asks Katherine to leave her "elde heresye" (5.641), and repeatedly accuses her of witchcraft (5.1019, 1121) and necromancy (5.1464), terms often used for Lollards. In an astute analysis of these rhetorical moves Karen Winstead suggests that Capgrave himself stood in an ambiguous position in relation to both political authority and religious orthodoxy, "eschewing certitude" and critiquing zealotry of all kinds—both Lollard and orthodox—rather than identifying with a single position.[76] Capgrave is an evasive and elusive commentator, presenting Katherine as an appealing and sentimentalized touchstone in a long commentary on the political and social scene. In separate studies James Simpson and Kathleen Kamerick have both recently added to Winstead's observations and further examined the relationship between Capgrave's St. Katherine and the Lollard image question, noting that Katherine's attacks on idols blur the boundaries between orthodox and heterodox positions.[77]

These analyses of Capgrave's position work well, I think, for helping us understand the complex rhetorical uses of images in his text. In Capgrave's *Katherine*, the performance of images also shows how easily objects can be mistaken for essences. Whereas Knighton and Hilton mobilize devotional images in the service of an ethical or devotional agenda, Capgrave seems interested in Katherine as an illustration of incarnate spirituality. Deflecting assaults on her own paradoxical carnality, she is the embodiment of spirit in action. While Knighton exploits the traditional iconography of idolatry to illustrate the horrors of Lollardy and Hilton echoes the materialist critique of images to underwrite an ascetic spirituality, Capgrave narrates a story about idolatry to comment on the status and work of devotional images. If both Maxentius and the wheel, along with the literal idols within the story, perform as idols in their failures of agency, they also offer a curious mirror of images as framed in Lollard critique. As the narrative point of view slips between orthodox and heterodox and as Katherine, Maxentius, and the philosophers each voices reversed positions in the image debate, the text offers a metacommentary on the troubling similarity between images and idols. Katherine, remarkable for her aggressive verbal assault on idols, takes on the role of Lollard by attacking devotional objects, even as she herself acts out the agency and efficacy of Christian devotional image. In the *passio* of Capgrave's text the central philosophical questions circulate around the inner life of objects. Though prolix—his Katherine is close to eight thousand lines of rhyme-royal verse—Capgrave is a skilled storyteller who structures his narrative around the drama of a remarkable, troubling, and quite believable heroine who resists assimilation into customary practices—whether those customs, as in the *vita*, are marriage, or, as in the *passio*, are public forms of worship. In many respects Capgrave treats the story in conventional ways; and indeed, the worship of idols is a common trope in medieval saints' lives. Nevertheless, by importing rhetoric from the image debate and by casting his narrative as a romance whose central players, Katherine and the emperor, act *as* images, Capgrave nuances his Katherine *passio* with hints about the uses and powers of objects: idols, Katherine herself. As the story unfolds, the balance between the emperor's worldly power and Katherine's mysterious agency progressively tips. As Maxentius tries, with increasing aggression, to claim her as property, his own powers diminish, until finally he is literally abandoned by both intellectual, martial, and domestic supports—his philosophers, his guards, and even his wife. Katherine, in contrast, takes on increasing agency. With the exception of the emperor, everyone she meets converts to Christianity. More dramatically, she activates a set of incendiary holocausts that leave her remarkably unharmed, even in her final decapitation, when milk pours out instead of blood. In the escalating drama of their interaction, Maxentius not only worships idols but also performs as an idol, demonstrating in his own powerlessness the same ineffectuality as his wheel. Katherine, to the contrary, operates like a devotional and even wonder-working image—not stock or stone but devotional alloy, conductor for powers but herself impervious to damage. She is not a dead image. The conflict between Katherine and the pagans frames the issues as ones of valuation and efficacy, or even of vivacity: What does this image do for you?

In Capgrave's *Katherine*, the worship of idols appears at multiple points in the text, fueling dramatic tension between Maxentius and Katherine as

they spar over his offer to make an idol of her and grounding a philosophical problem in her debate with the philosophers. Maxentius's offer to have
a statue made in Katherine's likeness contributes to the romance story,
the temptation of the heroine. It also offers a bit of comic relief. After the
martyrdom of the converted philosophers, Maxentius professes his love
for Katherine and makes a second offer to set an image of her in the market place, in which he will "counterfete youre face." She will be "deyfyed"
(5.401, 415). In her rebuke and refusal, Katherine laughs. How, she asks,
can any workman make an image that is living? "But this wold I knowyn
or we this thinge make: / Of what matere schall my legges be? / What
manere werkman that dare undyrtake / To make hem to meve and walke in
her degré?" (5.449–52). The statue will be a waste of money and time, for
it will be dead. It will have problems with birds: "Ther shall comyn sumtyme a full grete rowth / Here unclene dunge shall thei there put oute /
And lete it falle rith on the ymage face" (5.473–75).[78]

The central tension, as Capgrave's reprisal of the image debate makes
clear, lies in the vivacity of matter. Idols are dead images. In her disputation with the philosophers, Katherine consistently defends incarnate form
and trinitarian doctrine as the coexistence of body and spirit. When one
of the philosophers argues that pagan gods only represent abstractions, he
offers an argument startlingly similar to orthodox defenses for Christian
devotional images: "Thus are oure goddys in manere of allegorye / Resemble to natures whech that be eterne" (4.1583–84); that is, images only
resemble abstractions. Refuting him, she points to the closed circle of matter that defines his "allegorye," since his eternal "natures" to which images
refer are the planets, the pagan pantheon: "Ye worchep the schadow and
leve the substauns" (4.1615). Her defense of images, in contrast, lies in an
argument for vivacity. Images couple an object with promises of extended
life, much as the incarnation joins manhood (the body) with divinity (the
abstraction) (4.1912 ff.). In the arguments of the philosophers Capgrave
plays out the very questions about images that were circulating as part
of a public debate in the mid-fifteenth century about images, arguments
that Katherine not only refutes by logic but by performance. Much of the
drama of Capgrave's account lies in its picture of a romance heroine gifted
with powers of extraordinary and compelling animism, whose refutation
of paganism in all its forms equates the infidel or Other with death: the
closed circle of matter ("schadow" and "substauns"); the wheel; the idol that
Maxentius wishes to make of her and for her. In her own spirited bodiliness, Katherine performs Christianity. She is both woman *and* image.

While Katherine's assault on idols is directed to Maxentius's statues in the marketplace, the attack also implicates the emperor as well, whose foiled actions imitate the failures of his idols or his wheel. Her repeated critique of idols as items of human manufacture, devoid of internal or external agency, predicts the failures of Cursates' wheel toward the end of the narrative. It also evokes the very actions of the emperor in his ineffectual attempts to convert and seduce her. Wheel, idols, and emperor are all equally impotent, and their failures illustrate the narrative's broader discussion of idols and images. In the tradition of tyrants in hagiography, Maxentius is finally helpless, unable to harm anything other than form or flesh. Katherine, on the other hand, can be said to embody the miracle of incarnate union that she describes in her long discourse with the philosophers on the superiority of the Trinity as a coupling of body and spirit, and indeed, to enact herself properties of the Trinity, the image most often condemned in Lollard polemic. Though Katherine articulates a broad-based critique on images in her attack on idols and in her riposte to Maxentius when he offers to make an image of her, she in fact performs as wonder-working image. Agency is effected through her but not by her—or in the terms of Pauper in *Dives and Pauper*, by God and not the object: "Wurshepe hym [God] abouyn alle thyngge, noughte þe ymage, noughte þe stok, stoon ne tree, but hym þat deyid on þe tree for þin synne and for þin sake, so þat þu knele, 3yf þu wylt, aforn þe ymage noughte to þe ymage."[79] Placed between the wheels, the saint becomes a performative and an intercessionary; she prays to God to burn or break this "newe torment," and God sends a fiery thunderbolt (5.1330)

Katherine as image presents, however, a curious set of contradictions. The superior agency promised by Christianity, as she explains in her debate with the philosophers, lies in a relational transaction of the body, or more exactly, a sort of genetic miracle that allows double or even triple (trinitarian) life in one body, better because you get three for one. In the text, the very hyperbodiliness of the saint performs this miracle, even though the text seems to voice anxieties about the uses of images. By unsettling subject positions in the image debate, Capgrave's text gives both sides in the question brilliant play. Katherine operates as a kind of idealized image. Curiously deflecting harm, impervious to pain, she performs as a nonmaterial conduit for divine effects mobilized through prayer. Yet her own bodiliness consistently belies her own iconic status. Maxentius desires her. He offers to make an idol of her. Her spectacular appeal makes her most at risk, as her own story plays out the very seductions of devotional images. It is all too easy, her story says, to turn an image into an idol.

Tokens

If images as man-made objects are in fact almost indistinguishable from idols, what is the currency of Katherine in her ubiquitous form, the iconic queen with wheel? The miniaturized saint's attribute, with its overt disavowals, allows a vivid replay of this border zone and paradox. In visual representations of Katherine, circulating widely in Capgrave's day, the wheel clings to the body, continuing to trouble the boundary between the image/imaginary and the material form. Like other attributes of saints, the wheel haunts the image. Naming Katherine by its presence, the wheel also represents or we might say performs essential contradictions, disavowing death and harm even as reifies them, yoking matter with spirit.[80] In fourteenth-century stained glass from Christ Church Cathedral, Oxford, the wheel appears almost as a toy held in the hand, not an object of techno-terror at all but almost an ornament (fig. 10). The motif catches the eye through its

Figure 10. St. Katherine of Alexandria. Stained glass. Christ Church Cathedral, Oxford, 1330–50. Photo: V. Raguin.

hints of pain and pleasure, for the wheel, however evocative of rings held up by courtly lovers on medieval ivories, is edged with sharp teeth, so even though its menace is dramatically reduced in the miniaturization, it is not entirely voided. This motif, the wheel held up almost playfully in Katherine's hand, recurs throughout deluxe illustration. Similar in gesture and posture, Katherine holds up the wheel in a miniature from a fourteenth-century manuscript. Her triumphal posture, touched with *amour courtois* as well a bit of s/m, is furthered by the figure of Maxentius, squashed beneath her foot (fig. 11).

Throughout these images, the wheel remains, a material foil to the saint's body. However naturalized, it is always there. In its persistent presence, the wheel is like all attributes of saints: Barbara's tower, Lawrence's grill, Mary Magdelene's ointment jar. Following the "reliquary encryption" of saints' lives in the death of hagiography in the sixteenth century and beyond, to borrow a term from Julia Lupton, the sign of the saint remains as the enduring trace.[81] Saints' attributes articulate the very problem of materiality that the official discourse of the image seemed to be at such pains to disavow. Necessary visual markers of identity, so we can know which saint it is we are looking at—or donating to—attributes nonetheless haunt the image in highly physical and proximal ways. St. Mary Magdalene holds her ointment jar. Margaret steps on the dragon. Barbara leans against her tower or holds a miniaturized version in her hand. One of the most striking features of the attribute is its own denaturalization into a minilogo, remarkably toylike, a transformation that is especially queer when the object represents an instrument of torture. Whereas narrative sequences, such as wall paintings, will often picture saints enduring torment, in the iconic image the object serves chiefly as sign of the absent story. While such miniaturizations no doubt are intended to illustrate the saint's victory over death or torture, they nonetheless evoke a certain haptic pleasure—the pleasures of holding and of having.

If we can speak of the pleasure of touch, part of that comfort no doubt lies in our recognition of the familiar in the object. The griddle of St. Lawrence, a modestly popular saint, can illustrate the curious status of the object in a story of transcendence, for the griddle evokes both the familiar object, implement of the barbecue, as well as the horrific torture by roasting that the saint's triumph both evokes and disclaims. Indeed, *vitae* of St. Lawrence give the torture on the griddle a memorable if macabre humor; put to roast on the griddle by Decius, Lawrence finally asks to be flipped so that he can be evenly grilled on the other side. None of this drama, however,

Figure 11. Katherine stands on Maxentius. Brewes-Norwich Commentary on the Liber Sextus. St. John's MS A 4, fol. 36r. By permission of the Master and Fellows of St. John's College, Cambridge.

is recorded in the iconic image. In a fifteenth-century alabaster panel, Lawrence holds the handle of his griddle, or gridiron, with his left hand, while
in his right he holds a book (fig. 12).The gridiron is both large and presumably heavy, yet does not appear to weight him down. It is the size
you might use for roasting a side of mutton, not a person. It touches the
folds of his alb but of course does not singe it. The gridiron functions as

Figure 12. St. Lawrence and grill.
Alabaster panel, fifteenth century.
Courtesy Victoria and Albert Museum.

an oxymoron, in part, to remind us that it has no lasting power over the saint's body, resurrected intact after death. Yet its presence is a reminder that the saint is in effect signed and determined by his relationship with the object—and an object he chooses to grasp in his hand. The object is vital to his triumph and even to his very being; Lawrence cannot be identified without it.

This alabaster represents St. Lawrence in fully conventional ways. When Lawrence is pictured the grill is almost always present, though its form can change. In a window from York Minster, dated c. 1380, Lawrence displays the grill with both hands, the object reduced to the size of a musical instrument (fig. 13). In a panel from the fifteenth-century screen at Ranworth, Lawrence supports the gridiron with his left hand and in his right palm supports a book, the two objects balanced by opposing gestures (fig. 14). Indeed, in fifteenth-century East Anglian parishes, with their proliferation of saints on dados in parish churches, saints *and* attributes became dramatically present, facing the congregation even as they marked the threshold between laity and clergy, as in the screen at Ranworth, the best preserved of Norfolk examples. In the iconic form, the saint's body trumps matter: the object invites us to see the saint as victorious over corporeality. Material attributes are present, in part, to indicate this paradoxical inversion in structures of permanence. The saint's spirit, represented in a body, is that which lasts, triumphant over the objects that define the body's life or death in the world.

Yet the attribute, by its inevitable presence, interrogates that triumph. Haunting the body, a fragmentary idol, the object is always a trace pleasure. Disavowed by the saint's survival, it nonetheless remains as a remnant to question the very relation between images and their material form— the troubled line of demarcation repeated as *Dives and Pauper's* cautionary line: "worship before the image and not to the image." The saint's image, always defined by its material or corporeal logo in the late Middle Ages and increasingly signed by a label commemorating a named bequest, *orate pro*, brings together bodies, objects, and often money with dramatic visibility. Disavowed but never disappeared, Lawrence's grill touches his body as images in general would touch the social body. Like other attributes of the saints, it is the material *thing*—the object that condenses the key issues at stake in the image debate, the most impassioned form of fetish discourse in fifteenth-century England.

When I first became interested in saints' attributes it was in the context of the absent story: how did these little objects carry meaning to viewers—

Figure 13. St. Lawrence. Stained glass. York Minster, North choir, c. 1380.
Photo: V. Raguin.

Figure 14. St. Lawrence. Painted screen, c. 1450. Church of St. Helen, Ranworth, Norfolk. Photo: V. Raguin.

familiar as they must have been: How did viewers respond to or even *see* the commonplace? We would expect the attribute to have special and heightened meaning when it is a sign of torture, but that does not always appear to have been the case. Datini's recommendations that houses should be fitted with pictures of the saints such as Agnes with her lamb, Dorothy with her flowers, and Katherine on her wheel appear unaware of any difference between a lamb and an instrument of torture.[82] In some instances, as Katherine Lewis's recent study of the Katherine cult indicates, the wheel even became incorporated into pieces of jewelry. One will from 1529 records the bequest, from a woman to her daughter, of "a Katherine wheale of dyamontes with iiij perles sett in yt."[83] Miniaturized, as in the Oxford window, and morphed into a gem-encrusted bauble, this little wheel shows its harmlessness but also its material persistence. As a jeweled brooch, touching the body of its wearer, it even turns the woman who wears it into a performance of St. Katherine herself.

Responses to the question of how attributes might have been understood by late medieval viewers can be found in fifteenth-century writings as they attempt to grapple with the very problem of materiality and essence—the thing and the idea behind the thing. I would even suggest that the issue with saints and their attributes, or how to read the saint through its attribute, is a question of reading praxis, the method of allegory versus the discourse of the fetish. All discourses of the fetish, from de Brosses to Baudrillard, turn an eye on things as magically or hyperkinetically charged with attributed values. Allegorical reading or method takes the object as a starting point and moves to history and spirit, leaving questions of materiality behind. Or, we might say, allegorical reading, in parsing levels of meaning, denounces the fetishization of things for their qualities of lack and excess. Objects read through methods of allegory reverse Robert Stoller's definition that a "fetish is a story masquerading as an object."[84] *Dives and Pauper* makes it clear that attributes of saints are "tokens" of the absent story, signs that stand in for missing narrative and operate in a system of allegorical reading. Peter's keys signify the kingdom of heaven, Paul's sword is a token of how he was beheaded, John's camel skin is a sign of camel's hair, hard and sharp, St. Katherine's wheel a sign of the horrible wheels that the tyrant Maxentius devised for her torture. As tokens, attributes should be read the same way we read saints themselves—that is, as signs to make us think of the idea behind the image and not the image itself. The methods of allegory attempt to neutralize materiality. Through allegory the attribute becomes a shared cultural object, its objecthood disavowed by the communal narrative, or what we might call its allegorical real, shared in group memory.

Although Lollard texts rarely single out saints' attributes for specific attention, their concerns about the distractions of the object seem to fold together attribute and saint as a single problem. While Lollard writings generally privilege allegorical interpretation, what the *Lanterne of Liȝt* calls "þe wit of allegory," over the seductions of narrative, they nevertheless express little confidence that viewers could make the leap from the object to its absent real.[85] The only way most people can read devotional images is through the body, or as a body, an obsessional fetish form. As the Lollard "Tretyse of Ymagis" puts it, "God dwellis by grace in gode mennus soulis, and wiþoute comparesoun bettere þan all ymagis made of man in erþe, and better þan alle bodies of seyntis, be þe bones of hem never so gloriously schreynyd in gold."[86] The best way to deal with devotional images, then, is to reject them altogether or, we might say, out of hand. "Be þe bones of hem never so gloriously schreynyd in gold" wryly acknowledges the replicating properties of matter; images and relics invite gifts of money and then assume the aura of its glitter. In this twist we are reminded once again that the discourse of the image is a problem of the object. The lure of the image is the magic of the *thing*.

2

The Despenser Retable and 1381

IN 1847, IN ONE OF THE ANCILLARY CHAPELS in Norwich Cathedral, a chance discovery revealed that what was being used as a table was in fact the back side of a fourteenth-century altarpiece, a five-panel sequence of the Passion (fig. 15).[1] Shortly thereafter, for the special volume on the *History and Antiquities of Norfolk and the City of Norwich*, Albert Way wrote the following account of its discovery:

The preservation of this work of art is wholly due to the fortuitous circumstance that the well-compacted piece of joiner's work, whereon the painter so elaborately displayed his skill, had happily been found suitable to form a large table for one of the subordinate chambers or vestries, adjoining the choir of the cathedral. It had, accordingly, on the removal of all superstitious imageries, been cut to adapt it to the desired purpose; the painted side being reversed, and by that means rescued from further injury. It had thus remained long time wholly forgotten, whilst the back of the picture served conveniently as the top of the required table.[2]

Way's account, which quickly moves into a study of the work's stylistic affiliations, leaves out a good part of the story we might like to know—namely,

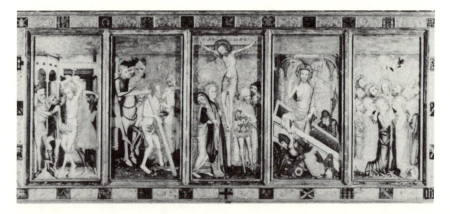

Figure 15. Despenser Retable, c. 1385. Norwich Cathedral. Photo: V. Raguin.

who found it and how, what the table was being used for, or speculations about how the painting got to be there. This large and elaborate five-paneled and framed altarpiece, constructed from oak boards and a molded oak frame,[3] had been used as a table, with the narrative on its underside long forgotten. Doubtless the story of the panel as a table is a piece of Reformation history—a skilled and large devotional piece, which Pamela Tudor-Craig suggests would have been appropriate for a high altar,[4] recycled during the Reformation into furniture. It is a story of creative reuse—and of the shift in uses according to altering contingencies of value: first an important devotional object, a statement of wealth and orthodox pieties; next a table in an annex; and then a masterpiece of East Anglian art.

Way's account of the retable, however, focuses not on its role in Reformation history, except to say that it was "preserved by this singular accident from the fury of iconoclasm,"[5] but instead on its prehistory, and chiefly on speculations about its stylistic origins and affiliations. Much of the literature on the retable conforms to traditional art historical praxis (the naming of an object according to stylistic origin), which in this case masks a larger imperative of using the object in the staking of nationalistic/stylistic claims. For Albert Way, whose interpretation was confirmed by his colleague Digby Wyatt, just returned in 1847 from an artistic tour of Italy, the altarpiece was unmistakably Italian in origin; and his language makes it clear that origins are deeply vested in value. Italian is good (sophisticated, Latinate, complex); northern is rustic.[6] Later descriptions of the altarpiece emphasized, quite to the contrary, the Englishness of the panel, a reversal that was prompted chiefly by a vastly increased information base about fourteenth-century panel painting and East Anglian style, but also, of course, by a project of reclaiming. An important Victorian account of the altarpiece, written in 1897 by W. H. St. John Hope, points to the "gigantic strides" in archaeological knowledge that now allow him to confidently speak for the English origins of the retable and to claim it as "genuine English art"—and even more locally, as Norwich art.[7] More recent studies continue to affirm local production, as evinced by Pamela Tudor-Craig in the 1987 *Age of Chivalry* Exhibition Catalogue, who concludes, based on stylistic parallels, that the piece was "executed by local craftsmen."[8] That the art historian has a stake in the project of local aesthetic and material claims is evidenced by Andrew Martindale's conclusion to his entry on the altarpiece in Lasko and Morgan's 1973 catalogue, *Medieval Art in East Anglia 1300–1520*: "One thing remains to be said, however. It is of remarkably high quality and quite able to bear comparison with other works of an international standing."[9]

I point to the critical history on the altarpiece to highlight that it is a history with its own imperatives and stakes, and one in which the aesthetics of an individual object serve, at least in part, in the construction of regional or even national canons. My interest in the altarpiece, however, lies in a rather different sort of claiming—and even with questions about the very project of *claims*: what we talk about when we talk about regionally inflected aesthetics; what catches the eye and how, and what passes as normative when we look at a familiar devotional form. In the critical history on the altarpiece there is little mention of the ways that this altarpiece—either as aesthetic object, as narrative, as icon, or as social text— might have engaged its first Norwich viewers, or even shaped the way they saw it.[10] The altarpiece has been dated to the last two decades of the fourteenth century and represents an important commission at a time of reformist concerns about the uses and display of sacred art. What were the claims that this altarpiece made from its position at the high altar?

This set of claims begins with a conjecture by W. H. St. John Hope in the late nineteenth century that the retable was given as a thank-you offering to the people of Norwich for their help in suppressing the rebellion of 1381, a conjecture that has been repeated by numerous scholars.[11] Hope's supposition is based on the existence of an unusual series of armorial banners in the frame; only three of the original twenty-eight coats of arms remain, and another three can be made out by trace markings on the frames.[12] The top is a recent reconstruction, the top board having been cut off, presumably when the altarpiece was made into a table. The altarpiece before its reconstruction can be seen in a line drawing by Digby Wyatt made shortly after its discovery (fig. 16). Several of the banners, now pictured with instruments or signs of the Passion, were destroyed when holes were cut in the corners for table legs. Of the identifiable six banners, three can be traced to families that played prominent roles in the suppression of the 1381 rebellion—namely, Sir Stephen Hales, Sir Thomas Morieux, and most significantly, Henry Despenser, bishop of Norwich from 1370 to 1406.[13] The Despenser arms appear in the center of the left side of the frame: "Quarterly argent and gules, the second and third quarters fretty or; over all a bend sable," distinguished as the arms of the bishopric by an azure border and golden mitres.[14] The arms of the Hales family appear in the bottom left of the frame: "sable, a chevron between three lions rampant argent"; and the arms of Morieux are next to Hales: "gules, a bend argent billety sable."[15] While there is no evidence to connect the other families whose banners appear in the frame with the uprising or its suppression, they too represent important local East Anglian families: Kerdeston, Gernon, and Howard.[16]

Three banners hardly constitute evidence that the altarpiece was given as a thank-you gift for suppression of the revolt; in her entry on the altarpiece in the *Age of Chivalry* catalogue, Pamela Tudor-Craig does not even mention this supposition, stating instead that "no doubt the heraldry commemorates not only those who contributed to the altarpiece itself, but those who had helped fund the reconstruction of the eastern arms of the church."[17] Nevertheless, the retable is exceptional for this unusual frame, which visually encloses the narrative of the Passion, itself enacted in Ricardian court style, with emblems of Norwich political and social power. Study of the retable indicates that the frame was made with the panels; both frame and panels are of a piece in imagination and execution, with the gilt ornament of the frame consistent in workmanship with the gilding on the panels. Splendid in its use of painted glass to imitate enameling, the frame effectively wraps the Passion narrative in a neat and orderly package, one that is hieratic, hierarchical, and above all local. The banners painted on the frame, coupled with the absence of any mention of the altarpiece in the sacrists' rolls, strongly suggest that it was a lay gift.[18]

Even if we cannot connect the retable to a specific event, the particular nature of this framed narrative suggests that it is a rich social text. The retable was painted and presented to engage a contemporary audience, as the coats of arms in the frames indicate. Narrative as well as iconic—or in Walter Benjamin's terms, carrying both cult and exhibition value[19]—the

Figure 16. Despenser Retable. Norwich Cathedral. After Digby Wyatt in Albert Way, "Notice of a Painting of the Fourteenth Century, Part of the Decorations of an Altar: Discovered in Norwich Cathedral," in *Memoirs Illustrative of the History and Antiquities of Norfolk and the City of Norwich*, Proceedings of the Archaeological Institute, 1847 (London: Archaeological Institute, 1851), 198.

five panels of the Despenser Retable also form a powerful linear narrative
that operates in tandem and in dialogue with the fixity of its coats of arms.
I have briefly outlined the aesthetic and regionally chauvinistic claims that
nineteenth- and twentieth-century art historians have made on the altarpiece and will suggest that we may also speak about a sophisticated overlay
of regional claims that the altarpiece makes on its viewers, specifically its
fourteenth-century viewers in Norwich Cathedral. In the visual dynamic
in which this piece engages its audience, the frame is its most locally situated feature, mediating between the viewer, powerful local families, and
a set of conventional Passion scenes. What does the frame communicate
about practices of social self-representation in the late fourteenth century?
In a recent study on the late medieval English parish Paul Binski has
suggested that altarpieces functioned as "labels" and were closely connected with the lay community in discourse with church authority: "Reta-
bles were never, in the period of their most rapid formation in England
or elsewhere, the object of 'top down' clerical control . . . they appear to
have been principally, and silently, a matter of 'bottom up' provision"—
that is to say, purchased and given by lay families.[20] In as much as churches
of late medieval East Anglia offer a remarkably rich record of donor portraits, chantry chapels, and tomb monuments, this frame with its banners
is testimony to local practices that memorialize the community in the
monument—and can and should be understood through the history of lay
self-representation.[21]

Peasant Violence and Englishness

Before discussing the frame, I would like to take a closer look at the Passion narrative itself. This chapter argues that the panels of the Despenser
Retable individually and collectively play out a narrative of social order—
or more precisely, of disorder and harmony. Temporally, the panels as a
sequence move from left to right: from the scourging or flagellation, to
Christ carrying the cross, to the crucifixion, to the resurrection and ascension. Each of the frames is crowded, with Christ in the middle of a busy
scene of action and interaction. Each of the panels tells a story about
community and about community types, making complex and intricately
rendered distinctions among class and ethnicity. In the far left panel, for
instance, Christ is imprisoned in a scene of wild, almost demoniacal punishing (fig. 17). His body, held to the pillar, is taut, graceful, and almost

Figure 17. Flagellation of Christ. Despenser Retable. Norwich Cathedral.
Photo: V. Raguin.

balletic; one early commentator even thought that the panel was representing him as suspended from the pillar by his hands. In dramatic contrast to his entrapment and bodily exposure, of course, are the figures of
the scourges, who whip him in a frenzy of pleasure as an older man, doubtless Pilate, looks on. Of the many contrasts portrayed in this scene, however, one of the most graphic is rendered through markers of class and
physiognomy. These scourges, as is conventional in scenes of the flagellation, are clearly peasants—swarthy, rustically dressed. The scourge on
the left reveals his class status as a laborer through the exposure of his
naked calves and thighs, which ripple in dark muscularity. The faces of
both scourges are almost caricatures of the peasant type as represented, for
example, in the Luttrell Psalter—heavily featured and dark from work in
the sun. In body type the scourges contrast markedly with Christ, whose
light-skinned and almost naked body singles him out from all three of the
figures in the scene.

The contrast between the captive and exposed body of Christ and
the animated violence of the peasants is dramatic and may well articulate
a local commentary of the kind that Jonathan Alexander has speculated
is voiced in the representation of peasants in the *Très Riches Heures*, the
famous illuminated calendar painted for the duc de Berry (before 1416).
Responding to earlier critics who have understood the depiction of peasants in the *Très Riches Heures* to be informed by both nostalgia for rusticity and by the new techniques of "northern realism," Alexander argues that
the peasants are shown to be "uncultured, boorish, and vulgar" and that
they contrast throughout the calendar with aristocrats, who are uniformly
elegantly dressed and mannered.[22] Peasants are even pictured as obscene,
as in the image for February, where two peasants famously lift their skirts
and expose their genitals before the fire. In the cycle of illustrations, he suggests, the Limbourg brothers have pictured peasants as the duc may well
have understood them: dehumanized subjects laboring for him beneath the
spires of his lofty castles. Alexander's analysis of the *Très Riches Heures* is
useful for reading the representation of the scourges in the Despenser flagellation, for it suggests that visual traditions existed for representing peasants
as a class endowed with traits—and in this case, traits of sadistic violence.
Certainly the depiction of the scourges as violent, subhuman, and peasantlike might well evoke descriptions of the rebels in chronicles of the 1381
revolt, which the Westminster Chronicle calls a "rising of the peasant rabble" ("ignobilis turba rusticorum surrexit") who behaved like "the maddest
of mad dogs" ("ut rabidissimi canes").[23]

In its representation of class disorder, the flagellation panel may also be said to represent a choice within a set of artistic or schematic choices; and while it displays "no irregularities," as Pamela Tudor-Craig says in the *Age of Chivalry* Exhibition Catalogue, it displays a singularity that is not mandated by the conventions of Passion iconography.[24] Texts that form the sources for the scene include John 19:1 and Matthew 26:8, both of which name Pilate as the scourge, as well as the *Meditations on the Life of Christ*, source for much late medieval Passion iconography, which pictures Pilate as an ambivalent figure and identifies the scourges as generalized torturers among the "sons of men":

The Lord is therefore stripped and bound to a column and scourged in various ways. He stands naked before them all, in youthful grace and shamefacedness, beautiful in form above the sons of men, and sustains the harsh and grievous scourges on His innocent, tender, pure, and lovely flesh. The Flower of all flesh and of all human nature is covered with bruises and cuts. The royal blood flows all about, from all parts of His body. Again and again, repeatedly, closer and closer, it is done, bruise upon bruise, and cut upon cut, until not only the torturers but also the spectators are tired.[25]

In the visual arts, representations of the flagellation generally follow the *Meditations* but display great variation in the way they visualize the social identities of both Pilate and the scourges. As Ruth Mellinkoff has shown in her generously illustrated study, *Outcasts*, some scenes contemporary with the Despenser altarpiece depict Pilate as similar in social class to the scourges, as in the fourteenth-century French *Petites Heures* of Jean de Berry, where Pilate seems to instruct while two men, dressed as fashionable courtiers but marked as enemies of Christ by their particolored hose, beat Christ with flails.[26] Pilate is sometimes absent altogether, as in a flagellation scene from the thirteenth-century Chichester Psalter, c. 1250, notable for signs of physiognomic or even racialized difference, a visual commonplace in Passion iconography to mark enemies of Christ. In Chichester the scourges are markedly dark, contrasting in both skin tone and in facial features with the light-skinned, northern-featured Christ (fig. 18). These contrasts are repeated and even amplified in the miniature of Christ brought to Pilate in the Fitzwarin Psalter, c. 1350–75 (BN Lat. 765), where virtually all of Christ's jailers, and Pilate as well, are pictured as dark, a sign of their enmity to Christ.[27]

This latitude in representing the class of the scourges and in the options for Pilate suggests that the altarpiece, in spite of "no irregularities," actually manifests complex aesthetic and narrative decisions. By representing Pilate

Figure 18. Flagellation of Christ. Chichester Psalter, England, c. 1250. Manchester, John Rylands Library MS Lat. 24, fol. 151r. Reproduced courtesy of the University Librarian and Director, The John Rylands University Library, The University of Manchester.

as a well-dressed and courtly figure and the scourges as peasants reveling in sadistic powers, the Despenser artist has made a choice to underscore class differences even while affirming, however paradoxically, collusions among groups in torturing Christ. Although their clothing communicates quickly that they are clearly not of the same estate or class, both Pilate and the scourges participate together in the physical punishment. As the peasants whip Christ, Pilate pulls Christ's hair with his left hand. The pulling at Christ's hair in scenes of the flagellation, according to Mellinkoff, is conventional, though normally Christ's hair would be grasped by the scourges themselves.[28] Mellinkoff also notes that from the early Middle Ages to the fifteenth century, long hair was a sign of upper-class identity[29]—a fashion "fact" that may help to explain the violence and animus of the attacks on Christ's hair in flagellation iconography. As Pilate, dressed in the courtly clothes of the late fourteenth-century gentry, grasps Christ's hair while two peasants whip him with flails, he participates with the scourges as a like tormentor, perhaps attempting to violate the intrinsic "class" immanent in the hair of the true Christ.

However much the left panel plays out a story of punishing social role reversals—even suggesting, in the well-dressed figure of Pilate, that peasantry and gentry are wrongly colluding in this act—the right-hand panel radically reconfigures both class and spatial order. In the ascension Christ is disappearing as the apostles, together with the Virgin, kneel in orderly worship in a scene that visually echoes the ritual of the Mass itself (fig. 19). In its presentation of orderly devotion, framed around and looking up at the mandorla-encircled Christ above, the panel evokes the elevation of the host, often pictured in contemporary art through a similar visual scheme. In images of the Mass surviving in varied media, from missals to baptismal fonts, a priest will frequently be shown holding up a monstrance while parishioners gather around him. In an illuminated initial in a late fourteenth-century English Carmelite missal the artist has painted both the biblical last supper and the eucharistic rite to emphasize their figural relationship (fig. 20). In the bottom register of the initial of the Corpus Christi Mass, a priest raises the host before a congregation, while in the top, Christ breaks bread with his disciples. The top/bottom ordering and the imagistic echo work to convey a picture of parochial order, the mystery of the Mass that draws the eye upward to the founding moment of the last supper.[30]

Through its linear narrative focusing, the Despenser altarpiece thus directs the viewer's gaze toward closure in this last panel and underwrites closure as order, specifically the order of worship, as the community gathers around Mary and John in a scene that is familial, parochial, aristocratic, and above all English. One commentator has remarked that the faces in this panel are of an "unmistakeably English type."[31] Presumably "English type" refers to late medieval English style; but the faces also represent a homogeneously English or north European physiognomy—blond, angular in feature—at least if we define "English gentry" as such in contrast to the ethnic or class others in the altarpiece as a whole: the broadly featured scourges of the first panel; the swarthy officials and even swarthier soldiers of the second and fourth panels. The community of twelve apostles in the ascension panel, a community that ultimately even comes to stand in for the absent body of Christ, is itself a carefully articulated social grouping.

Figure 19. Resurrection and Ascension, Despenser Retable. Norwich Cathedral. Photo: V. Raguin.

Clustered around an icon of familial male/female order, it is a body of worshippers that represents, in the richness of the clothes and in the homogeneity of its features, gentrified upper-class family values.

If we look at the altarpiece as a study of the management of bodies, the five panels thus articulate a linear figural drama and social typology. The left and right panels establish the plot as a narrative about social chaos redeemed or converted into social order, a reading that would seem to be

Figure 20. Top: Last Supper. Bottom: elevation of the host; initial of the Corpus Christi Mass. English Carmelite missal, completed 1393. London, BL Add. 44892, fol. 38r. © British Library Board. All rights reserved.

illustrated as well in the central crucifixion panel, where John holds the swooning Virgin on the left as doubters move into faith or speculate about its possibilities: the richly clad centurion with his banner, "truly this is the son of God," speaking to two Jews, presumably, who look and evaluate. Similarly, the second and fourth panels, with carefully staged dramatic sequencing, prepare for the orderly affirmation of Christian, and also English, community in the ascension scene. In the second panel life, vitality and energy are all embodied in the smartly dressed chevaliers, the officials and the sargeant-at-arms jostling around Christ, who staggers impassively under the weight of his cross. In a dramatic reversal, the fourth panel, separated from the second by the crucial interval of the crucifixion, rewrites this scenario as Christ emerges from his tomb with a crusader's cross, stepping on the sleeping guard. Visual gesture confirms the vivacity of bodies. In the second panel the gazes of the officials are focused, intense, directed; in the fourth, however, their eyes are shut or staring off vacantly into space, while Christ fixes us with his gaze as he steps from his tomb. The paired panels tell a story about inverted agency, a charivari played out in the second panel with social order righted in the fourth.

Markers of ethnicity or race also have a part in this drama of social order.[32] In speaking of a "racialized" identity, I am using the term broadly to refer to an iconography of "otherness" in which groups are identified by skin color or physiognomic traits—though there has been little consistency in how those bodily traces have been historically interpreted.[33] In her encyclopedic study of the visual representation of otherness, particularly of Jews, Ruth Mellinkoff has assembled powerful testimony to the ways that northern religious painting in the Middle Ages linked physiognomic traits with character, and did so in ways that are often uncomfortably legible when viewed through the history of racism and anti-Semitism. In the second and fourth panels, but even more so in the fourth, the bodies of the soldiers are swarthy, even Latin, contrasting markedly with the whiteness of Christ's body, whose very exposure and nudity, in fact, underscores his difference. Similar in skin tone and facial contour to the congregated apostles and Virgin in the ascension, Christ is marked by his bodily difference from nearly all the cultural and social "others" in the altarpiece. To be both prosperous and English is to be among the saved. The Passion narrative, centerpiece of the Church, affirms the transformative power of faith through the consensus of a monied class.

If we return to the frame, how then is this powerful linear narrative held or contained within it—and contained in part by the arms so conspicuously inscribed on it? Most immediately, the frame underscores the power of orderly eucharistic devotion: community order, the frame affirms, is co-extensive with the Church's most fundamental sacrificial ritual and also with its public webs of power. Furthermore, a striking feature in the costuming of the figures also reveals this symmetry between faith, authority, orderly worship, and powerful patronage. Discussions of the retable have remarked that the unusually fine gesso and gilt work of the background and the frame would seem to represent work of single hand.[34] Also in gilt, in visual symmetry with the background of panels and frame, are the undergarments of the figures of the saved. The gold work in the robes of Mary and John in the crucifixion panel is echoed in the gold embroidery of the centurion's tunic, carefully exposed for us to see as he holds aside his red mantle. Similarly, in the ascension, all of the apostles, as far as we can tell, wear gold-embroidered clothing beneath their mantles—affirming what would seem somewhat more than the medieval trope that faith is worn as a garment. Here the mark of faith, also a mark of economic privilege, visually extends beyond the borders of the panels themselves and into the frame. The frame and the painting form an elegant unit.

Despenser, the "Warlike Bishop"

But how might the retable's visual narrative of order and class be related to the hypothesis that the retable was commissioned and given to the cathedral as an acknowledgment or thank-you for help in suppression of the rebellion of 1381? The suggestion has been based on the identification of three armorial banners, and chiefly on the inclusion in the frame of the arms of the bishopric of Henry Despenser, bishop of Norwich from 1370 to 1406. While the bishop's martial role is best known from the disastrous crusade that he led in 1383 to Flanders, he also played a memorable part in the suppression of the rising of 1381.[35] Despenser's success in persuading the commons to back his Flanders crusade may have been due in part to his victory, brief but decisive, in suppressing the 1381 rebellion in his diocese. As Capgrave describes in his Henrician chronicle, Henry Despenser was at London with the king when he heard of the outbreak of the rebellion in East Anglia, led by Felmingham dyer Jack Lister who was accompanied by three others, Sceth, Trunch, and Cubith. Quickly departing for home, Despenser skirmished with some of this "wicked mob" at Cambridge where he "slew some, imprisoned others, and others he sent back

to their homes," and then continued on to Icklingham where he met lord
Thomas de Morley and a knight named Brewes, who handed Sceth, Trunch,
and Cubith over to him. Capgrave notes that neither Morley nor Brewes
dared execute the rebels without the permission of the king, though
Despenser, "having the zeal of Phineas in his breast," took the three to
Wymondham and had them beheaded. After that he went on to Norwich
to find out that Jack Lister and his followers, just like "a ribald fellow from
Kent, named Wat Tyler," had "committed many horrid deeds," especially
in the destruction of homes of "certain nobles . . . who were friends of the
law or of the king." In response, Despenser, leading an ever-growing group
of supporters, tracked Jack Lister to Walsham, where Lister's supporters
surrendered and Lister himself was captured, beheaded, quartered and his
four parts sent to Norwich, Yarmouth, Lynn, and Lister's home so that
"that rebels and insurgents against the peace might learn by what end they
will finish their careers."[36]

The social program of class-based order that is visually articulated in the
Despenser Retable would certainly be consistent with—and richly suggestive for—a gift commemorating the suppression of the rebellion, particularly as it unfolded in East Anglia through the actions of Bishop Despenser.
As J. A. Tuck notes, the fifteenth-century chroniclers of the rebellion consistently focus on the absence of retaliatory leadership among the gentry,
with the noted exception of Bishop Henry Despenser, marshaling men
of money and power behind him.[37] In his biography Capgrave accuses
the nobility of cowardice and singles out Despenser as the single individual able or willing to gather gentry support: "Whilst lords, and knights,
and others of the nobility, were hiding themselves for fear, he went forth
openly."[38] Walsingham also glamorizes the brutality and decisiveness, particularly in executing leaders of the rebellion, of Despenser, the "warlike
bishop" and "man quite capable of bearing arms."[39] Despenser's willingness
to engage in combat, especially in situations in which the historical rights
or prerogatives of the Church and his bishopric were concerned, is also
attested by accounts of a skirmish with the people during a procession in a
visit to Lynn in 1377, where Despenser insisted on having the civic staff carried before him rather than before the mayor. In spite of repeated warnings
by the aldermen that it would be dangerous, since Lynn had a long history
of conflict with the Norwich bishopric, Despenser persisted, for the common people, he said, were of no account.[40] He, his horse, and some of his
company were wounded during the predicted melee, which was finally dis-
persed by royal intervention. As Lynn Staley puts it in *Powers of the Holy*,

"the bishop personified the aggression, the temper, the noblesse oblige, the power (even when threatened) of the male aristocrat."[41]

Perhaps of even greater pertinence to the representation of social conflict in the Despenser altarpiece, the chroniclers all dramatize narratives of class role reversals in the revolt in East Anglia, with Despenser, at least for Walsingham and Capgrave, appearing as an avenging angel restoring social order—and particularly mobilizing the gentry against the Norwich dyer Jack Lister, self-styled "king of the commons," whose effrontry included coercing members of the gentry into his rebellion. Stephen Hales, whose arms appear in the frame of the altarpiece, played a key role in a brief but explosive charivari that is described in Walsingham's chronicle. Hales, a knight of the shire who held overall twenty-four commissions during the reign of Richard II and who may have been singled out for hostage by leaders of the rebellion for his role as controller of the poll tax for Norfolk,[42] was forced by Lister to become an accomplice. Walsingham describes Lister's camp on Mousehold Heath:

The names of the knights forced to follow the rebels were Lord Scales, Sir William Morley, Sir John Brewes, Sir Stephen Hales and Sir Robert Salle. This Robert did not last long in the rebel band, as, unlike the others, he did not know how to dissimulate but began publicly to condemn their deeds and to express his horror at them. As a result he was suddenly pierced through the brain by a peasant who was his own bondsman and died on the spot, though being a knight who, if he had had the chance of fighting against them in open combat, would have terrified a thousand rebels on his own. His companions, learning from the danger that had overtaken Sir Robert, realized that they had to dissimulate or die a similar shameful death, and so decided to praise everything praised by the rebels and to pour scorn on what displeased them. And so when they were graciously received by that rascal, John Lister, who called himself "King of the Commons," they found that they were judged suitable to be appointed tasters of his food and drink and to obey his commands on bended knee as he sat at meat. Indeed he specially chose out that honourable knight, Sir Stephen Hales, to carve his meat and to taste the food that he was about to eat, with other knights being appointed to other duties.[43]

Whether or not Hales and others were as fully coerced as Walsingham claims is certainly open to question; in any case Walsingham yokes Stephen Hales, singled out by Lister to be his personal carver and taster, with Bishop Henry Despenser through Despenser's ensuing bloody suppression of the uprising at North Walsham. Walsingham's account, which tells of a knight-as-peasant and then of a bishop-as-knight, is even more dramatic than Capgrave's in its picture of Despenser's heroics: "Dressed as a knight, wearing an iron helm and a solid hauberk impregnable to arrows as he wielded a real two-edged sword," the bishop led the battle against Lister's camp at North Walsham, capturing Lister, whom he personally absolved and led to the gallows.[44] Walsingham's dramatization of the event suggests a bloody battle, with Despenser himself slaughtering the commons ("grinding his teeth like a wild boar")[45]—though Capgrave, in his more measured account, tells us that the commons, on Despenser's arrival, immediately surrendered, and Lister hid in a cornfield.[46]

A key feature of all of the chronicles, whether they choose, like Walsingham and Froissart, to dramatize and even fictionalize the martial conflict in their versions of the rising in East Anglia, is a fascination with class role-inversions and rebel challenges to hierarchy, restored through Despenser's zeal as avenging angel. In his account of the rising in Suffolk, John Gosford, almoner to the Abbey at Bury St. Edmunds, describes the mocking of the prior of Bury at Newmarket in terms that echo the Passion: "Here, we are told, they all night long most blasphemously mocked him: kneeling before him they cried 'Hail Master!' and striking him with their hands cried to him, 'Prophesy who smote thee.'"[47] In his description of Lister's rebellion, Froissart focuses on the story of the physically massive Sir Robert Sale—"one of the biggest knights in all England"—killed in a dramatic sword fight while resisting inscription into Lister's commons.[48] Walsingham and Capgrave both note Despenser's restoration of hierarchy in accounts that make it clear as well that the bishop made rapid-fire distinctions among classes in his suppression of the rebellion, sparing lords Morley and Brewes and summarily executing rebel members of the commons, "Sceth, Trunch and Cubith," and sending their heads to be fixed on the pillory at Newmarket.[49] Walsingham concludes his entry with a paean to Despenser's personal embodiment of Christlike compassion and martial zeal:

The bishop listened to his confession, absolved him by virtue of his office and went with him in person to the gallows, showing he could do works of mercy and piety even on a defeated enemy. Indeed as John was being dragged off for his hanging, the bishop even held up his head so that it should not knock against the ground. Even after this the bishop did not rest until he had sought out all the rebels throughout his whole area and justice had been done on them. We should praise the goodness and applaud the boldness of the warlike bishop who in this way brought peace to his region and indescribable benefit to the whole community.[50]

This episode in the *Chronica* ends like a fairy tale. The soldier of Christ, merciful yet zealous in his Christian mission to punish the infidel, returns order to his community.

*   *   *

If we had firmer evidence for the claim that the Despenser Retable was given as a gift to the people of Norwich for help in suppressing the uprising of 1381, the story of social disorder and even charivari that is played out in the altarpiece, especially in the flagellation, would certainly take on vivid topical significance—even if stylistically the piece displays "no irregularities." Even without that evidence, however, I believe it is warranted to speak of the retable as a framed narrative about social disruption and the restoration of order—as a story as much about orthodoxy, community, and class in late fourteenth-century Norwich as it is about the Passion. Certainly it tells a story. An important commission following a conventional devotional plan, produced at a time of challenges from multiple quarters to clerical authority and ritual, the altarpiece may well articulate a brilliantly crafted counter to voices of disruption and even of dissent. Anne Hudson suggests that Wyclif may have been at least partly instrumental for the revolt, and even if his own writings and teachings had little direct impact, authorities and chroniclers shortly after 1381 noted the similarities between Wycliffite teaching and the anticlerical aims of participants in the rebellion.[51] As a narrative, the altarpiece may be understood as a visual document in a contest over the very rights to literacy, an authoritative charter or deed responding to the massive destruction of documents by the commons in the revolt.[52] The armorial banners, circling the altarpiece with a sigillary story, lend weight to its claims. The frame is a narrative composed of signs, each of which says, through its very condensation, that the family to which it refers is far more widely connected, owns far more, has far more power and influence, than a sign can figure. We might even think of the frame as offering a heuristic similar to marginal illuminations in medieval manuscripts, which often, as Michael Camille has argued, offer a meta commentary on the text they surround:

In this respect, marginal images are *conscious* usurpations, perhaps even political statements about diffusing the power of the text through its unraveling. . . . Another important aspect of the way marginal motifs work is by not reference to the text, but by reference to one another—the reflexivity of imagery not just across single pages but in chains of linked motifs and signs that echo throughout a whole manuscript or book.[53]

Following Camille's logic of the edge, we might read the banners as signs that speak with each other, telling a story about families, community, and alliances between gentry and clergy even as they communicate with the narrative of the Passion in the painting itself, though not to unravel but to underwrite. This inscription of signatory authority is brilliantly furthered through the parallel between the frame of the altarpiece as a whole and the resurrection panel, an image whose iconography signifies the reconstitution of the broken community.[54] Carrying his crusader's cross, perhaps even evoking Bishop Despenser himself, Christ steps out of his tomb below the banners of the Passion, gesturing to the viewer beneath Christian armorial shields that echo the coats of arms in the frame. Christ and the Church are affirmed by local power; local power, in turn, is affirmed through the authority of the resurrected Christ.

To read the Despenser Retable thus requires in a sense not only turning it over, but also returning it to its congregation—or congregational gaze, which may have even been directed toward the high altar, a place of marked pomp and circumstance in Norwich Cathedral, a building itself notable for grandeur, with its massive Norman stone work and ancient bishop's chair. The altarpiece, whose elaborate Norwich framing circles a Passion sequence that moves linearly from a picture of irruptive bodily energy to one of measured containment, also bespeaks grandeur as well as orderly communion between clerical and lay power. The frame effectively contains that sequential narrative as well as the gaze of its viewer. We kneel with the worshippers beneath the mystical body, looking up at the ritual elevation; the frame with its reassuring arms of familial power holds us close.

3

Chaucer and Images

IN *VOIR DIT*, GUILLAUME DE MACHAUT'S *Book of the True Poem*, the lover
Machaut is revived from his lovesickness by the arrival of a long-awaited
gift. Trembling in heart and limb, he unwraps the kerchiefs to find the gift
that the Lady has promised: an image of her "fait au vif," made from life.[1]
He studies the image, pleased with its beauty. He names it Toute Bele, "All
Beautiful." Later he places it on the wall high above his bed, where he
can gaze on it and touch it when rising in the morning in and turning in
at night.

Machaut's account of the image of his beloved, "made from a living
study," owned by a lay individual and placed for viewing within a private
chamber, appears to offer us an unusual early account of a secular portrait—
1360s France, long before the development of portraiture as a popular genre.
It quickly presents some ambiguities, however. Is it a painted panel or a
sculpted image in a niche? In medieval texts the term "image" most often
refers to a sculpted figure,[2] an equivalence suggested by the first of several
miniatures in the manuscript to depict this "ymage." As evidenced by the
messenger's beard peeking around the backside of the frame (fig. 21), Toute
Bele appears to be a piece of framed statuary. In later miniatures, however,
Toute Bele appears more like a painting or stained-glass picture in a gothic
niche-shaped frame. Even more puzzling, if Machaut's term "ymage" is
meant to refer to a likeness or portrait, we would expect it to have the representational promise of the surrogate: The value of a portrait lies at least
partly in its successful imitation of physiognomy. Rather like a photograph
of a pen pal, which takes at least part of its value from mimesis, the fact
that it "looks like" someone, a portrait should be simultaneously authenti-
cated and trumped later by the arrival of the prototype, the real thing.
("You look just like/are even prettier than your picture.") In *Voir Dit*, however, the image of Toute Bele does not participate in a realist drama of this
type. When Toute Bele finally appears in the flesh long after sending the
lover her image, he registers no confirmation or surprise, and in fact says

nothing to indicate any connection between her person and her portrait. He is pleased with her face, her manner, her body; but whether or not she looks like the image to which he has performed reverent oblations and services of devotion, he says not a word.

This disjunction between the image and the lady, the representation and its real, suggests that this story about the gift of a lover's portrait may not be as familiar or prosaic as it first appears, in spite of its remarkable apparent humanism. The economy or value of this image, this is to say, does not appear to reside in its likeness or verisimilitide to a living body, and its function as image is structured within a rather different set of conventions. It is *not* a portrait. Portraiture as we understand it today, in fact, was rarely practiced in northern Europe in the fourteenth century. While some images were judged acceptable for display in private homes, it is clear from letters and manuals of domestic advice that they were almost exclusively devotional; images for domestic display would have been understood to be models for behavior and would be drawn from biblical and

Figure 21. The messenger hands Machaut an image of Toute Bele. Paris, Bibliothèque Nationale, fonds français, MS 1584, M7. Courtesy Bibliothèque nationale de France.

apocryphal stories—the life of the holy family, the saints.[3] For a non-royal woman to have sat for her portrait, commissioning her image to be made "au vif," describes an astonishing act of artistic self-representation for its time and place in 1360s France—so unusual, in fact, that we should be careful how we read this artful fiction.[4] Close to fifty years later, Hoccleve will explain his famous portrait of Chaucer, which Derek Pearsall says may be "the first nonroyal English portrait that claims to be an accurate likeness," through the logic of iconic devotion.[5] Immediately after claiming to have portrayed Chaucer's "liknesse" in the miniature inserted in the margin of the *Regiment of Princes*, written in 1411, Hoccleve invokes the image debate:

> The ymages that in the chirches been
> Maken folk thynke on God and on his seintes
> Whan the ymages they beholde and seen,
> Where ofte unsighte of hem causith restreyntes
> [where often the lack of seeing of them causes hindrance]
> Of thoghtes goode. Whan a thyng depeynt [painted] is
> Or entaillid [carved], if men take of it heede,
> Thoght of the liknesse it wole in hem breede [nurture].
>
> Yit sum men holde oppinioun and seye
> That noon ymages sholde ymakid be.
> They erren foule and goon out of the weye;[6]

Even though some people (for example, Lollards) claim that images should not be made, images in churches serve to make people think on their "liknesse"—that is, God and the saints. By following the Chaucer portrait with this defense of religious images, Hoccleve thus seems to be endowing Chaucer with iconic status as a literary saint for England.[7] As with images of the saints, the purpose of the likeness is to prompt a recollection of its exemplar. It is within a humanist project, many years after Machaut's long epistolary romance and Hoccleve's Chaucer portrait, that we find fully developed conventions for portraits "made from life," with subjects that singly command the frame and occupy the picture space.[8]

If Machaut's "ymage" is not a portrait, then what is it? Toute Bele invites us to consider her image as a performative in a relationship—an image that is not simply an object but an object whose meaning occurs through its relationship with the viewer who looks at it. With the image of Toute Bele, this relationship clearly exceeds aesthetic appreciation. Kneeling before it, dressing it in expensive robes, the lover treats the image in ways that mime Christian devotional practices in the 1360s. At the same time, however, he worships the image not just as an icon but also as a pagan idol. Making sacrifice, not with bull or calf but with his own body, hands, mouth and heart, the lover kneels before the image and worships her as his sovereign goddess, "ma souvereinne deesse," a Venus, better than the saints because of her power to heal.[9]

*   *   *

The likeness of Toute Bele that the Lady sends her lover in *Voir Dit* offers an unusual example of a portrait but also an example, in a rich devotional parody, of an image. It also offers a graphic context for considering Chaucer's description of devotional or "artistic" images as well as his accounts of visual responses to those images in his poetry. The *Voir Dit*, it has been suggested, may have even been a source for Chaucer as he reshaped Boccaccio for *Troilus and Criseyde*.[10] In the years following the writing of *Voir Dit*, the relationship, or fine line, between between idolatry and orthodox uses of devotional images would become became the subject of focused and increasingly heated debate. Many of the positions in this the debate were set and sharpened between the 1380s and the 1390s in England, the period in which Chaucer was most productive as a writer.[11] It is hard to imagine that Chaucer would not have been familiar with this debate as it developed in the 1380s and 1390s. Scholars have long maintained that Chaucer was well acquainted with at least certain points of Wycliffite doctrine, particularly positions on the Eucharist.[12] Eucharistic controversy quickly became part of a public lexicon and even subject for stand-up comedy—especially if we countenance the joke from one of Wyclif's own sermons that the faithful should forbid friars to enter their cellars lest the wine be transubstantiated into nothing.[13] Paul Strohm has argued that a comment about substance and accident in the *Pardoner's Tale* owes much of its humor to Wycliffite controversies over the Eucharist, a position that has been echoed in Fiona Somerset's recent comment that the joke, such as it is, about the wagon wheel and the division of the fart in the *Summoner's Tale* also alludes to issues of substance and accident in the eucharistic controversy.[14] Among the so-called Lollard Knights who are believed to have comprised part of Chaucer's circle, Walsingham names Sir John Montagu, who is recorded as having packed up his devotional images and stored them away.[15] Montagu was a poet—a "gracieux ditteur," according to his acquaintance

Christine de Pisan[16]—a fact that makes it even more likely that Chaucer would have known him or at least heard the story of his alleged action against his own statuary. An odd detail for a chronicler to record, it suggests that Montagu's image removal was the topic of some public discussion and worth recording as evidence for Lollardy's influence. Even a man as well connected as Sir John Montagu could be swayed, by this cult, to move his furniture. Other evidence that points to Chaucer's familiarity with the image debate would include Gower, Chaucer's friend, who speaks of "this newe secte of lollardie" and who appears to reference the debate, at least obliquely, in his discussion of the history of idolatry.[17] The *Vox Clamantis*, Gower's long moral and political treatise begun after 1378 and continued into the 1380s, includes a discussion of images that takes up many of the central issues of the debate: whether the viewer worships the image or the idea behind the image; whether richly decorated images deceive worshippers into giving false offerings. Although Gower does not mention Lollards directly in relation to images, the argument itself seems clearly inflected by the controversy and walks a reformist though carefully orthodox path, critiquing images while also defending their utility to the faithful, condemning rich images yet locating blame in the producers and stage managers rather than in the lay worshipper.[18] Chaucer's writings themselves suggest familiarity with the controversy. Sounding like a Lollard iconomach, Cecilia in the *Second Nun's Tale* attacks Almachius for worshipping blind and senseless idols. And as Carolyn Collette has argued, the excursus on painted Nature in the *Physician's Tale* may also refer obliquely to the discourse.[19]

It is impossible to measure with any precision what pressures learned debates on the uses of devotional images might have exerted on descriptive conventions in the poetry of secular writers such as Chaucer. We might expect it to have been considerable, though, for insistently at stake in the image debate is our relationship to the image: How do we look at it? What is it to us? In Wycliffite polemic, our relationship with the represented body bespeaks our relationships to both spiritual beliefs and material forms as well as to the social life of the community. In late medieval meditative writings, devotional images often seem to come to life in acts of animation that may override any risk that their powers are intrinsically vested in their material nature. In fourteenth- and fifteenth-century poems of the Passion a crucifix will often speak to a passerby, as in Julian of Norwich's meditation, where the literal sight of a crucifix quickly leads to her first revelation, animate and immediate: the "rede blode trekelyn downe fro under

the garlande hote and freisly and ryth plenteously, as it were in the time of
His passion."[20] Indeed, notably absent from late medieval English writings
are descriptive or ekphrastic accounts of devotional images, except as
transformed, as in Julian's text, into visions. This lacuna may represent a
careful dodge of the temptation to worship the object. It may also represent a strategic avoidance of a dangerous subject. Kathryn Kerby-Fulton
has noted that Langland avoids describing icons of affective piety and that
the scribe/illustrator of the Douce *Piers Plowman*, the only extant illustrated
Piers manuscript, was deeply iconophobic, or what she calls "an iconomach
in the atelier."[21] To describe a devotional image is to risk coveting it.

For a striking contrast we can look at Roger Martin's account of Long
Melford Church from the 1580s, a nostalgic description in which he recalls
the images of his parish before their removal in the Reformation. A fascinating exercise in devotional ekphrasis, Martin's account is valuable for its
documentation of church holdings but perhaps even more for its voicing
of a transformed valuation of ritual objects, in which the devotional now
blends with a new aestheticized consciousness of the object in ways that
would have been impossible two hundred years earlier. Speaking of an
altarpiece once in his family's chapel and now in his home, Martin writes,
"there was also in my ile [aisle] called Jesus Ile, at the back of the altar, a
table with a crucifix in it, with the two thieves hanging, on every side one,
which is in my house decayed, and the same I hope my heires will repaire,
and restore again, one day." And later in the same document, an ekphrasis
of a carved pietà: "And, in the tabernacle at the south end, there was a faire
image of our Blessed Lady, having the afflicted body of her dear son, as he
was taken down, off the Cross, lying along in her lapp, the tears, as it were,
running down pittyfully upon her beautiful cheekes, as it seemed, bedew-
ing the said sweet body of her son, and therefore named the image of our
Lady of Pitty."[22] "As it were," "as it seemed," "the said sweet body": in terms
that differ markedly from Julian's focused animism, Martin is speaking of
an object from the world of likenesses. This is clearly an object whose pleasures lie in representation.

*   *   *

For Chaucer, the controversy over images in his own time provides a fascinating discursive backdrop against which to look at his construction of
textual bodies, or his arts of describing the human form. In techniques
of description of person, of course, Chaucer exhibits formidable and even

unparalleled talents. To what extent, this chapter asks, is Chaucer's descriptive practice contoured by a contemporary culture of visual affective piety—and specifically by a discourse with increasingly high ethical and political stakes about the uses of sculpted and painted devotional images? To address these questions I would like to take a look at just a few of Chaucer's "iconic" images, descriptions of objects or persons that are represented as the object of a devotional or worshipful gaze, even when that look, like the gaze of Machaut on Toute Bele, expresses erotic desire: the narrator's look on Venus in the *Knight's Tale*, Troilus's on Criseyde, and the narrator's on the daisy in the *Prologue to the Legend of Good Women*. Does the act of looking risk idolatry or even animate its object? In Wycliffite discourses on images, we are repeatedly reminded that images are dead, with the phrase "dead images" a common lexical register of the debate. In the Pardoner's *Prologue*, devotional objects in the form of relics are even grotesquely inert. To what extent do acts of visual devotion in Chaucer bring the object of the gaze to life?

Tellingly, Chaucer consistently invests the act of gazing with potent and often dramatic affective agency, and the act of gazing as an eyewitness often risks the seductions of both icon and idol. For instance, when Chaucer describes one character's gaze on another, that attention to the act of watching will often be followed by a statement that the person seen is too beautiful to describe, as in the *Squire's Tale* (34 ff.) or the *Book of the Duchess* (895 ff.). More frequently acts of gazing occur elsewhere, legitimizing or perhaps deinstitutionalizing the gaze by express transposition to exotic places: the pagan locales of the *Knight's Tale* and of *Troilus and Criseyde*; the fictive and atemporalized locations of the dream visions. Paradoxically, the disengagement of description from a textual eyewitness dramatically licenses "portraiture" as the practice of a Diane Arbus–style photorealism, a record of both the appealing and the grotesque details of human bodies and actions side by side. While Chaucer is perhaps best known to many for techniques of description that give us the portraits in the General Prologue or of Alisoun in the *Miller's Tale*, those portraits are pictured independent from a recording gaze or focalizer within the narrative. We see them, but not as perceived by an eye of the beholder in the text. Chaucer's most "visual" descriptions of person, that is to say, are also his most virtual.

When Chaucer includes a direct eyewitness, we can often expect dynamic change to the viewer or even serious trouble. The link between an imagined visual image and erotic desire, an image and the passions of the body, is perhaps most expressly conveyed in the story of Lucrece told in the *Legend of Good Women*. In this tale, the passion for an image leads to sexual violence and death. For Colatyn, Lucrece's husband, an evening of wife-sharing peeping with Tarquinius leads to erotic rescue, as he jumps, after listening to his wife's fears for his safety, from his hiding place with a shout, "Drede the nat, for I am here!" (F 1742). For Tarquinius, however, the evening incites a darker act of possession. Infatuated by the object of his voyeurism after the spying party, Tarquinius imagines Lucrece as an image, "th'ymage of hire recordynge alwey newe" (F 1760), picturing her first in one posture and then another. This image, the "plesaunce of hir forme" (F 1769), remains with him like the quiver of the waters after the storm, a disturbance in the field that stirs his passions to a disastrous pitch. The story rings with echoes of legends of the virgin martyrs, some of whom, like St. Katherine of Alexandria and St. Margaret, refuse to worship pagan idols. After her death Lucrece is carried on a bier and later worshipped as a saint. In Chaucer's tale, Lucrece, becomes herself an idol in the eyes of her stalker. In the familiar medieval lexicon of idolatry and eroticism, to worship a woman as idol is to become an idolator and to desire a woman as an image or idol is to destroy her.

With less catastrophic outcomes, Chaucer also describes a gaze on living images in the ekphrastic accounts of the statues of Venus, Diana, and Mars in the *Knight's Tale* or the images that decorate the Temple of Glass in the *House of Fame*. The presence of an eyewitness in many of Chaucer's most detailed and animate descriptions of pagan deities also underscores the uncanny resonance of these depictions with Christian visual theater. Chaucer's pagan deities often engage with a narrative viewer whose very act of seeing appears to animate them; in the *Knight's Tale* that eyewitness is a curiously unidentified "I" who records the ornament of the temples, reminding us repeatedly that his is a record of a first-person visual experience: "ther saugh I." Hardly idols with sightless eyes or deaf ears, the objects of that gaze appear to come to life before him as well as before the oblations of worshippers: In the *Knight's Tale* the statue of Venus shakes and makes a sign; the fires burning before the statue of Diana sputter and revive as the logs drip what looks like blood; the chain mail on the statue of Mars rings and whispers "Victory." Indeed, we might argue that Chaucer shifts the pleasures, and pressures, of Christian devotional objects—images of the saints, the Trinity, and the crucifix, the contested objects in the image debate—to images at a historical and devotional remove. Pagan idols in ancient Troy and Athens behave much like Christian images.

A closer look at the description of Venus, a pagan idol, in the *Knight's Tale* reveals the powers of the act of witnessing that animates the image and even seems to bring it to life. A notable feature of this description is its three-dimensionality, conveyed through attention to extremities, supports, and attachments. Rhetorical manuals in the Middle Ages offer formulae for describing the human body, the most common of which are the top-to-toe catalogues, where the writer is advised to begin first with the eyes and then move downward in a list of idealized attributes. In the description of Venus, however, Chaucer expressly articulates an appreciation of three-dimensional sculpted form. The description begins with the base and moves briefly downward and then up, but not through the center but rather the extremities:

> The statue of Venus, glorious for to se,
> Was naked, fletynge in the large see,
> And fro the navele doun al covered was
> With wawes grene, and brighte as any glas.
> A citole in hir right hand hadde she
> And on hir heed, ful semely for to se,
> A rose gerland, fressh and wel smellynge;
> Above hir heed hir dowves flikerynge.
> Biforn hire stood hir sone Cupido;
> Upon his shuldres wynges hadde he two,
> And blynd he was, as it is often seene;
> A bowe he bar and arwes brighte and kene. (1955–66)

For shape and dimensionality the statue grows in a sense from its foundation on a painted and sculpted sea, its contours defined by its props—the right hand carrying a stringed instrument, the head circled by first a rose garland and then a grouping of doves. Providing depth of field is Cupido, standing before Venus and himself defined by borders and edges: the wings on his shoulders, his bow and arrows.

Repeated references to the action of sight in this ekphrasis also seem to activate the senses, even bringing the statue to life. The parenthetical "glorious for to se" in the first line of the description interrupts the objective account of the statue's nudity, a coy splicing that emphasizes the pleasures of looking. When the narrator describes Venus's head, the parenthetical "ful semely for to se" similarly leads to the rose garland, "fressh and wel smellynge," as if the action of the gaze or attention to one sense activated another, breathing life into the garland; metaphoric slips into virtual. The flowers seem to be literally fragrant.

In the descriptions of the temples that follow, the boundaries between art or image and reality increasingly blur as the imagined eye that constructs the ekphrasis of Venus becomes a literal eyewitness ("saugh I ther," 2005) and as the images described increasingly seem to take on animation and dimensionality. Within the temples, images and "portreyture" repeatedly slip out of the representational into a textual real, a kind of virtualizing that plays out as a struggle for control between the maker and the artifact, the artist as fabricator and the text (or image) that takes on a life of its own. Readers have noted this shift, pointing to the inexplicable intrusion of the Knight into the text as if he were present as a character in the story and also the shift whereby images and paintings seem to take on life. Lee Patterson and H. Marshall Leicester explain this forfeiture of control as emblematic of the tale's general commentary on the seductions and paralysis of chivalry, an institution that, as Patterson puts it, "submerges the self in a surface pattern of ritual and replication"—and in this text, a giving over of the individual or collective will to Theseus, who not only builds the amphitheater, but purports to stage-manage the events of the tale in general.[23] Chaucer is a disenchanted maker, offering up the *Knight's Tale* as a critique of the chivalric institutions it memorializes, with the Knight, dupe to stage-mastered spectacle, as the nostalgic spokesman for an anachronistic social form.

I would want to nuance these readings by pointing to the close relationship between the deities in the temples and devotional figures in a culture where all images were to some extent iconic. The complex commentary on art, spectacle, images, and subjectivity generated through the temple ekphrases suggests we should also include Chaucer among the voices of the subject; and that voice, I believe, also takes the occasion to play out both the pleasures of "art for art's sake" as well as the complex entanglements of a gaze on devotional objects. If Chaucer details the images and paintings in the temples to comment on the Knight's willing subjection of judgment to the institutions of a destructive chivalric order, he still illustrates the pleasures of the gallery—on the one hand a love of images, their three-dimensionality, their sensuality, and on the other a distrust that may echo the voices in the image debate that critiqued images as dead "stocks and stones."

The description of the temples also presents the seductions of images as a developing process, a drama of sorts that increasingly entangles its viewer. Following the description of Venus, recounted with an attempt to capture the pleasures of three-dimensional form, the lines between art and reality blur and images and murals take on increasingly malevolent agency. The final lines of the description of the temples brilliantly focus this set of tensions around an image whose verisimilitude troubles the boundaries not only between art and narrative but life and death. In front of the statue of Diana is an image of a woman in childbirth:

> A womman travaillynge was hire biforn;
> But for hir child so longe was unborn,
> Ful pitously Lucyna gan she calle
> And seyde, "Help, for thou mayst best of alle!"
> Wel koude he peynten lifly that it wroghte;
> With many a floryn he the hewes boghte. (2083–88)

The image is so lifelike it appears to speak. Or is it that the image is so lifelike it *does* speak? The image might be said to illustrate the drama of life-likeness, but also—in the picture of the woman trapped in childbirth—a terrible stasis, the place of the undead, the inability to bring to life. This final ekphrasis bespeaks a number of very different responses, highly ambivalent, toward images as it resolves on an image, lodged between life and death, of death-dealing nascent life. In the final two lines of the account of the temples, the narrator retreats suddenly and entirely to disavow the drama he has just enabled, turning from the plea for help and changing the subject. At the end he speaks about art production: "wel koude he peynten lifly that it wroghte." If the image is painted "lifly," in a lifelike manner, it is done so with purchased pigments, "many a floryn." It is just a representation.

In the description of the temples in the *Knight's Tale* the ekphrastic mode thus seems not only to engage techniques of the observer but also to license them. In this long descriptive piece, the gaze of the viewer, "there I saw," organizes the frame in an oscillation between detachment and engagement, although as we have seen, detachment is always tenuous. When Chaucer describes the gaze on another person, rather than an image from pagan antiquity, the image brought to life in a human form through visual intersubjectivity, it is often to record that act as one of particular potency—so much so, in fact, that the object is even indescribable. In the *Squire's Tale*, the squire begs off describing Canacee on the grounds of rhetorical inadequacy. A similar excuse also appears, with direct reference to a textual eyewitness in a complex discussion of White's gaze intercalated with his own, in the *Book of the Duchess*, when the Black Knight says he is incapable of describing White's beauty except to say that she "was whit, rody, fressh, and lyvely hewed" (905). In the *Legend of Good Women*, the dynamism involved in the act of looking renders the God of Love even expressly unseeable: The narrator is so blinded by his face, "But of his face I can not seyn the hewe, / For sikerly his face shon so bryghte / That with the glem astoned was the syghte" (G 162–64). In the *Knight's Tale*, the non-description of Emily may also be reflex to a visual animism that evacuates its target. The gaze on Emily is of course the action that sets this story going: Palamon and Arcite spot Emily out of their prison window as she is walking in the garden, and both are stung to the heart with amorous rays. Readers have noted that Emily is peculiarly absent from the story, even though she is its catalyst; beyond a few formulaic terms her description is also absent. The only distinctive attribute we see about Emily, in fact, is her long blond braid. The single detail recorded about Emily sees her from the back.

For Chaucer's most complex drama of a gaze on an iconic object of attachment, we would have to turn to *Troilus and Criseyde*, a poem that, like the *Knight's Tale*, was also written in the 1380s, at a time of increasingly heated controversy about Lollardy and signs of devotion. While the poem is of particular interest for its dramas of intersubjectivity, it also may marshal language from the debate itself to nuance its human relationships. One instance may be found toward the end of the poem where Troilus himself seems to transpose into an image. In Book 4, after he has learned that Criseyde is to be traded away for Antenor, Troilus goes home and locks himself in his room, shuts all the windows and doors, and sits on his bedside "ful lik a ded ymage, pale and wan" (4.235). As we come to see when the terrible betrayal unfolds from here, the catastrophe has begun, and it is perhaps psychological realism that he first responds to the news with a kind of paralysis. The wraithlike shock suggested by the picture of Troilus as a dead image, in fact, follows curiously from the prior stanza, for before he shuts the windows and doors he first rushes to his room and hurls himself on his bed—a gesture where we hear, in a simile borrowed from Dante's picture of damned souls waiting to cross Acheron, he is like a leafless tree in winter, "ibounden in the blake bark of care" (4.229). First black, then pale or ghostlike, Troilus also takes on forms of both death and stasis. Whereas Dante's leaflike souls then swoop across Acheron, Troilus is figured as substance, trapped in the tree itself, and going nowhere.

Or, we might say, first he is wood, encased in bark, and then a carved figure, the tree or "stock" morphed into a statue—or even an idol. The term "dead image," made strangely material in this case through its evolution from a tree trunk, the black bark of grief, appears, as we have seen, with increasing frequency in Wycliffite texts, often naming the particular deadness of idols. Phrases marking insensate idols are echoed frequently in saints' lives, in Lydgate, and notably in Chaucer's *Second Nun's Tale*, where Cecilia rebukes Almachius for blindness to their queer masquerade:

> Ther lakketh no thing to thyne outter yen
> That thou n'art blynd; for thing that we seen alle
> That it is stoon—that men may wel espyen—
> That ilke stoon a god thow wolt it calle.
> I rede thee, lat thyn hand upon it falle
> And taste it wel, and stoon thou shalt it fynde,
> Syn that thou seest nat with thyne eyen blynde. (498–504)[24]

Idols delude as simulacra with no life. To worship idols is to worship things that, in their circulation on a devotional market, blur the boundaries between body and spirit. Indeed, Lollard insistence that images are dead voices an uneasy protest, for it also suggests that they might at any moment come to life. Knighton's story of Lollards Smith and Waytestathe, who cut off the head of a St. Katherine statue to see whether or not it will bleed, condenses and overlays a number of cultural narratives, perhaps most troubling among them host desecration; but the main thrill of this lurid story lies in uncertainty about the bodily status of the statue. Is it alive or dead?

Whether Chaucer's picture of Troilus as a "dead image" takes its language from this debate is uncertain; but as readers have noted, Lollard sect vocabulary generated a set of terms that many writers, among them Chaucer, borrowed, and not always to the expected purpose.[25] When Pandarus, earlier in the tale, is setting in place the tryst between Criseyde and Troilus that will follow dinner at his house, he swears to her "by stokes and by stones" (3.589) that he will look out for her interests. The phrase "stocks and stones"—stumps of wood and rocks that serve as base matter for carving—also appears throughout Wycliffite image discourse as a term to denote the base materiality of pagan idols, and also, derisively, devotional images. Sworn on stocks and stones, Pandarus's vow may be historically appropriate for the pagan setting, but given the circulation of the phrase in Chaucer's time the use in this context seems nevertheless suspect; and if we did not wonder before—along with Criseyde—about the nature of Pandarus's intent, we might after this vow. Similarly, the comparison of Troilus to a "ded ymage" in Book 4 may underscore, through the resonance of the phrase in a growing public discourse, Troilus's dramatic paralysis. Like the idols of the psalm, who have eyes but cannot see, ears but cannot hear, Troilus is helpless.

This picture of helplessness and powerlessness stands in marked contrast with the visual animation earlier in the work, which draws complexly on optics as well as on devotional iconography to represent the process by which Troilus and Criseyde fall in love. In Book 1 of *Troilus*, Chaucer details the process by which Troilus falls in love with Criseyde in explicitly visual terms, even as a drama of the "look," *le regard*, that exploits the language and terminology of devotional worship and optics to forfeit agency to the object of the gaze. Like Machaut before the image of Toute Bele in *Voir Dit*, Troilus is given over with remarkable suddenness to a woman-as-image. Following the decisive or fateful instant when Troilus's glance falls on Criseyde at the festival of the Palladium, one of the terms repeated most often is "look" or "lokynge." With Troilus's gaze Chaucer takes up the familiar trope of the lover's gaze that pierces the eye to wound the heart but reverses it to exploit the illusion that Troilus's gaze has agency over its object, piercing Criseyde rather than himself. Looking over the ladies at the festival, Troilus spots Criseyde, and his self-wounding is imagined as an action of violence on Criseyde's body:

> And upon cas bifel that thorugh a route
> His eye percede, and so depe it wente,
> Til on Criseyde it smot, and ther it stente. (1.271–73)

He is suddenly conscious of her and of "looks" which refer variously to her demeanor, her gaze, and to his gaze on her:

> To Troilus right wonder wel with alle
> Gan for to like hire mevynge and hire chere,
> Which somdel deignous was, for she let falle
> Hire *look* a lite aside in swich manere,
> Ascaunces, "What, may I nat stonden here?"
> And after that hir *lokynge* gan she lighte,
> That nevere thoughte hym seen so good a syghte.
>
> And of hire *look* in him ther gan to quyken
> So gret desir . . . (1.288–96; italics mine)

"Look" in this passage and beyond participates in the doubled register of the word in modern use: we look at; we also bear a look (an attitude) that is the record of someone else's look on us. The way I look registers my face and demeanor in the gaze of another. The coupling of the term in Troilus with the metaphor of love-through-the-eyes exploits this elision of the transitive with the intransitive—to the extent that Troilus's own gaze on Criseyde fictively mobilizes her gaze. He imagines its agency on him:

> Lo, he that leet hymselven so konnynge,
> And scorned hem that Loves peynes dryen,
> Was ful unwar that Love hadde his dwellynge
> Withinne the subtile stremes of hire yen;
> That sodeynly hym thoughte he felte dyen
> Right with hire look, the spirit in his herte: (1.302–7)

Although he feels himself struck dead "with hire look," there is no indication that she looks at him. Troilus controls the gaze in this account. Her gaze has only been invoked to indicate her sense of entitlement, the look aside that claims her right to be there: "What, may I nat stonden here?" (1.292). The look is dramatized as a metphysical ligature, the "subtile stremes of hire yen," not tears but affective visual "species." Love through the eyes electrifies this temple with visual rays. Dynamically phallic, piercing the crowd and then Criseyde, Troilus's gaze blurs the lines between voyeurism and exhibitionism as it turns around to slay the messenger. To look at with desire is to imagine being seen.

In his use of the language of optics and of visual rays in Book 1, Chaucer thus performs a brilliant sleight of hand, reproducing agency as victimization, action as passivity, Troilus who looks and desires as Troilus a captive.[26] Through this illusionistic shift Chaucer establishes some of the central issues of his romance: is Troilus a victim or a maker of his fate? Do we shape our fortunes or are we acted upon? By drawing on visual tropes that ground, as we have seen, the science of optics and the language of affective devotion in Christian ritual, Chaucer not only plays out a convincing psychological drama ("this is what it feels like to fall in love") but also valorizes the erotic story with evidence from anatomy and metaphor from religion.

The spatial representation of Criseyde also contributes to a system of resonances and an overlay in modes or even genres. Standing within the temple, Criseyde is located in a place clearly exotic (a pagan temple) but also curiously familiar—as indeed the city of Troy, as readers have remarked, seems very much like a fourteenth-century town, and its buildings seem remarkably similar to late medieval English palaces.[27] Within the temple on a high holiday, she occupies a place not unlike a church; she even seems framed within it, occupying space as an image in a niche, but also sequestered among the laity at the back near the porch: "And yet she stood ful lowe and stille allone, / Byhynden other folk, in litel brede, / And neigh the dore, ay undre shames drede" (1.178–80). She is among them but separate from them, still and curiously detached, as if framed, "in litel brede," a little space—a space that later she appears to claim with her "look a lite aside" (1.291). As object of Troilus's gaze, she is iconized within this temple rather like an image in a niche, within a space she also appears to claim as her own.

But if as a temple, does the spatial framing of Criseyde as a kind of image suggest she stands in relation to Troilus as pagan idol? Readers of *Troilus* have often commented on the text's highly ambiguous treatment of love and its shift from the apparently benign and domestic to an increasingly public and destructive sphere, in which the very cultural formations, such as chivalry and courtly love, that construct the subject and give him or her over to desire also vitiate will to give the subject over to betrayal and death.[28] The moment of apprehension of Criseyde, brilliantly recreating the press of real bodies and human energies, also evokes ritual forms of worship, either of pagan goddesses or of Christian devotional images. Whether as idol, icon, or bodily woman, or all in one, as I believe, Criseyde in Book I mobilizes an extraordinary excitation of the air; she stands still in her little space as the temple seems to reverberate with visual rays. In *Troilus* as elsewhere in Chaucer's poetry, vision is an act of agency and potency, a performative that transforms the self, subjecting the will in dramatic acts of fealty. And in *Troilus*, as in the *Knight's Tale*, the very act of visual apprehension tends to iconize its object; recorded in the action of the gaze, images become people and people become images.

Word and Icon in the Prologue to the *Legend of Good Women*

Within Chaucer's later poetry, a devotional object comes dramatically to life, in ways that are richly evocative of the intellectual debates in his time about images, texts, and authority, in the Prologue to the *Legend of Good*

Women, which is the text I would like to turn to here. Two rather different Prologues exist, without clear critical agreement on which one came first. From internal references to Chaucer's writings it seems clear, however, that the first must have been written around 1386–88 after the composition of *Troilus* and before the *Canterbury Tales*.[29] When the other was revised is uncertain, but it could have been quite late in Chaucer's life; most readers have believed that F is the earlier and that G could only have been written after 1394, or after the death of Queen Anne, since in G all references to the queen have been deleted.[30] Both, in any case, appeared in a climate of concern about postures of worship and at a time when members of Chaucer's own circle were inspired by Wycliffite reformism. While Chaucer may have borrowed terms from the image debate in *Troilus* to sharpen his text's contemporary resonance, in the Prologue to the *Legend of Good Women*, a work that he most likely drafted right after *Troilus*,[31] he develops a critical aesthetic that, I believe, engages directly if ironically with the debate. Readers have argued persuasively that the concerns with language, vernacular writing, and textual authority that structure the Prologue echo Wycliffite language and articulate some of its most pressing concerns. A foil to the many texts or books referenced in the Prologue, however, is its devotional image, pictured in the form of an iconic daisy. Are pleasure and authority vested in the daisy or in old books? The debate on images, along with discussions of vernacular translation and textual glossing, may equally inform the Prologue's commentary on authority. What do we trust, the text or the image? Where does authority reside, in the dead image or in the living word of the text—or even in a "devotional" image come to life in the form of Alceste?

If there is an overt topic or theme to the Prologue, it would be Chaucer's literary production, or more exactly, Chaucer's ironic self-critique, in the eyes of imagined judges, of his own work. This critique centers on Chaucer as a love poet but clearly encompasses more, since the writings that Alceste names in Chaucer's defense include ones that have little to do with love, particularly his translation of Boethius. Chaucer's commentary on his own writing, as it proceeds through a kind of courtroom prosecution by the God of Love with Alceste as intercessor, uses language that had developed, by the late 1380s and 1390s, certain topical connotations. Many of the terms that appear in the Prologue, particularly in the G text, Helen Phillips argues, are charged "buzzwords" that resonate within contemporary debates about textual authority, or texts and authority, particularly as vested in the Lollard translation project.[32] Similar arguments have been made for other Chaucer texts, such as the Wife of Bath's Prologue, which draws heavily on Lollard sect vocabulary.[33] Perhaps the most markedly Lollard of these phrases in the Prologue is "naked text":

> But wherfore that I spak, to yeve credence
> To bokes olde and don hem reverence,
> Is for men shulde autoritees beleve,
> There as there lyth non other assay by preve.
> For myn entent is, or I fro yow fare,
> The naked text in English to declare
> Of many a story, or elles of many a geste,
> As autours seyn; leveth hem if yow leste. (G 81–88)

When the narrator claims that his intent is to write "the naked text in English," he is using a metaphor used commonly to designate writings in the vernacular, and clearly that meaning is in play in this passage. "Naked text" also appears throughout Wycliffite writings in reference to the unglossed or unvarnished words of the Bible, which through translation into the vernacular should be available to all, as in a Lollard tract on translating the Bible that speaks of the "naked tixt of the Soundaie Gospel."[34] Applied to Chaucer's textual project, however, the intent behind his "naked text" is anything but transparent. As the narrator says, the goal of his naked text is to foster belief in old books—stories and histories—even if there can be no test that assures their truth, no "assay by preve" (G 84). As Kathryn Lynch comments, the Prologue thus opens on "epistemological quicksand" as a "paradoxical house of lies" that borrows terms from contemporary discourses on the authority of the scriptural word as transparent sign of epistemic certainty and then builds instead a house of cards, where the one certainty about old books is the absence of truth-value.[35] The phrase "naked text," which resonates with disputes that were coming to take on weighty political implications, thus seems deliberate and even provocative, sandwiched as it is between two statements that call the veracity of those stories into doubt. "Naked text" heightens the Prologue's comic send-up of the credulous narrator, but at the same time, it underscores the seriousness of the critical commentary. Since stories and gestes are clearly *not* the naked text of Scripture, what then can be their claims to truth?

Throughout the opening of the Prologue, the narrator's meditation on books also leads him, in what seems a compulsive need to tell or need to know, away from books and to the daisy, the flower that he worships. Indeed, these two topics are even causally spliced and both couched in the language of belief and of devotion. The only thing that can draw him away from his books, he tells us, is spring. Later, after he returns to the topic of the authority of books, asserting that he will tell stories ("leveth hem if yow leste," [G 88], believe them if you want to) he segues back again to daisy worship, "Whan passed was almost the month of May. . . ." (G 89) as if the very question of belief in textual truths prompts a return to another kind of faith experience. Or to put it another way, he is slave two forms of pleasure and authority, one of them a book and the other an icon of devotion, the visual and sensory thing. But the pleasures of seeing things are also couched in a discourse on sight as a mode of knowledge. Both versions of the Prologue begin with a rather lengthy proclamation that one should believe in more than one can see, a statement that the narrator then goes on to use as justification for reading. These assertions of truth, as readers of the Prologue have noted, lead not to clarity but to a dizzying uncertainty. At the outset the narrator asks what is most authoritative, visual or textual knowledge, then asserts books are the answer—but then heads out to worship a flower. His is a wonderful comedy, the credulous believer in books wandering off to the meadow as the even more credulous devotee of a flower. He rises before dawn to be at the "resurreccioun" when the daisy opens, and gets down on his knees as he awaits its opening (F 110, 115).

If it can be argued that the discussion of texts, authority, and reading in the Prologue is inflected by contemporary discourses in Wycliffite writings about loci of truth, it can also be argued, I believe, that the daisy, in all its potent daisyness as an object of worship, is informed by debates in those writings about the uses of images. For the narrator worships this daisy, and it is not clear at all that he adores it for its idea or for itself. He seems to fall into the posture warned against in the contemporary *De adoracione ymaginum (On the Worship of Images)*, a treatise attributed to Hilton, which asserts that we do not worship the substance of the image but the meaning or idea: "Seeing the images of Christ's crucifixion and coming into remembrance of his saving suffering and prostrating ourselves, we worship not the substance, but the image. In this manner, we do not adore the substance of the gospels or that of the cross, but their model, that is, their significance or essence." Images of the crucifix or of the saints are "revered as symbols, not as things."[36] The treatise even comments that the most enlightened of the laity even know enough to shut their eyes when worshipping before images: "And so they are moved by no affection or reverence toward the wood itself, as far as the material of the wood goes, or how carefully it has been painted. They value such things not at all, but they use images as a remembrance; lying down in the presence of images, but forgetting their presence, they send their prayers to God and his saints. . . . And so those who wish to pray spiritually are accustomed to close the outer eye or turn it away from the object of the images, lest the intention or attention of the mind be dragged through the sensual grasp of the object."[37] Images are mnemonic guides, reminders of spiritual truths or essences. Remembering, paradoxically, requires that we forget the images in front of us. We can use them, but to use them we should not even see them.

The narrator's daisy worship, in contrast, is acutely visual, pandering to the pleasure of the eye. Throughout both prologues, we are in a dazzling or even blinding visual world. The God of Love, crowned with the sun, is so bright the narrator is nearly blinded; but even before the God of Love appears, the narrator's primary obsession is to see the daisy, "to seen this flour ayein the sonne sprede" (F 48). When spring lures him away from his books—"Farewel my bok and my devocioun"—he is off to sensory and visual pleasures, or as the Prologue keeps reminding us, to truths. With the daisy, however, substance and accident seem to be one: its pleasures are immanent, and the narrator revels in them. As he says in the F Prologue, "And I love it . . ." and "Al swere I nat, of this I wol nat lye, / Ther loved no wight hotter in his lyve" (F 56, 58–59). The devotional parody is particularly marked in the F Prologue, where the language of prostration is developed, as Helen Phillips says, with an "erotic-religious register" and with "frivolously blasphemous imagery."[38] The flower is his mistress and muse: "She is the clernesse and the verray lyght / That in this derke world me wynt and ledeth" (F 84–85).

* * *

Not long after Chaucer's death Edward Langley, the second duke of York, dedicated a hunting manual to Henry IV, in which he refers to the Prologue to the *Legend* and specifies that in it Chaucer not only defends writing as the key to memory but also promotes writing over visual documentation: "for as Chaucer saith in this prologe of the xxv good women. Be wryteng have men of ymages passed for writing is the keye of alle good remembraunce."[39] Through writing, that is, men have dispensed with the need for images; writing, Langley seems to say, offers a more reliable or secure record of the past, a key to memory. Yet Langley imputes to Chaucer a rejection of images that the Prologue itself does not sustain, for in its own metaphoric recursivity the text repeatedly circles back to its daisy. In the *visio*, the daisy or originary devotional object, what we might call the text's object of extreme attachment, morphs into the voice of his own defense in the form of Alceste, who seems herself to be a daisy incarnate. Alceste may be the dream form of the daisy, but she cannot be simply identified as the meaning behind the metaphor or, to borrow language from the image debate, the idea behind the image. Even if she may be the metaphor's primary form, the woman and subject of discourse figured forth in the image of the daisy, we can never be clear where the daisy ends and Alceste begins. As Peter Travis remarks, the text provides a "pinwheeling of correspondences" without a clear subject and predicate—or as he puts it, "what the dreamer discovers in his dream is that distinguishing between a principal subject and a subsidiary one is such a fuzzy proposition that it is impossible to determine,"[40] among other things, whether Alceste or the daisy comes first.

This is not to suggest that the Prologue reprises, in parodic form, contemporary debates about devotional images and naked texts, at least as its chief concern; the play with metaphor in the Prologue owes its most direct debts to marguerite poems by Chaucer's contemporaries Froissart, Machaut, and Deschamps, and the Prologue and legends that follow are voiced principally within that movement or artistic contest.[41] Nevertheless, from a carefully framed allegorical remove Chaucer gestures to the image debate, borrowing language from Wycliffite discourses, among others, to charge the Prologue with a contemporary and specifically English set of resonances. Wycliffite horror of images is deeply antimaterial, an ethical critique that equates worship of devotional images with attachment to things; and as part of the movement's social radicalism Wycliffite writings condemn images as material goods, unequally apportioned and divided. In contrast texts, at least the naked text of Scripture brought to readers through the Lollard Bible, can be available to all. As the site of truth, the word trumps pictures, objects, and ritual display. Chaucer's Prologue, however, offers no such clear epistemological hierarchy or certainty. The iconic daisy turns into Alceste, the muse for his poetry.

And indeed, in Alceste's transformation the flower even comes to life, animated by the narrator's act of worship. If Lollards insist that images are dead, it may be because of this uncanny habit of coming to life. Chaucer has few doubts about this property. The drama of the image in the Prologue tells us little directly about Chaucer's own attitude toward icons of popular piety, but it does give a remarkably clear picture, through a playful recapitulation of postures of idolatry, of their dynamic hold on the psychic and imaginative life. This quality of pleasure, or playfulness, is perhaps the most surprising feature of the Prologue, particularly if we can situate its discussions of texts and images within a serious set of public discourses. Sheila Delany suggests that phrase "naked text," which only appears in the G Prologue, may offer evidence that G was the earlier version; when official hostility to Wyclif's position lent a sectarian charge to vocabulary and phrases identified with him, the phrase was removed.[42] The claim that the "naked text" is one of a cluster of Wycliffite terms, a register of buzzwords, may suggest rather the opposite, however; Chaucer may have used terms from the Lollard sociolect in order to capitalize on those very connotations. Fiona Somerset's contention that recent scholars have exaggerated the risks of engaging in religious controversy in the later years of the fourteenth century would also further this argument.[43] Both Prologues seem remarkably casual or offhand in their glancing references to Lollard concerns. Both Prologues, as well, make capital on truth, images, and texts. In the Prologue's send-up of contemporary philosophical, literary, and Lollard discourses, we find out quickly that neither image nor text can guarantee truth. Both, however, deliver on pleasure.

And it is this quality of pleasure or enchantment that may also be the most compelling feature of Chaucer's iconic images. Characters in Chaucer's poetry repeatedly submit to the pleasures of images as if to a seduction, as in *Dives and Pauper*, where Dives anxiously records the difficulty of knowing how to position himself before images in ritual spaces where the gestures of most worshippers suggest they love the object itself like a living god.[44] For Chaucer, the pleasures of vision repeatedly entangle the subject in a similar ethical dilemma, conditioning the apprehension of form in terms that may well be inflected by the anxieties of the object. The gaze on the body demands a sacrifice, the giving over of self to what is seen. In *Troilus* this sacrifice is direct, dramatic, and immediate: he is an instant victim. With descriptive accounts of images from antiquity, descriptions in which Chaucer clearly seems to take a good deal of pleasure, Chaucer allows a recording eye to roam more freely, but even there detachment repeatedly slips into entanglement and objects transform into living bodies. In the Prologue to the *Legend*, this gaze on an icon that transforms into a book lover's goddess is enacted in delightful parody. Like the stocks and stones of the image debate, whose trouble lies in the worshipper's unwillingness to see them in their essences, Chaucer's images never stay fully in the gallery.

The Pardoner's Relics

Chaucer offers a far darker take on devotional paraphernalia, however, in the Prologue to the *Pardoner's Tale*. The Pardoner's relics are objects, the General Prologue and the Prologue to the *Tale* repeatedly show, that are grotesquely inert. The language insists on their materiality: what they are made of, where they are kept. In the General Prologue we hear that he has a pillowcase that he calls the Virgin's veil which he keeps in his "male," perhaps the same "walet" in his lap that is "bretful" or brimful of pardons "al hoot" from Rome in which he stashes his own hood. He has a "gobet" of St. Peter's sail, a metal cross "ful of stones," and pigs' bones in a glass. In the Prologue to the tale itself he tells his listeners that his "relikes" include glass cases "ycrammed ful of cloutes and of bones" and a shoulder bone of the sheep from a holy Jew mounted in "latoun," a brass alloy. Some of his relics, moreover, need to touch something to be activated, as if their powers were engaged only when matter meets matter. The shoulder bone goes to work for you once it you dip it in a well; the mitten has the power to increase your store if you put your hand in it. Rather than coming to life, these objects seem fully inert. Like stocks and stones that reformists invoke to describe dead images, these are bits of things that are contiguous to other bits of things—fragments, pieces of the body, objects even of disgust. Stones rather than gems cover the cross; scraps of bones fill his glass cases, along with rags, or "cloutes." The nature of "cloutes" is vividly evoked by their fate in the *Merchant's Tale* when May tears Damian's note into "cloutes" and drops it down the privy (1953).

These falsified objects are relics, of course, and not devotional images. As relics, their materiality is crucial to their efficacy, for the relic, unlike the image, contains matter and spirit in a miraculous fusion that exemplifies the resurrection of the body.[45] In late medieval reformist polemic relics receive much less attention than devotional images, but when relics are mentioned it is to focus on their physicality. Wyclif comments in one sermon that the Church has been seduced in the cult of "dead bodies and images" and in another he critiques the cult of relics in language often mobilized in polemic against rich images: "it would be to the honour of saints and the advantage of the church were the jewels with which the sepulchers of saints have been foolishly and uselessly adorned, to be distributed to the poor."[46] One of the tenets of William White, tried for heresy in the late 1430s, is that worship of relics is a form of idolatry: "that the relics of saints, namely bodies and bones of dead men, should not be worshipped, neither taken from the stinking tomb nor stored in a box of silver or gold. . . ."[47] In his depiction of the Pardoner's false relics Chaucer pictures them as fragments that circulate only in economic transactions, and those lead only to death or morbid circulation. This is their inertness and their horror. Even the old man, searching to exchange the "cheste" in his room for the earth, seems like a relic, "flessh, and blood and skyn," longing for its reliquary (732–34). For him, as for the revelers, no transaction can exchange the body for the spirit: No one will change youth for his age. As Lee Patterson observes, the tale's relentless materialism signals its most explicit clerical critique. The great failure of the Pardoner's vision is that matter remains only matter.[48]

A closer look at the Pardoner's devotional paraphernalia demonstrates its inert materiality. Perhaps the most appealing of all the Pardoner's devotional trinkets is the one that, as described in the General Prologue, looks most like an icon: the vernycle, or veronica, that is sewn on his cap. This object, a pilgrim's badge that he wears to show he has just been in Rome where veronicas were popular souvenirs,[49] takes meaning from its descriptive contingencies, or indeed, like relics themselves, from touch:

> But hood, for jolitee, wered he noon,
> For it was trussed up in his walet.
> Hym thoughte he rood al of the newe jet;
> Dischevelee, save his cappe, he rood al bare.
> Swiche glarynge eyen hadde he as an hare.
> A vernycle hadde he sowed upon his cappe;
> His walet, biforn hym in his lappe,
> Bretful of pardoun comen from Rome al hoot. (General Prologue,
>   680–87)

The Pardoner's veronica is foremost an object of display, displacing his hood, which he has trussed up, for fashion or "jolitee" in the knapsack in his lap—a sexual stew of stones, scraps of cloth and, as he names the pardons in the tale itself, hot holy "bulles"—a term that was as raunchy in Middle English as it is today.[50] Yet direct bodily contingencies, recorded in the following line that takes us to his lap, also show this veronica's inversion. Topping his eyes, which glare or stare like those of a hare, the veronica on his cap seems even to double for his eyes as well. Wearing the veronica, the Pardoner becomes perversely the face of Christ. The doubling of his eyes with the face on his cap also gives us a demonstration of practical idolatry. He provides both the icon and the eyes with which to adore himself.

The veronica is not the only garment of the Pardoner that bears a bodily imprint. At the end of the tale Harry Bailly famously rebuffs with a curse the Pardoner's invitation to offer to his relics:

Thou woldest make me kisse thyn olde breech,
And swere it were a relyk of a seint,
Though it were with thy fundement depeint! (948–50)

The Pardoner's "olde breech," his underwear, is another article of clothing imprinted, like the veronica, with an image, but here the imprint is not the face of Christ but the stain of excrement as decorated by his anus, his "fundement." He wears two items of clothing painted with images, with his underwear the nether side of the visual icon on his cap. His breechcloth decorated with excrement also may comment as well on the nature of spiritual change afforded by the Pardoner's relics. Indeed, the only transactions the Pardoner even promises are material: give money, use objects and get things, the "creauncing" of stock or grain. Readers have noted the complex ways in which the tale echoes eucharistic controversy and have argued that the tale offers, in the death-delivering feast of the rioters, a sacramental parody.[51] The Pardoner's relics and clothing also participate in this drama of substance and accident, with the final transformation to excrement.

When the Pardoner asks Harry Bailly to "offre first anon, / And thou shalt kisse the relikes everychon" (943–44), he is asking him to believe that the objects he has been shown have a surplus beyond mere matter—that they have powers, can work magic or change. He is asking, that is, for the Host to believe that his inert objects have the powers of fetishes or even asking him to act as a fetishist who believes even though he knows better. The very imputation that he is a fetishist, in fact, may be what gets Harry so exercised, for fetishism, even in the Middle Ages, marks the fixations of others and never of ourselves. Fetishes always remain outside the limit. A fetish contains an outlaw surplus; there is more to the object than we know. Introducing the term "fetish" in the first chapter of *Capital*, Marx draws an analogy to religion, the "mist-enveloped regions of the religious world. In that world the productions of the human brain appear as independent beings endowed with life, and entering into relation both with one another and the human race. So it is in the world of commodities with the products of men's hands. This I call the Fetishism."[52] In the European discourses of religion from which Marx appropriates the term, "fetish" refers to the magical talismen of primitives and hence is already tainted with aberrancy. A fetish is an object of desire that we love out of measure, and thus its uncanny or unknown meanings, its surpluses, are suspect: what is it we desire that exceeds what we choose to acknowledge?

None of this excess attaches to the Pardoner's presentation of his relics, even if he simultaneously attempts to invoke a spiritual presence when he asks the Host to step up and sanctify his relics with a kiss. "Gobets," "cloutes," stains, bones, rocks and metals: The Pardoner reduces objects of devotion to fragments of matter and bits of the body. Their materiality, stripped of representational artifice, communicates not only Chaucer's position on clerical corruption but even seems to voice a deep skepticism about the mobilization of icons of popular piety in worship. As William Kamowski has argued, since fake relics circulated virtually everywhere in Chaucer's time, the Pardoner is only asking the pilgrims to give his particular objects the same credit—in the form of literal cash—that people give unquestioningly to relics, real or otherwise, in the spiritual marketplace.[53] In the Pardoner's Prologue, Chaucer's most graphic account of devotional objects in action, images are spectacularly dead.

Yet as we have seen, Chaucer elsewhere imbues devotional images, though in pagan or atavistic form, with vivacity, bringing them to life when he looks at them. The debates about objects of popular piety in Chaucer's time and beyond point to an increasing public discomfort with the uses and claims that people, both clerical as well as lay, make of those objects. Why is it we love them? They "compel us to have a relation to them," to borrow a phrase from Bill Brown, writing recently of the status of things in twentieth-century American fiction.[54] Disciplinary discourses about images as voiced in Chaucer's time imply that people imbue them with the uneasy surplus intrinsic to the sexual fetishes of Freud, the commodity fetishes of Marx, or the publicity fetishes of Baudrillard. Those who worship images imbue them with false powers. Wrongly they seem, in Marx's terms, "independent beings endowed with life." The image debate of late medieval England, that is to say, gives us remarkably nuanced discourses of the fetish. Like the fetishes of modernity, devotional images in texts responding to the vision contest are suspect as objects of attachment, of desire, and of surplus. As Lollard writings note, images even have secret and illicit ties to capital. The economics of false relics in the *Pardoner's Tale* certainly suggest that Chaucer was sympathetic to these critiques. Nevertheless Chaucer may also respond to images with the fetishist's disavowal: I know, but even so. His return throughout his writings to accounts of quasi-devotional daisies and pagan Venuses that wonderfully come to life and even speak out, as Alceste, to defend his writings indicate that he was well attuned to their enchantments and willing to credit devotional images with uncanny powers over love, faith, and even imagination. As an ethicist and cultural critic Chaucer may assert their deadness, but as a writer Chaucer kneels before them and lets them do what they will.

4

Translating Griselda

WHEN CHAUCER'S PILGRIMS ARRIVE AT CANTERBURY, they sort themselves, quite literally, into the sheep and the goats. During the sprinkling with holy water at the cathedral door, which includes a tussle for the sprinkler by the Friar, the pilgrims present themselves one after the other according to rank, "everich after other, righte as they were of states."[1] Following this, they proceed inside, sorting themselves this time by an instinctual, or really classed, wisdom about protocol. The Knight and his cohorts head straight toward the shrine "to do that they were com fore" (146), while the Pardoner and Miller "and other lewde sotes" behave like "lewd gotes" (147–48) and find themselves distracted by the images in the glass, peering at the pictures and counterfeiting gentlemen as they attempt to identify coats of arms in the glazing and interpret the meaning. Finally the Host, chiding them for gaucherie, has to send them toward the shrine with a verbal shove to "Get up and do your offering!" There, still "goglyng [ogling] with hir hedes," they pray to St. Thomas and kiss the relics as the attendant monk recites the names and martyrology. Finally brought under control, they attend to process and protocol, brought to appropriate postures before the martyred body. In a quick sequence of steps ("and sith," and then) the text passes with a brief sweep over the discipline of ritual, of bodies chastised even as they look ahead to dinner: "And sith to other places of holynes they raughte / And were in hir devocioun tyl service were al doon, / And sith they drowgh to dynerward, as it drew to noon" (168–70).

This account comes, of course, from the *Canterbury Interlude* that precedes the *Merchant's Tale of Beryn*, an anonymous fifteenth-century Chaucer continuation. Dated to about 1420,[2] this description of the ends of pilgrimage, however fictionalized, represents one of the most graphic contemporary accounts describing how pilgrims in the fourteenth and fifteenth century would have encountered the relics in Canterbury. A striking feature of the text is its embedded narrative about class and the encounter of classed bodies with other forms of matter, most graphically with matter that is not the saint's body but other bodies of evidence—first the glazing, a mystified heraldic text, and later, after all the pilgrims leave the church, the tokens that they buy and stash in their shirts and pockets, postponing dinner as they quite literally stuff themselves with portable relics. The social critique in this text is leveled squarely at the untutored. Throughout, the narrative marks its rubes as unruly bodies, people who cannot contain their appetites for food, sex, or objects and who cannot even regulate their own bodies within sacred space but have to be guided about like children. In contrast, the material substance of the cathedral and the relics within it are curiously quiet—indecipherable, like the images and heraldry that the Pardoner and Miller struggle to interpret, or even absent from the story. About the bones, hair shirt, brains, and other relics that wait as the goal of the Canterbury pilgrimage, the poet tells us almost nothing, distancing himself from the hieratic moment whose time stretches out (or is compresed) into an unmeasured devotional and unparsed "service." The central moment, the evidentiary and ritual centerpiece of the pilgrimage, is paradoxically its least visible event, glossed by the text in quick *seriata*, "and then": "And were in hir devocioun tyl service were al doon." Time shapes up after, and they all head off to lunch.

Not so with the account of the Canterbury ritual in Erasmus's colloquy, *A Pilgrimage for Religion's Sake*, written one hundred years later, where materiality and its horrors shift to the relics as well as to the gold and jewels in which they are encased. In this famous critique of clerical corruption, the pilgrims—Ogygius (aka Erasmus) and his companion—walk through the cathedral's ritual theater as shrewd commentators, disembodied into talking heads through the form of the colloquy. Matter, in contrast, takes on a strikingly physical form in the "linen rags," many of them still showing traces of "snivel" with which "the holy man wiped the sweat from his face or neck, the dirt from his nose, or whatever other kinds of filth human bodies have."[3] This encounter in the sacristy with Becket's handkerchief, in all its putrefaction, follows closely on the pilgrims' visit to the shrine, which Ogygius recounts as a ritual adoration of riches, the purest form of idolatry. Once the golden chest is drawn up by ropes, it reveals, he says, "inestimable treasure": "Everything shone and dazzled with rare and surpassingly large jewels, some bigger than a goose egg. Some monks stood about reverently. When the cover was removed, we all adored. The prior pointed out each jewel by touching it with a white rod, adding its French name, its worth, and the name of the donor. The principal ones were gifts from kings."[4] In this ritual elevation and adoration, a rich parody of the Mass, the bones, which cannot be seen, seem nevertheless present in surrogate form. Erasmus yokes barnyard to sacristy in his image of the goose-egg-sized gems that stir the pilgrim's awe. Becket's bones are overlaid with, and even lost within, other forms of matter and clerical capital: "we all adored."

The shifting locations of matter—and of satiric energy—in these two pilgrimage narratives can be bracketed, of course, by the history of dissent in the fifteenth century and in particular the tensions circulating around relics, pilgrimage, and the riches of the Church. For Erasmus, the saint's relic has become metonymic with clerical corruption and specifically with riches held by the Church. It is corruptible, itself corrupting, a performative that generates physical disgust when Ogygius's companion Gratianus Pullus (John Colet), presented one of the rags as a gift, carefully picks it up with a grimace of disgust and "scornfully" puts it back in the box. For the poet of the *Canterbury Interlude*, in contrast, matter is elsewhere. The saint's relic remains the sacred sign. His clerical figures, along with the Knight and even the Host, move in his text with the disembodied ritual authority of the saint's relic at the heart of his story—a role transposed to Erasmus's two savvy narrators in the later text. In the earlier account of the Canterbury spectacle, that is, the body that centers the ritual content of the journey cannot really be described—a lacuna that itself may itself record a certain nervousness about describing religious images. After the unruly bodies of the nonelite classes have been brought to task, the ritual performance itself, when those characters see and touch the relics, is not even described.

For Chaucer, always moving toward Canterbury but never arriving, the ritual encounter with the saint's body remains in a narrative imaginary. In one sense, of course, the encounter *is* imagined, carnival style, in the Pardoner's venomous display of his rags and bones and in the Host's retort that the Pardoner would "make me kisse thyn olde breech," doubtless an oblique reference to Becket's britches, on display at Canterbury.[5] Yet many of Chaucer's tales are haunted by the ends of pilgrimage, in particular by the ritual performance of the sanctified body. We return, throughout the tales, to bodies of women and children that, transformed, become signs of faith or doubt and that become public sites of pilgrimage or even literal shrines. Donald Howard has described the *Canterbury Tales* as an "antipilgrimage" in which the deepest reality is displaced from actual sights or objects to the "heart of the individual pilgrim."[6] Yet sights and objects are curiously not lost but recreated within the structure of narrative to turn some of his tales into the very performance of pilgrimage itself. Certainly literal pilgrimage is the promise at the end of the *Tale of Saint Cecilia*, a tale that describes the transformation of a woman into a relic. This tale begins and ends with a female body, hair-shirted at the outset and dismembered in a boiling bath at the end, whereupon the remains, in the final stanza, are collected and moved to consecrated ground.

The transposition of pilgrimage from an event that is destined to happen, or never to happen, at a moment in an unreached narrative imaginary to an event that is framed within the structure of storytelling itself defines the central drama of both the *Clerk's Tale* and the *Prioress's Tale*, the subject of this chapter and the next. In the *Knight's Tale* Chaucer begins the *Canterbury Tales* with a romance of chivalry that explores the collusions between the spectacle of the tournament, despotic power, and even the desires of both its characters and its readers. In his sacramental tales, Chaucer also contrasts private will with public performances, though these performances echo practices of liturgical rather than chivalric spectacle. In the *Prioress's Tale*, the overlay of liturgical ritual commonplaces is condensed, rich, and multivalent, such that the body of the Litel Clergeon, singing with the eucharistic "greyn" upon his tongue, itelf enacts the sacrament of Corpus Christi as he is carried, with "greet processioun" to the abbey, where he then recalls and performs the sacrificed body of Christ in the Lamentation as his mother swoons, like Mary, next to his bier. In the *Clerk's Tale*, the "translation" of Griselda from peasant to queen is also shaped as a bodily translation that resonates with echoes of liturgical ritual. She becomes a form of cultural property, the body or even relic at the center of communal pilgrimage. Griselda is the centripetal force at the center of the story; Walter, the people, even the murderous-looking sergeant repeatedly come to her. With both of these tales, in particularly unsettling ways, Chaucer seems to echo public discourses of images and of the sacraments to dramatize the theatrics of faith. Both tales locate a sacrificial subject at the center, surrounded by those who believe and those who doubt.

One of the questions that repeatedly unsettles readers of both the *Clerk's Tale* and the *Prioress's Tale* is the affiliation of the narrator with the story that is told: both tales are carefully and even theatrically staged. They are voiced by speakers with whom we have already been brought into a relationship of sorts through the General Prologue. Since we have been given this knowledge, or encoded within a relationship, can we entrust our responses to the speakers Chaucer gives us? Nevertheless, both tales have at their center a figure whose language appears to be driven by piety—the

boy's love of the Virgin or Griselda's marital promise to Walter.[7] The piety
of Griselda and the Litel Clergeon seems unassailable, even if we hold
ourselves at a remove in suspicion of the Prioress or the Clerk. In each of
these tales, the pious speaker is the nerve center of the story, however
unnerving the sacrificial commitments may be. In both of these tales pilgrimage is performed as a powerfully enfleshed drama that forcibly yokes
sacrificial subjects to contemporary ritual practice: Chaucer gives us subjects who enact sacramental ritual within their communities, even as the
pathos of their stories and the complex tissue of narrative lines of sight
invite the reader to inhabit the places of the sacrificed body and of the torturers alike.[8]

These chapters take as a point of departure the gravitas of pathos in
Chaucer's poetry and ask how Chaucer understands the private utterance
or experience in relation to communal ritual practices. In arguing that
Chaucer identifies with pathos or legitimizes pathos, I am also inviting a
consideration of Chaucer's uses of pious language and of the relationship
between language and public ritual practices, such as marriage, that codify
private verbal contracts into law. In the *Prioress's Tale*, the Clergeon incites
murderous rage by pious song, and the story comes to dramatize the risks
of that action in worlds governed by money, or money lending, and by law.
In the *Clerk's Tale*, language that articulates fidelity, or what we might call
domestic piety, also puts its speaker dramatically at risk, inciting a drama
of interrogation fueled by suspicion of the speaker's word. Marriage, a
sacrament of consensual *will*—a key term that appears repeatedly throughout the Griselda story and that receives special emphasis in Chaucer's version—depends on a voluntarist and invisible contract. Chaucer transforms
his sources to invent Griselda as a sacramental and sacrificial body and in
so doing heightens issues of trust in marriage, an institution that was itself
being redefined in a new sacramental role in his own time. Walter's doubts
articulate the paradox at the heart of the private sacrament: When we give
our willing consent to fidelity in marriage, who is to know if we mean what
we say and if we will remain true to our word? The pious speaker becomes
a powerful performative, not simply an agent staged by others, but a self-
staging, a speaking self, that provokes extraordinary and even murderous
responses. Against the scrim of Canterbury and the relics that the pilgrims
never reach, these tales resonate or fairly bristle in their fictive dramas of
pilgrimage, sacrifice, and reliquary witnessing and encryptment. Word is sacrament, the outward sign of inward grace. Word is uttered at extraordinary
risk. If faith can be mapped so neatly onto the speaking body, what then is

the relationship between linguistic risk and public performances of knowledge and evidence that drive communal will?

In what follows I will first explore the "translation" of Griselda from peasant girl into sacred site or sign, a devotional image of sorts, attributed with cultic powers. That transformation, I will also argue, underwrites a commentary on marital sacrament and on the related problematic of private trust and verbal contracts. The final section of this chapter then offers a reading of Griselda's language, what I call her sacramental poetic, in relation to larger issues of discursive poetic lineage that frame the tale as a whole.

*   *   *

Describing medieval clerical practices in which the presence of the deity is revealed, Charles Zika uses the term "visual theophany." Zika's term brackets cultural imperatives similar to those that Gail Gibson has called an "incarnational aesthetic" and that Sarah Beckwith has termed "sacramental theater."[9] With reference to narrative, all of these terms describe the fictive imitation or echo of clerical performances in which the sacred is made manifest, such as the elevation of the host during the Mass or ceremonial unveilings of sacred relics, performances that varied from shrine to shrine but apparently followed similar patterns. As we have seen, textual echoes of ritual performances often appear to speak in dialogue with larger cultural debates on the location of the sacred within matter and on the authority of the priest to reveal it. The *Clerk's Tale* also exploits, recasts, politicizes, and domesticates the visual theophanic by placing a transformed and tortured individual at the center of collective adoration and study. Late medieval ritual spectacles of a suffering or transformed body as encountered daily in the Mass, as well as countless other cultural productions, such as stories and images of the saints, no doubt played an important role in fueling the late fourteenth-century preoccupation with the Griselda story, a tale that was translated numerous times and retold across Europe in the form of exemplum, poem, and drama. Yet the *Clerk's Tale*, I will argue, itself stages a kind of sacramental theater, borrowing from clerical rituals of evidence—the elevation of the host in ordinary or even daily performances of the Mass and the demonstration or presentation of holy relics at pilgrimage sites—as a backdrop or frame for an interpretive drama about marriage and about the fate of language, the poet's utterance, his *parole*.

The questions that I would ask for Chaucer address not so much how his narrative secularizes a story of faith and pathos but rather how his tale relies, in profound and also contradictory ways, on contemporary ritual performances of the public body and overlapping practices of sacramental ritual to frame a performance that crosses boundaries between the religious, the political, and the domestic.[10] As I argue in Chapter 3, Chaucer may have negotiated the image debate in the 1380s and 1390s in part by techniques of avoidance, reserving his descriptions of what might be thought of as "devotional images" for pagan deities in his antique tales and dream visions. In several of his tales, however, he reveals a keen interest in spectacle, both liturgical and chivalric, and uses these performances or stagings as a backdrop against which to explore the operations of public and private will. Through the transformations and devotional uses of both the Clergeon and of Griselda, Chaucer may even be said to contribute to the vital public discourse in the 1380s and 1390s about devotional objects and their cultic powers. Chaucer's religious tales need to be understood within contemporary public discourses on piety, as David Aers has argued—discourses that, Aers claims, are also political ones; expressions of piety never "simply" voice an expression of faith but articulate responses to social, cultural, and economic conditions.[11]

Several studies of the *Clerk's Tale* have seen in Walter and the Commons refractions of English political theater in Chaucer's time.[12] We might also see in the *Clerk's Tale*, as well as in the Prologues to the *Legend of Good Women* and the *Pardoner's Tale*, a response to both clerical spectacle and the contemporary public discourse surrounding objects of veneration. How Chaucer's own faith can be graphed in relation to Lollardy has long been the subject of scholarly attention; it is, as most scholars agree, an immensely complicated issue, since Wyclif-like reformism was voiced not only in Lollard circles but from within orthodox ones as well.[13] In a recent circumspect contribution to this topic, William Kamowski argues that Chaucer shared with Wyclif a belief that miracles of the contemporary Church are smoke and mirrors, tricks to gull the innocent and line the pockets of the clergy; and even though Chaucer did not necessarily ascribe to all of Wyclif's views, Wyclif had a "significant influence" on Chaucer's own anticlericalism.[14] Taking a similar position, David Aers comments that Chaucer's writing should be situated within the contemporary "webs of interlocution" that were fueled by Wyclif's attacks on clerical corruption and absolutism.[15] Among these discursive webs would certainly be the debate on relics, images, and the Eucharist, the key devotional objects used in Christian devotional ritual. In his satire on phony relics in the *Pardoner's Prologue*, Chaucer seems to take a position close to that of Wyclif, who writes, "For certainly in the worship and veneration of the Eucharist along with the worship of dead bodies and images, through corrupt tradition the church is deceived."[16] While he dramatically repudiates false relics (Wyclif's "dead bodies"), as I discuss in Chapter 3, Chaucer gives few overt clues to his position on the Eucharist or on devotional images. Nevertheless, his sacramental tales dramatize responses to a transformed body that seem to echo contemporary reformist positions on devotional images in general, including the Eucharist. As Lynn Staley puts it, Chaucer "used his poetry to ask questions about urgent social issues that were invariably related to his politics of devotion or sanctity."[17] Through stories of belief and doubt, translation and transformation, as we shall see, the *Clerk's Tale* and the *Prioress's Tale* both engage profoundly with issues of sacramentality. Whereas devotional icons and vernacular authority get parodic play in the Prologue to the *Legend of Good Women*, in these two sacramental tales questions of piety are hardly comic. Where is the sacred located, how can we know it, and what are its powers over the public will?

The Griselda story, which both Petrarch and Chaucer frame within a dialogic structure, itself constructs a dialogue among contemporary sacramental practices as an enaction of the very tensions that it refuses to resolve. Certainly there is little consensus on how we as readers are to respond to Griselda or to interpret Chaucer's subtle changes in his translation of Petrarch and the anonymous French *Livre de Griseldis*, although most agree that Chaucer mounts a series of protests to Petrarch's reading through his additions and alterations.[18] As evidenced by responses to the tale from readers as early as the Paduan and Veronese friends Petrarch mentions in his letter to Boccaccio, one of whom bursts into tears halfway through the story and the other of whom refuses to be moved by the tale's obvious lack of verisimilitude,[19] to my own colleague who tells me that he never quite knows how to read or teach the *Clerk's Tale*, discomfort with this tale does seem consistent over time. The story refuses to let us down gently on one side or the other, neutralizing its own polarities of Walter's unexplained impulses to sadism and Griselda's uncanny resiliance. Walter, who is repeatedly humanized, ultimately even assumes a sort of heroic status with his return of the children and his accompanying disclaimer: This was a test. It was only a test. Because she capitulates with domestic violence and refuses to conform to hagiographic or romance norms of resistance, Griselda, alternatively, never fully engages our compassion, or at least not until the moment she collapses in a swoon when reunited with her children. Certainly we never quite understand her.

In part the text's resistance to resolution is created by its rapid shifts in positionings between investigative subjects and its sacrificial and sacramental body. If were to look for a Jamesian center of consciousness, we would find, I believe, that the center oscillates within the text between Walter, a Commons whose position is chiefly defined by its being Not Walter, and Griselda—that is, by an absence of a center for a complex set of positionings. The compulsions of its story are generated, in part, by these swings between collective and single lines of sight around a body that is studied, undressed, dressed anew, translated, rehoused (and later warehoused), approached, revered, and investigated—even as it tells a story about a body that cannot be known.

The transformation of Griselda from single and simple peasant girl to sacramental center is virtually as rapid as her marriage. Readers have repeatedly remarked on Chaucer's introduction of biblical allusion and overtone to describe Griselda; as Elizabeth Salter notes in her oft-cited essay, these include a set of echoic references to Griselda's origins in an ox stall, her resemblance to Job, and her likeness to a lamb before the will of the cruel sergeant.[20] While readers have wrestled with the allegorical Griselda, they have paid less attention to the performative Griselda who evokes not only Christ but also the devotional practices through which the iconic status might be known or witnessed. Allusions to sacrifice, promissory notes of her performance in a martyrology, are also shaped by processes of communal witnessing that invest her with an altered and sacramental role. Transformed into a queen, Griselda suddenly takes on public visibility; she is the object of speculation, a public surmise that invests her with a new identity to the point of even discounting her biological lineage. Even those who have known Griselda all her life can hardly believe that this new woman is Janicula's daughter: "for, as by conjecture, / Hem thoughte she was another creature" (405–6). Even as the public thinks she has become a new person ("hem thoughte"), she seems to morph herself and take on the virtues that the public attributes her:

> For though that evere vertuous was she,
> She was encressed in swich excellence
> Of thewes goode, yset in heigh bountee,
> And so discreet and fair of eloquence,
> So beneigne and so digne of reverence,
> and koude so the peples herte embrace,
> That ech hire lovede that looked on hir face. (407–13)

Is this ironic double-talk to suggest that seeming stands in for being and that in fact her new being is just a construct of public opinion, like the emperor's new clothes? I think not, but rather a recognition that she has been subject to a sacramental transformation of the kind that shapes medieval ritual theater in arenas as different as the *elevatio* in the Mass and ceremonies of investiture or coronation. Her own transformed status acts quickly as a social performative that influences the public's response to her. Her fame spreads; people come from afar:

> So spradde of hire heighe bountee the fame
> That men and wommen, as wel yonge as olde,
> Goon to Saluce upon hire to biholde. (418–20)

In the process of her transformation, Griselda becomes an object of pilgrimage, drawing in the community who come "upon hire to biholde"— coming later for counsel but first, it seems, just to witness the miracle of transformation. Grielda becomes the center of a "visual theophany," a relic of sorts, whose miracle lies in her performance of a central transformation that is at once material (she is the same body) and invisible (her new qualities, her "thewes good").

The description of the bodily transformation that leads to this new status, the ritual investiture in which her clothes are removed in public and she is dressed in new attire to prepare her for her new role, itself suggests dramatic status change and ceremonial transpositions of the body: "Unnethe the peple hir knew for hire fairnesse / Whan she translated was in swich richesse" (384–85). In his discussion of the tale, David Wallace points out that Chaucer most often uses the term "translaten" to refer to language practices, the translation of texts.[21] Chaucer's uses of the term, however, are somewhat anomalous in his time, for "translate" most often meant "to move" and was commonly used to designate the relocation of the bones of a saint, as in "þe gode Kyng Edward . . . was translatede, & put into þe shryne," or from the *South English Legendary*, "his swete body . . . Unto þe cite of Ediss translat it was with pes."[22] By rendering the line from the French text, "transmuee et changie" and Petrarch's Latin, "subito transformatum" with the preterite "translated," Chaucer in effect mobilizes his term so that it implies not just a quality of inner change but also a shift in status that can be mapped both on and across the body.[23] "Translated" would even be likely to recall, in historical memory if not in actual experience, accounts of ritual processions and relocations of sacred bones, such as the triumphal *adventus*, a procession which itself recalled the arrival of a prince, in which sacred bones were brought for the *depositio* in the ceremonial consecration of a church.[24] Through linguistic resonance, the term could also place Griselda's translation within accounts of famous processions in which saints' bodies were moved, such as Becket's famous *translatio* in 1220 when his bones were moved from the crypt to behind the high altar; the huge procession of 1239 when St. Louis carried the Crown of Thorns to St. Chapelle; the procession when Henry III (d. 1272) carried the relics of Edward the Confessor to Westminster; or the spectacle when Edward I (d. 1307) carried the body of St. William.[25] "Whan she translated was," Chaucer's version suggests, she is also moved and rehoused—and, as the following stanzas detail, visited by a widening community of pilgrims.

I suggest, therefore, that Griselda's translation into Walter's palazzo plays to familiar structures or performances of faith that share, as a central motif in their visual theophany, the placement of a miraculous body at the center of a group of spectators, such as the public witnessing and veneration as orchestrated, for instance, by Love's *Mirror* or the Despenser Retable. As G. J. C. Snoek argues in a recent study, *Medieval Piety from Relics to the Eucharist*, these clerical performances of the Eucharist themselves had prior housing in the traditions and rituals related to holy relics.[26] In the late fourteenth-century *Instructions for Parish Priests*, John Mirk notes that the sight of the eucharistic host offers protection for the rest of the day against fire, blindness, disease, or sudden death—guarantees that were also commonly attributed to relics.[27] Reconstructing how pilgrims would have encountered the relics in Canterbury in a distillation of accounts that includes, among others, St. Cuthbert's Shrine at Durham Cathedral and Stow's chronicle of Canterbury, Arthur Stanley suggests that pilgrims entering Canterbury to view Becket's bones were likely to experience a highly theatricalized event, one that, with its tinkling of bells, elevation of a canopy, and collective worship, followed a script similar to the moment of the elevation during the Mass:

The lower part of the shrine was of stone, supported on arches; and between these arches the sick and lame pilgrims were allowed to ensconce themselves, rubbing their rheumatic backs or diseased legs and arms against the marble which brought them into the nearest contact with the wonder-working body within. The shrine, properly so called, rested on these arches, and was at first invisible. It was concealed by a wooden canopy, probably painted outside with sacred pictures, suspended from the roof; at a given signal this canopy was drawn up by ropes, and the shrine then appeared blazing with gold and jewels. . . . As soon as this magnificent sight was disclosed, everyone dropped on his knees, and probably the tinkling of the silver bells attached to the canopy would indicate the moment to all the hundreds of pilgrims in whatever part of the cathedral they might be.[28]

The translocation of the "visual theophany" from relics of various local saints to the ritual elevation of the eucharistic body of Christ during the Mass represented, according to Snoek, a centralization of diffuse and local sanctities. Similar arguments have been advanced by Charles Zika, who points out that the sacred powers of the host "were largely indistinguishable from the growing power of the clergy," and by Sarah Beckwith in her argument that Christ's body became "the focus and medium through which clerical control seeks to establish itself."[29]

Once she takes on the raiment of queen, however, the translated body of Griselda becomes an object of pilgrimage outside structures of control or display. Her draw is cultic; her fame spreads by rumor: "if oon seide wel, another seyde the same" (417). Indeed, Chaucer develops this section from his sources, emphasizing her role as a public attraction and a kind of relic that draws folk from all around the region. How are we to understand Chaucer's investment in Griselda's sacramental transformation? Certainly in part we are to understand her as the authentic miracle. In her internal transformation that communicates itself through cultic dissemination, she metamorphoses into the outer self that is constructed through marriage and investiture; the "nowches" or ornaments that adorn her clothing alchemically seem to transform into "thewes good," the "personal qualities" that increase within her. In the reliquary depository of the pilgrimage to Canterbury, her transformed essence contrasts sharply with the Pardoner's dry bones. In her translation, that is to say, Griselda becomes the real thing.

Yet if she signifies the real presence, or rather if the echoes between her transformation and sacramental ritual suggest the possibility of the sudden visit of transforming grace, that process takes its meaning through its effects on others, where like a relic or Cecilia's tortured body, she becomes an action on the bodies of others. Her dynamism engages the "people" who come to Saluzzo "upon hire to biholde." I referred earlier to centers of consciousness that shift between positionings around Griselda as a sacramental object; following her marriage the text sweeps its own readers into the text's Commons, to whom she assumes the status of an enhanced being. But of course, the chief significance of this view on Griselda lies in what comes next. When the narrative redirects its gaze through Walter's line of sight, the story becomes one of an unreadable body or a body that masks a set of motives that Walter tries fruitlessly to interpret by her words and "chiere" (576; 599–600). The shift, which redirects the text and lines of narrative sight away from public assessment to the private and domestic, also transfers the rule of the sacramental body from rituals of use known through clerical rite and through regal investitures to marriage. This shift to marriage and to a story about a husband's inability to read his wife's motives is haunted, I believe, by the sacramental frame in which Chaucer sets it, for within this mythic narrative of ritual transformation and testing, resonant with biblical echoes, lie two very different versions of sacrament—both sharing a dramatic contrast between a public gaze or will to see and know and the object of that gaze, whose "truth" must be taken on faith. One is the Mass and the other is marriage, enacted in the *Clerk's Tale* by a story that seems in some respects like the ordinary film noir, the Bluebeard story: can we ever really know the thoughts, desires, body of the person that we are closest to?

Marriage and the Private Will

A number of studies of the *Clerk's Tale* have pointed to its debt to philosophical traditions current in the late fourteenth century, especially nominalism, and have suggested that the tale explores philosophical constructs of knowing, chiefly through the capricious shifts in Walter's own thinking. As Kathryn Lynch argues in a particularly lucid account of the tale as a dramatized epistemological crisis, when he first recognizes Griselda at her home Walter immediately recognizes her truth, performing an act of intuitive cognition that recognizes truth without contingencies of proof—a moment of knowing by grace that is soon replaced by "a secondary, abstractive, experimental knowledge that has curiosity as its motive force."[30] I would add to this account of epistemological contrasts the contrast between Walter and the public, as each shapes itself around Griselda in dramatically different postures of faith and doubt. More importantly, however, I would also suggest that the Clerk directs us to practices of popular piety as well as to the university for the epistomological constructs of this story, which echoes, with its simple domestic horrors and folk-tale plot, ritual practices of faith and knowing. Griselda's ritual investiture and incarnation into both a queen and a cultic center draw the public as docile bodies around her and early on split the world of the story between those who believe and those who do not. However simplistic this division may seem, in its extremes the story divides its community between those of faith and those (or the one) of doubt—between those who accept a miracle of a sanctified body and those who would interrogate it. This is not to suggest that we should read the *Clerk's Tale* as an allegory of orthodoxy and dissent; but it is to suggest that we read it as a story that uses practices of ordinary and habitual faith as a framework against which to construct a drama about knowing the other in marriage, a sacrament of the body and consensual will.

In suggesting that Chaucer sketches a picture of Griselda as she is transformed through marriage that draws heavily on popular rituals of faith, I am also proposing that Chaucer evokes sacramental ritual to underscore the ways that this story plays to a powerfully embodied class-passing fantasy. The powers of the host during the elevation during the Mass were engaged in both intromissive and extramissive ways: its powers were those of a mutual action and even a mutual gaze. When it was raised by the cleric to be witnessed, it also emitted its powers.[31] Central to the operations of the *sacrum signum* and particularly of the sacrificial body is a disrupted and heightened metonymic in which meaning not only exceeds the matter in which the sacred is embodied but also in which the fleshiness of matter itself also exceeds or mutes whatever allegorical readings we might make of it.[32] Encounters with signs of sacred bodies in pilgrimage and in the elevation of the host in the Mass are marked by this dialogue between the body and communal ideology or fantasy. Whether visual, as in the Mass, or tactile, as in pilgrimage, medieval ritual encounters with the sacred body operate as a form of touch, as the Passion scene in Love's *Mirror* so forcibly demonstrates. When we cluster around the theophanic body, we also take it in. Its materiality is essential to this process, for it allows us to absorb both its abjection and transcendence. The relic that is kissed offers a confirmation of a double process of absorption and transcendence: the elite are mere mortals after all. The relic also affirms that ordinary beings can live on; the sanctified ordinary body can also leap across class boundaries to become permanently housed among the clerical elite. Saints' bodies repeatedly reconfirm the miraculous possibilities of the ordinary self.

In the *Clerk's Tale*, Griselda's transformation in marriage and her transformation into a sacred sign offer this hope and this participatory pleasure. We not only watch her and identify, as we might watch TV stories of lottery winners and imagine how that Powerball fortune would change our lives; we also take her in through her imitation of familiar performances of sanctified bodies. Griselda's translation in a fairy-tale leap of class passing occurs against familiar narratives and even public performances of female assumptions, either actual or legendary: the assumption of the Virgin; the martyrdom of St. Katherine; or even ritual processions, such as Anne of Bohemia's passage through the city in 1382 or the reconciliatory procession of Richard II and Queen Anne in 1392, as described in Richard Maidstone's *Condordia*.[33] Contemporary accounts of Anne's own arrival, in fact, may offer a particularly pertinent illustration of public responses to the queen's body. The chroniclers first demean Anne as a rather worthless foreign body, arriving with insufficient funds: "But to those with an eye for the facts it seemed she represented a purchase rather than a gift, since the English king laid out no small sum for such a small piece of flesh," "pro tantilla carnis porcione."[34] Later accounts of Anne, however, emphasize, as Andrew Taylor comments, her "reputation for prudence, charity, and the devout reading of Scripture," allowing her an assumption of sorts into the theophanics of queenship as Anne the Good or Anne the Wise.[35] The Westminster Chronicler's account and later paeans offer a striking contrast in embodiment, for in the later descriptions Anne's body is absorbed into a role, one defined by the expectations of intercessory behavior. First a "carnis porcione," she becomes an icon whose flesh is abstracted into virtues.

Whereas the extraordinary body of the saint or queen performs its own class-passing miracles, ordinary bodies in marriage, intimately known, contain very different promises and resistances; and it is this doubling of public sign and private sacrament that Griselda herself embodies. Recent studies of *Piers Plowman* by Teresa Tavormina, and others, have pointed to the importance of a new cult of domesticity in the late fourteenth century. Marriage came to be increasingly idealized through a rhetoric of sanctity around its human laws—what Tavormina identifies, in *Piers*, as "the social relations of mutual support, governance, obedience, and love."[36] For Langland, marriage also interpenetrates with reformist models for the state, and the singular heterosexual bond that joins two people through an act of consensual will becomes a model for an expanding system of social and political relationships.[37] Even more directly pertinent to the *Clerk's Tale*, Philippe de Mézières's *Livre de la vertu du sacrement de marriage*, written between 1385 and 1389, defends marriage as an institution for social ordering. Philippe includes the Griselda story, translated from Petrarch's Latin, as an exemplum to celebrate patient suffering, which itself can be sanctified by its service to a sacramental union. Philippe's vision of marriage, according to a recent argument by Lynn Staley, is deeply social and conservative, invested in female conciliation to compassionate structures of masculine authority. Because her obedience is undertaken through a sacramental vow, Griselda's patience, "both conventional and pacific," shares with the heroism of Job.[38]

At the same time, however, fundamental contractual arrangements of marriage remained private and consensual. As James Brundage puts it, "in contrast to all of the other sacraments, marriage required no special form for validity," but relied for its validity on words of consent.[39] Although the Church sought to outlaw marriages not sanctified by its clergy, it also recognized the validity of private or clandestine marriages.[40] This absence of official form, which included the absence of any specific words or even any words at all, resulted, furthermore, in numerous contractual uncertainties, as indicated in surviving records of late medieval marital litigation. According to Michael Sheehan's study of the Ely Register from 1374 to 1382 and also to Shannon McSheffrey's edition of depositions in two London courts in the fifteenth century, most suits were brought not, as one might expect, to dissolve marriages but rather to enforce private contractual agreements. Surviving records of marital litigation from the fifteenth century appears designed to discern, McSheffrey explains, "whether or not consent had been properly exchanged and a contract made."[41]

In the *Clerk's Tale*, the story of doubts in marriage, performed as that marriage is within a privately contracted ceremony, also becomes a story about evidence that voices contemporary tensions about marriage ideology and the proof of consent. Even as Griselda functions as a sacred sign, that translation into a sign is effected by Walter alone; he is a single agent—both orchestrator and maestro. Following her ritual dressing, when she is "translated in swich richesse," "this markys hath hire spoused with a ryng" (386) in a marriage ceremony of a form known technically as private and clandestine and validated, in the terms of marital depositions, by "the public voice," rather than solemnized by the Church.[42] Unlike the *Merchant's Tale*, where January and May "to the chirche bothe be they went / For to receyve the hooly sacrement" (1701–2), the *Clerk's Tale* makes no mention of a ceremony within the church, solemnized by any clerical authority, but only of a sharing of vows in public view.[43] Indeed, the fragility of the verbal contract is itself powerfully underscored by Walter's fabricated dissolution of the marriage with the fake papal bull, an action that dramatizes not only the power of public cermonial and written text to trump private vows but also to shape the public will, as evidenced in the public's rapid betrayal of Griselda for the new queen. Framed within a culture where lawsuits aimed at validating marriage contracts appear to have been common practice, Walter's compulsion to test Griselda bespeaks certain anxieties within the institution of marriage itself. How can a verbal marriage contract hold up in the face of public pressures and especially written documents that

would validate it or dissolve it? Even more profoundly, in a marriage contracted under a new domestic ideology of mutual trust, who is to guarantee that the other party will remain true to its terms?

With a saint's body, the evidence lies in the bones. The transformation
is by magic, a kind of assumption, and the evidence lies in the body itself,
the body of evidence, Griselda's presence in the body that "translated was."
Unlike the clever and learned skeptic that Erasmus describes, who sees the
remains of the shrine as mere "stocks and stones," to borrow a term from
Lollard denunciations of images, the pilgrims who flock to Saluzzo to see
and seek advice from Griselda accept her transformation not because they
are gulls but because that transformation is really an assumption of sorts, a
transformation of total presence and being, one that is effected, in part, by
their own faith: Chaucer's additions to this section suggest the dual inter-
penetration of faith and substances. The body *is* the evidence; beyond faith
that is affirmed in the witnessing, there is no further need for proof. Just
how central questions of substance and evidence were to the very concept
of the sacramental is expressed by Roger Dymmok in his refutation of the
1395 Lollard *Conclusions*. Nothing, Dymmok says, shows the body's change
at moments of sacramental transformation: "For if this [Lollard] argument
should thrive, all the sacraments of the church, all the oaths of kings, and
all the political exchange should be completely destroyed. . . . I ask, what
sensible change do you see in a boy newly baptized, in a man who has con-
fessed, in a boy or man who has been confirmed, in consecrated bread, in
a man ordained into the priesthood, in marriageable persons betrothed or
joined?"[44] What all the sacraments share, that is, is a miraculous but invisible transformation whose effects can only be taken on faith. At the risk
of proposing another version of what Linda Georgianna has dubbed the
"Protestant Chaucer," I would also suggest that Chaucer as skeptical fideist
strips the mediation from his ritual encounters to confront his readers
directly with the sacramental. Whereas the Beryn poet elides the encounter
with the relics in Canterbury, focusing instead on faulty forms of interpretation and relic purchasing as a way of illustrating the "visual theophany"
itself, which cannot quite be told, Chaucer imagines versions of the visual
theophanic in his sacramental tales, using a miraculous, if human, body as
a scrim against which to perform dramas about knowledge and of trust.

Marriage, even if it guarantees a body, carries no assurances about its
sanctity, however. Elizabeth Salter, explaining the tale's imbalance in terms
that many critics have echoed, claims that we are in two virtually irrecon-
cilable worlds, one of ideal values, the other of actuality in which the story

is "cruel, unnatural and unconvincing."[45] Doubtless this is true. But, I would also suggest, Walter's testing of Griselda is disconcertingly *natural*, if cruel and extreme, framed as it is within performances of sacramental knowledge and faith, or we might say, framed by the sacramentalizing of a human bond. Griselda's "translation" into a sacred sign levies an extraordinary promise of revelation and sanctity even as that translation, contracted through the verbal promises of marriage, highlights the dilemma of ordinary knowledge of the other. In real time, living bodies that give themselves to us by private consent in marriage cannot be kept or fully known.

Language in Petrarch's Shadow

In Part 3 of the *Clerk's Tale*, when Walter conceives of his plan to test Griselda, the narrative moves from public vision, spectacle, and assessment to a much darker private interior. This shift is marked in Petrarch; it is even more overtly dramatized in Chaucer, who touches his story with hints of his male characters' sinister motivations and with an overall ambience of an ominous and unexplained secrecy. Chaucer spatializes the story to locate Griselda in her chamber where she is visited at night, first by Walter, then by the sergeant, and privatizes these moments to emphasize the secrecy surrounding the events. In Petrarch's story, Walter sends for Griselda in his chamber; Chaucer reverses this action, highlighting Griselda's vulnerability by presenting her as passive recipient to Walter's sinister visitation in the night: "He cam allone a-nyght, ther as she lay / With stierne face and with ful trouble cheere" (464–65).[46] Furthermore, Chaucer repeatedly points to the secrecy of Walter's designs. Walter makes certain that Griselda realizes that no one can hear what he is saying to her, documenting their privacy: "Taak heede of every word that y yow seye; / Ther is no wight that hereth it but we tweye" (475–76). Secrecy also surrounds the sergeant, whom Chaucer names as "this privee man" (519) and to whom Walter tells his plan: "he prively hath toold al his entente" (517).[47]

Walter's orchestration of privacy and secrets takes curious shape on the body of Griselda, who now becomes, until the moment that her children are restored to her, a secret from the reader as well. The text becomes extraordinarily dark and psychologized; Walter's motive for testing Griselda, Chaucer's translation suggests, lies in losses, or more precisely in absent spaces of loss in domestic relations. His sudden impulse to test her "whan that this child had souked but a throwe" (450) suggests that his impulse to frighten her, to "affraye," results from feelings of displacement and envy, an explanation that the Clerk briefly appears to support in his offhand comment that things like this often happen: "as it bifalleth tymes mo" (449).[48] Men, the Clerk seems to say, often have an impulse to hurt or test their wives, especially when there is a new baby at the breast. A marriage in full view of the people, one in which Griselda has transformed herself both inwardly and outwardly to conform to a public role and to take on a public role as an icon or even devotional relic, suddenly shifts, or really is pulled back by Walter, into the private life and even into a darkened bedchamber, and its dramas and terrors suddenly arise out of affiliative impulses. Griselda is also withdrawn from view. The window into her thoughts—"she thoghte" (281)—that we are given before her marriage when she plans where to stand with the other girls so that she will be able to spot the marquis's new bride closes abruptly for us as well.

This shift in visibility, in which Griselda is withdrawn from a role as public sign or icon into the private life where she becomes in essence a kind of private study for Walter, is I believe one of the most carefully orchestrated and unsettling moves of the narrative—and one that is particularly dramatized in Chaucer's translation, with his emphasis on the sudden privacy and secrecy in which Walter's actions, and Griselda's very presence, are cloaked. Walter insistently studies Griselda's face for signs, though precisely what Walter is searching for, or what he would do with the evidence if he found it, remains one of the troubling unknowns of the story. In Part 2, she is transparent. She stands at a literal and metaphoric threshold, her thoughts exposed, her layered being visible to both Walter's gaze and the public's scrutiny. The transformation that is reflected in her clothing is, as I have noted, etched on her being, her "thewes good." Even her body appears transparent, a kind of Visible Woman whose virginity paradoxically functions as a lens, a hymen unbroken but permeable, to reveal her heart: "Yet in the brest of hire virginitee / Ther was enclosed rype and sad corage" (219–20).[49]

When she is withdrawn from view in Part 3, Walter's agency as a private inquisitor thus stands against a public moment of sacramental exposure, or even revelation, and immediately casts him as infidel. As the one who challenges and tests what the audience believes to be the "real" thing, he plays a role not unlike that of pagan persecutors in lives of the virgin martyrs or of Jews testing the host in the continental precursors to the Croxton *Play of the Sacrament* or even, in real time, of Jews testing the host in continental host desecration accusations, which I discuss in Chapter 5.[50]

He also creates a system of untruths. In his private theater, he shapes whatever reality he chooses. Invoking the people, who have repeatedly demonstrated only their trust of her, "they seyn," he tells her that it is shameful to be subject to one as lowly born as Griselda. She is not dear to them, but only to him. He desires, he tells her, to live his life with them in rest and peace—a curious wrenching of desire in domestic relations from the private to the public sphere. At the opening of the tale Walter has been presented as somewhat at odds with his subjects and only agrees to marry in response to their direct and even coercive petition. In Part 3 he claims he must do not what he would like to, but what his people wish. Suddenly Walter is a pious servant of a public will, even though we were told at the beginning that his interest was entirely centered on his own pleasure: "but on his lust present was al his thoght" (80).

Walter's distortions of the truth in Part 3 play a role in Griselda's sacramental drama, for they bracket her own role as a sign of truth, embodied both in gesture, in body, and in language. Whereas Part 2 features Griselda as a sign that is fully knowable, Part 3 features the withdrawal of evidence from the body and from language, at least as visible to Walter's inquisitorial gaze. With this shift, the tale brings to the fore fundamental conflicts of affiliative trust and truth that were central to new ideologies of marital sacrament in the late fourteenth century. Griselda's sudden inscrutability enacts the problem of the verbal contract: what are its guarantees? This shift in the text also foregrounds the instabilities of language itself. Through the doubts that circulate around the oral contract (Griselda's word) the text invites us to consider questions of linguistic and even poetic risk taking. Griselda's oath of extraordinary fidelity, a promise that is reiterated in response to Walter's tests, is itself situated within a complex metacommentary on poetic language, the discourse on Petrarch that surrounds the story itself. The complex asides to Petrarch invite us to consider Chaucer's own translation project and transformations to the story, as readers have argued; they also invite us to weigh, I would suggest, the various speech acts performed within the poem, particularly Griselda's speech, as a form of sacramental poetry, and the uses of language by her interlocutors in relation to the Petrarchan commentary on poetic debts and affiliations. When the word, language itself, provides the evidence, what indicates its authenticity?

The remainder of this chapter focuses on language as a medium of ethical accountability. In a reading of Griselda's own speech as well as of the discourse on poetry that surrounds the tale, I argue that Chaucer elides marital sacrament with poetry; poetry enunciates a sacramental gesture that challenges public, ritual practices of evidence. By withdrawing Griselda as a visible icon and by introducing Walter's inquisition and distortions of the truth, Chaucer directs our attention to the risk of plain speaking. Through Griselda's verbal contract, voiced in a set of extraordinary utterances, Chaucer dramatically underscores the risks of language—and specifically the risks of vernacular poetry.

*   *   *

As readers have repeatedly noted, Chaucer's most significant changes to the Griselda story emerge not in his translation of the tale itself but in the framework with which he surrounds it—the Prologue, the Clerk's comments at the end, and in the Envoy. The subject that grounds the Clerk's Prologue is language. The Prologue in fact offers one of Chaucer's most detailed and sustained commentaries on language and on his sources, a commentary that develops as well as a meditation, however tongue-in-cheek, on the relative merits of high style and plain speaking through the consideration of Petrarch as a powerful authority. In the Clerk's response to the Host's request for simplicity and lucidity in his tale, and in his elaborately deferential acknowledgment of Petrarch as his "auctor," lies an invitation to read the story as a performance, the tale itself as a staged response to this double demand. On the one hand it attempts to fulfill the desire of the Host, the figure from the vernacular with his anticlerical needling, and on the other it bows to Petrarch, the model of Latinate and humanist learning.

In explorations of the tale's rhetoric of translation, readers have noted Chaucer's uneasy relationship to Petrarch and recognized that Chaucer's translation levels a critique at the Petrarchan academy. In her analysis of arts of translation, poetic figuration, and processes of interpretation as patriarchal activities practiced over the body of a woman, Carolyn Dinshaw, for instance, argues that Chaucer uses the voice of the Clerk to explore—and critique—the ways that language institutes social relationships.[51] More specifically attentive to Chaucer's political critique, David Wallace argues that Chaucer's vernacular translation exposes forms of tyranny endorsed by Petrarch's own political affiliations in Lombardy and also by his implicit valorization of domestic tyranny in his version of the Griselda story. Although each of these approaches sets the *Clerk's Tale* on a slightly different axis, both imagine Griselda as a kind of still center, the unfigured or "real" around which terrorizing acts, linguistic and otherwise, circulate. Indeed, the very act of translating the tale into English may have had a decidedly

political and controversial edge in the early 1390s, when the tale was probably written. By the 1380s the act of translating had become associated with
Wyclif and "consequently demanded a certain amount of rhetorical care."[52]

I would also argue that Griselda, as the unfigured real whom, as Wallace says, shows "no gap between her public face and her private feelings,"[53]
is also a radical voice of vernacular plain speaking whose words embody the
spirit of the Host's mandate to the Clerk: "Speketh so pleyn at this tyme,
we yow preye, / That we may understonde what ye seye" (4.19–20). When
Walter hints that he might take some action on her daughter, Griselda responds in dramatically plain language, asserting her loyalty and locating
her heart or "corage" as both a geographic and moral center:

> Ther may no thyng, God so my soule save,
> Liken to yow that may displese me;
> Ne I desire no thyng for to have,
> Ne drede for to leese, save oonly yee.
> This wyl is in myn herte, and ay shal be;
> No lengthe of tyme or deeth may this deface,
> Ne chaunge my corage to another place. (505–11)

Although Walter refuses to take on faith the consonance between her words
and her will, the reader never doubts that her words, free of rhetorical
flourishes, are consistent with her desire; and in this seamless overlay her
language contrasts radically with Walter's own twisted distortions of the
public will. Her language is remarkable for a simplicity and directness characterized by active verbs and short nominals: thing, dread, soul, heart, will,
time, death, place. It is voiced with the linguistic directness of a vow; the
end rhymes join "me" and "ye" with "ay shal be."

As a voice for simplicity, for plain speaking at its most direct, Griselda
thus ventriloquizes the voice of the Clerk, at least as the Host has directed
him, "speketh so playn"; and in some respects this voice also speaks for
Chaucer, I would argue, in agreement with readers who hear Chaucer pro-
jecting a poetic persona onto his feminized or feminine subjects.[54] We
can understand what she says—or at least should—for she is the one constant in the story. Other figures in the text either overtly distort truth, as
does Walter, or else use rhetorical flourishes, the "termes, colours, and figures . . . as whan that men to kynges write" (16–17) that the Host asks the
Clerk *not* to use in his story.[55] The spokesman for the Commons builds a
complex metaphor into his appeal to Walter to marry:

Boweth youre nekke under that blisful yok
Of soveraynetee, noght of servyse,
Which that men clepe spousaille or wedlok. (113–15)

Couching his picture of the delights of marriage in a richly self-canceling
oxymoron, the yoke of sovereignty, the spokesman hints that marriage is
a form of law and power even as he trenchantly points to its disciplines.
Clearly we hear in this speech a collective wish not just to get Walter married to produce an heir but also to domesticate him; marriage is a yoke
with which to produce a more lawful and nurturant form of rule. Nothing,
however, is said directly. The speech is a demonstration of linguistic servil-
ity, the strategic hedging of terms in the language of the sycophant. In addition, the appeal is Latinate and conventional, the "heigh style" one adopts
when appealing to kings: "Accepteth, lord, now of youre gentillesse / That
we with pitous herte unto yow pleyne, / And lat youre eres nat my voys
desdeyne" (97–98). It is, perhaps, no accident that the sergeant's speech when
he arrives to take Griselda's daughter echoes the words of the spokesman.
Both speak a rhetoric of deference, however different the ends of deference might be. Asserting that his will is subject to Walter's command, the
sergeant's rhymes produce an apology trapped in a net of courtly passives:
"constreyned," "yfeyned," "compleyned" (527–30). In this case Latinate and
courtly language clearly bears little relationship to apparent intent, as he
adopts the demeanor of a terrorist, grabbing the child and making as if to
kill it, "as though he wolde han slayn it er he wente" (536).

To hear in Griselda's plain speaking Chaucer's voice or at the very least
an idealized poetic utterance, and not just the voice of the Clerk fulfilling
the Host's mandate for "some murie thyng" (4.15), we need to pause over
the Clerk's Prologue. The Prologue effects a curious merging of personae
in that the Clerk and the Host, even though they represent very different intellectual and social allegiances, take up a collusive posture against
Petrarch. Chaucer's edgy and ambivalent relationship to Petrarch and the
Petrarchan academy has been insightfully explored by David Wallace, and
I will not rehearse that ground here; but I would read in the Prologue an
even sharper and more troubled set of responses than Wallace accords in
his account of the homage demonstrated in the Prologue's deference: "the
cultural achievement of Petrarch is here accorded great respect, but is insistently brought up hard against the brute facts of mortality."[56] Mortality,
or Petrarch's death, indeed seems crucial to the Clerk's own project as a
storyteller:

I wol yow telle a tal which that I
Lerned at Padowe of a worthy clerk,
As preved by his wordes and his werk.
He is now deed and nayled in his cheste;
I prey to God so yeve his soule reste!
   Frannceys Petrak, the lauriat poete,
Highte this clerk, whos rethorike sweete
Enlumyned al Ytaille of poetrie,
as Lynyan dide of philosophie,
Or lawe, or oother art particuler;
But Deeth, that wol nat suffre us dwellen heer,
Hem bothe hath slayn, and alle shul we dye. (26–38)

Clearly the Clerk allies himself with the practice of poetry that Petrarch represents and with Petrarch's famous claims on classical learning and courtly high style; and in this voicing of the ends and definitions of poetic authority he also comes back to the fact of death, what Wallace calls its "brute facts," both times slipping himself into the imaginative space of the dead poet. In his prayer to God to "yeve his soule reste," he speaks as Petrarch's intercessor from an almost familial position; and then, after his reflection on the illumination of Italy by both Petrarch and canon law professor Lignano, the Clerk includes himself as the third of an enlightened trinity of writers: "and alle shul we dye."

The punctuations of Petrarch's praise by assurances of his death thus not only link the Clerk—or Chaucer—to Petrarch in a fantasy of shared poetic immortality but also to Petrarch in a murderous struggle with a literary father. This ambivalent filial relationship, voiced through the repeated citation of Petrarch's death, is even more assuredly articulated in the Prologue's critique of Petrarch's own proem. It is worth pausing over these lines. Recounting the description of Saluzzo and of the river Po's course eastward from Mt. Viso, the Clerk repeats Petrarch only to discredit him. According to the Clerk, "er he the body of his tale writeth" Petrarch first describes the landscape and in particular the river Po. Springing from a small well on Mt. Viso, the river

Taketh his first spryngyng and his sours,
That estward ay encresseth in his cours
To Emele-ward, to Ferrare, and Venyse,
The which a long thyng were to devyse.

And trewely, as to my juggement,
Me thynketh it a thing impertinent,
Save that he wole conveyen his mateere;
But this the tale, which that ye may heere. (49–56)

The use of the term "conveyen" in the penultimate line in the Prologue
means "introduce," as in the sense of forming the introduction to the following story, though Chaucer uses it elsewhere to mean "accompany,"
"escort," or "communicate." "Conveyen" here carries as well a metaphoric
aptness to the description that the Clerk has just translated, for the account
of regional topography builds as a series of contingencies that moves
toward the rush and growth of the river, which ends itself not in the Adriatic but in a critique of Petrarch for his poetic excesses in describing the
river at too great a length: "the which a long thyng were to devyse" (52).

Discrediting the account he has just written as irrelevant except as it
"wole conveyen" the story, the Clerk has also recounted a description remarkable for the crescendo of its own contingencies, a story about topo-
graphic forces and even more precisely, about the hydraulics of water, in
a sixteen-line unbroken poetic utterance. What the Clerk appears to find
problematic about Petrarch's proem is the representation of a landscape for
its own sake, the deracination of the description from the prescriptions of
epideictic oratory that demand that description convey praise or blame.

When the Clerk cuts short the description even before the Po reaches
the Adriatic, he reasserts control and effectively redirects the narrative back
toward the overt production of praise or blame. Petrarch, in contrast, concludes his description with an account of how the river empties into the
sea and uses description as an entree into the tale itself, allowing the tale to
emerge as an embedded narrative within a travelogue. The story of Walter
and Griselda, this opening suggests, is as natural as the landscape itself:
"Through Liguria its raging waters cut their way, and then, bounding
Aemilia and Flaminia and Venetia, it empties at last into the Adriatic sea,
through many mighty mouths. Now that part of these lands, of which I
spoke first, is sunny and delightful, as much for the hills which run through
it and the mountains which hem it in, as for its grateful plain. From the
foot of the mountains beneath which it lies, it derives its name; and it has
many famous cities and towns. Among others, at the very foot of Mount
Viso, is the land of Saluzzo, thick with villages and castles."[57] Chaucer, however, inserts a stop that severs narrative from geography and that also re-
aligns both the mood and the tempo through a shift from couplets to rhyme

royal. In the opening to the Griselda story that immediately follows, the narrator places his story on the west side of Italy, away from the Po that itself never quite reached the Adriatic in the east:

> Ther is, at the west syde of Ytaille,
> Doun at the roote of Vesulus the colde,
> A lusty playn, habundant of vitaille. (57–59)

Emphasizing a geographic shift in the location of his story, the Clerk makes a marked shift in tone, both from the tenor of the Prologue and from either of his sources. The reference to Mt. Viso as cold, which appears in neither Petrarch nor in the *Livre de Griseldis*, sets the Clerk's Tale in a less hospitable landscape than Petrarch's; it also separates the action of the tale from the natural contingencies that appear to orchestrate the setting for Petrarch's story. Though the narrator records Petrarch's comments about the fertility of the Saluzzan plain, he also begins with a clear statement of a different locale; this tale is set in "west side" of Italy and with his own cautionary note: "Vesulus [Mt. Viso] the colde."

Coupled with his multitiered critique of Petrarch—the Clerk's choice to bend to the Host's request and tell a story that speaks plainly rather than in Petrarchan Latin, his proclamations of Petrarch's death, his discrediting of Petrarch's introductory description as "impertinent" or irrelevant—the Clerk's revisions of Petrarch's proem and the opening of his own tale point to a markedly different poetics, one chiefly defined, I believe, by "pertinence." The Clerk's critique of Petrarch's description of the Po and the Saluzzan plain for irrelevance would seem to include as well a recognition of the seductions of descriptive narrative that would naturalize human events: for Petrarch, the Griselda story, embedded within Italian geography, is also embedded cataclysmically within human and geophysical hydraulics as if to suggest that Walter's actions, and other forms of domestic and political tyranny, will be as natural and as inevitable as the falling waters of the Po. The Clerk, however, demands of language ethical accountability, in terms that allow him to continue as the schoolman even as he bows to the Host's "yerde" that demands "som murie thyng" for a story.

The chief voice for ethical accountability in the tale, of course, is Griselda, whose plain speaking is completely and transparently aligned with her will. Chaucer's double move to both humanize Griselda, emphasizing her pathos as a human and suffering subject, and to allegorize the story serves, I would argue, to sacralize suffering and perhaps also to give

the writing of vernacular poetry special status as an act of personal risk.[58]
I hesitate to say that Griselda is speaking "for" Chaucer or "as" the Clerk;
yet what marks her language is the risk that it takes and its stripped-down
consonance with the Clerk's apparent quest for a form that will encompass
both simplicity and "pertinence." As a speaking subject within the darkened and domestic space of Walter's designs, she becomes only language,
a cipher of evacuated visual signs. The graphic disembodiment of Griselda
within the central section of the tale points, however ironically, to the radical stakes of language, whose truth carries no visible evidence.

Among the many dissonances in the tale is the moral provided by the
Clerk at the end, when he follows Petrarch in arguing that the story is not
told to encourage wives to imitate Griselda's humility but to encourage all
of us to "be constant in adversity" and take what God gives us:

> This storie is seyd nat for that wyves sholde
> Folwen Grisilde as in humylitee,
> For it were inportable, though they wolde,
> But for that every wight, in his degree,
> Sholde be constant in adversitee
> As was Grisilde; therfore Petrak writeth
> This storie, which with heigh stile he enditeth. (1142–48)

The dissonance arises from the failure of this reflection to accord with the
radical agency of Griselda's will, which is not submissive at all; as Jill Mann
notes, "Griselda's unquestioning obedience to her husband is not the simple result of her marriage vow, but something that she takes upon herself
with the unique promise that is the special condition of her marriage."[59] Yet
certainly the Clerk's highly self-conscious voicing of literary/critical intent
in these final passages places on the table issues of how we are to interpret
the story's meaning—why it "is seyd." Most readers have assumed that the
Clerk's repetition of Petrarch's moral indicates that he is asking us to read
the tale in the same way; yet acknowledgment of Petrarch's intent in writing the story does not necessarily have to be read as an endorsement of that
same ethical poetic, especially if we read these lines in the context of the
anxious critique of Petrarch leveled in the Prologue. Even as he presents
us with Petrarch's moral, the Clerk's citation allows him to acknowledge
Petrarch's while marking an alternative space for his own intent.

Why the Clerk has told the story, therefore, can be another matter,
and his pointed references to Petrarch's thematic and didactic goals with

the tale can act as a proem for his own meditations on contemporaneity and the Wife of Bath that return his story to the Canterbury pilgrimage. In returning, it is an entirely different spirit from the one adopted in the tale, and it is one, as I read it, of determined or even overdetermined play. In his final aside to the pilgrims, "But o word, lordyngs, herkneth er I go" (1163), and in the Envoy, the Clerk moves his story into a fallen present in which Griseldas cannot exist. Griselda and her patience, "bothe atones buryed in Ytaille" (1178), in fact share with Petrarch and Giovanni da Lignano the fact of being dead, as if to idealize Griselda as somehow unrecoverable. The proclamation of Griselda's death is sudden and unexpected; nothing in her story tells us of her end, and the tale itself appears to occur in a time contemporary with the telling. Who is to say she is dead? The proclamation expresses a sort of violence in affirmation. It is also the opening line of the Envoy, which stands as an alternative text to the tale itself and especially to Griselda's own uses of language. In this quixotic ballade, which rollicks along with an ill-fitting pastiche of metaphors drawn from bestiaries, courtly adventure, classical mythology, and ordinary life ("clappeth as a mille"), Chaucer moves to play—and perhaps it is here that the Clerk most fully adopts the mandate of the Host to "telle us som murie thyng of aventures." Through the excesses of its language the Envoy also preserves the tale itself, even as it demonstrates the kind of misogynist joke that often serves as an antidote for piety or truth.[60] Clearly this song of linguistic aggression is offered as a model of verbal impotence. In the Envoy, women's language is representable and easily understood through commonplace, if stock antifeminist, metaphor; women are counseled to "clappeth as a mille"; their "crabbed eloquence" is an arrow that can pierce chain mail; with tongue "unnailed" they are like Chichevache and Echo. Imagining woman's speech through its similarity to commonplace and especially masculine things, the Envoy asks women to be familiar and knowable—more, as Henry Higgins laments, "like a man"—a move that effectively showcases Griselda's uses of language. If the Envoy expresses a wish for Griselda to be dead, that wish voices a public or shared longing for the familiar. As a speaker of violence, aggression, and just plain noise, the woman invoked in the Envoy presents a much less formidable adversary than Griselda.

In the concluding lines and in the Envoy, the Clerk thus draws two possible lessons from Griselda's behavior, both of which he effectively disavows. Through these disavowals he protects his own position from either extreme—from Petrarch's suggestion that the tale urges women to take a posture of silent endurance and to be "constant in adversitee" and also from

the Envoy which urges women to the other extreme: "holdeth no silence."
Griselda has chosen to be constant *before* adversity and has adopted a linguistic model that yokes piety, plain speaking, and will. Derek Pearsall, writing of Griselda as an embodiment of ideals of free will, argues that Chaucer
is "less interested in faith and the sentiment of piety than in questions of free
will and determinism that had always preoccupied him."[61] I would agree
that questions of will and free choice are of abiding importance to Chaucer
but might also add that will and piety are not necessarily in opposition. In
the figure of Griselda, will is inextricably bound together with piety and
pathos, and through Griselda, in fact, Chaucer can be said to offer ideal-
izing definitions of these concepts: piety, an operational sense of self as
devoted to and governed by Christian or family law; will, a forfeiture of
self to choices dictated by piety; pathos, the probable outcome of joint acts
of piety and will. In the figure of Griselda, and of Griselda as a speaker,
piety and will are also nostalgically imagined to emerge from domestic and
especially familial relations—expanded to include spousal bonds as well as
filial devotion. When Walter recognizes Griselda's virtue before his decision to seek to marry her, he does so by watching how she cares for her
father (230–21). At the end of the tale, likewise, the transformative drama
that moves Walter to pity—and hence the text to a comic resolution that
reunites children, wife, and state—has at its core Griselda's love of her children. However ironically, her most suspicious act, the one Walter cannot
trust, is the extension to a husband, to Walter, of the kind of unconditional
love that the text imagines as properly or "naturally" given to children or
to parents; when she says she dreads losing nothing "save oonly yee," she
has expanded the circle of deep affiliative bonds to include her husband as
well. It is perhaps no accident that the text and Walter as well always name
the children as belonging to one parent or the other, usually Griselda, and
never as belonging to them both.[62] Maternity, that is, offers no intrinsic
bond to link marital partners and in fact brings a wedge between them. Will
and piety in this tale are naturally housed in filial relations; Griselda's radical choice lies in her extension of that same practice of piety to marriage
as well.

    If we hear in Griselda's language an idealized form of plain speaking,
it is also a voice of poetic resistance, or of the poet whose choices both to
translate and to speak plainly in the vernacular can subject him, if not to
violence, at least to critical censure. Certainly the tale is centered in issues
of marriage, and the Clerk's disavowal of Petrarch's generalizing explanation of the tale as a commentary on humanity's relationship to God may

also be seen as a redirection of his tale toward the particularly complex demands of marriage as both a private and a public sacrament.[63] Yet through the metacommentary on language and poetic style that surrounds the tale, Chaucer's telling of the Griselda story moves beyond marriage to include as well reflections on the risks of writing poetry. Griselda chooses to speak for trust and truth to her word within marriage; her fidelity to Walter results from choice, rather than from a will constrained, like Criseyde's, by prior emotions of love or desire. Griselda's word is *langue* versus *parole*, the semiotic versus the symbolic order represented by the language of Walter, the sergeant or the spokesman for the Commons—and also by Petrarch. As the voice, in the vernacular tongue (*langue*) of a speaking subject, her word eclipses her body and stands in for her absent body in the center of the poem; she becomes, we might say, the word made flesh—or the flesh made word. This is the center of the story's drama of sacrifice: Griselda becomes word, in all the terrible vulnerability of the word before those who would doubt it. Just as the viability of the verbal promise given in marriage depends on the partner's choice to trust it, so does the poet's word, once given or written, require its reader to enter into a promissory contract of sorts. And, this text suggests, certain kinds of plain speaking ratchet up the risks in the public eye.

In this sense, then, Chaucer creates in the *Clerk's Tale* a sacramental poetic. By linking the language of the marriage vow with the vernacular poetic espoused by the Clerk and also by Chaucer, the tale sacralizes vernacular poetry. Word as sacrament in this text is mobilized in relation to or against other, perhaps more familiar, performances of the sacramental—and especially of Griselda's own public performance as "translated" relic or saintly body. If the text generates more questions than it answers—and is told, as many readers would agree, in order to raise those questions—it may well be that it is also told to throw into relief forms of performance: public performances of sacramental ritual in relation to private contractual agreements; aureate public poetry in contrast to newer vernacular forms. Certainly the text exposes the fickleness of some devotional gestures. The people who flock to Griselda as a public shrine early in the text quickly turn elsewhere once Walter suggests they could have a new queen of more suitable rank. Stripped of her clothes, her husband, her children, and her relation to her public, Griselda's power or credibility persists through her word; she is, finally, only word. The sacramental hermeneutic is, at the end, performed by language as much as it is by any visible display—or perhaps even more. Some of the discomfort readers may feel with the "happy ending" may come from the disparity between the story's fairy-tale resolution and the sacrificial veracity of Griselda's word. While the Prologue to the *Legend of Good Women* may leave it uncertain whether icons or old books are the proper objects of devotion, the *Clerk's Tale* hangs on the word. Griselda embodies the naked text and speaks it in a powerful vernacular.

5

The Clergeon's Tongue

IN HER WELL-KNOWN DISCUSSION of pollution taboos and bodily margins, Mary Douglas cites Jean Genet: "if I can fervently drink his tears, why not the so limpid drop on the end of his nose?"[1] One reason Douglas offers for our contrasting responses of desire or disgust to bodily emanations is that "nasal secretions are not so limpid as tears. They are more like treacle than water." More significant, she posits, is that tears are not related to bodily functions, such as digestion and reproduction, that are already signified with sets of taboos. Liquids emanating from the mouth and from organs of reproduction come from orifices that themselves signify exits and entrances, the fragile margins of the body and also culture. This is Kristeva's abject. The horror arises at the place of uncertainty: "what disturbs identity, systems, order. What does not respect borders, positions, rules. The in-between, the ambiguous, the composite."[2]

In the *Prioress's Tale*, boundaries of the body are violated at the moment the body is sanctified. This is the moment at the end of the tale when the abbot plucks the grain from the Clergeon's tongue and allows the boy to die. Chaucer does not abstract this event in the same way that he removes the boy's murder to a point offstage; instead he turns it into a graphic demonstration that positions the reader, the Canterbury pilgrims, and the Christian public within the story as witnesses to the event. We watch as the abbot pulls out the tongue to extract the grain: "This hooly monk, this abbot, hym meene I, / His tonge out caughte, and took awey the greyn" (670–71). The abbot does not simply pluck out the grain but instead reaches in to grasp the tongue. How do we see this? The abbot is groping the body of the living dead. The child has willed his own death and has in effect begged the abbot to remove the grain, but nonetheless the body itself resists. The abbot has first to subdue the tongue, holding it in his hand.

This scene is admittedly very brief, a small flash in the narrative. Yet its status as the coup de grace and the evidentiary moment that causes the abbot to fall prostrate and still and the rest of the convent to fall weeping to the floor invite us to take note. What disturbs the story at this point is a violation of the body at its margins, or really a willed violation that involves taboo touch. Tongues are not for touching with the hand, unless they are licking our own fingers. Tongues themselves oscillate between profane and sacred. As profane parts, tongues are sexual fetishes and signifiers, organs of outlaw and sodomitic pleasure. The tongue is the facial mime of the fist or the finger; we spit on things to defile them. We stick out our tongues to insult people. This is the obscenity of the gargoyle, the animal heads at Notre Dame with their tongues out, or the corbel head at Reims, mouth open and tongue hanging to the side.[3]

Yet as the producer of language, the tongue is sacred, the organ that most closely allies the sexual body to the speaking soul. Psalter iconography commonly shows King David pointing to his mouth or touching his tongue, illustrating in his gesture the verse from Psalm 38: "I said I will take heed to my ways, that I sin not with my tongue [in lingua mea]: I will place a guard on my mouth when the sinner comes before me."[4] French "la langue" is the word for both a body part as well as for language or speech. Modern English usage for the most part has severed the terms for speech from the bodily organ, though English has retained a number of archaisms, such as "mind your tongue!" "speaking in tongues," or "mother tongue." Centering language in the body, these phrases resonate uneasily with a bodily surplus: the language of the tongue is disruptive, incoherent, presymbolic. In Middle English, however, all speech can be "tonge." In most of its uses in Middle English, in fact, "tonge" refers to language instead of a body part and often brings to life, as a kind of somatic speech-agent, the ethics of language use: in "tonge" language takes on both flesh and a moral animus. In Langland, for instance, tongues are usually true or false, "Fals Fikeltonge," a "neddres tonge," or "Trewe-tonge."[5] Chaucer's tongues serve much more often as agents of language than as agents of digestion; they are "sely," "deslavee," "wikked," or "rakel." Yet "tonge," even when it is used to signify language or speech, remains connected to the body. We need to discipline the tongue, to "naille" it down (*Clerk's Tale*, 1184), to "keep" it (*Manciple's Tale*, 315); to wall it in with "teeth and lippes" (*Manciple's Tale*, 323). As an agent of the body, language also can take action on the world: the tongue "kutteth freendshipe al a-two" (*Manciple's Tale*, 342).

When the priest removes the grain, his action on the tongue literally severs language, and by holding the tongue he masters it into an inert organ, a pillow really, for the grain in which language has been invested. The metonymic link between tongue and language remains intact, or at least intact until broken by the abbot, who enters the body for an act of removal. Yet this is also the sacred moment, or the moment that defines the body of the boy as sacred object, fit for burial in a marble tomb where it will become the site of pilgrimage, "God leve us for to meete!" (7.683). How can we explain this coalescence between sacrament and bodily violation? The moment, with its pederastic and sodomitic echoes, releases the boy to eternal life, yet only by bringing death. In part we can explain the abbot's role in this sacrifice through typology; the Christlike child, nurtured and given language by the Virgin, is killed by a figure of the established Church who stands in for the Christian community—that is, the boy, like Christ, is killed by us. Or looked at another way, the abbot represents the redemptive action of a law that brings eternal life with death, unlike the fate meted out by the Jewish homicide that consigns the Clergeon to life-in-death. If both Jew and Christian literally participate in killing the boy, that act resonates with larger patterns of death and redemption in salvation history, the old law replaced by a new, as Sherman Hawkins has outlined in his study of typological patterns in the tale.[6] And if the abbot appears to violate the child's body by reaching into his mouth to grab his tongue, that action can be typologically justified or at least explained by the move of the narrative toward severance and salvation. The body is inert, dead matter signifying the split between corpus/corpse and eternal life. The abbot cannot violate the body, since that body, in part through the very sacramental action of the abbot himself, is now supremely unimportant. Life is elsewhere.

If life is typologically elsewhere, as we are to understand through the boy's reporting that the Virgin will fetch him once the grain is removed from his tongue, that new space of eternal life nevertheless remains outside the story, which concludes in a collective gaze on the body or, more exactly, on its tomb as a site of evidence. The conclusion of the tale allows a curious disjunction between its set of symptoms and its typological promise. Certainly this paradox or coalescence is central to Christian liturgical ritual. The body, specifically Christ's body in the form of the Eucharist, is the paradigmatic sign of life beyond the body or the body's providential inessentiality. In the *Prioress's Tale*, however, the story of martyrdom maps life anterior to sacrifice and contrasts liturgical evidence (severed from life) with vivacity. The narrative splits in fact into two parts and parallels speech with vivacity and death with liturgical spectacle. The first part tells a story of the emergence of language from familial relations and the willed choices the boy makes, focusing a narrative gaze, that is, on the domestic world of affective and especially familial relations, which in this case have produced

a form of radical piety. The second part of the narrative turns the body over
to the world. We hear the story of the boy's murder, the legal proceedings,
and the move to liturgical ritual and spectacle as the miracle is demonstrated and the body housed into pilgrimage site.

The contrast between the individual speaker and the communal and
clerical uses of his body constitute, I believe, one of the central tensions of
the tale. In its dramatization of tensions between the private will and public spectacle the *Prioress's Tale* is strikingly similar to the *Clerk's Tale*. Like
Griselda, the Clergeon's language, his song, springs from family nurture,
or a radical subjection of the will to family law—even though the parent
romanced in the *Prioress's Tale,* the Virgin, belongs to a holy family rather
than an earthly one. Both narratives subject an individual—whose agency
paradoxically emerges from a giving over of the self to an other—to forms
of scrutiny that range from inquisition to cultic worship. Even though the
production of the sacred by the sacrifice of the living is squarely centered
in Christian liturgical practice, the rehearsals of that process in the *Prioress's
Tale* leave the sacramental ending strangely corporeal, and even, as I have
suggested, at least briefly grotesque. With the spectators in the tale, the
readers are locked in a mesmerized gaze on the body, watching as the abbot
touches its interiors, even as the text declares the unimportance of that body.
Of all the *Canterbury Tales*, the *Prioress's Tale* most explicitly describes the
making of the shrine through martyrdom; this tale envisions, within the
framework of the narrative, the ends of pilgrimage. Yet through a play of
pathos that the tale's ritualized conclusion never satisfactorily resolves, the
tale juxtaposes rather than joins sanctity and vivacity: liturgical ritual seems
curiously at odds with the passion for language that sets the plot in motion.

"Construen" and Vernacular Piety

Following the account of its setting, the tale opens with the desire for language. Through the voice of the Prioress Chaucer devotes more than five
stanzas to describe how the boy learns the song. He hears the older children singing the "Alma Redemptoris" while he is sitting in school learning
his primer, learns the first line by heart, and though he cannot understand
the Latin he begs, on bended knees, an older boy to "expounde" the song
to him in the vernacular ("his langage"). The older student tells him he
cannot really translate the song except to say that it was made to greet the
Virgin and pray for her help. The Clergeon then decides to memorize it

even if he will be scolded for not learning his lesson, so the older boy teaches it to him on the way home from school. With the Latin song memorized the Clergeon sings it "ful murily" as he walks to school through the Jewry—with, of course, disastrous consequences. As this story is told, the acquisition of song or language carries personal risks, risks that extend catastrophically beyond the act's feared outcome. The punishment the boy fears is an immediate disciplinary one, a beating "thries in an hour" for not learning his primer, a childish concern that underwrites the narrative's dark punitive twist: his singing does not bring down the rod of his schoolmasters, as far as we know, but it does incite a far more dire punishment.

For a short tale, the *Prioress's Tale* devotes rather a lot of space to the learning of a song, enough to suggest that the pedagogical practices described in such detail deserve close attention.[7] The Clergeon's linguistic heroics lie not only in his pious singing of the song but also in his acquisition of the song to begin with. His sacrificial piety becomes that of a David taking on a Goliath in the form of a number of formidable authorities, among them the schoolmasters and Latin as an authoritative and, for a seven-year-old boy, inaccessible language. His language skills are ultimately partial but also surprisingly advanced, since he masters the literal text through memorization and moves directly to translation and interpretation. That is, while he cannot learn the meaning of the words, he is able to extract an explanation that serves as a kind of translation; he sings the words, "fro word to word, acordynge with the note," but the meaning for him is something else again: "on Cristes mooder set was his entente." In studies of pedagogy in late medieval England, Rita Copeland has argued that writings on pedagogy traditionally make a sharp distinction between the literal sense, which is appropriate for children, and symbolic interpretation, which can be the work of more advanced students. By privileging the literal sense of Scripture the Lollard classroom, Copeland further argues, breaks down these time-honored distinctions, unmaking "long-standing distinctions between the symbolic domains of childhood and adulthood."[8] Chaucer's Clergeon seems to be a practitioner of both of these registers, the literal and symbolic, as he works to learn the words themselves and also to acquire their essence.

I am not suggesting here that the Clergeon is meant to represent a small Lollard, but I would argue that the attention to translation and interpretation bespeaks some of Chaucer's most abiding concerns. When the Clergeon asks the older student to "construe" the Latin meaning, he is using a term that commonly means "to translate into English";[9] and hence

when he asks his fellow student to "construe and declare" he is asking him
to both translate and also to explain the Latin song. These terms are quite
marked in the second stanza devoted to the song:

> Noght wiste he what this Latyn was to seye,
> For he so yong and tendre was of age.
> But on a day his felawe gan he preye
> T'expounden hym this song in his langage,
> Or telle hym why this song was in usage;
> This preyde he hym to construe and declare
> Ful often tyme upon his knowes bare. (523–29)

When he begs the older boy to "expound" the Latin hymn he is asking
him to explain it, yet in terms that also suggest the process of translation.
"Expositio," the art of interpretation, as Rita Copeland has also pointed
out, was central to Chaucer's ideas about translating.[10] To translate is not
simply to reproduce or mime an original in a word-for-word equivalent
but to explicate or interpret it—a practice that was at the heart of Chaucer's
translation project throughout the *Canterbury Tales*. In this stanza of the
Prioress's Tale Chaucer endows the Clergeon with a powerful need to know,
expressed through desires to understand and make meaning that were close
to Chaucer's own poetic work. In the tale's analogues the boy learns the song
in school, whereas in Chaucer's version he learns the song outside, walking
to and from school, a change that heightens the melodrama surrounding the
boy's passion for language. Most seven-year-old boys, this change seems
designed to remind us, leave book learning at the schoolhouse door.

The boy's desire to make meaning from the Latin song also has a broad
cultural resonance, of course, with issues of textual translation that, in the
1380s and 1390s, were acquiring a political edge. The heightened political
and ethical importance of access to vernacular texts in the 1380s has been
ably explored in recent scholarship, but it will serve us here to look quickly
at a few key markers of changing public attitudes toward the politics of
translating in the years preceding Chaucer's writing of the *Prioress's Tale*.
Steven Justice and Susan Crane have demonstrated how fundamentally
the uprising of 1381 altered the public perception about access to written
materials, as the zeal of the rebels to destroy Latin documents of all kinds
alerted the public to the authority of official written texts and the political implications of lay literacy.[11] Access to literacy became, in a moment, a
political issue. The Bible translation project undertaken by the Lollards in

the 1380s, which explicitly aimed to make Scripture available to all, can be
said to take up this mandate. It also dramatically increased the risks associated with devotional translation of all kinds. Historical records from the
1380s suggest that scriptural translation was increasingly regarded with suspicion, primarily through association with the Lollards: Lollard schools
were outlawed in the 1380s[12] and the 1382 order of the Blackfriar's Council that Oxford seize all books by Wyclif and Hereford was expanded in
1388 to include English as well as Latin writings.[13] The chronicler Henry
Knighton, vehemently anti-Lollard in his own sentiments, documents these
changing attitudes in the 1380s as he tells the story, with vitriol, of the work
of two Lollards Smith and Waytestathe, whom I discuss in Chapter 1. In
what may have been a Lollard school or study group Smith had been copy-
ing English texts of the gospels, epistles, and the fathers, "in maternal lingua de evangelio, et de epistolis et aliis episcopis et doctoribus," since the
early 1380s, apparently unbothered or at least undiscovered, but was arrested
and forced to abjure in 1389.[14]

What these events collectively document is a developing climate of suspicion around the politics of Bible translation in the 1380s, suspicion that
in the early years of the 1400s would become formalized into Arundel's
Constitutions, new legislation classifying as heretical the possession of vernacular Scriptures and curtailing translation and ownership of books in
English.[15] The *Prioress's Tale*, written most probably in the late 1380s to early
1390s, does not document translation per se, since the boy never learns
the "Alma Redemptoris" in English, but only its essence. Because he only
learns the song by rote and does not understand the meaning of the words,
his relationship to Latin song as sung by the older boys stands, however,
in a kind of vernacular relationship furthered, as I have suggested, by the
hermeneutic verbs "expounde," "construe," and "declare." His is a translation to a simpler tongue. In this way his rendition of the "Alma Redemptoris" is a translation; the meaning he has supplied is his own.

The boy's pedagogical heroics, viewed through the lens of public anxieties about scriptural translation, are thus even magnified. The disciplinary risks he faces from his teachers and ultimately realizes at the hands
of the Jewish homicides echo certain risks that may have been at large in
the world at that time, a synergy that invites us to read his drive to understand and sing as part of a broader translation project in the last decades of
the fourteenth century, one that also came to voice widespread public
interest in questions about access to Latin learning of all kinds. In the Clergeon as a speaker we may even detect some of Chaucer's own desires about

linguistic transparency. Like Chaucer the Clergeon is a translator; very much unlike Chaucer, however, who has often been credited with the instincts of a canny survivalist well aware of the risks of speaking his mind, the boy gives no thought to the consequences of his singing. If there is nostalgia in the *Prioress's Tale*, it may lie in part in this desire for transparent language and freedom from self-censorship.[16] Part of the generalized protest voiced in the boy's song is directed against powers that would limit both the form and meaning of what we say.

It is this quality of radical intuitive *protest* that returns us to the question: Where does Chaucer locate piety, within liturgical performances, or within language? Liturgical ritual and language are not necessarily opposed, of course; yet in Chaucer's four most overtly religious tales, as H. Marshall Leicester points out in reference to essays by Elizabeth Robertson and Elizabeth Kirk, the reader's sympathies lie with a victimized and feminized pious speaker who opposes institutional powers.[17] In the *Prioress's Tale*, the contrast between an individual, small and powerless, and institutional powers is reinforced on every level: the little boy's passage through the Jewry; his passion to memorize the "Alma Redemptoris" in spite of the risk of punishment at the hands of schoolmasters for not learning his lessons; and (after his murder) the mobilization of law (the provost) and then increasingly official circles of the Christian community. In this regard, it is symptomatic that the Clergeon's song angers not just a single Jewish homicide but, as the text suggests, the entire Jewish community ("the Jues," 565), which then collectively hires out the murder. As the "serpent Sathanas" says to them, the boy's song violates their "lawes reverence"—that is, their structures of piety as scripted into law.

That the *Prioress's Tale* should be read as an exercise in piety or "pite" is by no means a given among Chaucer critics. Numerous essays on the *Prioress's Tale* have attempted to explain the tale's contrasts, most often its anti-Semitism and its contrasts between piety and violence, in an effort to locate, through the ventriloquizing voice of the Prioress, Chaucer's voice.[18] Many influential readers in the last half century, among them R. J. Shoeck and E. Talbot Donaldson, have argued that Chaucer displays the Prioress's sentimentality, piety, and attractions to violence and bigotry in an artful and vicious parody.[19] Other readings of the tale have been less certain of Chaucer's distance from the Prioress, yet many still have argued that piety is trumped by violence:[20] The text is a kind of performance piece, a tale that makes virtuoso uses of the tropes and language of religiosity to mask regressive or even infantile violence—even to the point of seducing the tale's readers.[21] Louise (Aranye) Fradenburg has argued that in focusing on piety, readers have ignored the story's understructure of violence; is violence against a demonized other (the Jews) lends the Prioress's infantilized narrative, "in which all change can only be imagined as crisis," a sentimental veneer that masks its own regressive fears.[22] The object of this terror, displaced onto the Jews, is actually paternal violence, itself sanitized in the violent, son-sacrificing founding myth that is central to Christianity. Whereas Fradenburg seems unclear about Chaucer's own position, allowing the "text" rather than either the Prioress or Chaucer to be the engine of violence and anti-Jewish hatred, Lee Patterson—somewhat like earlier readers—has recently argued again for a disenchanted Chaucer who has given the Prioress a tale that voices a longing for an impossible and regressive innocence.[23] By evoking, in the fate of the Clergeon, Jewish heroic martyrdoms that were reported to have occurred across Europe in the fourteenth century, the tale performs a double act. Even though Christianity cannot be purged of its complicity with the violent deaths of Jewish martyrs, the Prioress tries to imagine a "pure" and sanitized Christianity, recalling historical events even while changing them with an inverse narrative.

What both of these readings share is a vision of the contrasts between Christian and Jew or between good and evil as self-canceling. Piety, especially as deployed in the Prioress's prayer and the boy's song, is tainted by that which it attempts to exclude. While I agree that the lines dividing good from evil in this tale are far more muddied than they might at first appear, I would also argue that Chaucer preserves the Clergeon, whose language, like Griselda's, has been endowed with a radical agency, from corporate collusions between Christians and Jews. Chaucer gives us little purchase from which to critique the affective piety with which he endows the boy and the Prioress, though we might further consider its ethical agenda. In her essay "The Protestant Chaucer," Linda Georgianna has argued that post-medieval—which often means post-Catholic—readers have brought their own habits of skepticism to the overt emotionality of Chaucer's religious tales, which "seem to promote religious beliefs that are hard to account for either by liberal humanist critics or by conservative, exegetical critics, for both of whom the greatest sin is credulity."[24] The essence of religious belief in these tales, Georgianna further argues, lies in its "intuitive, non-rational" character—though as David Aers points out in his counter to Georgianna, medieval theology understood reason as central to faith.[25] Yet perhaps even more germane to the representation of affective piety in this tale, and far more problematic for literary scholars today, is emotion. For Chaucer, "pite" (a term he uses frequently) always invokes qualities of mercy or emotions of pity—intuitive and immediate. Never does Chaucer use "pite" to mean "piety" as in the sense of devotion to one's faith, even though that meaning was available in his time.[26] In Wycliffite texts contemporary to Chaucer, we can frequently find "pite" used in the sense of "religious piety" or faithful observance of the tenets of religious dogma or social mores: "I wolle that wymmen ben in convenable abite [clothing] . . . not in writhen here [curled hair], ne in gold . . . ne in precious cloth, but that that bicometh wymmen bihetynge pite [piety] bi good works."[27] H. Marshall Leicester even suggests that Chaucer uses affective, emotional, and even vernacular "pite" to oppose a "piety" that evokes Latinate institutional values: "affective piety is the site of resistance to *pietas*, and vice versus."[28] In the *Prioress's Tale* "pite" is the central drive of the Clergeon's work in expounding the "Alma Redemptoris" and rendering it in his own form, which joins mimicry or rote learning and exegesis.[29] Articulated, his affective (emotional) "pite" not only expresses his love of the Virgin but also becomes a form of social protest directed against institutions and their official practices.

Prague, the "Greet Citee"

The fundamental structural contrast between innocence and power also creates homologies among powers themselves and complicates any neat divisions between Christian and Jew as polarized forces of good and evil. As the studies by Fradenburg and Patterson mentioned above have argued, the violence and anti-Semitism of the *Prioress's Tale* implicates not only the Jews. Sylvia Tomasch has recently carried these arguments further to show how well the tale dovetails with arguments about cultural codependency that have been mounted in postcolonial studies. The fantasies of pollution and purity through which we collectively imagine a racial or religious other are constituted through a double process of displacement and condensation. Christianity is dependent for its very existence on imagined qualities of Jewishness: "a polluted Asia—polluted through Jewish presence and actions—is implicitly contrasted with a purified England, whose sanitized state is founded on the displacement of the Jews."[30] As cultural theorist Slavoj Žižek explains it, the stereotype of the Jew absorbs social antagonisms, and it does so, at least in the twentieth-century imagination, by condensing opposing features of the upper and lower classes—oppositions that are expressed in the contradictory nature of the stereotypes: the Jew is both impotent *and* lecherous, filthy *and* cerebral/intellectual. How can this be? A sign embodying society's own fundamental lack of coherent ideology and practices, the Jew also permits society (or Christianity) to imagine its integration: "'Jew' is a fetish which simultaneously denies and embodies the structural impossibility of 'Society'; it is as if in the figure of the Jew this impossibility had acquired a positive, palpable existence."[31] In medieval miracle tales such as the *Prioress's Tale* or the Croxton *Play of the Sacrament*, the fetish of the Jew's body gets dramatically corporeal play, in terms that underscore the fundamental categorical homologies between both Christian and Jew: each needs the other to exist. According to Steven Kruger, reading the Jew's body and the violence repeatedly enacted against it in medieval narratives as a reflex to the anxiety about bodies expressed in Christianity, "the violence of Jewish body makes possible the miraculous suffering and survival of the Host; the miracles of Christian body lead inexorably to Jewish dismemberment and disintegration."[32]

In the *Prioress's Tale*, the homologies between Jew and Christian, the ghetto and the Christian community, are enunciated from the outset in a rhizomatic network of geographic hailings and imagistic echoes that suggest not only contrast but also complicity. Complicity is built into the structure of Christian/Jewish/Muslim relations from the start. The central distinctions are not only Christian and "other," but the Clergeon and all "others"—or the Clergeon's radical vernacular "pite" in opposition to adult authority of all kinds. While the Clergeon is a part of the Christian community, he operates as a lone agent, ultimately acted upon by authorities from both Jewish and Christian worlds. From the beginning the tale imagines a geographic location that is defined by an interaction of Christian, Jewish, and—by implication of the Asian locale—Muslim communities, with an emphasis on their proximity and even codependence.[33] It is worth looking at this opening closely, for it is atypical for the *Canterbury Tales*, which generally open with a brief geographical naming as an introduction to the central character or characters: "In Flaundres whilhom was a compaignye / Of yonge folk that haunteden folye" (*Pardoner's Tale*, 462–64); "In Armorik, that called is Britayne, / Ther was a knyght that loved and dide his payne / To serve a lady in his beste wise" (*Franklin's Tale*, 729–31). The *Prioress's Tale*, however, takes a cryptic tour through exotic urban geography before bringing us to the boy, postponing his introduction behind a rather elaborate initial stage-set that tells us that place and relationships among communities seem to be significant. Opening with what we might call a progressive geographic diminution, the story commences with a centripetal gaze that begins broadly (somewhere in Asia) and goes on to focus on smaller and smaller units: a large city, a Christian community, a Jewry within the Christian community, a street in the Jewry—until we come finally to the Litel Clergeon, the smallest, it seems, of the small Christian boys at the small school at the end of the street:

> Ther was in Asye, in a greet citee,
> Amonges Cristene folk a Jewerye,
> Sustened by a lord of that contree
> For foule usure and lucre of vileynye,
> Hateful to Crist and to his compaignye;
> And thurh the strete men myghte ride or wende,
> For it was free and open at eyther ende.
>
> A litel scole of Cristene folk ther stood
> Doun at the ferther ende. . . . (488–96)

Mapping ethnic communities in circular or nested form around the "free" street that intersects the Jewry, the description of place opens by announcing the proximity of Christian and Jewish communities, with a suggestion (though it is never stated explicitly) that usury involves the Christians as well. Most readers have understood that the "lord of that contree" must be pagan, since the tale is set in Asia; the Jewry is "amonges" Christians, and both Christians and Jews are located in a pagan land. The language of the opening description is notably unclear about relationships and identities, however. Even if a city in medieval Asia would have a Muslim as its local lord, overseer of both communities, as Sheila Delany and others have argued, the syntax of this description allows the unidentified "lord" homology with the Christians who are also living close to the Jews; and the absence of any mention of pagans or Muslims of any kind does not, to my mind, imply that they exist as an absent presence, but rather that they are absent, and that the world pictured really is all about Christians and Jews.[34] In the opening lines geographic proximities are mirrored in a grammar that allows a certain confusion between the lord who "sustains" the Jews and the Christians who surround or mingle with them. A point of information that this opening gives us rather pointedly is that the Jews are maintained by the lord for usury: "for foule usure and lucre of vileynye."[35] This rather convoluted opening explicitly describes the practice of mutual benefits and symbiosis between the Jews and an "other" that surrounds them and does so in ways that implicates Christians, even to the point of suggesting that the "lord of that country" who maintains the Jews for usury is himself a Christian.

What this prefatory geography accomplishes is to show the workings of big powers, whose mutualities isolate the text's single agent, the Litel Clergeon. The use of an Asian locale to focus a critical gaze on the actions of Christians is hardly a novelty in the fourteenth century, for one only has to look at *Mandeville's Travels* for a study in the uses of the exotic for the purposes of self-scrutiny pitched toward the reformation of Christians, where, as Iain Higgins says in his study of Mandeville, the author's "ethnographic portrait of the Other suddenly shifts to become a Self-critical mirror."[36] The text of the *Travels* develops through a series of these contrasts, often sudden, a move that even at one point levels a joint critique of Christians and Jews through the eyes of the sultan, whose shrewd attack on their corruption is itself preceded by the narrator's "objective" account of an Islamic commentary on the moral failings of both Christians and Jews: "Also the Sarazines seyn that the Iewes ben cursed for thei han defouled the lawe that God sente hem be Moyses. And the Cristene ben cursed also, as thei seyn, for thei kepen not the commandementes and the preceptes of the gospelle that Ihesu Crist taughte hem."[37] Certainly the *Travels*, with its tremendous popular readership in the late fourteenth century and beyond, helped establish Asia and the Orient as a textual space for behavioral exoticism; according to Kathryn Lynch, "many features of Orientalism were clearly present in Chaucer's day as well: the Orient, so called even by Chaucer (e.g., Monk's Tale, line 2314), as monstrous, mysterious, exotic, sensual, sexually deviant."[38] As a distant place of indeterminate and shifting values, the East offers a safe location for a comment on contemporary affairs.

This particular Asian locale might evoke, in addition to the exotic places of the East, cities much closer to home, and in particular Prague, a city if not in the East at least to the east. Prague was home to one of the largest urban Jewries in medieval Europe, part of which remains today, its walls intact, as a troubling and disenchanting tourist site.[39] Prague was also childhood home of Anne of Bohemia and hence very much within the background of the London court imaginary in the 1380s and 1390s. Bohemia was a sophisticated and cosmopolitan center, far more so than London, which, as Alfred Thomas puts it, might have seemed like a "tawdry and provincial" backwater in comparison.[40] Events from Prague, and especially controversies that involved the king, would doubtless have made their way to London. In a provocative set of speculations, in 1981 Sumner Ferris entertained the idea the *Prioress's Tale* might have been an occasional piece written on the 1387 visit of Richard II and Anne of Bohemia to Lincoln Cathedral[41]—and if this were so, then the opening reference to the Jewry would evoke an immediate geographic "home": a large city to the east with a Jewry maintained for usury would doubtless call Prague to mind. Prague not only had one of the largest Jewries in medieval Europe, but in the last decades of the fourteenth century and first decades of the fifteenth, Prague was also at the center of controversy for practices of moneylending. As Miri Rubin documents in *Gentile Tales*, in the 1380s these tensions became particularly heated, when the university rose up against Wenceslas IV, the son of the university's founder and half-brother to Chaucer's Queen Anne, in a denunciation of usury.[42] Jews were particularly targeted in this polemic, but Christian patrons of Jews were also implicated as well; the 1381 synodal statutes claim that "men of high status, in all sorts of ways" profit from the "sin of usury . . . a horrible and detestable crime."[43] If we entertain Ferris's argument, we can see how the tale's opening description might give us a snapshot of the Prague Jewry as Anne would have remembered it, updated by a critique of the "lord," Wenceslas IV, for usury.[44]

Prague suggests itself as a locale for this tale in far more disturbing ways than just the reference to usury, however. I refer to the host-desecration accusation of 1389, one of the most violent incidents of anti-Jewish violence in Prague's medieval history.[45] This event, which was recorded by several contemporary chroniclers and gave rise to Rabbi Avigdor Kara's famous lament, "All the Afflictions," developed from an alleged attack on the Eucharist on Easter, which in 1389 also coincided with Passover. The incident in Prague unfolded not unlike other host-desecration events occurring across Europe in an epidemic of allegation and ensuing violence, and it appears to have evoked the threats to clerical order that are depicted so clearly in the Lovell Lectionary, where an initial shows a bishop raising the host in the Corpus Christi procession while at the bottom of the page, in an antitype to the consecration, two men, armed with long spears, attack a host as blood seeps across a white tablecloth (fig. 22). In Prague it was alleged that stones were thrown at a priest carrying the Eucharist on a street through the Jewry; some accounts claim that the stones were thrown by children. The accusation of desecration led to mob violence and massacre. Some accounts reported that all the synagogues but one were burned, and over three thousand Jews killed.[46] Stories of this massacre would no doubt have found their way to London, steeped as it was in Bohemian connections at this time. One document emerging from the incident even seems to evoke the opening of the *Prioress's Tale* with startling directness. Following the events of 1389 a polemic by John Lange, supporter of Archbishop John of Jenstein, rails against King Wenceslas for usury: "O king, kings! Be shamed for such a crime! The usurious gain on the capital which is earned by the accursed people, in which you yourselves are proven to be accursed usurers."[47] Very like the "lord of that contree," Wenceslas is accused of sustaining Jews for—in the words of the *Prioress's Tale*—"usure and lucre of vileynye."

Figure 22. Corpus Christi procession and host desecration. Lovell Lectionary, c. 1400. London, British Library, MS Harley 7026, fol. 13r. © British Library Board. All rights reserved.

As an imaginary urban backdrop for the *Prioress's Tale*, Prague would thus add a rich set of resonances to the tale's opening and also to its picture of Jewish/Christian complicity. Usury, named so particularly in the story's opening, invokes a system of corrupt mutual benefits. Yet exempt from usury, and its benefits, is the Litel Clergeon, who walks through the free street, bisecting this system. Joining an exotic Asia with the geography of real cities and picturing adult communities as both complex and corrupt, the opening thus sets as its central contrast not Jews and Christians, but rather adult communities and children—or we might say, institutional systems and innocence—pictured not as the nostalgic infantilism that has been derided by the tale's critics, but rather as unconflicted, oppositional desire.[48] Adult structures (institutions) of law, education, finance, and even faith work to oppose the agency, and voice, of this radical, self-immolating piety. The Clergeon is like a saint, who as subject outside the law follows the ethical mandate of pleasure—which as Žižek says, is to "not give way on one's desire."[49]

The opening of the tale also introduces, however quietly, the idea of pilgrimage. The infrastructure of the urban ghetto that opens the *Prioress's Tale*, mapping the idea of usury across a community of Jews and Christians, also contains within it an open street. Christians occupy the space in which the Jewry is located and also use the street as a passage through the Jewry: they are both among the Jews and through them. This street, a free passageway through which "men myghte ride or wende" evokes pilgrimage as a *via* to a Christian destination, the Christian school at its end, through a place peopled by Christians, Jews, and also the Asian "other." The language of community even recalls the pilgrimage frame of the *Tales* as a whole; the "companye" with Christ that opposes the Jewry echoes the grouping of Canterbury pilgrims, comprised of "nyne and twenty in a compaignye" (General Prologue, 24). If the *Prioress's Tale* ends in a description of a new pilgrimage site, it also begins by evoking a paradigmatic journey. But both pilgrimage and pilgrimage site, structuring the beginning and end of this story, are tainted or we might say "disenchanted" from the start by usury. While the *Prioress's Tale* describes the street through the Jewry in ways that resonate with protection, freedom, and eschatological promise, the structure of the Jewry, both in its proximities of residence (who is living next to whom) and in its economic infrastructure (who is using whom) belies this annexation of the clean from the unclean.

Liturgical Drama

The contrast established at the beginning of the tale, where language or song challenges systems of adult authority and even pilgrimage, as I have suggested, reappears at the end, where the loss of language leads to the body's encryptment. After the Clergeon's voice is silenced—interrupted first by the Jews who cut his throat and then again by the abbot who removes the grain—his body is conscripted into a public shrine in ways that reenact liturgical performances on many levels. Since Marie Hamilton's 1939 essay, scholars have recognized the debt of the *Prioress' Tale* to the liturgy of Holy Innocents Day and also to the Little Hours of the Virgin.[50] The first lines of the Prioress's Prologue, "O Lord, oure Lord, thy name how merveillous / Is in this large world ysprad," translate Psalm 8:2–3, which serves as the opening psalm of matins in the Little Office of the Blessed Virgin Mary as well as the Introit for the Mass for the Holy Innocents or virgin martyrs on December 28: "Ex ore infancium Deus et lactencium perfecisti laudem propter inimicos tuos."[51]

In addition to its liturgical allusions, the ending also dramatizes, through a kind of theatricalized citation, clerical as well as scriptural performances of sanctity. It is, above all, a performance. The raising of the grain from the Clergeon's tongue evokes the elevation of the host, grain to miraculous bread; the swoon of the mother by his bier suggests Mary's swoon, as any fourteenth-century reader would recognize from countless representations of the Passion. Commenting in *Chaucer and the Liturgy* on Chaucer's antisacramental faith, Beverly Boyd argues that although Chaucer displays a detailed, quotidian knowledge of liturgical forms, he appears antipathetic to ritual displays, choosing to name rather than enact them in his poetry: "Chaucer's references to the Mass sometimes touch on liturgical details but they do not describe."[52] I would agree generally with this observation, but suggest that, like the *Clerk's Tale*, the *Prioress's Tale* pictures liturgical practices in considerable detail, and even performs them. When the child is taken up and carried, singing, to the next abbey by the "Christian folk," this public processional is saturated with liturgical echoes; indeed, processionals marking the onset of the Mass and the movement into sacred space would have been among the most familiar rituals of the Catholic liturgical calendar, occurring every Sunday at the High Mass with a procession around the church where the altars and congregation were sprinkled with holy water,[53] and also on special occasions in far more elaborate form. Beginning in 1264, when Corpus Christi Day was officially added to the liturgical calendar in England, the annual festivals would commence with a procession in which the host, not unlike the miraculous body of the Litel Clergeon, was carried in a monstrance and displayed to the community on its way to its deposition in a church at the end of the processional route.[54] With even greater pertinence to the procession described in the *Prioress's Tale*, elaborate processionals, more like public political parades, were also organized to accompany the movement or "translation" of a saint's bones to a place of burial. For the "translation" of the bones of Thomas Becket in 1220 from a crypt to a place behind the high altar of the cathedral, "it is reported that the people of England had never seen such a large number of people gathered together in one place."[55] G. J. C. Snoek summarizes this record:

The sources speak of the translations as drawing huge crowds to the church square, in the streets and in the trampled fields round about. All attention was focused on what was going to arrive, as the bells began to ring to signal that the procession was moving off. A sea of silver and gold crosses rose above the uncovered heads, a long line of monks, priests, deacons and subdeacons made its way forward, with each in their distinctive garments and carrying torches in their hands; then came the candle-bearing abbots, bishops and archbishops, clad in richly ornamented choir capes and wearing magnificent mitres that glittered with precious stones. . . . Through the incense smoke, finally, the outlines of a beautiful reliquary, borne by monks, princes of the church or kings, was seen approaching.[56]

Also contributing to the liturgical drama in the *Prioress's Tale* are figural citations that link the Clergeon with Christ and his mother with the Virgin, citations that echo far beyond the narrative to evoke familiar cycles of devotional imagery. The ending affirms or, we might say, compensates for the trauma of the boy's murder; like Christ, he has been killed by the Jews; and like Christ, his body, even before he is fully dead, serves as both a holy sign, even to providing a kind of eucharistic wafer in its "greyn."[57] When the provost arrives, he first praises Christ, then the Virgin, and "after that" has the Jews bound, as if vengeance on the Jews for the death of the Clergeon were directly prompted by Christ and Mary. The provost's command for the Jews to be bound replays—and repays—the binding of Christ by his torturers, a popular topic in Passion painting. We might say that the reference transforms the scene, almost inevitably, according to familiar visual schema, and organizes our responses by locating us within a devotional space in which such a picture would be displayed. At the same time we are also invited to process within the narrative frame as members of an unspecified grouping of Christians who look on.

Chaucer thus uses liturgical spectacle in this tale as a performance that masks collusive practices of power, the central metaphor for which is usury. Clerical ritual offers consolation; yet the primary desire (or *pleasure*) that drives the tale and centers its pathos is a desire for language, both the Prioress's prayer for "song" in the Prologue and the Clergeon's "Alma Redemptoris." As in the *Clerk's Tale*, language (either speech or song) carries risks of death. Even though martyrdom is the central drama of Christianity, the dramatization of martyrdom in the *Prioress's Tale* fails to make a clear distinction between the clean and the unclean, we might say, and fails to provide liturgical spectacle that fully compensates for death. Of all the *Canterbury Tales*, the *Prioress's Tale* most explicitly describes the making of a shrine; this tale imagines both pilgrimage and its ends. Chaucer suggests that liturgical spectacle opposes, rather than expresses, vernacular piety. The performance of liturgical and eucharistic ritual opposes the living articulation of sanctity through language. Language (song) is ethical action; vision (the spectacle of the martyr's body) is public display. Piety may live in Becket's bones—but anterior to martyrdom.

6

Nicholas Love's *Mirror*:
Dead Images and the Life of Christ

IN NICHOLAS LOVE's *Mirror of the Blessed Life of Jesus Christ*, "ymagina-cion" is a key term by which the narrator structures the meditation. We are to picture the sequential events of Christ's life by "deuoute ymaginacion" (14.40) as if we were present, setting ourselves visually in place and experiencing a set of pre-scripted emotions as those scenes unfold. Epiphany gives a good example of how we are to picture the text of the gospel: "And so ymagine we & set oure mynde & our þouht as we were present in þe place where þis was done at Betheleem; beholdyng how þees þre kynges comen with gret multitude" (43.28–31). In his demands on the reader's visual imagination, the narrator invokes a dramatically involved kind of meditation, one that repeatedly relies on mental pictures to stir emotion. "Ymaginacion," as a noun, is the faculty by which we are to visualize Christ's life—through processes of "ymagining" or "beholding," verbals that both describe acts of mental picturing. In a guided meditation, the narrator places us close to the scenes we are watching and then sets them in motion, creating not a set of *tableaux vivants* but a dramatic reenactment. We watch as Christ's life imaginatively comes to life.

The appeals to visual imagining in the *Mirror* are not in themselves unusual. Love's *Mirror*, an immensely popular translation and adaptation of the *Meditationes Vitae Christi*, emerges from a long tradition of Franciscan visual meditation and English vernacular piety that stressed emotional and bodily imitation of Christ through meditation on his humanity.[1] More surprising, however, is Love's choice to translate a highly visual enactment of the gospels at time when the literal uses of devotional images in worship had become the subject of impassioned and even high-risk debate. By 1410, the probable year the *Mirror* was published, denunciation of image worship had been long associated with the Lollard heresy. In the record of his heresy trial in 1407, just three years earlier, William Thorpe writes that he was accused of having preached that images should not be worshipped in any way. For this Archbishop Arundel had condemned him as a vicious and cursed priest, denouncing as well all Lollards for their plots against "ymagis þat mouen þe peple to deuocioun."[2] Arundel, who had held posts as the bishop of Ely, archbishop of York, and archbishop of Canterbury by the time of Thorpe's trial and was no stranger to images used for spectacular aesthetic, narrative, and emotional effect, went on to lament, "Losel [scoundrel], were it a faire þinge to come into a chirche and se þerinne noon ymage?"— what would it be like to come into church and not see any images?[3]

While the *Mirror* offers few direct comments about devotional images that would answer this question or place it polemically within the image debate, its articulations of "ymaginacion" and "ymagining" could hardly have failed to evoke the controversy. Indeed, the attention to imaginative visualizing is so precise and pervasive as to suggest that the text is intended to be part of the discourse. In other ways the *Mirror* announces a position on the side of orthodoxy and takes Lollardy as a direct target. It had even received Arundel's express endorsement. A "Memorandum" appended to numerous manuscripts notes that the *Mirror* was presented by Love to Archbishop Arundel, who returned it with the decree that it "be published universally for the edification of the faithful and the confutation of heretics or Lollards."[4] In adapting the *Meditations* for an English audience Love added material that directly addressed Lollard positions on the Eucharist, auricular confession, and obedience to the hierarchy of the Church.[5] As Nicholas Watson even suggests, "it is tempting to speculate . . . that it was written in part to order,"[6] a vernacular gospels thoroughly mediated by the voice of a priest, to counter the outlawed Lollard Bible. The term "devout ymaginacion," Richard Beadle has shown, almost invariably introduces a recreated scene of biblical narrative and is a term that Love appears to have coined to offer clear directives to the process of imaginative embellishment.[7] Licensing great freedom with imaginative recreation of biblical narrative, the *Mirror*'s uses of a "devout imagination," Beadle claims, are designed to counter Lollard insistence on literal reading: "Love plainly recognised that his *haute vulgarisation* of the originally abstruse and esoteric . . . meditative tradition was, in the years following upon the turn of the fourteenth century, distinctly vulnerable to the rationalistic insistence of the Wycliffites upon the self-sufficiency of the 'naked text,' as they called it, of the scriptures."[8] This argument is a persuasive one that might be extended as well to include a metacommentary on art as imaginative intermediary. Love's creation of moving images, replete with clear instructions on how to engage imaginatively with them, also seems strategically pitched to engage debates about literal images themselves.

*   *   *

When Lollard writings say why we should be suspicious of devotional images, the reason most frequently cited is that images are dead. Yet the phrase "dead image" is peculiarly spectral, as we have seen, for if images are "dead," then they might also have life. Even if "dead" is understood to simply mean inanimate, the possibility of life is never far off. In modern English when we speak of things as metaphorically dead, it is often to imply that they ought to be otherwise, as in dead ends, a dead party, or even—as the phrase "dead image" is now—a dead metaphor. Deadness is a quality of absence, the lack of vivacity that marks both the normative and the real. In late Middle English, "dead" was used adjectivally in much the same way as we might use it today: Common fourteenth-century usage includes "dead coals," a "dead swoon," or as in Mandeville's *Travels* and in *Cleanness*, a "dead sea," all terms that invoke absence of heat and movement or even a violation of properties of nature.[9] Absence is often implied in Lollard uses of "dead images" as well. The Wycliffite "Tretyse of Ymagis" says that people who give to images should instead give alms to the "quicke ymagis of God, þat ben pore folc,"[10] the poor who are living images of God, and the Prologue to the Wycliffite Bible contrasts dead images with the "image made of God's hands, that is, a Christian man or Christian woman."[11] That this particular deadness lies on a continuum is suggested by frequent references to their sensory impairment; even when they are not precisely dead, images are deaf and blind. As described in the eighth conclusion of the Lollards, they are idolatrous blind crosses and deaf images.[12] Even the base materials—dead stocks and stones—used to carve panels and statuary can hint of an absent vivacity. In a kind of proto-ecocritical complaint, William White writes that "trees growing in a wood are of greater virtue and vigour, and bear a clearer likeness and image of God, than stone or dead wood carved to the likeness of man."[13]

In the *Meditations* Nicholas Love found a text that was brilliantly suited to negotiate the image contest, for his adaptation allows scenes from the life of Christ extraordinary vivacity even as the directed meditations bypass the image as material object. The *Tretise on Miraclis Pleyinge*, a Wycliffite condemnation of the performance of miracle plays, condemns the "living" quality of theater as even worse than the "deadness" of devotional images, for plays are "quike bookis to shrewidnesse."[14] In contrast the *Mirror*, in a defense of the "quickness" of devotional scenes, dramatizes images in action. Yet rather than offering a defense of devotional images or engaging in a debate pro and con, as we see in contemporary works like *Dives and Pauper*, the *Mirror* gives us a demonstration of images in use, scripting a drama of the object that is unassailable from either the most orthodox or the most radical reformist position. Several recent scholars have suggested that Love was uneasy in his response to Lollardy and that rather than addressing Lollard demands directly he strove for certain accommodations while confuting Lollard doctrine. Arguing that the *Mirror* orchestrates Christ's body in a strategic display of clerical authority, Sarah Beckwith also notes that the text effectively empowers the very lay audience it seeks to control: "By helping to introduce and expand the notion of the radical reflexivity of the human will, such piety ultimately gave an extraordinary dynamism to lay piety."[15] Other readers of the *Mirror* have suggested that Love was actively sympathetic to some points of Lollard doctrine. According to Kantik Ghosh, the *Mirror* is an exercise in practical dualism that emphasizes "the hermeneutic authority of the Church, and of the devout reader operating within the Church." [16] In his representation of visual devotion Love might also be said to cast a wide net that accommodates the social critique on images even as it captures the concerns of a lay audience that loves the pictures and carved alabasters in the church. Bypassing the problem of the materiality of images (dead stocks and stones) the *Mirror* instead invites the reader to become part of imagined communities witnessing what we might think of as episodes from the Christian primal scene. Even as they are dematerialized, images come to life.

The few explicit references to images in the *Mirror* offer little in the way of clear guidance to Love's own position on images. Some of Love's changes to his source even seem to express concerns about the literalism of images in popular devotion. To take one example, in the account of events leading up to the incarnation the *Mirror* tells the reader to picture God in dialogue with Gabriel: "Now take hede, & ymagine of gostly þinge as it were bodily, & þenk in þi herte as þou were present in þe siȝt of þat blessed lord, with how benyng [benign] & glad semblant he spekeþ þees wordes" (21.30–33). Even though this passage tells us to imagine God speaking in bodily form, the *Meditations* goes even further and describes him. Love leaves out that description, an editorial decision that Michael Sargent suggests is to avoid "the excessively literal visualizations" of his source.[17] Love also adds an explicit warning against visualization in his commentary on the Trinity, an addition that seems designed to accommodate Lollard concerns: "Bot now beware here þat þou erre not in imaginacion of god & of þe holi Trinite, supposyng þat þees þre persones þe fadere þe son & þe holi gost ben as þre erþly men, þat þou seest with þi bodily eye" (22.7–10). The problem with the Trinity, that is to say, is that you might suppose that the three persons are like three earthly men that you can see with your bodily eye. Love's concerns about literalizations of the Trinity seem to accord remarkably with Lollard complaints. Wyclif objected to literal representation, claiming "Thus laymen depict the Trinity unfaithfully, as if God the Father was an aged paterfamilias, having God the son crucified on his knees and God the holy spirit descending as a dove," and further objecting that people think "the Father or Holy Spirit or Angels to be corporeal."[18] This complaint about the Trinity was echoed elsewhere; the Lollard eighth conclusion says "þe ymage usuel of Trinite is most abhominable," presumably meaning by "usuel" the representation as Wyclif described it, and that would become, in the fifteenth century, a favorite subject for alabaster carvings: God the father seated holding the son between his knees, and above both a dove, the holy spirit, fluttering down from heaven (fig. 28).[19]

Yet even though these editorial decisions register discomfort with the exuberant literalism or even bodiliness of certain kinds of images, the theatrical structure of the text as a whole overrides those concerns to underwrite the dynamically imaged world of the fifteenth-century parish and the veneration of its devotional objects.[20] Another editorial deletion in the *Mirror* even seems to speak *for* the value of images in stirring people to devotion. In one of his major alterations to his Latin exemplar Love abridges the portion of the "Thursday" section of the work in which the active and contemplative life are described, and refers the reader instead to Hilton.[21] The section of the *Meditations* that Love deletes includes a paraphrase of Bernard's refutation of visual meditation: "The fourth impediment [to contemplation], he [Bernard] says, is phantoms of corporeal images. And this is more irksome than all the others named above [poor health, care, and sin]. . . . Thus it is suitable for the contemplator to be mute, deaf and blind, so that in seeing he does not see and in hearing he does not understand and in speaking he does not delight; that in order to be abstracted from these transitory things and joined to God, in hearing, seeing and speaking, he does not abate his course, but flees when he can."[22] Love deletes this passage, explaining that his deletion is motivated by considerations of audience; he will "pass over" sections on the active and contemplative life "lest þis processe of cristes blessed life sholde be tedyouse // to comune peple,

& symple soules, to þe whech it is specialy writen" (107.40–41). In leaving it out, he also excises a statement overtly critical of imaged devotion and even images themselves. The insistence that the contemplative be "mute, deaf, and blind" echoes the very language in which Lollards condemned material devotional objects—stocks and stones that are deaf, blind, and dumb. Love's envisioned audience for the *Mirror*, to the contrary, is emphatically not blind, deaf, or mute, but engaged as a full sensory participant in Christ's daily life.[23]

　　That act of participation seems to blur the boundaries between images and imagining as the text's visual process mirrors the mental work that devotional scenes themselves set in play; this is a dynamic form of visual glossing that offers a dramatic alternative to the Wycliffite "naked text." As Ghosh puts it, "one of the devotional advantages of images—for the Lollards, one of their many disadvantages—is their appeal to the 'imagination' and their frequent indeterminacy of significance."[24] It is precisely this appeal to imagination that Reginald Pecock points to in his long anti-Lollard defense of images. On Good Friday people creep toward the image of the crucifix as to the person of Christ, "which bi þer ymaginacioun was bodily strei3t forth with the bodi of the ymage."[25] Through the faculty of imagination our mental picture can be identical with the image. We find a similar defense of both image and imagination in Thomas Netter, a contemporary of Love who defended images on the grounds that God took on human form: "A most beautiful reason" we should turn to images is that "Christ is now known in the express image ['in expressa imagine'] of his body naturally on the altar."[26] For Netter, this mirrored corporeality is itself revelatory, a sign that also is a defense of signs in the world of Christ; yet for Lollards, the visual imagining of devotional scenes can be construed as a form of textual glossing and hence a threat to the integrity of the biblical text. In an apt phrase, James Simpson comments that Love's uses of "moving images" may even operate, as part of an assault on the linguistic tyranny of Lollard literalism, "to dissolve the textuality of words."[27]

　　In the *Mirror* this textual "dissolve" occurs without ekphrasis of devotional objects but in many ways enables the same effect through immediate connection between the spectator and scenes from Christ's life. In his guided meditation, the narrator repeatedly gives play to his own imagination in analogies that erase historical distance. He converts currency from the gospels into fifteenth-century value: Describing Judas's reward of "þritty grete pens" he notes that "euery peny was worþ tene commune pens, as now our grote is worþ foure commune pens" (145.7–9). In the absence of detail in his sources he also pictures what could be happening; on the Wednesday of Christ's betrayal the narrator asks, "Bot on þat oþere part, what dide oure lord Jesus & his blessed company þat day. . . . Me þinke is reasonably to be trowede, þat he was þan for þe moste part occupiede in praiere," first speculating and then offering his own suggestion for what happened that day (145.21, 25–26). One of the most striking and coercive features of both the *Meditations* and of Love's *Mirror* is the use of the vocative, the voice of an invisible authority that not only orchestrates the story and commentary but also tells us how to see it, coaxing us to "behold" landmark events in Christ's life. The first of these directives occurs at the moment that the narrative will begin to explore the conversion of immaterial to material—that is, in the account of the annunciation: "Now take hede, & ymagine of gostly þinge as it were bodily, & þenk in þi herte as þou were present in þe siȝt of þat blessed lord" (21.30–32). Throughout the remaining text, similar directives control the narrative by telling us to be present in Mary's private chamber during the annunciation (22.33), ordering us to contrition and compassion as when we are told to "beþenk þe & haue in mynde" (32.36) the Virgin's poverty. Above all, with a marked development in intensity as we approach and experience the Passion, we are ordered to "behold." In portions of the Friday section of the text, which narrates the Passion, directives on how to behold and how to respond to what we see appear every few lines; "beholdeth" how Christ prays (164.10); "and also beholde" how he let himself be taken and bound (167.25); "now . . . beholde" how he is led to Jerusalem (167.36); now with inward compassion focus on his youth as, naked, he gathers his clothes—"beholde him here in maner as I seide before onelich after þe manhede" (173.4); "beholde & se" (174.31) the torments as one takes him, another binds him, another blasphemes him, another scourges him, "& so forþ now one & now anoþer" (175.1–2) as he is taken hither and thither, in and out.

The act of beholding these scenes is not a static process for either observer or the scene observed. We are to imagine Christ's life in action. To take almost a random example in the annunciation, the narrator gives precise instructions on visualization, focusing attention on what he calls the "bodliness" of the scene—and as part of that bodiliness, its animation. When we picture Gabriel it is to see him in action: "And on þat oþer side, how Gabriel with a liking face & glade chere vpon his knen knelyng & with drede reuerently bowing receueþ þis message of his lord" (21.33–35). Once Gabriel receives his orders he flies to earth and takes human likeness before Mary, who is also imagined in an act, "perauentur redyng þe prophecie of ysaie" (21.40). The relationship of the spectator with the scene is direct, although, as we shall see, carefully orchestrated; we are to watch as if we were present in the room. Describing the Last Supper the narrator says "Now þen beholde oure lord Jesu after he was come to þe foreside place, how he stant in sume part beheþen, spekyng with hese disciples of edification, & abiding til it was made redy for hem in þe forseid house aloft" (147.17–20). When Lazarus is raised from the dead, the narrator gives even more explicit instructions for participatory spectatorship: We should "make vs by ymyginacion, as þei we were present in bodily vonuersacion not onely with oure lord Jesu and hees disciples. Bot also with þat blessed & deuout meyne" (128.7–10). In the room as a member of the company, we are even to be part of the conversation.

In scenes such as these, which recur throughout the text, the narrator urges the reader to participate, as voyeurs and players, in the lives of the text's characters. To picture the Virgin reading the prophecy of Isaiah is to look over her shoulder. Through its animation of biblical scenes the *Mirror* seems to exemplify the dictum that people should worship not the image but the idea behind it, a refrain echoed throughout orthodox defenses of image veneration. In the *Mirror*, "idea" is turned into a moving picture, in effect working as a *demonstrandum* of the image as sign. In their animation scenes from the *Mirror* give a dynamic response to the insistence that images are dead. Imagined as if vibrantly and intimately contemporary, they offer an embodied answer to Wycliffite demand that people worship not images, but the "quick" image of Christ. In the *Mirror*, Christ is vitally and engagingly "quick"—even, we might say, in the dramatic process of his death.

Devotional Images, Moving Pictures

The directives to "devout imagination" may also work to legitimize devotional images through their narrative echoes of pictures and images of the gospels as Love's lay audience would have known them from the material fabric of parishes and cathedrals. In the *Mirror* images take on life as scenes of participatory spectatorship and in this way may work to validate the very postures of image veneration. Readers have pointed to the influence of the *Meditations* and of the *Mirror* on drama and on visual art in the fifteenth and sixteenth centuries.[28] The interest in the *Mirror*'s powerful legacies to later art and drama has had the effect of diverting attention from its own programmatic debts—or more aptly for the point of this chapter, from its *habitus* in both imaginative space and in the physical structure of the church. In many ways the visualized meditation of the *Mirror* echoes contemporary devotional art, valorizing practices of imaged devotion in its very plan. Fifteenth-century readers would have seen these scenes represented countless times in wall painting and stained glass in the local parish. That is to say, many of the scenes so carefully described in the *Mirror*, such as the annunciation, epiphany, the ascension, and scenes from the Passion already had their material prototypes. As it gives instructions for positioning ourselves in relation to the imagined life of Christ, the *Mirror* gives an affirming nod to the troublesome objects themselves.

Moreover, the very postures of "devout imagination" mimic the representation of spectatorship in scenes from Christ's life. Instructed to imagine scenes from the life of Christ and the holy family as if we were there, we are told to adopt a pose and a gaze that mimes the posture of spectators in many gospel scenes decorating English parishes: the magi, the witnesses at the presentation in the temple, and especially the crowd that typically surrounds scenes of the Passion. While the peopling of these scenes with venerators dramatically intensifies in fifteenth-century painting, schema for focusing biblical scenes through the gaze of spectators, a feature particularly marked in representations of the Passion, were thoroughly conventional. These schema are perhaps most dramatically displayed in deluxe manuscript paintings such as the Lytlington and Sherborne missals, c. 1380s, both of which throng their crucifixion miniatures with spectators, after practices in Italian painting.[29] As we see in Chapter 2, the Despenser Retable, an important late fourteenth-century altarpiece in Norwich Cathedral, also fills its panels with witnesses and participants. In each of the panels Christ is framed by a group of viewers—and we might even include in that the 1380s Norwich congregation for which the altarpiece was painted: in the resurrection scene Christ rises from his tomb over the bodies of the sleeping soldiers to look out and face the viewer. In other scenes, spectatorship is contained within the panel; in the flagellation, Pilate and others stand and watch; as Christ carries the cross to cavalry he is accompanied by others; and as he ascends to heaven his disciples gaze upward at his disappearing feet (fig. 15). Pictures of the Passion on English wall paintings, the visible media of the lay audience that seems to be targeted in the *Mirror*, adopted similar symbolism and patterns, though the scenes of choice most often were the nativity and the Passion and were often painted in simpler, more schematic form.[30] Wall paintings may even offer the most direct narrative parallel to the images in the *Mirror*, for they provided, like the *Mirror*, access to biblical stories for ordinary people—simple souls of "simple vndirstondyng" (10.22–23), as Love describes his target audience—and also guided the emotional piety of parishioners in their direct appeals to sentiment and empathy. Yet these are not simply parallel universes but crossovers or eidetic ones. As it recalls familiar visual images through its precise directives on how to look at biblical scenes, the *Mirror* also documents and validates their public display and veneration.

The postures of reverent beholding we are told to assume before gospel scenes may even evoke poses adopted by donors, a new form of self-representation that appears in late fourteenth-century English sculpture, wall painting, and stained glass and continues well into the fifteenth.[31] Donor images, which typically represent a man or woman kneeling below a devotional picture, such as a saint, the Passion, or the Trinity, affirm the validity of contractual relationships between members of the congregation and the material structure of the church. Linking the worshipper or viewer materially with the image he or she has given, donor images commemorate lay endowments and build a vital, highly visible link between lay parishioners, the physical world of worship, and the larger church community. In her *Book*, Margery Kempe seems to picture herself in the posture of a donor, as I argue in Chapter 7. The *Mirror*'s instructions for reverent beholding organize the gaze in similarly devout postures: If one wants to have "swete vndurstandyng" of the biblical stories, the narrator says, "him behoueþ to make himself by deuout meditacion as he were bodily present in alle places and dedes" (202.1–2). That presence in a worshipful or devout posture can suggest the bodily veneration assumed by donors kneeling before devotional images—a gesture graphically lampooned in the Lollard *Pierce the Plowman's Crede*, where the eagerness of would-be donors, hoping to see their names painted visibly on the windows they have given, is the subject of a sharp critique, as I discuss in Chapter 1. It may be, of course, that developments in lay patronage and vernacular piety that led to the popularity of donor images were themselves influenced by the conscripted veneration of the *Meditations*, years before Love's translation—yet that would only further underscore this synergy. A reader of Love's text in 1410 would have many models for "devout imagination," among them pictures within pictures, donors represented in acts of kneeling before the very images they have commissioned.

In multiple ways the directives for imagining Christ's life thus work to underwrite a world of images. The scenes we are told to imagine mimic prototypes in devotional art, the troubling dead matter of Lollard critique, and the postures of spectatorship that we are urged to adopt echo acts of witnessing and veneration widely represented in many of those same scenes. In engaging directly with episodes from the life of Christ, we also follow to the letter a widely voiced concern about the literalism of images; we go straight to the living. Yet the text's most subtle and strategic intervention in the image debate might lie in its careful construction of what we today might call "viewing communities." In orchestrating a drama of communal witnessing, the *Mirror* reenacts theatrical relationships fundamental to traditional Christian liturgical practice, particularly the congregation's veneration of the consecrated host. In this way the *Mirror*'s responsive structure furthers its own sacramental theology; our acts of visual veneration, in postures carefully and theatrically blocked by a pastoral voice as our guide, are as important as the scenes that we witness. The *Mirror*'s oblique commentary on images may even be best understood through its dramatic meta-commentary in defense on the Eucharist, the most troubling of all images in Lollard theology. In its management of communal postures around living images of Christ, the *Mirror* offers a dramatic demonstration of transubstantiation, enacted in direct form for its intended lay audience. What we watch is not a sign, but the living body.

Communities

In its eyewitness technique, the *Mirror* not only positions its readers as spectators but also locates them as members of communities. As we "behold" the gospel, we do so as part of a group. One of the achievements of the *Meditations* is to present a comprehensive history of Christ's life, one to which the narrator and the reader are both eyewitnesses, from the early life of the Virgin through the resurrection of Christ. Where Love adapts this program, as Gail Gibson puts it, is to "perform the transformation of this contemplative text into a model for the lay devotions of men and women who lived very much in the world."[32] This transformation occurs through an increased emphasis on the physical meditation seen before the eyes, miracles of the Mass that express themselves in visible, highly concrete form, and even on direct transfusions of bodily sensation from Christ to the eyewitness. Whether we understand this display of an exemplary life to function, as Gibson says, as a "model for the lay devotions of men and women who lived very much in the world" or as a means of separating, as Sarah Beckwith says, spiritual from bodily and high from low in a strategic display of clerical authority,[33] the meditation is directed through commands that appear to dissolve hierarchy even as they place the audience—whom most readers agree is consistently feminized—within carefully constructed social communities.[34]

The express aim of these ocular directives is to stimulate affective piety through a powerfully experienced incarnational aesthetic, creating a highly personalized and one-to-one engagement or even identification of the spectator with the Virgin or with Christ.[35] The voice at the ear is intimate, sharing in our sorrow even as it leads us to even more painful sights: "Oo my lorde god, what is alle þis? Loo þenke þe not here a fulle harde & continuele bitter bataile? Ʒitte abide a litel while, & þou salt se hardere" (175.7–9). The organizing, intimate voiceover of a narrator who directs what appears to be a personalized meditation only creates the illusion of an individuated devotional self, however. The framing of this meditation across a transhistorical narrative to which we are fixed as spectators with a scripted participatory role continuously defines personal experience as collective ritual and organizes individual will through acts stage-managed by the clergy. Several of the directives are even quite explicit about how we are to place ourselves imaginatively among the company in the gospel: As we picture the events of epiphany, "so ymagine we & set oure mynde & our þouht as we were present in þe place where þis was done at Betheleem" (43.28–30); in the story of Lazarus, we are told to "make vs by ymyganacion, as þei we were present in bodily conuersacion not onely with oure lord Jesu & hees disciples; bot also with þat blessede & deuout meyne, that is to sey, Martha, Marie & Lazare" (128.7–10). In this way Love's text becomes in effect a demonstration, through its own mirroring, of the spectacle of the Mass itself, with the voice of the narrator who directs us to "beholde" speaking for an invisible cleric displaying the bodily miracle in the mystery of the Eucharist. Raising the visible host in the directives that guide the narrative, the text becomes a reiterated *demonstrandum*, the text-as-image repeatedly fixing the individual in various communal and sacramental postures. Individual agency is parsed and reconstituted as a collective will.[36]

The group identity that the text both imagines and creates takes on various personae, but it is primarily a female one. Even though Love suppresses the addresses in the *Meditations* to "dear daughter"—the Poor Clare for whom the Latin exemplar supposedly was written—he retains other directives that would target a primarily female audience. Even as he extends the application of his translation to both men and women, he acknowledges in the Prohemium that "Bonaventure's" text was written for a woman, "a

religiouse woman" (10.10). Neither does he suppress the "incipit" in which
the entire project is likened to the meditations of St. Cecilia, who kept the
events of Christ's life in her heart so that she could meditate on them night
and day (11.24–33). Even more important, though, the text feminizes its
spectators through appeals to emotional response and domestic or maternal acts. The text emphasizes homely details, urging the reader not only
to participate in the events of Christ's childhood and later life but also to
participate in them as a woman.[37]

The orchestration of community is particularly skillful in the Passion
scene. The reader being directed to "behold" adopts a variety of positions
from which to watch the events of Christ's torments and death; often,
however, we watch through the eyes of the Virgin, and even more exactly,
from a position among a group of women who wrestle for Christ—and
even for Christ's body—against similarly constructed and oppositional male
groupings. For instance, when Christ is imprisoned and bound to a pillar,
the narrator first takes an intimate view of him, telling us to "take heed"
how he holds his peace and looks toward the ground in spite of what they
do to him: "and so stode he bonden vnto þat pilere vnto þe morowe"
(168.33–34). Then the scene shifts. "In the mean time" John, who has followed Jesus, goes to the Virgin and Mary Magdalen and others who are
gathered at Magdalen's house, and when he tells them what has happened
"and then was there vnspekable sorowe, criyng, & wepyng" (168.35–40).
This move into Magdalen's house is dramatic, given to us in set of cues that
organize our identification through contrasts between types of helplessness,
first Christ's and then the group at Magdalen's house: "Take nowe entent
to hem, & haue compassion of hem, for þei bene in þe grettist disese &
hyest sorowe for hir lorde" (168.41–42). The command displaces Christ's
passivity onto a community of women, "beholdyng alle þat shale be done
aȝeynus þi lorde" (176.9), helpless to stop the action. The narrative vocative, shifting between distance and intimacy, tells us how to act and react
as it places us among women who are identified by familial and fraternal
bonds—and in the Passion episode, by their shared helplessness.

The rest of the Passion repeats a similar pattern in which space is constructed through the action of groups, a system in which the singular body
of Christ occupies center stage in a community struggle with clearly identified agents. Christ's body is handled and essentially passed among groups,
who struggle to glimpse him, to torment him, or to hold him. When he is
led to Pilate, it is by a group composed of "princes and souereynes of þe
peple" (169.20–21). While he follows this group "as an innocent lamb" the

women who come to see him and meet him at a crossroads are part of a crowd. "His moder & Jone & oþer women of hir companye" (169.28–29) approach and stop, confronted by the sight of him "with so grete a multitude of peple" (169.31). The compassion we ought to feel, the narrator tells us, should be a group experience: "And so in þat metyng to gedire of oure lorde Jesu & hem; & siht of oþere; þere was grete sorowe on boþe parties" (169.34–35). This collective response and action on the body of Christ is even more explicitly framed in the scenes of the torments and of the deposition. In the torments, we are brought into the scene as passive witnesses to "behold and see"; and what we see is defined through collective agency, a group action that positions us also as collectively helpless: "First one dispitesly leiþ hande on him & takeþ him. A noþer is redy & harde byndeþ him. A noþer criynge putteþ vpon him blasfeme. A noþere spitteþ in his face. A noþer sotely askeþ of him many questiones in deceite fort accuse him . . . & so forþ now one & now anoþer & diuerse & many" (174–5.32–2). The deposition repeats this kind of shared action in a scene in which group spectatorship is paramount. As it is taken from the cross Christ's body becomes sacrament, parsed and passed among Nicodemus, Joseph of Arimathea, and the Marys:

And than Nichodeme comeþ done fort drawe out the þridde naile of þe feete, & in the mene tyme, Joseph susteneþ þe bodye. Soþely wele is him þat may susteyne & clippe þat holiest body // of oure lorde Jesu. þerwiþ oure lady takeþ in hir handes reuerently oure lordes riht hande, & beholdeþ it & leþ it to hir eyene & deuoutly kisseþ it, sore wepyng & sihhyng. And when þe naile of þe feete was drawe out. Joseph came done softly & alle leiden to hande, & token oure lordes bodie, & leide it done on the erþe, & oure lady toke þe hede & þe sholderes & leide it in hir barme, bot Maudeleyn was redy to take & kysse þe feet, at þe whech she fonde so miche grace before in his life. (185.18–29)

I cite this passage at length, for it offers, in condensed form, a particularly vivid example of the text's strategic control of sacramental spectacle. This scene, which first describes communal touch, rewrites itself through a shift from touch to sight. Immediately following this description, we see how the scene is framed by communities of beholders. First the watchers are identified as generalized members of the group, "oþere of that cumpanye stoden about beholdyng" (185.30). The account then identifies its central watcher, "his blessede modere . . . beholdyng the wondes of hands & feet" (185.35). First Christ's body is known through touch, surrounded by a group that essentially fragments and shares it. Then it is known through sight, as spectators in the text, among them the Virgin, watch—just as the reader has been told to do throughout the text. Yet this narrative of enlarging frames paradoxically occludes the body at its center, or at least places our identification with the group, chiefly of women, that looks at it. The beholding that we have been instructed to perform throughout the Passion sequence is thus repeated, frame within frame, as communal action around a shared body, almost as the act of sharing the body. In this way the scene, and indeed the text as a whole, engages its readers in communal relationships centered around Christ that mirror the eucharistic rite itself, in which the living body of Christ is held up before a congregation. The text demonstrates, in narrative form, its most clearly articulated polemical argument.

If it can be said that the *Mirror* as a whole, with its orchestrated performance of reverent beholding, implicitly enacts the miracle of the Mass, the "Treatise on the Sacraments" gives an explicit argument for miraculous transformation. The *Mirror* brings images to life most graphically in this interpolated treatise, a text that is appended to nearly all of the manuscripts of the *Mirror* and, as Michael Sargent has convincingly argued, should be considered an integral part of the work. In the "Treatise," a defense of transubstantiation, Love explains that there are three types of miracles associated with the sacrament: transubstantiation itself, miraculous eucharistic visions that move people to more fervent love of God, and miraculous reprieves from illness, prison, or other misfortunes. Although the false heretics say that we "honouren & maken brede oure godde," in the miracle of transubstantiation there is no fear of heresy: "For we seyen & beleuen, þat in þat holy sacrament brede is turnede in to goddus bodye, by vertue of cristes wordes. And so we alle holely honouren not brede; bot god & his body in forme of brede, þat is to sey in þat likenes of brede þat we sene with oure bodily eyene; we honouren goddus body þat we seene by trewe byleue in soule with oure gostly eyene" (228.16–22). Love's defense of the sacrament echoes terms writers typically use to defend images in general—to honor not the image but the idea behind the image—and can be paralleled to the *Mirror*'s own drama of Christ-in-action as imagined with the ghostly eye. In the sacrament, as in the text of the *Mirror* itself, we go directly to the real in the evidentiary image. Just as Lot's wife was changed to salt, God can perform miracles that change things in their substances, Love says. Host miracles witness similar mutations, the "Treatise" continues: A clerk of Hugh of Lincoln saw God's body rising from the chalice in the sacring; a woman was converted in a Mass performed by St. Gregory when the eucharistic bread turned into a finger. In the late Middle Ages, stories of wonder-working images flourished side by side with an often dense clerical discourse that attempted to distinguish among proper and improper uses, among *latria* and *dulia*, or between worshipping the image or the idea behind it.[38] In the "Treatise on the Sacraments," as throughout the *Mirror* as a whole, Love creates the kind of pious and direct encounter that we find in stories of the saints. Questions about whether we worship the image or the idea behind the image are quietly bypassed in the text's active demonstration of images in action—and especially of the Eucharist at the moment of sacring, where food becomes a living body.

In the Prohemium to the text Love explains that he has chosen his title in order to recreate an image of Christ's life as a man's face is reflected in a mirror (11.15–19). "Mirror" is an appropriate name, he says, because the life of Christ can only be described the way an image of man's face is shown in a mirror, "in a maner of liknes as þe ymage of mans face is shewed in þe mirroure" (11.17). Directly preceding this somewhat enigmatic explanation, Love also says that Christ's life cannot be described as lives of other saints, a distinction that seems to suggest that Christ's life defies the techniques of narrative distance that we use when we turn someone's life into a story. Christ's life must be seen, rather than told; it must also be seen in direct encounter "as þe ymage of man's face is shewed in þe mirroure." An even fuller explanation for his title, one that defines the sacramental project optically as one of a visual multiplication of matter, is suggested in the "Treatise on the Sacraments." In the "Treatise" Love explains that the miracle of the Mass is like a mirror that, even when broken, represents the self as whole in each piece; thus the host can be infinitely fractured and infinitely multiplied, with Christ's body intact and entire in every morsel (229.22–26). Love's translation and adaptation of the *Meditations* gives us a similarly perceptible demonstration, one whose sacramental potency is defined by an erasure of boundaries between individuals and communities and between images and the living bodies they represent. Just as the mirrored body is one and many, so is the individual self organized as one member of a shared and transhistorical family.

And what, we must ask, is this community, and what does it do? Central to the pleasure of the text is a forfeiture of will, both to clerical authority and to community. Through the highly controlled spectacle of Love's *Mirror*, the viewer expresses shared experience by responding to orders. Yet the terms of visual identification elide the text's systems of authority. Displacing its own agency by holding us in engaged passivity before a spectacle that unfolds before our eyes, the clerical vocative organizes us into a community defined by our circulation around the centrally individuated

Christ. Even though the narrator's voice often appears within the narrative as well, sometimes taking the viewer's position as just another spectator, it nevertheless remains authoritative and even intrusive. The popularity of this text may, I believe, result from its manipulation of the pleasure of looking; it may also derive in part from the pleasure of being seen. Love's text enacts the Mass through display of the body of Christ; it also evokes the Mass through a fragmentation of the beholder and reconstitution of the singular self into a congregation, defined through the collective power and pleasure of both looking and of being seen. As individual spectatorship multiplies into a collective gaze on a family narrative, the gaze thus fragments the action of visual identification and visual suffering into reenactments of mirrored passivity.

In its representation of direct encounters between communities of witnesses and episodes from Christ's life, the *Mirror*—and indeed the symbol of the mirror—may also be said to encode a kind of "ocular communion," to borrow a term from a study on medieval visuality by Susannah Biernoff.[39] Desires to see God or to suffer when we look at a crucifix have a graphic physical dimension in the optical link joining viewers and objects through the agency of visual rays.[40] Seeing is not simply believing but sharing and touching. In the *Mirror*, "reverent beholding" is also a form of touch. The text builds multiple kinds of contiguities: the reader participates in scriptural communities even as she shares directly in the demonstration of Christ's life, bodily taking in, we might say, the Eucharist through the eye. And this experience, particularly in the Passion sequence, is expressly to be shared. In one of his interpolations in the scene of the crucifixion, Love directs our gaze first to Mary Magdalene, then to the Virgin's grief, and then to our own—followed by an excursus on visual pleasure: "Soþely þis siht of oure lord Jesu hangyng so on þe crosse by deuoute ymaginacion of þe soule, is so likyng to sume creatours; þat after longe exercise of sorouful compassion; þei felen sumtyme, so grete likyng not onely in soule bot also in þe body þat þei kunne not telle, & þat noman may knowe, bot onely he þat by experience feleþ it" (181.15–21). The pleasures ("likyng")—and horrors—of looking, that is to say, are shared. The text, blending moral directives and good storytelling, fixes our identification on parish fabric and community through its recreation of family relationships, particularly as experienced by women whose actions circulate around nurturance and care of the body.

* * *

And what does the *Mirror* suggest that might shed light on Love's own attitudes toward images? As a Carthusian prior at Mount Grace charterhouse in Yorkshire, Love held an important post in an order that was historically opposed to images, though it is unclear how fully regulations for simplicity were upheld. An inventory done under Henry VIII of the Carthusian charterhouse in London reveals a significant accumulation of plate, ornaments, and images.[41] William of Worcester, describing the church at the Charterhouse at Sheen, writes that "on the walls on each side of the nave of the church hang *many* devotions and good reminders to devotion and the arousing of all Christian souls to God," and recent excavations at Witham and Beauvale have exposed fragments of painted glass, indicating that those houses were not entirely austere.[42] Nevertheless, images were officially proscribed; a treatise on the Carthusians written in 1310 notes that they had no pictures, sculptures, or painted images of the saints but only a single crucifix in "a solemn and eminent place" over each altar. The Chapter of 1424 gives an ordinance against "curiously" painted pictures on altars of some charterhouses and pictures in windows showing coats of arms.[43]

Of course the rules of the order, however they were officially scripted or followed, may have had little bearing on the kinds of devotional practices Nicholas Love might have envisioned as appropriate for lay people outside the cloister. In the later fifteenth century Mount Grace also seems to have been a center for the kind of emotional piety exemplified in the *Mirror*, producing works of markedly affective or even ecstatic devotion by Richard Methley and John Norton.[44] For Love's own attitudes toward images in the early part of the fifteenth century the primary evidence is the *Mirror*; and there, as we have seen, his concerns about devotional images, particularly his interpolation warning against literal representations of the Trinity, echo those of Wycliffite writers. Nevertheless, by urging his readers to imagine scenes that were common subjects of painting on walls and glass in contemporary parishes, Love presents a complex affirmation of an image culture; and by conscripting his readers in a variety of devotional postures venerating those scenes, the text creates a strategically articulated meditation attentive to the ways images should be used. As Love goes on to say in the excursus on the Trinity, when we find ourselves thinking too much about abstract concepts that we cannot see with our bodily eye, such as the godhead, the Trinity, angels, or souls, we should just stop and take their reality on faith: "And þerfore when þou herest any sich þinge in byleue þat passeþ þi kyndly reson, trowe soþfastly þat it is soþ as holy chirch techeþ & go no ferþer" (22.23–25). Love may well share with the

Wycliffites concerns about the appeal of images to private "ymaginacion"—
and hence consistently conscripts imagination into collective devotional
postures. Go no further, he says; believe as holy Church teaches. Part of this
creed, in an argument on which both reformist and conservative ecclesiasts
would agree, is that we should worship the idea behind the image, not the
image itself. The *Mirror* performs a strategic bypass to get, we might say,
to the heart. Its images are living stories. The community of the parish,
comprised of venerators and images, is never far off. In its specular politics,
the *Mirror* defines vision through the object; each time we look at Christ's
body we are claimed as a corporate body ourselves.

7

Arts of Self-Patronage in *The Book of Margery Kempe*

A LINCHPIN IN ARTS PROGRAMMING is the benefactor list. Discreetly tucked away toward the end of the program, this list draws the eye through its conspicuous ordering, a ranking that brackets orders of patronage with clear dollar amounts. It might begin in the thousands, with the Seraphim, as in "Seraphim (gifts of $10,000 or more)," followed by Cherubim, then Angels, and finally the Patrons and then the Friends—gifts of $100 or less. This list serves its cause through its polite and careful acknowledgment of material gifts. The list also serves the benefactors by circulating their names and dollar attachments among a select readership. Its networks are strategic. If I am among this celestial hierarchy, I would be likely to look for my own name and also scan the list to see who else is on it. The benefactor list, taking up its pages in the program, claims public space for its patrons, designating a cultural network and transforming the private individual into a nominal corporate identity.

But what if I am not on the list? This list, like all roll calls, serves to mark who is in and who is out, or, we might say, states of being or nothingness. A mechanism of cultural envy, the patronage list suggests, with a curious reverse turn, that those who are named have been chosen—and leaves us feeling that we are excluded from the circle even if we have never considered giving to this cause. Or it might do so, I should qualify, if the names on the list had the potential to include me: a neighbor on the list, and my name is absent.

For women, the claiming of a public name and public space historically has involved a complex negotiation between private and public identity. To have one's name recorded as the patron of a public space or building is also to leave a record of influence in the public sphere, announcing material purchase power, with a name listed as a form of enduring symbolic capital. Increased opportunities for public roles for women in the recent past have led, of course, to sometimes traumatic, often comic confrontations with the politics of self-naming: What do I even call myself? A recent program from the Boston Symphony Orchestra, reflecting changing protocols that themselves signify a profound transition in the terms in which women claim public space, permits a variety of ways for female patrons to list their names: Ms. Ruth Russel Smith; Mrs. Joan D. Wheeler; William and Deborah Elfers; Joseph Hearne and Jan Brett, or the conventional and common form, Mrs. George R. Rowland, Mr. and Mrs. Peter Brooke, wives whose gifts are recorded through the patronymic. Certainly some of the anxieties about naming arise from genre, and in this case the genre of named donation with its subtle protocols. A group of women I know started meeting together as a consciousness-raising group in the early 1980s and continues to meet together to this day. A few years ago a member of the group, a dancer, died, and the group as a whole decided to give a joint gift in her memory to a local arts center. Their donation was to be acknowledged by a plaque on a wall. The problem they faced with the plaque, however, was how to record their identity. They had always called themselves by the name "Stitch and Bitch." Should "Stitch and Bitch" be etched on the plaque, the enduring record of donation? I do not know how the plaque was finally printed. I tell this story, however, because it seems to illustrate the tentative, often transitional claims women continue to have on public space. In the case of the Stitch and Bitch, anxieties about public naming were recorded not only in the question over the plaque but also in the very choice of a name to begin with, which itself playfully acknowledged the group's transitional identity, in a time of unparalleled change in the visibility of women in public roles, between a women's sewing circle and something very different: stitch, the private life; bitch, the complaints about it.

While the benefactor list, along with the conventions for recording the names of its patrons, both male and female, continues to develop its own protocols in the twenty-first century, it has deep affiliations with forms of conspicuous patronage in the late Middle Ages. Recent research on fifteenth-century English material culture has revealed a flourishing growth in the production of devotional artifacts of all kinds, with a corresponding interest in visible bequests. As we have seen, studies of lay patronage have documented generous endowments to rebuild local parishes with new roofs, reglazed windows, and private chapels, with many of these gifts commemorated by plaques and inscriptions. Tangible evidence of patronage, such as the coats of arms in the frame of the Despenser Retable, was so widespread as to suggest that patronage itself took on cultic status in late medieval England.[1] Names and portraits of benefactors, both male and female, appear nearly everywhere, from stained glass to rood-screen panels and bronze plaques. The devotional ornament and furnishings of fifteenth-century parishes became signally entailed, marked by the incision of a self, whether named or emblematized with a coat of arms, in a passion for self-portraiture.

This chapter focuses on a quixotic and highly localized fifteenth-century benefactor list—*The Book of Margery Kempe*. It is of course an unusual list, for one name appears over and over in all the categories, and that is Kempe's ("this creature"); and the amount of her gifts are registered not in dollars or pounds but in hundreds of thousands of souls she saves with her prayers.[2] Kempe's *Book*, a hybrid between autobiography and spiritual or mystical memoir, also borrows conventions from the saint's life and spiritual confession, constructing a personal history defined, in part, by the worldly pleasures she has come to renounce. One of the continuing pressures of her text, however, is the need to have a public identity, even though she claims to renounce that goal; and it is a public self that also is deeply indebted, I will argue, to contemporary donor images, themselves signs of subtle but crucial shifts in attitudes toward self-representation in fifteenth-century England. The Creature whose life story Kempe recounts makes astonishingly territorial claims over public space, demanding audience with powerful clerics and interrupting church services repeatedly with her crying and weeping. Acutely conscious of her social position, she also seems strategically invested in creating an enduring public image.[3] In the mystical portions of her text, Kempe even claims physical space, imagining herself in a complex set of postures as a donor of means. Kempe pictures herself in the very fabric of the buildings themselves.

It has been widely recognized that Kempe's visions are contoured by contemporary iconography, both as transmitted through the *Meditations on the Life of Christ* or in its local version, the *Mirror* by Nicholas Love, and through the drama.[4] The debts of her visions to images that she would have seen in Lynn, Norwich, York, and elsewhere have been less fully addressed, in part because her *Book*, in spite of its detailed mapping of her travels, offers few concrete details about the spaces she inhabited and visited, either in England or in her pilgrimages. In a recent study that attempts to situate Kempe within a culture of images Kathleen Kamerick argues that Kempe's sensory mode of visualization links her bodily with modes of imaged devotion such as we see in Love's *Mirror*.[5] I would agree with this assessment but also argue that Kempe's visualizing makes concrete uses of parish space and of conventions for lay participation in the veneration of images. Certainly Kempe responds energetically to images. In the few references she provides to images or devotional objects, she indicates that they produce powerful, even visceral reactions. She marvels at a vision of the host and chalice trembling during a Mass (20.1514), weeps at the stations of the cross in Jerusalem and collapses in a fit at Calvary (28.2204). She sobs and cries out when she sees the Virgin's kerchief in Assisi (31.2284), when she looks at a crucifix in Leicester (ch. 46), or when she sees a pietà at a church in Norwich (60.4956).

Nevertheless, there is little in the way of descriptive detail and attention to place in Kempe's *Book*, and while she tells us a great deal about where she goes and with whom she talks, she gives us little information about the surface texture of either people or places.[6] Repeatedly she locates herself within clerical spaces that would have been richly or even lavishly ornamented in the fifteenth century: the Prior's chapel in Lynn (56.4656),[7] the Chapterhouse at Beverly (54.4394),[8] the high altar at St. Stephen's in Norwich (60.4936) and at All Saints in Leicester (48.3789), the choir (23.1714) and the chapel of the Gesine in her home church of St. Margaret's (63.5204).[9] Nonetheless she does not catalogue the surfaces of these sites, which would have been decorated with altarpieces, windows, statuary, and textiles describing sacred history. Rather, she appears to interiorize this complex and absorbing imagery.

As she narrates her visions and dialogues with Christ, however, Kempe repeatedly constructs tableaux that can imaginatively flesh out the spaces that she has visited. Kempe transposes the exterior to an interior life, authenticating her sanctity through imagined participation in important moments of Christ's life as she would have seen those events represented in alabasters, glazing, and panel painting.[10] This feature of narrative style, perhaps a strategic choice made in the interests of constructing an "authoritative" visionary history, may also be driven by late medieval aesthetic practice, specifically a generalized prohibition on description of devotional objects. As we have seen, in early fifteenth-century England writers did not casually describe "works of art" or devotional objects. The image debate and the shadow of heresy made any discussion of images and their devotional uses a potentially risky topic in the early fifteenth century, especially following 1409, the year of Arundel's Constitutions. Much of the *Book of Margery Kempe* takes place during the years in which prosecution of Lollards reached its zenith—between 1409 and 1410, when she prayed for an end to sexual relations with her husband, and the early 1420s—and during those years she appears to have been a suspect for Lollardy. Yet the dual pressure of her meditations not just to picture herself within scenes from the gospels or to picture Christ as modeled after current devotional forms but also to imagine herself as a donor in those scenes, as I will argue, constitutes an extraordinarily complex act of border crossing. In a move pitched toward the dynamic and embodied experience of a spiritual life, Kempe uses her visions to lay claim on local space, turning herself into an image and images into her own text. Margery Kempe's textual imaging may use "art" in ways similar to familiar arts of social connoisseurship, in which one can claim social status through the very knowledge of high art, though for Kempe, the contingencies of value are social rather than aesthetic.[11] Her text, which has often been called the first autobiography in English, becomes a form of cultural capital. Her constant self-aggrandizement, repeated references to her intimate contract with Christ, and detailed accounts of interviews with the powerful ecclesiastics of her time all contribute to turning her *Book* into a kind of accreditation or deed legitimizing Kempe's life and even purchasing her well-being in the afterlife.

This chapter raises questions about the role of objects in her text—or more exactly, the role of absent things that take on life when they are transformed into visions. To what extent does Kempe borrow from emerging traditions of visual signatures to describe a self that is both donor and self-portrait, creating a kind of autoportrait?[12] To what extent does Kempe's *Book* depend on contemporary arts of patronage—and in effect transform the material culture of fifteenth-century East Anglian churches into the very fabric of her text itself? As it has long been recognized, the elision of mental and material images is characteristic of medieval devotional imagery.[13] Studies of female devotional practices have also recognized the concrete quality of the meditations of medieval women, often articulated through imagined pictures that were explicitly based on material objects.[14] The ekphrastic and self-dramatizing form of Kempe's meditations, however, allows her to use images in ways that seem even more materially efficacious than has been suggested. Kempe's personalized uses of iconographic schema and of devotional images in her *Book* raise fascinating questions about the currency of visual objects as they circulate through language and are claimed and publicized through personal use.

The pressure to exhibit the self in the act of supporting the material life of the parish was a familiar and widely sanctioned social impulse in the late Middle Ages and has been the subject of increasing attention by the work of art historians interested in the interplay between images and their local production and use.[15] In England, the impulse to exhibit the self, whether as a single, family, or corporate identity in the form of a name, coat of arms, or portrait, has left its traces widely on objects that have survived Reformation iconoclasm.[16] A signal feature of fourteenth-century East Anglian manuscript illumination is the display of heraldic ornament, visible, for instance, in the Gorleston Psalter, a richly illustrated early fourteenth-century manuscript from the Norwich region. The coats of arms in the four corners of the border of the *Domine exaudi* page, most likely displaying the arms of important local families, are typical of the uses of armorial signatures throughout the manuscript, and indeed, in East Anglian manuscript illumination in general.[17] As we have seen with the Despenser Retable in Norwich Cathedral, coats of arms of local families are included prominently in the frame. Coats of arms also appear prominently in fifteenth-century East Anglian glass; in his study of the Norwich school of glass painting, Christopher Woodforde lists more than 130 identifiable coats of arms appearing in the glazing.[18]

While coats of arms display the patronage and power of noble families, names and portraits of donors commemorate the gifts of individuals and families of merchant classes. Work on lay patronage and devotion in the late Middle Ages has increasingly drawn attention to the deeply imbricated relationships among laity, clergy, and material culture, such that fifteenth-century East Anglia was, as Gail McMurray Gibson puts it, a highly material "theater of devotion," with the emphasis on theatricality and display. Kempe, who repeatedly recounts events in her home parish of St. Margaret's in Lynn, would have seen the huge commemorative brasses marking the tomb of Robert Braunche, mayor of Lynn in 1349 and 1359, and his wives Letitia and Margaret and also of Adam de Walsoken, mayor in 1335 and 1343, pictured with his wife Margaret.[19] We can only speculate how Kempe might have responded to these larger-than-life memorials to mayor's wives when her family, and she herself, a mayor's daughter, left no such records in the material life of the parish. Gail Gibson's discussions of John Baret of Bury St. Edmunds, John Clopton of Long Melford, and Ann Harling of East Harling are illuminating in this regard for their assessment of strategically visible patronage in fifteenth-century East Anglia. Names from the family of John Clopton, a wealthy clothier who helped finance the rebuilding of Long Melford church from the 1460s to the 1490s, appear in inscriptions around the exterior walls of the church and lady chapel, in effect emblazoning the church with the name of its principal sponsor (fig. 23).[20] Illustrating the power that women could wield as patrons in fifteenth-century

Norfolk, Ann Harling of East Harling left a highly visible legacy in the beautiful parish church of St. Peter and St. Paul. Ann Harling donated its windows, which remain some of the finest examples of fifteenth-century glass work in England, contributed to the rebuilding of the steeple of the parish in 1449, and in the 1460s founded a chantry chapel dedicated to St. Anne in the north aisle.[21]

Patronage in fourteenth- and fifteenth-century English cathedrals and parishes was at its most strategically visible in the use of donor portraits. Richard Marks's work on patronage in glazing indicates that images of donors most commonly appear in medieval stained glass from the thirteenth to the fifteenth century as small figures, hands pressed in prayer, kneeling below or beside a devotional scene.[22] The spectacular fourteenth- and fifteenth-century windows at York—some of which Kempe may well have seen and noted, since she recounts, in chapter 50, spending fourteen days in the minster—display numerous donor figures from not only the elite estates but also from the merchant class, a relationship strikingly illustrated in a window in the nave north aisle, which depicts goldsmith Richard Tunnoc presenting his window to St. William of York.[23] In this window both the saint and the goldsmith are so prominently displayed that it seems

Figure 23. Flint inscription, "Pray for the sowle of William Clopton esqwyer . . . ," c. 1496. Lady Chapel, Holy Trinity Church, Long Melford. Photo: V. Raguin.

fair to ask which of them is the real object of the gaze or even of devotion, the saint of the socially pious Richard Tunnoc.

The line between venerator and venerated, often flexible in a picture where both are represented, becomes even more ambiguous in the windows in Holy Trinity Church at Long Melford (Suffolk), which are packed with figures representing members of the Clopton family and people tied to them by important social links.[24] The extant images, originally from the clerestory, have been relocated to the north aisle. Suggestive for Margery's localization of herself within the space of the church, these donor images represent both men and women, offering a striking visual record of female patronage and influence in a late fifteenth-century Suffolk town. Members of the Clopton family, their heraldry constructing the very fabric of their dress in a public display of familial networks, make a commanding frieze across the fifteenth-century glazing. Images of family members include Anne Danvers, Elizabeth Fray, Margaret Fray, Catherine Mylde, Elizabeth Tilney, and Elizabeth Talbot (fig. 24) the source, so it is said, for the duchess in Teniel's illustrations for Lewis Carroll's *Alice in Wonderland*. In these windows the object of veneration is even absent. The images suggest that object of their veneration is the sanctuary that the figures face, or even the Clopton family network itself.

*   *   *

A closer look at the dialogue with Christ in the *Book* as well as the iconography of her visions points to the ways that Kempe participates in this culture of patronage. In *Christ's Body*, Sarah Beckwith argues that Kempe's "identification with Christ's body may be seen as a subversive and dynamic private appropriation of an imagery that was subject to intense and jealous clerical control."[25] While Kempe's uses of devotional imagery are no doubt appropriative on many levels, she positions herself in relation to an imagery that was also subject to an intense, and perhaps even jealous, *lay* control. Even though she claims to have transcended material desires when she describes her fashion requirements as a young woman, money continues to play a key role in her history, and needs for stylish clothing shift subtly to desires for money that she can use to endow churches and religious foundations. At several points in the *Book*, Kempe negotiates financially with Christ for money to make public endowments.[26] Although Christ repeatedly praises Kempe for the gift of souls, at other points in the text he even points to more material forms of patronage that she would have performed

Figure 24. Elizabeth Talbot and Elizabeth Tilney, late fifteenth century. Holy
Trinity Church, Long Melford. Photo: V. Raguin.

if she had the means. For instance, after she has missed the ferry and hence failed to make an expected visit to the nuns at Denny, Christ consoles her, saying that he, who knows "every thowt of thyn hert" (84.6869), also realizes that, if she had had the money, she would have liberally endowed churches and abbeys: "And I knowe wel, dowtyr, that thu hast many tymys thowt, yyf thu haddist an had many chirchys ful of nobelys [money/nobles], thu woldist a yovyn hem in my name. And also thu hast thowt that thu woldist, yyf thu haddist had good anow, a made many abbeys for my lofe, for religiows men and women to dwellyn in, and a yovyn iche of hem hundryd powndys be yer for to ben my servawntys" (84.6857–63). Christ's discourse, rich with consolation, is also rich with the language of payment and reward, even parsed in a specific figure, the generous hundred pounds a year with which she would endow the abbeys. The language of imagined charity throughout the chapter is contractual, Kempe's reward in heaven purchased either by the endowments to the abbeys and churches, by endowments for priests (84.6864), or purchased, as in Christ's discussion of lepers, by gifts of twenty pounds a year to each leper, so that each one could love and praise Christ (84.6871).

The explicitly contractual nature of this exchange, not unlike the contract Kempe negotiates with her husband to secure her sexual autonomy, is echoed in Christ's discourse throughout the book and often expressed in fantasies of patronage that blur distinctions between contractual spirituality, the private contract with God, and public benefice. When Kempe describes her struggles with exclusion from St. Margaret's because of her excessive weeping, Christ consoles her with a picture of the power of immaterial goods, with a play on "price" (63.5263) and poverty in reference to the beatitude, "Blessed are the poor": "Dowtyr, thu seyst oftyn to me in thi mende that riche men han gret cawse to lovyn me wel, and thu seyst ryth soth, for thu seyst I have yovyn hem meche good wherwyth thei may servyn me and lovyn me. But, good dowtyr, I prey the, love thu me wyth al thyn hert, and I schal yevyn the good anow to lovyn me wyth, for hevyn and erde schulde rathar faylyn than I shulde faylyn the" (63.5270–75). In his role as spiritual director/confessor and alter ego, Christ both acknowledges and soothes Kempe's preoccupation with her own poverty, her inability to endow and give, by promising her "good anow," goods enough that in this passage presumably are spiritual. Nevertheless, the language of the passage, "meche good" with which rich men serve and love God, draws from market economics. The longing for goods seems also to voice a longing for the religious clout that can be bought with cash.

The material inflections of longing in this passage may even specifically invoke the spectacle of "goods" possessed by the priory, to whose cloister she retreats when she fears her crying will get her ejected from the church (63.5220). A preoccupation of this section of the text, which deals with her rejection from parish communities for her excessive weeping, concerns Kempe's ability or right to occupy space; after she has been thrown out of the church, Christ speaks to her and promises that the friar who has preached against her will be outside the church and she will be in (63.5250–51). A few chapters earlier in the text Kempe speaks, with particular intensity, of the moment of her houseling in the prior's chapel (56), painting a brief and suggestive picture of herself first ejected from a public space and then received and welcomed, even physically embraced, in a decidedly masculine and private clerical space:

. . . but than encresyd hir cryes and hir wepyngys in-so-meche that prestys durst not howselyn [give communion] hir openly in the chirche, but prevyly in the Priowrys Chapel at Lenne, fro the peplys audiens. And in that chapel sche had so hy contemplacyon and so meche dalyawns of owr Lord, in-as-meche as sche was putte owt of chirche for hys lofe, that sche cryed what tyme sche schulde ben howselyd as yyf hir sowle and hir body schulde a partyd asundyr, so that tweyn men heldyn hir in her armys tyl hir cryng was cesyd, for sche myth not beryn the habundawns [abundance] of lofe that sche felt in the precyows sacrament, whech sche stedfastly beleyved was very God and man in the forme of breed. (56.4655–65)

Kempe's ecstatic record of this moment, focused on her desire for the Eucharist, also recounts a process by which she gains access, perhaps strategically, to a clerical space that would have displayed a wealth of devotional objects and images. Rejected from the church as a liturgical pariah, Kempe is then fostered in a private ritual within a private chapel which, according to Hope Emily Allen's note, may have contained the library as well as the "liturgical furniture."[27] Subsequently rejected from there as well (57), she is permitted, in a negotiated settlement between her confessor and the prior, to take the sacrament at the high altar at St. Margaret's every Sunday. To what extent is Kempe's own sense of literal poverty sharpened by her surroundings, and especially the priory, with its display of material wealth and ecclesiastical purchase power?

While Kempe does not answer this question directly, her appropriations of devotional imagery throughout her narrative suggest that the power of meditative images in her text is inseparable from other contingencies that lend those images value, and specifically contingencies of corporate and symbolic ownership in the culture of fifteenth-century East Anglia: prerogatives of class and gender that mediated not only ownership of but also physical access to images. While studies of ownership, inheritance, and donation indicate that some women in the fifteenth century owned private devotional images, especially Books of Hours, ownership and access to elite representation was largely restricted to women of the upper classes who possessed, unlike Margery Kempe, both literacy and money.[28] The chief distinction that would allow anyone more frequent and more intimate visual access to expensive and beautiful religious art was clerical privilege. The high altar within the chancel space was traditionally the site of the most lavish endowments;[29] and this space, according to custom, was restricted to the clergy.[30] A curious exception that would seem to affirm this restriction for Kempe's home church of St. Margaret's is even indicated in a bylaw of the Corporation of Lynn, 1424–25, where the ordinance for the obit of John Burghard includes, according to Lynn historian Henry Hillen, "a strangely digressive clause which insists upon the attendance of the whole Corporation at feast days generally. Special permission was accorded the mayor and Jurats [aldermen] — 24 only — to sit in the chancel."[31] The twenty-four lay people allowed to sit in the chancel on feast days, that is, would be men.

Within the nave, access to images was determined in part by class, since well-to-do families often commanded private pews and chapels that were close to the chancel or that had their own liturgical furnishings.[32] Pamela Graves argues that late medieval parish churches, as recipients of increasingly rich donations from both merchants and gentry, expressed corporate hierarchy and conflict in their very design.[33] While the architectural division between chancel and nave conventionally constituted and replicated a social division between clergy and laity, who were variously responsible as well for the upkeep of the two spaces, a jostling for status through visible marks of patronage and the strategic siting of ones' tomb altered these divisions, transforming all parts of the church into memorials for lay families. The Despenser Retable, as we have seen, presents a highly visible statement about local lay patronage and may have done so from the high altar in Norwich Cathedral, where Kempe might even have seen it displayed. In another example, Graves cites a church at Ashton, in Devon, which was rebuilt in the fifteenth century to accommodate a private chapel in the north aisle for the local manorial family. Whereas the nave was decorated with saints marked by their signs and attributes, chancel and chapel were decorated with images carrying text banners inscribed with the Sarum rite and new fifteenth-century liturgical developments. As Graves interprets this program, the chapel images offered the manorial family marked access to the power of clerical ritual: "The family sat visually and physically separated from their tenants and viewed their religion as integrated with the textual form, whereas for the rest, it was dominated by image and action."[34]

The Man of Sorrows

The most important image structuring Kempe's *Book* is the speaking Christ, Kempe's companion throughout much of the text. While Kempe's dialogue with Christ can be chiefly characterized by verbal intimacy with Christ as a lover and counselor, the relationship repeatedly locates Kempe in the position of a donor, even keeling below the image she has given. The narrative and iconographic detail with which Kempe endows Christ may suggest the Man of Sorrows, one of the most popular new devotional images to appear in Kempe's time.[35] Typically portraying Christ, simultaneously both living and dead, as a half-length figure, hands crossed over his torso,[36] the Man of Sorrows evolved into an important cult image in the fifteenth century, capturing the miracle of embodiment and transformation—the speaking Christ that is simultaneously flesh and eucharistic wafer, the body and the Mass.[37] The image also became an important indulgenced figure, especially in the form of the Gregorian Man of Sorrows, one of the most important eucharistic images of the fifteenth century. This legend, appearing around 1400 and becoming a popular subject for representation in glass, woodcuts, panel painting, and manuscript illustration in the fifteenth century, told the story that Christ, blood flowing from his wounds into the chalice at the altar, appeared to St. Gregory when he was saying Mass.[38] Many images representing the miracle include inscriptions explaining that an indulgence of thousands of years, said to have been granted by a Pope Clement, would be granted to those who prayed before it.[39]

Images of the Man of Sorrows in the Gregorian form as a half-length figure rising from the tomb and showing his wounds are extant in fifteenth-century English glazing at several sites.[40] In East Anglian glazing the figure also takes the form of the pietà, the Man of Sorrows held in the Virgin's arms, as well as the Throne of Mercy with God the Father holding the body of his son in his arms, important new images in fifteenth-century English devotional art. Although most extant images postdate Margery Kempe's *Book*, the figure was present in the early fifteenth century and widespread by the end of Kempe's life.[41] Particularly suggestive for its elision of the image with a figure of donation is a hybrid Man of Sorrows/pietà or Lady of Pity, from Long Melford, with a donor in blue below (fig. 25). In this image Christ, his body speckled with blood, looks up at his mother who is holding him in her lap and gestures with his right hand in what is likely a speech gesture. Most arresting in this window is its representation of emotional dialogue between the mother and son. Both are dramatically displayed. Her face reflects pain, and his body and gestures both work to suggest his attempt to explain his pain to her.[42] Miniaturized below this scene, the

Figure 25. Lady of Pity, with donor, late fifteenth century. Holy Trinity Church, Long Melford. Photo: V. Raguin.

donor, a cleric—or, as Woodforde suggests, John Clopton, chief patron of
the rebuilding of Long Melford church in the late fifteenth century—maintains a prominent place in this devotional drama.[43] The donor's placement
below one of the central images in the glazing is above all a speech act for
public continuity, a visual record to ease his soul through purgatory even
as it entrenches his family's prominence.

It is most probable that Kempe would have encountered an image
of the Man of Sorrows in early fifteenth-century England. In her travels
in Rome she could also have seen the image, or even the famous wonder-
working icon in Santa Croce in Gerusalemme, even though she does not list
this particular church among her inventory of churches visited in Rome.[44]
The *Prayer Book of Humphrey Duke of Gloucester*, whose dates (1390–1447)
are close to Kempe's own, contains a Man of Sorrows that offers a parallel
for Kempe's imagined Christ, one that also suggests how such images were
being understood and used in her time. In this image (fig. 26), which is
combined with a Trinity, the duke is presented by St. Alban to the Man
of Sorrows, and carries a Latin scroll that reads "Your pity [pietas] O Lord
has been worked in me."[45] The characteristics with which Kempe endows
Christ in their dialogue—bleeding wounds, the ability to speak, the powers of indulgence—suggest that she has constructed her narrative image
after visual models such as this, popular on the Continent and newly available in England in her time. In the first episode in which Kempe describes
Christ speaking to her, she recounts how she kneels below him, assuming
a pose suggestive of both a petitioner for indulgence as well a donor. Like
the donor in blue in the Long Melford window, Kempe's gives herself a
spot next to a speaking icon. Kempe also evokes the iconography of the
Man of Sorrows by picturing the speaking Christ as a hybrid figure of pity,
suffering, and eucharistic power:

Than on a Fryday beforn Crystmes Day, as this creatur, knelyng in a chapel of Seynt
John wythinne a cherch of Seynt Margrete in N, wept wondir sore, askyng mercy
and forgyfnes of hir synnes and hir trespas, owyr mercyful Lord Cryst Jhesu,
blessyd mot he be, ravysched hir spyryt and seyd onto hir:
"Dowtyr, why wepyst thow so sor? I am comyn to the, Jhesu Cryst, that
deyd on the crosse sufferyng byttyr peynes and passyons for the." (5.491–98)

The Christ that Margery hears and seems to see as she kneels in the chapel
of St. John in St. Margaret's evokes the Man of Sorrows by identifying
himself as dead: "Jhesu Cryst, that deyd on the crosse sufferyng byttyr
peynes and passyons for the." As his dialogue continues, Christ also speaks

Figure 26. Humphrey, duke of Gloucester, kneeling before the Man of Sorrows. *Prayer Book of Humphrey Duke of Gloucester*, 1430–47. London, BL MS Royal 2.B.I, fol. 8. © British Library Board. All rights reserved.

"A," sche seyd, "This is the Boke of Lyfe."

And sche saw in the boke the Trinite, and al in gold. Than seyd sche to the childe:

"Wher is my name?"

The childe answeryd and seyd: "Her is thi name, at the Trinyte foot wretyn," and therwyth he was a-go, sche wist not how." (85.6958–70)

The Trinity that Kempe sees is an image painted in gold, and the self that she demands to see in the image is a symbol of herself, her name, authorizing a relationship between herself and the Trinity. The image contains multiple social and iconic echoes: the angel bearing the Book of Life recalls the angel of Revelation, while his act suggests a ceremony of ritual presentation, a *liber vitae* presented to a wealthy patron. Imagining a Book of Life, Kempe may be echoing St. Bridget, who has a vision of a Book of Life;[48] she may also be aligning herself with St. Katherine, one of the saints frequently named in her text. In an early fifteenth-version of the *Life of Saint Katherine* that includes the mystical marriage, when the virgins and martyrs present Katherine to the Virgin Mary they say that "at your commaundement we present hur, our der sistre, whose name ys specially wrytyn in the [boke] of euerlastyng life."[49] To have one's name written in a "Book of Life" is to have one's name recorded in a necrology. English monasteries kept registers known as *Libri Vitae,* which were lists of benefactors for whom masses would be recited.[50] The *Liber Vitae* or New Minster Register, for example, contains a list of the monks and benefactors to be commemorated during the services.[51] Kempe's insistence on seeing her own name etched below the image on the presentation page of a Book of Life thus transforms a conventional image denoting salvation into one of conspicuous patronage. She imagines the Book of Life as a literal book and locates her name visibly within it.

In beginning the set of visions of chapter 85 with this personalized dedication page, Kempe sets the stage for "reading" the visions that follow as pictorial moments, images that also have been lifted from the pages of a manuscript. With this first image in particular Margery dramatizes an anxious relationship between her vision and a devotional object, even establishing a pictorial hermeneutic for reading the following scenes as images as well. Present in familiar devotional scenes, Kempe is both a pious woman reliving crucial moments in the life of the holy family and also a powerful and socially visible patron of the devotional arts. With this image, indeed, as with her carefully constructed relationship to a speaking Christ, Kempe's meditations serve as a clearly material asset. They define her spiritual election as a special and privileged recognition by Christ and the holy family; they also give her a place among the donors and patrons of Lynn.

But what, exactly, is the Trinity that Kempe pictures in the Book of Life? Although she explicitly names the image in chapter 85, she does not describe it, nor does she describe the images of the Trinity to which she prays elsewhere in her text. Her reference could suggest an image such as the circular and textual Trinity that surmounts the Man of Sorrows in Long Melford (fig. 27) or the church's totemic rabbit-ear Trinity below. A more

Figure 27. Trinity, late fifteenth century, Holy Trinity Church, Long Melford. Photo: V. Raguin.

likely prototype for Kempe's reference, however, would be the closely framed grouping of God, crucifixion, and dove, a trinitarian form that survives widely in English alabasters, with over eighty extant examples.[52] As a common subject for altarpieces—so common, in fact, that in the fifteenth century the small alabaster triptychs designed to stand on an altar were quite inexpensive[53]—the image was both public and authoritative, frequently placed at the center of worship. In the most common scheme, God is seated, the crucified Christ between his knees (Throne of Mercy), with the central grouping often surrounded by attendant figures, usually angels. The image is generally frontal and magisterial in spite of its dramatic postural paradoxes. An unusually fine surviving early fifteenth-century alabaster from the Boston Museum of Fine Arts includes as well secular donors kneeling at the right and left of God's knees (fig. 28). The father is dramatically larger than the son; the son's crucified body is pendant, dead, in contrast to the seated muscularity of the father. The image conflates manly authority with maternal and even natal care, the small crucifix cradled between the father's knees. The similar format of a fourteenth-century wall painting from Oxfordshire, which shows a Trinity flanked by a kneeling donor at the side, suggests that this particular form of visible patronage was deemed appropriate for very different venues (fig. 29).[54] Kempe imagines her name below a Trinity in an elite manuscript, though from first-hand experience she would have been more familiar with the image from wall painting.

These records of surviving images and accounts of their placement and use in English parishes thus suggest that Kempe's vision is shaped around an image that is highly conventional and squarely centered in liturgical ritual. Her vision of a Trinity on a presentation volume signed by her would also seem to stake an important claim for her orthodoxy in the face of repeated accusations of Lollardy.[55] As we have seen in Nicholas Love's *Mirror*, the Trinity, in its most conventional form grouping God, crucified Christ, and dove, is an image to which, Anne Hudson writes, "Wyclif and his followers took particular exception."[56] In its condemnation of offerings to "ymages of tre and of ston" the Twelve Conclusions of the Lollards singles out the "usual" image of the Trinity as particularly offensive and problematic: "And þow þis forbodin ymagerie be a bok of errour to þe lewid [ignorant] puple, ȝet þe ymage usuel of Trinite is most abhominable."[57]

However Kempe pictures the Trinity in this scene, what seems to matter most to her is the inscription of her name beneath the foot, which presumably would mean beneath the feet of the crucifix, in terms that display her orthodoxy. The insistence on a gesture of donation, of finding her name

inscribed, repeats one of the most characteristic features of Margery's
Book—the drive to authorize herself, to name drop, (though here it is *her*
name that is dropped) and connect herself with powerful clerical figures.
Yet even though modern readers often perceive these concerns with public
recognition as idiosyncratic, similar desires are echoed widely in contemporary practices of patronage. The dropping of one's name, leaving visible

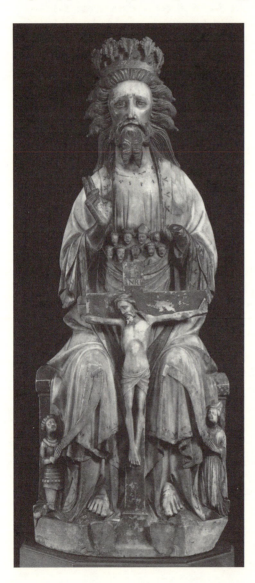

Figure 28. Unidentified artist,
English, fifteenth century,
English. *Bosom of Abraham*
Trinity. Object place: Europe,
Nottingham, England, 1420–50.
Stone and alabaster with poly-
chromy and gilding. 95.9 × 38.1 ×
12.7 cm (37¾ × 15 × 5 in.).
Museum of Fine Arts, Boston.
Decorative Arts Special Fund,
27.852. Photograph © 2007
Museum of Fine Arts, Boston.

Figure 29. Trinity with donor. Wall painting, c. 1325. St. Bartholomew's Church, Ducklington, Oxfordshire. After E. W. Tristram, *English Wall Painting of the Fourteenth Century* (London: Routledge & Kegan Paul, 1955), fig. 58.

traces on parish buildings, was as we have seen a gesture of wide currency in fifteenth-century England, even surviving in images of the Trinity that suggest parallels to her vision. In his study of donor images in late medieval England, Nigel Morgan writes that devotion to the Trinity through the use of donor images appears in England in the thirteenth century and continues with the International Gothic.[58] At the Church of the Assumption of the Blessed Virgin Mary in Attleborough, East Anglia, a Trinity painted on the right central panel of the chancel parclose sits above the names of the donors below, inscribed with the conventional tag "orate pro . . ." An image of a donor kneeling below the Trinity in a clerestory window on the north side of the nave at Ringland[59] and an image of a mitred bishop or abbot, presenting his heart to a trinitarian grouping in a fifteenth-century alabaster,[60] both picture a visible alliance between the image and its giver, as does a Carmelite Missal, c. 1393, which depicts a lateral Trinity with Virgin and donors.[61] Even more suggestive for Kempe's vision in chapter 85 (though it postdates her *Book)* is a late fifteenth-century window from Holy Trinity Goodramgate in which is displayed a Trinity hybrid with Man of Sorrows in the father's arms. The central image is flanked by the donor, John Walker, seen at the foot of the Trinity with a scroll, "Te adoro et glorifico O Beata Trinitas."[62]

Kempe's account of the presentation of the Book of Life suggests images of donation like these, picturing her as both the donor whose name is inscribed in the book and also the recipient of the gift. The larger textual context for this episode further underscores her role as patron. Kempe's vision of the Trinity in chapter 85, introduced by her customary paratactic folk formula "on a tyme" that structures each chapter as a self-contained narrative unit, is framed by a larger meditation on the spiritual rewards of material patronage. First Christ recognizes that she would endow the abbeys with one hundred pounds a year if she could; then an angel approaches with a magnificent book, as if to exhibit a specific devotional object that she has personally commissioned. Her name in the Book of Life thus resonates with complex forms of desire: the desire for sanctity that Kempe exhibits throughout her book; the anxious insistence on orthodoxy in the face of accusations of Lollardy; the desire for recognition by the socially elite, perhaps even by the locally prominent Trinity guild to which her father belonged. Most tellingly, through her vision of her name in the Book of Life and the surrounding discourse on the spiritual goods money can buy, Kempe claims a place within a local building campaign. Her question is poignant, even haunting, for it expresses exclusion from power and money. Perhaps she also asks "where is my name" because her name is there, but she is unable to read it.

*   *   *

What became of the *Book of Margery Kempe* immediately after its composition is unknown, but it by the late fifteenth century it appears to have come into the possession of the Carthusian Abbey of Mount Grace in northern Yorkshire. A notation in the manuscript in a late fifteenth-century hand reads, "Liber Montis Gracie. This boke is of Mountegrace."[63] Mount Grace was also the home of Nicholas Love, the first prior at the abbey's incorporation in 1410.[64] In both the *Mirror* and Kempe's *Book*, Christ plays a key and notably similar role. Parts of the Kempe's visions appear to be directly modeled after the life of Christ as represented in the *Meditations* and perhaps even the *Mirror* itself. While these connections have been well documented, less attention has been paid to echoes between the iconography of Christ in these texts and in Carthusian imagery in general, in which the Man of Sorrows or *imago pietatis* became, during the fifteenth century, a kind of icon of the order.[65] In Chapter 6 I have argued that Nicholas Love counters reformist polemic that decried images as "dead stocks" by imagining a living Christ and urging the reader to picture a narrative and dramatic Jesus who communicates with him or her in ways that are similar to the Man of Sorrows. A common feature of Christ as Man of Sorrows is the quality of engaged half-life; Christ is not a mortuary figure nor a figure of the living, but something in between, often speaking with the worshipper even as he displays his wounds.[66] These are the characteristics that are so vividly dramatized in the mid-fifteenth-century Carthusian Miscellany, British Library Add. 37049. Most likely from a northern Carthusian house, perhaps even Mount Grace, this cohesive manuscript is remarkable for its dynamic interchange between written text and pictures.[67] Its images, notably simple in quality, are insistently textualized, spliced with writing or appended with speech scrolls. Numerous drawings of Christ as a Man of Sorrows or *imago pietatis* appear throughout the manuscript in ways that are often developed far beyond the traditional posture of the half-length figure, arms crossed in front of him, which is the form taken by the Man of Sorrows in the manuscript's frontispiece. In some of these tinted drawings Jesus, bleeding profusely from all parts of his body, walks, gestures, and speaks, even pointing to his own heart as text. In fol. 20r Christ raises his right hand above a large heart in a gesture that combines prayer, the *demonstratio vulneratum* or display of his wounds, with a speech gesture[68] as the accompanying poem addresses the reader, "O man unkynde / hafe in mynde / my paynes smert / Beholde and see / that is for the / percyd my hert" (fig. 30). The heart, slashed with wounds, looks remarkably like a mouth, its lips inscribed with the words, "þis þe mesure of þe wounde I sufferd for oure redempcion." Although gestures indicating speech in medieval manuscripts are usually manual rather than oral, nevertheless the inscribed hearts in the Carthusian Miscellany, with their emblemlike symbolism, seem to invite viewers into a novel hermeneutic in which the heart literally speaks. The synergy between picture and speech is furthered by the lyric dialogue, "Querela divina" and the "Responsio humana," that the picture illustrates. Illustration and text are dynamically engaged, such that Christ and his heart have literally become speaking images. The similar text/image arrangement in fol. 24r may even pun on "here" to suggest that the heart is both the object of devotion and even a speaking agent to which we are invited to listen. The man of sorrows stands next to the heart, this time gesturing with his left hand, its wounded palm displayed. The text, "O mankynde / hafe in thi mynde / my passion smert / And thu sal fynde / me ful kynde / lo here my hert," is placed right next to Christ's head and above his gesturing hand; in effect this wounded Christ both shows the heart itemized with its number of wounds and drops of blood and also invites us to attend. Speaking directly to the reader in ways similar to Christ in Kempe's *Book* or the narrator in Love's *Mirror*, Christ in these pictures has transformed from devotional icon to dramatic agent. As the talking dead, he is almost the "quick" image of Christ.

Kempe's Jesus, who shares qualities of animation, wounds, and speech, may also have been imagined within this iconographic tradition. The fifteenth-century reader who contributed the *Book* to Mount Grace may have recognized, in the *Book*'s representation of a Man of Sorrows with a narrative donor, the aptness of her text for the monastery's library. What Love and Kempe share above all is an interest in a figuration of objects of popular piety through imaginative interaction with those objects in ways that dissolve their materiality and even bring them to life. Love's *Mirror* names few images, as we have seen, and even expresses unease with the use of devotional objects or the world of imaged piety, yet gives Jesus a vital if virtual presence through directed meditation. Kempe's book articulates a somewhat different response to imaged devotion by including its author as a participant in dialogue with Christ, enacting the *Mirror*'s directives to picture the scenes of Christ's life as if we were there. In neither of these

Figure 30. Man of Sorrows and heart, mid-fifteenth century. London, BL MS Add. 37049, fol. 20r. © British Library Board. All rights reserved.

texts, both of which assert orthodoxy in the face of the explicit threat of Lollardy, is Christ a dead image.

For Kempe, the animation of the image also involves acts of virtual patronage. The meditations that Kempe localizes at altars throughout the environs of Lynn color the panels, fill the niches, and glaze the main and tracery lights in a demonstration of a vividly imagined and enacted role as patron, donor, and—with her figuration of herself praying before indulgenced images—as spiritual intercessor. Kempe's "devotional theater" not only takes its form from the images in glass, panel painting, and ecclesiastical ornament that would have surrounded her in fifteenth-century East Anglia, but also takes its form from the dynamic rebuilding campaigns that were occurring throughout parishes and lay buildings in Norfolk and Suffolk.[69] Even some of the buildings she names were rebuilt within the scope of the *Book*. St. Nicholas's Chapel, St. Margaret's chapel-of-ease that figures so prominently in Kempe's text as the subject of a separatist plot, was rebuilt c. 1429;[70] and following the fire described in the *Book*, the guildhall in Lynn was rebuilt in the 1420s. Kempe's "contemplacyon" and "meditacyon,"[71] private acts in which she imagines herself talking with Christ or participating with the holy family, are thus also public displays that make startlingly assertive and keen-eyed claims on objects of popular piety. The interactive compositon of her "meditatacyons" repeatedly mark Kempe as phantasmatic donor, a visible patron gifted with the means and social power to endow and control the material life of the churches in which her meditations occur. Kempe's question reverberates as central to her *Book* and also to the East Anglian redevelopment project of the fifteenth century. *Hic iacet. Orate pro nobis*. Here is my name.

Notes

Introduction

1. Charles William Stubbs, *Historical Memorials of Ely Cathedral* (New York: Scribners, 1897), 116.

2. For theories about the date of the iconoclasm, see Nigel Ramsay, "The Dean and Chapter, Reformation to Restoration: 1541–1660," in *A History of Ely Cathedral*, ed. Peter Meadows and Nigel Ramsay (Woodbridge, Suffolk: Boydell, 2003), 173n. Ramsay dates the destruction to Bishop Goodrich's Ely Injunctions of 1541 for the suppression of images, while other historians have suggested dates as late as the seventeenth century during the Commonwealth.

3. Michael O'Connell, *The Idolatrous Eye: Iconoclasm and Theater in Early-Modern England* (New York: Oxford University Press, 2000), 3.

4. Nicola Coldstream, "Ely Cathedral: The Fourteenth-Century Work," in *Medieval Art and Architecture at Ely Cathedral*, Transactions of the British Archaeological Association 2 (Leeds: Maney & Son, 1979), 28–46. The narrative of the sculptures in the spandrels has been reconstructed by M. R. James, *The Sculptures in the Lady Chapel at Ely* (London: D. Nutt, 1895).

5. Coldstream, "Ely Cathedral," 38.

6. D. J. Stewart, *On the Architectural History of Ely Cathedral* (London: Van-Voorst, 1868), 141.

7. For general surveys on the multiplication of imagery in the late Middle Ages, see Margaret Aston, *England's Iconoclasts*: vol. 1, *Laws Against Images* (Oxford: Clarendon Press, 1988), 20–34, and for the Injunctions against images under Henry VIII, 222–46; see also Kathleen Kamerick, *Popular Piety and Art in the Late Middle Ages: Image Worship and Idolatry in England, 1350–1500* (New York: Palgrave, 2002), 4–5.

8. Duffy, *The Stripping of the Altars: Traditional Religion in England, 1400–1580* (London: Yale University Press, 1992), 156.

9. Richard Marks, *Image and Devotion in Late Medieval England* (Phoenix Mill, Gloucestershire, U.K.: Sutton Publishing Ltd., 2004), 86–87.

10. Paul Binski, "The English Parish Church and Its Art in the Later Middle Ages: A Review of the Problem," *Studies in Iconography* 20 (1999): 10.

11. Hans Belting, *The Image and Its Public in the Middle Ages: Form and Function of Early Paintings of the Passion*, trans. Mark Bartusis and Raymond Meyer (New Rochelle, N.Y.: Caratzas, 1990), 215.

12. Michael Camille, *The Gothic Idol: Ideology and Image-Making in Medieval Art* (Cambridge: Cambridge University Press, 1989), 219, 215.

13. Theories of extramission as propounded by Augustine argue that vision is accomplished when rays projected by the eye met with species (rays) emitted by the object. Intromission theory, propounded by late medieval optical theorists Avicenna and Bacon, among others, foreground the role of the object; as Michael Camille puts it, "the intromission model took the emphasis away from vision and onto the power of images themselves, whose eyes, as in cult statues and devotional images, could stare back," "Before the Gaze: The Internal Senses and Late Medieval Practices of Seeing," in *Visuality Before and Beyond the Renaissance*, ed. Robert S. Nelson (Cambridge: Cambridge University Press, 2000), 207. For the gaze on Christ, see Sarah Stanbury, "Regimes of the Visual in Premodern England. Gaze, Body, and Chaucer's *Clerk's Tale*," *New Literary History* 28 (1997): 261–90; on seeing God in medieval theater, see Sarah Beckwith, "*Sacrum Signum*: Sacramentality and Dissent in York's Theatre of Corpus Christi," in *Criticism and Dissent in the Middle Ages*, ed. Rita Copeland (Cambridge: Cambridge University Press, 1996), 264–88; and for a recent study that considers medieval optical theory and visual metaphor in relation to later visual theorists, see Suzannah Biernoff, *Sight and Embodiment in the Middle Ages* (New York: Palgrave, 2002), 102, "whether carnal or scientific, vision was a dynamic extension of the subject into the world and at the same time a penetration and alteration of the viewer's body by the object."

14. Studies of the eucharistic rite, especially by Miri Rubin, *Corpus Christi: The Eucharist in Late Medieval Culture* (Cambridge: Cambridge University Press, 1991), have demonstrated its importance, as strategically deployed spectacle, to clerical power in the late Middle Ages; see also Sarah Beckwith, *Christ's Body: Identity, Culture and Society in Late Medieval Writings* (New York: Routledge, 1993), 33–37; and David Aers and Lynn Staley, *The Powers of the Holy: Religion, Politics, and Gender in Late Medieval English Culture* (University Park: Pennsylvania State University Press, 1996), 24–27; Camille, *Gothic Idol*, 219, also comments on the breakdown between image and body at the moment of the elevation.

15. Aston, *England's Iconoclasts*, 123, notes that there is evidence for academic debates about the veneration of devotional images at Oxford as early as 1372–73 in the *Postilla super Mattheum* of William Woodford.

16. "Et patet quod ymagines tam bene quam male possunt fieri: bene ad excitandum, facilitandum et accendendum mentes fidelium, ut colant devocius Deum suum; et male ut occasione ymaginum a veritate fidei aberretur, ut ymago illa vel latria vel dulia adoretur . . . ," *Tractatus de Mandatis Divinis*, ed. Johann Loserth and F. D. Matthew, Wyclif Society (London: C. K. Paul, 1922), 156; trans. Aston, *England's Iconoclasts*, 99; see also W. R. Jones, "Lollards and Images: The Defense of Religious Art in the Later Middle Ages," *Journal of the History of Ideas* 34.1 (1973): 28–29.

17. Aston, *England's Iconoclasts*, 105; see also Jones, "Lollards and Images," 37–39; for a succinct review of late medieval texts that take up the image debate, see also Anne Hudson, ed., *Selections from English Wycliffite Writings* (Cambridge: Cambridge University Press, 1978), 179–81 (hereafter cited as *SEWW*). For an argument locating the short text of Julian of Norwich's *Revelations* in the 1380s on the basis of its reference to images and the image debate, see Nicholas Watson, "The Composition of Julian of Norwich's *Revelation of Love*," *Speculum* 68 (1993): esp. 659–65.

18. In *Sermons of Thomas Brinton*, ed. Sister Mary Aquinas Devlin, Camden Third Series (London: Royal Historical Society, 1954), 2:495, cited in Aston, *England's Iconoclasts*, 105.

19. Aston, *England's Iconoclasts*, 146.

20. *Dives and Pauper*, vol. 1, ed. Priscilla Heath Barnum, EETS, 275 (London: Oxford University Press, 1976). See also discussion in Aston, *England's Iconoclasts*, 144–45; and on its evasive orthodoxy see Anne Hudson, *The Premature Reformation: Wycliffite Texts and Lollard History* (Oxford: Clarendon Press, 1988), 418–20.

21. Barnum, *Dives and Pauper*, x.

22. Ibid., 81.

23. Ibid., 83, 85.

24. Ibid., 82.

25. A. J. Minnis, *Chaucer and Pagan Antiquity* (Cambridge: D. S. Brewer, 1982), 38–39, notes that this translation of Guillaume de Deguileville's *Le Pèlerinage de la vie humaine* is itself an elaboration of an episode in Wisdom 13:11–19.

26. John Lydgate, *The Pilgrimage of the Life of Man*, ed. F. J. Furnivall, EETS, e.s., 77 (London: Kegan Paul, Trench, Trübner, 1899), 556.

27. On this passage, see also Susan K. Hagen, *Allegorical Remembrance: A Study of The Pilgrimage of the Life of Man as a Medieval Treatise on Seeing and Remembering* (Athens: University of Georgia Press, 1990), 97–99.

28. Michael Camille, "The Iconoclast's Desire: Deguileville's Idolatry in France and England," in *Images, Idolatry, and Iconoclasm in Late Medieval England: Textuality and the Visual Image*, ed. Jeremy Dimmick, James Simpson, and Nicolette Zeeman (Oxford: Oxford University Press, 2002), 170–71.

29. London, BL MS Additional 24202, ff. 26–28v, in *SEWW*, ed. Hudson, 83–88 (at 84).

30. Camille, *Gothic Idol*, 197–220; and "Iconoclast's Desire," 151–71.

31. Kathleen L. Scott, *Later Gothic Manuscripts 1390–1490* (London: Harvey Miller, 1996), 1:44–45; and Camille, "Iconoclast's Desire," 169.

32. Hudson, *Premature Reformation*, 15–21, 355–56; Nicholas Watson, "Censorship and Cultural Change in Late-Medieval England: Vernacular Theology, the Oxford Translation Debate, and Arundel's Constitutions of 1409," *Speculum* 70 (1995): esp. 825–30.

33. Aers and Staley, *Powers of the Holy*, 43–76, 107–78; and Watson, "Composition."

34. Watson, "Censorship and Cultural Change"; Simpson, *Reform and Cultural Revolution*, esp. 383–457. For essays that respond to Watson and address ramifications of "vernacular theology," see cluster 1, "Vernacular Theology and Medieval Studies," ed. Bruce Holsinger and Elizabeth Robertson, in *Literary History and the Religious Turn*, *English Language Notes* 44 (2006): 77–137.

35. Paul Strohm, *England's Empty Throne: Usurpation and the Language of Legitimation, 1399–1422* (New Haven, Conn.: Yale University Press, 1998), esp. 32–62, 128–52.

36. Important contributions include Gail McMurray Gibson, *The Theater of Devotion: East Anglian Drama and Society in the Late Middle Ages* (Chicago: University of Chicago Press, 1989); Duffy, *Stripping of the Altars*; Rubin, *Corpus Christi*;

Beckwith, *Christ's Body*; and Jonathan Hughes, *Pastors and Visionaries: Religion and Secular Life in Late Medieval Yorkshire* (Woodbridge, Suffolk: Boydell, 1988); and Katherine L. French, Gary G. Gibbs, and Beat A. Kümin, eds., *The Parish in English Life* (Manchester: Manchester University Press, 1997).

37. Peter Pels, "The Spirit of Matter: On Fetish, Rarity, Fact, and Fancy," in *Border Fetishisms: Material Objects in Unstable Spaces*, ed. Patricia Spyer (New York: Routledge, 1998), 94.

38. Sut Jhally, *The Codes of Advertising: Fetishism and the Political Economy of Meaning in the Consumer Society* (New York: St. Martin's Press, 1987), 29.

39. For fetish discourse as a language of demystification, see James J. Kearney, "Trinket, Idol, Fetish: Some Notes on Iconoclasm and the Language of Materiality in Reformation England," *Shakespeare Studies* 28 (2000): 260; Webb Keane, "Calvin in the Tropics: Objects and Subjects at the Religious Frontier," in *Border Fetishisms*, ed. Spyer, 13; William Pietz, "The Problem of the Fetish, I," *Res* 9 (Spring 1985): 14.

40. Pietz, "The Problem of the Fetish, II: The Origin of the Fetish," *Res* 13 (Spring 1987): 23–45.

41. Pietz, "Fetish, II," 35.

42. "Sinnlich übersinnliches Ding"; see William Pietz, "Fetishism and Materialism: The Limits of Theory in Marx," in *Fetishism as Cultural Discourse*, ed. Emily Apter and William Pietz (Ithaca, N.Y.: Cornell University Press, 1993), 130.

43. London, BL MS Additional 24202, ff. 26–28v, in *SEWW*, ed. Hudson, 83; for a discussion of the treatise, see also Carolyn Collette, *Species, Phantasms, and Images: Vision and Medieval Psychology in "The Canterbury Tales"* (Ann Arbor: University of Michigan Press, 2001), 112–14.

44. *SEWW*, 182n.

45. Ibid., 87.

46. Ibid., 27.

47. In Lollard polemic images and relics are often folded together, as in the Twelve Conclusions; see *SEWW*, 27. Patrick Geary argues that in the West from the fourteenth century on images came to compete with relics as objects of devotional power, "Sacred Commodities: The Circulation of Medieval Relics," in *The Social Life of Things: Commodities in Cultural Perspective*, ed. Arjun Appadurai (New York: Cambridge University Press, 1986), 188. See also Alain Besançon, *The Forbidden Image: An Intellectual History of Iconoclasm*, trans. Jane Marie Todd (Chicago: University of Chicago Press, 2000), 152–53, for an argument that relics generally ranked above images in the hierarchy of worship.

48. Sarah Beckwith, *Signifying God: Social Relation and Symbolic Act in the York Corpus Christi Plays* (Chicago: University of Chicago Press, 2001), 70–71, in a comment on the sacramental theology of Dominican theologian Edward Schillebeeckx, *Christ: The Sacrament of the Encounter with God* (New York: Sheed and Ward, 1963).

49. Hugh of St. Victor, *On the Sacraments of the Christian Faith*, trans. Roy J. Deferrari (Cambridge, Mass.: Medieval Academy of America, 1951), 155.

50. Humbert of Romans, *Beati Umberti sermones* (Venice, 1603), fol. 59rb, cited by Miri Rubin, *Corpus Christi*, 36; see also Beckwith, *Signifying God*, 60.

51. John of Damascus, *On the Divine Images,* First Apostasy, section 16, trans. David Anderson (Crestwood, N.J.: St. Vladimir's Seminary, 1980), 23; cited in

O'Connell, *The Idolatrous Eye*, 39–40. For a succinct history of the Byzantine controversy, see David Hawkes, *Idols of the Marketplace: Idolatry and Commodity Fetishism in English Literature, 1580–1680* (New York: Palgrave, 2001), 59–66.

52. Besançon, *The Forbidden Image,* 126.

53. *Two Wycliffite Texts: The Sermon of William Taylor 1406; the Testimony of William Thorpe 1407*, ed. Anne Hudson, EETS, o.s., 301 (Oxford: Oxford University Press, 1993), 57.

54. ". . . quia licet ymagines ecclesiae non possunt representare oculis intuencium scilicet aliquam similitudinem diuine nature in seipsa, p[ossun]t representare tamen et significare similitudinem humane nature assumpte, in qua Deus operatus est salutem humanam. . . ," *De Adoracione Ymaginum,* in *Walter Hilton's Latin Writings*, vol. 1, ed. John P. H. Clark and Cheryl Taylor, Analecta Cartusiana 124 (Salzburg: Institut für Anglistik and Amerikanistik, 1987), 199, trans. Kathleen Derrig, (unpublished manuscript), 12.

55. Hilton, *De Adoracione Ymaginum,* "ut signa venerantur, non ut res," 199, trans. Derrig, 12.

56. *Trialogus*, ed. G. Lechler (Oxford: Clarendon Press, 1869), 247, cited in Strohm, *England's Empty Throne*, 48. The remark is by a commentator on Wyclif's *Trialogus*, completed after the Blackfriar's Council in 1382.

57. Strohm, *England's Empty Throne*, 138.

58. *The Voyages of Cadamosto, and other documents on Western Africa in the second half of the fifteenth century*, ed. and trans. G. R. Crone (London: Hakluyt Society, 1937), 68; also cited in Pietz "Fetish, I," 9. Cadamosto follows this observation with further details on differing standards of value in trading, describing how the Gambians traded baboons and apes for "objects of little worth, giving ten *marchetti* for the value of one," *Voyages*, 69.

59. Pietz, "Fetish, II," 36.

60. Anne McClintock, *Imperial Leather: Race, Gender and Sexuality in the Colonial Contest* (New York: Routledge, 1995), 184–87.

61. Ibid., "Soft-Soaping Empire," 207–31.

62. Aston, *England's Iconoclasts*, 124–32; and Margaret Aston, *Faith and Fire: Popular and Unpopular Religion, 1350–1600* (London: Hambledon Press, 1993), 219–29.

63. Hudson, *SEWW*, 83, 84.

64. Ibid., 85.

65. *Six Ecclesiastical Satires*, ed. James M. Dean. TEAMS (Kalamazoo, Mich.: Medieval Institute Publications, 1991), 12, lines 123–28.

66. Ibid., 25, lines 560–63.

67. Ibid., 12, line 129.

68. *SEWW*, 84; see Aston, *Faith and Fire*, 224. For the yoking of idolatry and commodity fetishism in Reformation rhetoric, see especially Hawkes, *Idols of the Marketplace*, 6–7, 17, 21.

69. *Dives and Pauper*, 83–113.

70. Ibid., 101.

71. William Langland, *Piers Plowman: The B Version*, ed. George Kane and E. Talbot Donaldson (London: Athlone Press, 1975; rev. ed. 1988), 3:48–50, 59–63.

72. *SEWW*, 87.

73. London, BL MS Harl. 211, fol. 48r; cited in Aston, *England's Iconoclasts*, 116.

74. *The Lanterne of Liƺt*, ed. Lilian M. Swinburn, EETS, o.s., 151 (London: Kegan Paul, Trench, Trübner & Co., 1917), 84.

75. Ibid., 84–85.

76. Joel Kaye, *Economy and Nature in the Fourteenth Century: Money, Market Exchange, and the Emergence of Scientific Thought* (Cambridge: Cambridge University Press, 1998), 15–36.

77. *Dives and Pauper*, 81.

78. Reginald Pecock, *Repressor of Overmuch Blaming of the Clergy*, ed. Churchill Babington (London: Longman, 1860), 1:183–84, also 136–37; see Margaret Aston, "The Use of Images," in *Gothic: Art for England 1400–1547*, ed. Richard Marks and Paul Williamson, with Eleanor Townsend (London: Victoria and Albert Publications, 2003), 69.

79. Gibson, *Theater of Devotion*, 26.

80. Francis Cheetham, *English Medieval Alabasters* (Oxford: Phaidon/Christie's, 1984), 11, 52.

81. Ibid., 28–31.

82. Richard Marks, "An Age of Consumption: Art for England c. 1400–1547," in *Gothic*, ed. Marks and Williamson, 22.

83. Duffy, *Stripping of the Altars*, 155–56.

84. Joel Rosenthal, *The Purchase of Paradise: Gift Giving and the Aristocracy, 1307–1485* (London: Routledge & Kegan Paul, 1972), 10.

85. Apter, "Introduction," in Emily Apter and William Pietz, eds., *Fetishism as Cultural Discourse* (Ithaca, N.Y.: Cornell University Press, 1993), 4.

86. Binski, "English Parish Church," 12, notes that screens started being painted with litanies of the saints between 1425 and 1450; on donor images in late medieval English manuscripts, see Nigel Morgan, "Patrons and Devotional Images in English Art of the International Gothic c. 1350–1450," in *Reading Texts and Images: Essays on Medieval and Renaissance Art and Patronage in Honour of Margaret M. Manion*, ed. Bernard J. Muir (Exeter: University of Exeter Press, 2002), 93–121.

87. For a recent summary of scholarship on responsibilities for maintenance of chancel and nave, see C. David Benson, *Public Piers Plowman: Modern Scholarship and Late Medieval Culture* (University Park: Pennsylvania State University Press, 2004), 169–71.

88. See Binski, "English Parish Church," 12; and esp. Eamon Duffy, "The Parish, Piety, and Patronage in Late Medieval East Anglia: The Evidence of Rood Screens," in *The Parish in English Life, 1400–1600*, ed. Katherine L. French, Gary G. Gibbs, and Beat Kümin (Manchester: Manchester University Press, 1997), 133–62; and Duffy, "Holy Maydens, Holy Wyfes: The Cult of Women Saints in Fifteenth and Sixteenth Century England," in *Women in the Church*, ed. W. J. Sheils and Diana Wood (Oxford: Blackwell, 1990), 176, who notes the importance of individuals and lay groups in the choice of imagery on painted screens.

89. Duffy, "Parish, Piety, and Patronage," 136, also 142.

90. From *Pre-Reformation Records of All Saints', Bristol*, pt. 1, ed. Clive Burgess, Bristol Record Society, 46 (Stroud: Alan Sutton, 1995), 15–17, 28–29; cited in Simpson, *Reform and Cultural Revolution*, 432.

91. Gibson, *Theater of Devotion*, 80–96.

92. *Things*, ed. Bill Brown (Chicago: University of Chicago Press, 2004), 5.

93. For instances see Hudson, *Premature Reformation*, 166.

94. *Select English Works of John Wyclif*, ed. Thomas Arnold, 3 vols. (Oxford: Clarendon Press, 1871), 3:462–63.

95. Pietz, "Fetish, II," 40.

96. Ibid.

97. In a critique of historical periodization as a form of colonialism, Kathleen Biddick points to Pietz's genealogy of the fetish as an example of the ways historical study continues to underwrite traditional epistemologies that draw a sharp line between medieval and modern. Pietz not only reinscribes these conventional divides, his history fails to acknowledge that the early modern notion of the fetish, emerging in European trade with west Africa, might also voice anxieties about slavery, a trade in the most problematic of incommensurables, "the exchange of people as objects and trinkets as things: African slaves and Portuguese trinkets": "Translating the Foreskin," in *Queering the Middle Ages*, ed. Glenn Burger and Steven F. Kruger (Minneapolis: University of Minnesota Press, 2001), 196. Steven Kruger has furthered this argument about historical periodization, arguing that the very idea of the Middle Ages emerged through a fetishizing of the past, disavowed for its lack and benightedness and contrasted with the plenitude of modernity; "Fetishism, 1927, 1614, 1461," in *The Postcolonial Middle Ages*, ed. Jeffrey Jerome Cohen (New York: St. Martin's, 2000), 193–208, esp. 200–202.

Chapter 1. Knighton's Lollards

1. *Knighton's Chronicle, 1337–1396*, ed. and trans. G. H. Martin (Oxford: Clarendon Press, 1995), 297; the story is told on pp. 292–99. Further page references will be given in the text.

2. E.g., a chapel of St. John. Hospitals customarily had chapels attached or close by. According to Knowles and Hadcock, "The hospital [of St. John] must have been already old c. 1200, when its master and poor are recorded, with brothers and sisters c. 1235. It was under Augustinian rule in the fifteenth century, and perhaps from the start. All the brothers, except two, died of a pestilence in 1361." David Knowles and R. Neville Hadcock, *Medieval Religious Houses* (London: Longman, 1971), 369.

3. "'En,' inquit, 'mi karissime socie, iam Deus nobis prouidit de focali pro caulibus nostris coquendis ut esuriem nostram saciemus. Hec sancta ymago certe iam erit nobis focale sanctum. Et sic per securim et ignem nouum pacietur martirium, si forte per inmanitatem nouorum tormentorum, uenire aliquando poterit ad regnum celorum'" (296).

4. Many later versions spring from the so-called Vulgate *St. Katherine* written in the mid-eleventh century. The Vulgate version has been edited by S.R.T.O d'Ardenne and E. J. Dobson, *Seinte Katerine*, EETS, s.s., 7 (Oxford: Oxford University Press, 1981), 144–203. The development of textual traditions in England is summarized by Jacqueline Jenkins and Katherine J. Lewis, "Introduction," in *St.*

Katherine of Alexandria: Texts and Contexts in Western Medieval Europe, ed. Jenkins and Lewis (Turnhout, Belgium: Brepols, 2003), 5–15; Saara Nevanlinna and Irma Taavitsainen, *St. Katherine of Alexandria: The Late Middle English Prose Legend in Southwell Minster MS 7* (Cambridge: D. S. Brewer, 1993), 7–10; for the cult and textual tradition in England, see especially Katherine J. Lewis, *The Cult of St. Katherine of Alexandria in Late Medieval England* (Woodbridge: Boydell, 2000).

5. *Life of St. Catherine by Clemence of Barking*, ed. William Macbain, Anglo-Norman Text Society 18 (Oxford: Blackwell, 1964); trans. Jocelyn Wogan-Browne and Glyn S. Burgess, *Virgin Lives and Holy Deaths: Two Exemplary Biographies for Anglo-Norman Women* (London: Dent, 1996).

6. For the text in the Katherine Group, see *Seinte Katerine*, ed. d'Ardenne and Dobson.

7. Oxford, Bodleian Library, MS Laud 108 (c. 1285–95), printed in the *Early South English Legendary*, ed. Carl Horstmann, EETS, o.s., 87 (London: Trübner, 1887), 92–101; the Auchinleck version is printed in *Altenglische Legenden, Neue Folge, mit Einleitung und Anmerkungen*, ed. Carl Horstmann (Heilbronn: Verlag Von Gebr. Henninger, 1881), 242–59; for Spaldung's hymn see Ruth Kennedy, *Three Alliterative Saints' Hymns: Late Middle English Stanzaic Poems*, EETS, o.s., 321 (Oxford: Oxford University Press, 2003).

8. Osbern Bokenham, *Legendys of Hooly Wummen*, ed. Mary S. Serjeantson, EETS, o.s., 206 (London: Oxford University Press, 1938); John Capgrave, *The Life of Saint Katherine*, ed. Karen A. Winstead, TEAMS (Kalamazoo: Western Michigan University, 1999).

9. E. W. Tristram, *English Wall Painting of the Fourteenth Century* (London: Routledge & Kegan Paul, 1955), 25, lists St. Katherine in twenty-four churches, with scenes from her history appearing in twelve of these. According to Eamon Duffy, a total of thirty-six St. Katherine wall paintings survive from before the Reformation: "Holy Maydens, Holy Wyfes," 185 n; for St. Katherine as a guild patron, see David Wallace, *Chaucerian Polity: Absolutist Lineages and Associational Forms in England and Italy* (Stanford, Calif.: Stanford University Press, 1997), 95–96.

10. See indexes to Lucy Freeman Sandler, *Gothic Manuscripts 1285–1385* (London: H. Miller, 1986), and Scott, *Later Gothic Manuscripts*.

11. Cited in *Italian Art 1400–1500: Sources and Document*, trans. Creighton Gilbert (Englewood Cliffs, N.J.: Prentice-Hall, 1980), 146.

12. Pecock, *Repressor*, 215.

13. Capgrave, *Life of St. Katherine*, 36 (bk. 1, ch. 7, line 424).

14. For a review of this discussion, see Aston, *England's Iconoclasts*, 134n. The dates of Knighton's account and of Lollard activity around Leicester and particularly the Chapel of St. John are also discussed by Geoffrey Martin, "Knighton's Lollards," in *Lollardy and the Gentry in the Later Middle Ages*, ed. Margaret Aston and Colin Richmond (New York: St. Martin's, 1997), 34 and 38, who argues that the incident that Knighton dates to 1382 must have been spread over a much longer period.

15. Aston, *England's Iconoclasts*, 131. See also Joy M. Russell-Smith, "Walter Hilton and a Tract in Defence of the Veneration of Images," *Dominican Studies* 7 (1954): 200–204; Jones, "Lollards and Images; *SEWW*, ed. Hudson, 179–82.

16. Watson, "Composition," 662; and Hudson, *Premature Reformation*, 76–78.

17. NLS Advocates 19.2.1, printed in *Altenglische Legenden*, ed. C. Horst-mann, 244, line 104. Citations from the Auchinleck *St. Katherine* are taken from this edition.

18. "Willemus . . . persona despicabilis et deformis. Qui cupiens ducere in uxorem iuuenticulam quandam set ab ea spretus, in tantam prorupit sanctitatis ostentacionem quod omnia mundi concupiscibilia despexit, muliebrem amplexum perpetuo abdicauit . . ." (292).

19. "Nam si capite percussa sanguinem emittat, amodo a nobis ut sancta adoranda erit. Sin autem sanguinem non eliciat, cibus erit ignis nostris coquendis oleribus ut tanta saturetus nostra esuries" (296).

20. The Auchinleck Katherine is incomplete, but the narrative is continued in Cambridge, Gonville and Caius College, MS 175/96, printed in *Altenglische Legenden*, ed. Horstmann, 258, line 754. See also BL, MS Harley 4196, printed in *Altenglische Legenden*, ed. Horstmann, 173, line 747.

21. In his rendition of Knighton's *Chronicle* into modern English verse, Martin provides an entertaining yet loose translation of the poem. For help with the translation I am grateful to Edward Vodoklys, S.J., who notes that the poem is dotted with sexual and scatological metaphors.

22. "'Sanguis percussa si manat uera uocetur / Si non, per iussa, nobis cibus ignis habetur,' Caule quo cicius mendici scruda coquentur / Esuries satius, et eis fames cito fugit" (298). The meaning of "scruda" is uncertain, but according to Vodoklys, may be slang for scrotum.

23. "Creuit populus credencium in ista doctrina et quasi germinantes multi-plicati sunt nimis et impleuerunt ubique orbem regni, et adeo domestici facti sunt acsi essent de uno die procreati" (298).

24. "Hec erat condicio Lollardis huius / secte quod ymagines oderunt et in-sidiabantur eis, et eas ydola predicabant et uelut simulacra aspernabantur. Cumque quis nominasset Sanctam Mariam de Lincolnia uel Sancram Mariam de Walsyng-ham, uocabant eas epialtes. Hoc est in materna lingua 'Wiche of Lincolle,' and 'Wyche of Walsyngham,' et huiusmodi" (296).

25. Huston Diehl, *Staging Reform, Reforming the Stage: Protestantism and Popular Theater in Early Modern England* (Ithaca, N.Y.: Cornell University Press, 1997), 163.

26. Ibid., 163-64.

27. For the uses of the vernacular as strategic contrast to Latin, see Ruth Evans, Andrew Taylor, Nicholas Watson, and Jocelyn Wogan-Browne, "The Notion of Vernacular Theory," in *The Idea of the Vernacular: An Anthology of Middle English Literary Theory, 1280–1520*, ed. Wogan-Browne et al. (University Park: Pennsylvania State University Press, 1999), 314–30.

28. Geoffrey Chaucer, *The Riverside Chaucer*, ed. Larry D. Benson, 3rd ed. (Boston: Houghton Mifflin, 1987), lines 358–59.

29. "Utrum fuit experiamur / Vera per arsentes hec alma uel ea uiolamur / Sanguis percussa si manat uera uocetur" (298).

30. Diehl, *Staging Reform*, 156.

31. E.g., "thu wikide wiche, Quhat wenis thu ws lang to preche?" *Legends of the Saints in the Scottish Dialect of the Fourteenth Century*, ed. W. M. Metcalfe, Scottish Text Society 25 (London: Blackwood, 1896), pt. 4, line 1088. A similar

accusation appears in the *South English Legendary*, ed. Horstmann, 100, lines 279–80: "Faste ȝe schulle þe wychche binde . . . And smitez of hire heued a-non."

32. Karen A. Winstead, *Virgin Martyrs: Legends of Sainthood in Late Medieval England* (Ithaca, N.Y.: Cornell University Press, 1997), 17.

33. *St. Katherine*, ed. Nevanlinna et al., 89, line 725.

34. Julia Lupton, *Afterlives of the Saint: Hagiography, Typology, and Renaissance Literature* (Stanford, Calif.: Stanford University Press, 1996), xxi, 46.

35. Jones, "Lollards and Images," 33.

36. Ibid., 29.

37. Ibid., 34.

38. Rosenthal, *Purchase of Paradise.*

39. Gibson, *Theater of Devotion*, 68–69.

40. Jacques Derrida, *The Gift of Death*, trans. David Wills (Chicago: University of Chicago Press, 1995), esp. ch. 2.

41. I take this phrase from Judith Butler's Raymond Williams Lecture at Cambridge University in May 2000; the subject of the lecture was Foucault's essay, "What is Enlightenment?" in *Essential Works of Michel Foucault, 1954–84*, gen. ed. Paul Rabinow, trans. Robert Hurley et al. (New York: New Press, 1994), 1:303–19.

42. Winstead, *Virgin Martyrs*, fig. 14, p. 91.

43. For an argument that Katherine functioned as a model for women's literacy and reading in the late Middle Ages, see Lewis, *The Cult of St. Katherine*, 175–226; see also Jacqueline Jenkins, "St. Katherine and Laywomen's Piety: The Middle English Prose Life in London, BL Harley MS 4012," in *St. Katherine of Alexandria: Texts and Contexts in Western Medieval Europe*, ed. Jenkins and Katherine J. Lewis (Turnhout, Belgium: Brepols, 2003), 153–70.

44. Lewis, *Cult of St. Katherine*, 184; for a discussion of the Katherine cult and English royal households, see 63–79.

45. This incident is discussed in Aston, *England's Iconoclasts*, 134–35; from Walsingham, *Chronicon Angliae*, 1328-88, ed. E. M. Thompson, Rolls Series 64 (London: Longman, 1874), 377.

46. *Virgin Lives and Holy Deaths*, xx.

47. Citations from *The Scale of Perfection* are taken from the edition by Thomas H. Bestul, TEAMS (Kalamazoo, Mich.: Medieval Institute Publications, 2000).

48. *The Scale of Perfection*, ed. Evelyn Underhill (London: Watkins, 1923), vi, l–li; *The Scale of Perfection*, trans. J. H. P. Clark and Rosemary Dorward (New York: Paulist Press, 1991), 33.

49. *Scale*, trans. Clark and Dorward, 25, 46; for Hilton's response to the *Cloud* author, see 24–27; and Nicholas Watson, who argues that on the topic of the image the *Cloud* responds to *Scale 1* and that *Scale 2*, in turn, replies to *Cloud*: "'Et que est huius ydoli materia? Tuipse': Idols and Images in Walter Hilton," in *Images, Idolatry, and Iconoclasm in Late Medieval England: Textuality and the Visual Image*, ed. Jeremy Dimmick, James Simpson, and Nicolette Zeeman (Oxford: Oxford University Press, 2002), 106–10. For Pseudo-Dionysius and the *Cloud* author see Wolfgang Riehle, *The Middle English Mystics*, trans. Bernard Standring (London: Routledge and Kegan Paul, 1981), 7–8.

50. J. P. H. Clark, "Image and Likeness in Walter Hilton," *Downside Review* 97

(1979): 204–20, quote at 204. "Likeness" is Hilton's term for the "similitudo Dei," which opposes the "imago peccati" (210).

51. Clark, "Image and Likeness," 210.

52. For Hilton's relationship with the *Cloud* author, see also *Scale*, ed. Clark and Dorward, 24–27.

53. *Scale*, ed. Bestul, 2.

54. Suggesting that Hilton moved in circles actively engaged in the prosecution of heresies, records from York indicate that the Prior of the Augustinian Priory at Thurgarton, where Hilton died as Canon in 1396, was authorized in 1388 to arrest and imprison heretics for "teaching and maintaining divers heresies and nefarious opinions subversive of sound doctrine and notoriously tending to impair the orthodox faith, stirring up other lieges and dwellers in the county to adhere to the same to the manifest peril of their souls." *Cal. of Close Rolls*, 1385–89, pp. 529, 550; trans. Russell-Smith, 203.

55. Watson, "Idols and Images," 97; see also the comment by Janel Mueller in her Preface to Clark and Dorward's translation of *Scale*, 7: "In one extended discussion remarkable for the wit and finesse applied to a hot topical issue, he appropriates—by thoroughly reinterpreting in a Pauline light—in that Lollard rallying cry that idolatrous images be dishonored and destroyed. Hilton identifies idolatry not with the veneration of images in churches (which he elsewhere explicitly defended) but with the 'body of sin and death,' the worldly, carnal self from which Paul cried out to be delivered and whose members he sought to break apart."

56. Watson, "Idols and Images," 97; for arguments for Hilton's authorship, see Russell-Smith, "Walter Hilton," 188; J. P. H. Clark, "Walter Hilton in Defence of the Religious Life and of the Veneration of Images," *Downside Review* 103 (1985): esp. 9–16; as Clark, 16, notes, the title of the Latin treatise indicates that the tract was written as an aid to counter Lollard pressures: "contra hereticos qui asseruerunt ymaginem Crucifixi ceterorumque sanctorum ymagines in ecclesia Dei statuere ydolatriam esse." The full text is printed by John P. H. Clark and Cheryl Taylor, eds., *Walter Hilton's Latin Writings*, Analecta Cartusiana 124 (Salzburg: Institut für Anglistik und Amerikanistik, 1987), 2:179; Watson, "Idols and Images," 97n, offers a dissenting voice, arguing that scholars "seem more confident of his authorship than the evidence quite warrants."

57. Watson, "Images and Idols," 110.

58. In an enunciation of the ways that boundary violation is central to the consolations of anti-Semitism, Slavoj Žižek, *The Sublime Object of Ideology* (New York: Verso, 1989), 125–26, argues that a society's sense of itself as an organic unity is sustained, in part, by naming outsiders as threats to that order and also endowing those outsiders with "traits" that embody the very contradictory and untenable extremes that the "cohesive" fantasy cannot fully accommodate. See also Homi K. Bhabha, "The Other Question: Difference, Discrimination and the Discourse of Colonialism," in *Out There: Marginalization and Contemporary Cultures,* ed. Russell Ferguson, Martha Gever, Trinh T. Minh-ha, and Cornel West (New York: New Museum of Contemporary Art, 1990), 71–87; Jeffrey Jerome Cohen, "Hybrids, Monsters, Borderlands: The Bodies of Gerald of Wales," in *The Postcolonial Middle Ages*, ed. Cohen (New York: St. Martin's, 2000), 85–104.

59. *The Creation, and the Fall of Lucifer* (York), in *Everyman and Medieval Miracle Plays*, ed. A. C. Cawley (London: Dent, 1956; rpr. 1974), p. 8, lines 149-50.

60. In the *Cloud of Unknowing*, which responds directly to *Scale 1*, "derkness" rather than "merkness" is the essential quality of unknowing: "For when I sey derknes, I mene a lacking of knowing; as alle that thing that thou knowest not, or elles that thou hast forgetyn, it is derk to thee, for thou seest it not with thi goostly ighe. And for this skile it is not clept a cloude of the eire, bot a cloude of unknowing, that is bitwix thee and thi God." *The Cloud of Unknowing*, ed. Patrick J. Gallacher, TEAMS (Kalamazoo, Mich.: Medieval Institute Publications, 1997), p. 35. Watson, "Images and Idols," 107, argues that in responding to *Scale 1* the Cloud author is particularly troubled by Hilton's emphasis on sin as an image. If that is so, the *Cloud's* consistent use of the term "darkness" rather than "merkness" may also be a choice to dematerialize spiritual experience. In *Scale 2*, ch. 24, "merknesse" becomes the paradoxical good and 'bright darkness' in which Jesus can be discovered.

61. *Dives and Pauper*, 86.

62. John Wyclif, *Tractatus de Mandatis Divinis*, ed. J. Loserth and F. D. Matthew (London: Wyclif Society, 1887), 166; in Aston, *England's Iconoclasts*, 102–3.

63. Wyclif, *de Mandatis Divinis*, 194; in Aston, *England's Iconoclasts*, 102.

64. Michael Camille, *The Gothic Idol*, 88, 94.

65. See the *Middle English Dictionary*, sense 1a.

66. Scott, *Later Gothic Manuscripts*, Index, s.v., St. Catherine of Alexandria.

67. *Dives and Pauper*, 92.

68. Capgrave, *St. Katherine*, book 5, lines 1242 and 1295. Citations from Capgrave's *Katherine* are from Winstead's edition. Further citations will be given in the text by book and line number.

69. Richard Von Dülmen, *Theatre of Horror: Crime and Punishment in Early Modern Germany*, trans. Elisabeth Neu (Cambridge: Polity Press, 1990), 80, 95; according to Pieter Spierenburg, *The Spectacle of Suffering: Executions and the Evolution of Repression* (Cambridge: Cambridge University Press, 1984), 71, breaking on the wheel originated in a Frankish mode of punishment.

70. For the *Book of Numquam* image, thirteenth/fourteenth century, see Mitchell B. Merback, *The Thief, the Cross and the Wheel: Pain and the Spectacle of Punishment in Medieval and Renaissance Europe* (London: Reaktion, 1999), fig. 44.

71. Quoted in Merback, *Thief*, 158; see also Lionello Puppi, *Torment in Art: Pain, Violence, Martyrdom* (New York: Rizzoli, 1991), 16.

72. Merback, *Thief*, 167–68, discusses this painting.

73. On the increasing importance of mutilated bodies and visualization in late medieval law, see Seth Lerer, "'Representyd Now in Yower Syght': The Culture of Spectatorship in Late-Fifteenth-Century England," in *Bodies and Disciplines: Intersections of Literature and History in Fifteenth-Century England*, ed. Barbara A. Hanawalt and David Wallace (Minneapolis: University of Minnesota Press, 1996), 34.

74. *The Early South English Legendary*, ed. Horstmann, 98, lines 222–27; see also *St. Katherine*, ed. Nevanlinna et al., lines 880–83; Spalding, "Ein mittelenglischer Katherinenhymnus," stanzas 10, 11; *Altenglische Legenden*, ed. Horstmann, 170, lines 515–18.

75. For images in Pecock's *Repressor*, see Simpson, *Reform and Cultural Revolution*, 433–44; and Aston, *England's Iconoclasts*, 147–54.

76. Winstead, *Virgin Martyrs,* 167–77, 177; Winstead, ed., *St. Katherine*, 7–8.

77. Simpson, *Reform and Cultural Revolution*, 420–29; Kamerick, *Popular Piety*, 64–67.

78. The incident gets similar ironic treatment in Clemence of Barking's Anglo-Norman treatment of the incident, trans. Wogan-Brown, *Virgin Lives and Holy Deaths,* 23. Maxentius's offer to make a statue is a common trope in the story; for instance, it is briefly mentioned in the Auchinleck MS, printed by Horstmann, *Altenglische Legenden*, 247, line 244; in *De sancta Katerina historia*, also printed *Altenglische Legenden*, 168, line 326, where the statue is described as Katherine's "awin lyknes;" and in a c. 1420 *Life of St. Katherine*, in *Chaste Passions: Medieval English Virgin Martyr Legends*, ed. and trans. Karen Winstead (Ithaca, N.Y.: Cornell University Press, 2000), 147.

79. *Dives and Pauper*, ed. Barnum, 85.

80. Making a similar point for relics, Caroline Walker Bynum argues that their essential materiality affirmed the possibility of resurrection: *The Resurrection of the Body in Western Christianity, 200–1336* (New York: Columbia University Press, 1995), 104–8.

81. Lupton, *Afterlives of the Saints*, xxi.

82. Text cited in Gilbert, *Italian Art,* 146.

83. Lewis, *Cult of St. Katherine*, 192.

84. Robert J. Stoller, *Observing the Erotic Imagination* (New Haven, Conn.: Yale University Press, 1985), 155, cited in Susan Crane, *The Performance of Self: Ritual, Clothing, and Identity During the Hundred Years War* (Philadelphia: University of Pennsylvania Press, 2002), 53.

85. *Lanterne of Lizt*, 120. For Lollardy and allegory, see Hudson, *Premature Reformation*, 271–72; Lee Patterson, "Chaucer's Pardoner on the Couch: Psyche and Clio in Medieval Literary Studies," *Speculum* 76 (2001): 670; Peggy Knapp, *Chaucer and the Social Contest* (New York: Routledge, 1990), 71–76.

86. *SEWW*, ed. Hudson, 84.

Chapter 2. The Despenser Retable and 1381

1. The retable was discovered by a Professor Willis in 1847, according to C. H. B. Quennell, *The Cathedral Church of Norwich* (London: G. Bell & Sons, 1898), 92.

2. Albert Way, Esq., "Notice of a Painting of the Fourteenth Century, Part of the Decorations of an Altar: Discovered in Norwich Cathedral," in *Memoirs Illustrative of the History and Antiquities of Norfolk and the City of Norwich*, Proceedings of the Archaeological Institute 1847 (London: Archaeological Institute, 1851), 199.

3. For the most detailed description of the altarpiece and its construction, see W. H. St. John Hope, "On a Painted Table or Reredos of the Fourteenth Century, in the Cathedral Church of Norwich," *Norfolk Archaeology* 13 (1898): 292–314. The entry on the altarpiece by A. H. R. Martindale, "Altarpiece, Scenes from the

Passion, Resurrection, and Ascension of Christ Norwich? C. 1380–1400," in the exhibition catalogue *Medieval Art in East Anglia 1300–1520*, ed. P. Lasko and N. J. Morgan (Norwich: Jarrold & Sons, 1973), 37, lists as the best available discussion of the altar an unpublished M.A. thesis by Joanna Symonds from the School of Fine Arts and Music at the University of East Anglia (now the School of World Art Studies and Museology) in 1970; but this thesis is now lost.

4. *The Age of Chivalry: Art in Plantagenet England, 1200–1400*, ed. Jonathan Alexander and Paul Binski (London: Royal Academy of Arts, Weidenfeld and Nicolson, 1987), #711, p. 516.

5. Way, "Notice of a Painting," 199.

6. On the draperies Way, ibid., 203, cites Wyatt: "They are cast with greater skill than was, I think, possessed of any other nation excepting Italy," and "I must express the conviction that no artist of any country but Italy, could have drawn the nude with the refinement exhibited in these paintings, at the period of their execution" (204).

7. Based on a letter from Mr. Alma-Tadema (Hope, "Painted Table," 310), and in an effort at identifying the painter as a local artist, Hope speculates that Robert Ocle, an artist working in Norwich in the early fifteenth century, might have painted the oak leaves and acorns of the second and fourth panels as "a rebus indicative of his handiwork" (311).

8. *Age of Chivalry*, ed. Alexander and Binski, #711, p. 516.

9. Martindale, "Altarpiece," 37.

10. On spectatorship and issues of the historian as beholder, see Michael Ann Holly, "Past Looking," in *Vision and Textuality*, ed. Stephen Melville and Bill Readings (Durham, N.C.: Duke University Press, 1995), 83: "What the discussion about the gaze in works of art has taught us is that perception always involves a circulation of positions, a process of movement back and forth that will forever undermine the fixity of the two poles, inside and outside."

11. Hope, "Painted Table," 302; Martindale, "Altarpiece," 36; and Joan Evans, *English Art 1307–1361* (Oxford: Clarendon Press, 1949), 93; it is also repeated by Sarah Beckwith, as a statement of fact, in her brief discussion of the retable in *Christ's Body*, 23.

12. For Hope's discussion of the banners, see "Painted Table," 299–302.

13. The role of Thomas Morieux in the rebellion is indicated through his possession of the indictments taken at Bury St. Edmunds; see Edgar Powell, *The Rising in East Anglia in 1381* (Cambridge: Cambridge University Press, 1896), 7; see also 31, 126.

14. Hope, "Painted Table," 300; Henry Despenser's arms also appear in the South East Transept Clerestory in Canterbury Cathedral, as described by Madeline Caviness, *The Windows of Christ Church Cathedral, Canterbury*, Corpus Vitrearum Medii Aevi, Great Britain, vol. 2 (London: Oxford University Press, 1981), 306.

15. Hope, "Painted Table," 300.

16. Ibid., 301.

17. *Age of Chivalry*, ed. Alexander and Binski, #711, p. 516. In 1362 the spire collapsed and fell eastward, damaging the presbytery. Although there is no record of the reconstruction of the spire (Quennell, *Cathedral Church*, 36), sacrists' rolls

for 1364, 1369, and 1386 record expenses for "opus presbiterii": Eric Fernie, *An Architectural History of Norwich Cathedral* (Oxford: Clarendon, 1993), 183.

18. Hope, "Painted Table," 302.

19. Walter Benjamin, "The Work of Art in the Age of Mechanical Reproduction," in *Illuminations*, ed. Hannah Arendt, trans. Harry Zohn (New York: Schocken, 1968), 225.

20. Binski, "English Parish Church," 7.

21. For East Anglian lay patronage, see Gibson, *Theater of Devotion*, especially ch. 2, "East Anglian Religious Culture in the Late Middle Ages."

22. Jonathan Alexander, "*Labeur* and *Paresse*: Ideological Representations of Medieval Peasant Labor," *Art Bulletin*, 72.3 (1990): 439. Alexander is responding chiefly to Johan Huizinga, *The Waning of the Middle Ages* (New York: St. Martin's, 1985), and, as he claims, to Erwin Panofsky, *Early Netherlandish Painting, Its Origins and Character* (Cambridge, Mass.: Harvard University Press, 1953 and New York: Icon, 1971), 1:66, 70–71—though Panofsky anticipates his argument about social class.

23. *The Westminster Chronicle*, 1381–94, ed. and trans. L. C. Hector and Barbara F. Harvey (Oxford: Clarendon Press, 1982), 2–3; see discussion in Strohm, *Hochon's Arrow*, 33–56.

24. *Age of Chivalry*, ed. Alexander and Binski, #711, p. 516.

25. *Meditations on the Life of Christ: An Illustrated Manuscript of the Fourteenth Century*, trans. Isa Ragusa and Rosalie B. Green (Princeton, N.J.: Princeton University Press, 1961), 328–29.

26. *Petites Heures*, BN MS. Latin 18014, fol. 83v; see Ruth Mellinkoff, *Outcasts: Signs of Otherness in Northern European Art of the Late Middle Ages* (Berkeley: University of California Press, 1993), 1:21–22; for the iconography of the flagellation, see also Gertrud Schiller, *Iconography of Christian Art*, trans. Janet Seligman (Greenwich, Conn.: New York Graphic Society, 1971), 2:68.

27. Mellinkoff, *Outcasts*, 2: figs. 1.38–1.40.

28. Ibid., 1:184.

29. Ibid., 189.

30. See Rubin, *Corpus Christi*, 298–302; and for representations of the elevation, see Duffy, *Stripping of the Altars*, figs. 42–43.

31. Hope, "Painted Table," 307.

32. On the interchangeability of the terms "race" and "ethnicity," see Robert Bartlett, "Medieval and Modern Concepts of Race and Ethnicity," *Journal of Medieval and Early Modern Studies* 31.1 (2001): 40.

33. In *Before Color Prejudice: The Ancient View of Blacks* (Cambridge, Mass.: Harvard University Press, 1983), esp. 63–87, Frank M. Snowdon Jr. has argued that peoples in the ancient world distinguished others by physiognomic markers and skin tone but rarely used those markers as signs of inferiority or superiority. In medieval Europe, although dark skin and African physiognomy had few of the racialized associations that they came to assume later through the slave trade, body type and character do frequently seem to overlap. In a recent study of race in the Middle Ages, Thomas Hahn has assembled numerous examples in which black skin is equated with exoticism or monstrosity: "The Difference the Middle Ages Makes:

Color and Race Before the Modern World," *Journal of Medieval and Early Modern Studies* 31.1 (2001): 1–37. Hahn, 5n, disagrees with Snowdon's central thesis that the absence of color prejudice was a distinguishing feature of ancient attitudes toward race.

34. Hope, "Painted Table," 297.

35. Despenser was sanctioned by Parliament in 1383 to take up the crusader's cross and lead an army into Flanders to fight the Clementist opponents of Pope Urban VI. The crusade, which began on May 16, 1383, with an early series of military successes, ended by October of that year in defeat and withdrawal. For the failure of the mission Despenser was impeached by the chancellors, and what had been a much-touted glorious campaign ended in a public disgrace that lasted until 1385, when he was restored his temporalities through his service to Richard II on the Scottish campaign. For a brief summary of the crusade, see Nigel Saul, *Richard II* (New Haven, Conn.: Yale University Press, 1997), 102–7. The crusade in Flanders also made Despenser the target of Lollard polemic, some of which seems to have endured far longer than 1385. The Lollard author of the *Opus arduum*, a Latin commentary on the Apocalypse written between 1389 and 1390, repeatedly mentions the Despenser crusade as a symptom of multiple ills of the Church. As Hudson summarizes, "it revealed all the evils of a clerical hierarchy more interested in political power and wealth than in Christ's flock, prepared to resort to war, offering indulgences to the laity for their support and participating themselves in bloodshed": *Premature Reformation*, 266. For other evidence of Lollard antipathy to Despenser, see ibid., 14, 78, and 91. Through the crusade, the bishop secured his martial reputation and also his status, among Lollard opponents, as a scion of a corrupt Church.

36. John Capgrave, *The Book of the Illustrious Henries*, trans. Francis C. Hingeston (London: Longman, Brown, Green, Longmans, & Roberts, 1858), 198–201.

37. J. A. Tuck, "Nobles, Commons and the Great Revolt of 1381," in *The English Rising of 1381*, ed. R. H. Hilton and T. H. Aston (Cambridge: Cambridge University Press, 1984), 194–95.

38. Capgrave, *Book of the Illustrious Henries*, 198; see also Tuck, "Nobles, Commons and the Great Revolt of 1381," 195. Despenser also descended from a distinguished lineage, one that, as George M. Wrong notes, "was such as to make his military tastes and even his imperious temper quite natural," *The Crusade of 1383, Known as That of the Bishop of Norwich* (London: James Parker & Co., 1892), 10; according to Capgrave, *Book of the Illustrious Henries*, 198, Despenser's warlike tendencies emerged from his youth, when he campaigned in Italy for the apostolic rights of the Church: "This Henry then was born of the race of Despensers; a soldier valorous in all things, and who in the vigour of youth seemed to thirst after warfare only."

39. Thomas Walsingham, *The Chronica Maiora of Thomas Walsingham, 1376–1422*, trans. David Preest (Woodbridge: Boydell, 2005), 145–46.

40. *Chronicon Angliae, ab anno domini 1323 usque ad annum 1388*, ed. Edward Maunde Thompson, Rolls Series 64 (London: Longman, 1874), 139–40; see also Wrong, *Crusade of 1383*, 13–14, and discussion in Beckwith, *Christ's Body*, 99–100.

41. Lynn Staley, "Julian of Norwich and the Crisis of Authority," in *Powers of the Holy*, 157.

42. For Hales's commissions, see Roger Virgoe, "The Crown and Local Government: East Anglia under Richard II," in *The Reign of Richard II: Essays in Honor of May McKisack*, ed. F. R. H. DuBoulay and Caroline Barron (London: Athlone, 1971), 228; and for his role with the poll tax see Edgar Powell, *The Rising in East Anglia in 1381* (Cambridge: University Press, 1896), 31n.

43. *Chronica Maiora*, 145.

44. Ibid., 146.

45. Ibid.

46. Capgrave, *Book of the Illustrious Henries*, 201. See also Powell, *Rising in East Anglia*, 39.

47. Trans. by Powell, *Rising in East Anglia*, 18; Powell, 139–43, transcribes the extract from Gosford's chronicle that deals with the revolt at Bury: BL Claudius, A. XII, fol. 131b.

48. *The Chronicles of Froissart*, trans. John Bourcher, ed. G. C. Macaulay (New York: Macmillan, 1895), 258. Froissart, curiously, does not mention Despenser's role in the 1381 rebellion, writing of Despenser's 1383 campaign in Flanders that he "never bare armour before but in Lumbardy with his brother," 297r. Froissart does dramatize the story of Lister's coercion of the gentry.

49. Capgrave, in Powell, *Rising in East Anglia*, 38, names the three victims, but Walsingham does not: *Chronica, 146.*

50. Walsingham, *Chronica*, 147.

51. Hudson, *Premature Reformation*, 66–69.

52. According to Christopher Dyer, the burning of court rolls was "one of the most widespread expressions of rural rebellion," with 107 identifiable incidents of destruction: "The Social and Economic Background to the Rural Revolt of 1381," in *English Rising*, ed. Hilton and Aston, 12. For the contest over literacy in the rebellion, see Steven Justice, *Writing and Rebellion: England in 1381* (Berkeley: University of California Press, 1994).

53. Michael Camille, *Image on the Edge: The Margins of Medieval Art* (London: Reaktion, 1992), 42; see Kathryn Kerby-Fulton and Denise L. Despres, *Iconography and the Professional Reader: The Politics of Book Production in the Douce Piers Plowman* (Minneapolis: University of Minnesota Press, 1999), 133–34.

54. Beckwith, *Signifying Signs*, 87–88.

Chapter 3. Chaucer and Images

1. Guillaume de Machaut, *Le Livre dou voir dit (The Book of the True Poem)*, ed. Daniel Leech-Wilkinson, trans. R. Barton Palmer (New York: Garland, 1998), pp. 110–11, letter 9.

2. Ellert Dahl, "Heavenly Images: The Statue of St. Foy of Conques and the Significance of the Medieval 'Cult-Image' in the West," *Acta ad Archeologium et Artium Historiam Pertinentia* 8 (1978): 175–91.

3. Hans Belting, *Image and Its Public*, 232n; David Freedberg, *The Power of Images: Studies in the History and Theory of Response* (Chicago: University of Chicago Press, 1989), 4.

4. According to Michael Camille, a fourteenth-century illustration from a French version of Bartholomeus Anglicus is "one of the earliest examples of what we would call a modern framed painting"; the image of Toute Bele may offer an equally early example; Camille, "The Image and the Self: Unwriting Late Medieval Bodies," in *Framing Medieval Bodies*, ed. Sarah Kay and Miri Rubin (New York: Manchester University Press, 1994), 66.

5. Derek Pearsall, "Hoccleve's *Regement of Princes*: The Poetics of Royal Self-Representation," *Speculum* 69 (1994): 401; see also Kerby-Fulton and Despres, *Iconography and the Professional Reader*, 105.

6. Thomas Hoccleve, *The Regiment of Princes*, ed. Charles R. Blyth, TEAMS (Kalamazoo, Mich.: Medieval Institute Publications, 1999), lines 4999–5008.

7. Pearsall, "Hoccleve's *Regement*," 401–6.

8. Norbert Schneider, *Art of the Portrait* (Cologne: Taschen, 1994), 6–9; Joanna Woodall, *Portraiture: Facing the Subject* (Manchester: Manchester University Press, 1997), 1.

9. Machaut, *Livre*, pp. 112–16, lines 1536–627.

10. Ibid., lxxxiii.

11. See Alistair Minnis, *Chaucer and Pagan Antiquity*, 39.

12. Hudson, *Premature Reformation*, 390–94.

13. Wycliffe, *Sermones*, 194; as noted in *Riverside Chaucer* in the note on the *Pardoner's Tale*, lines 538–39. Citations from Chaucer refer to the *Riverside Chaucer* and will be included in the text.

14. Paul Strohm, "Chaucer's Lollard Joke: History and the Textual Unconscious," *Studies in the Age of Chaucer* 17 (1995): 23–42; Fiona Somerset, "Here, There, and Everywhere? Wycliffite Conceptions of the Eucharist and Chaucer's 'Other' Lollard Joke," in *Lollards and Their Influence in Late Medieval England*, ed. Fiona Somerset, Jill C. Havens, and Derrick G. Pitard (Woodbridge, Suffolk: Boydell Press, 2003), 128.

15. Walsingham, *Chronica Maiora*, 250; see Aston, *England's Iconoclasts*, 134–35; for Lollard knights, see K. B. McFarlane, *Lancastrian Kings and Lollard Knights* (Oxford: Clarendon, 1971), 148–76; and for Chaucer's circle, see Paul Strohm, *Social Chaucer* (Cambridge, Mass.: Harvard University Press, 1989), 42. As Strohm notes, there is no evidence that Chaucer knew Sir John Montagu.

16. Paul Strohm, *Hochon's Arrow: The Social Imagination of Fourteenth-Century Texts* (Princeton, N.J.: Princeton University Press, 1992), 91; McFarlane, *Lancastrian Kings*, 182.

17. Alcuin Blamires, "The Wife of Bath and Lollardy," *Medium Aevum* 58 (1989): 225.

18. *The Major Latin Works of John Gower*, trans. Eric W. Stockton (Seattle: University of Washington Press, 1962), 109–11.

19. Collette, *Species, Phantasms,* 102–19.

20. *The Shewings of Julian of Norwich*, ed. Georgia Ronan Crampton, TEAMS (Kalamazoo, Mich.: Medieval Institute, 1993), 42, lines 114–15.

21. Kerby-Fulton and Despres, *Iconography and the Professional Reader*, 38, 26.

22. David Dymond and Clive Paine, *The Spoil of Melford Church: The Reformation in a Suffolk Parish* (Ipswich: Salient Press, 1992), 2.

23. Some readers have understood the ekphrases of the images and paintings in the *Knight's Tale* to represent various forms of entrapment: of the self by the fictions of chivalry, as noted by Lee Patterson, *Chaucer and the Subject of History* (Madison: University of Wisconsin Press, 1991), 227–28; of the individual will by transforming images of imprisonment (V. A. Kolve, *Chaucer and the Imagery of Narrative: The First Five Canterbury Tales* [Stanford, Calif.: Stanford University Press, 1984], 113–30); of the free choice to Christian charity by the seductions of pagan idols, and specifically Venus, the "mother of all fornication" (D. W. Robertson Jr., *A Preface to Chaucer: Studies in Medieval Perspectives* [Princeton, N.J.: Princeton University Press, 1962], 371); or even of the visual field by *le regard*, a socially constructed desire that endows the object of the gaze, however harmful, with an illusory will and wholeness, as H. Marshall Leicester Jr. argues (*The Disenchanted Self: Representing the Subject in the Canterbury Tales* [Berkeley: University of California Press, 1990], 268).

24. See Kamerick, *Popular Piety and Art*, 27; for Robert Holcot's commentary on these lines from Wisdom, see Minnis, *Chaucer and Pagan Antiquity*, 37–40, 85–86.

25. Helen Phillips, "Register, Politics, and the *Legend of Good Women*," *Chaucer Review* 37.2 (2002): 101–28; Anne Hudson, "A Lollard Sect Vocabulary," in *Lollards and Their Books* (London, Hambledon, 1985), 165–80; Collette, *Species, Phantasms*, 112.

26. Sarah Stanbury, "The Lover's Gaze in *Troilus and Criseyde*," in *Chaucer's Troilus and Criseyde: "Subgit to alle Poesye": Essays in Criticism*, ed. R. A. Shoaf (Binghamton, N.Y.: Medieval & Renaissance Texts and Studies, 1992), 225–38, and companion essay, "The Voyeur and the Private Life in *Troilus and Criseyde*," *Studies in the Age of Chaucer* 13 (1991): 141–58.

27. H. M. Smyser, "The Domestic Background of *Troilus and Criseyde*," *Speculum* 31 (1956): 297–315; Saul N. Brody, "Making a Play for Criseyde: The Staging of Pandarus's House in Chaucer's *Troilus and Criseyde*," *Speculum* 73 (1998): 115–40.

28. See, for example, Louise O. Fradenburg, "'Our owen wo to drynke': Loss, Gender, and Chivalry in *Troilus and Criseyde*," in Shoaf, ed., *Chaucer's Troilus and Criseyde*, 88–106; and Sheila Delany, "Techniques of Alienation in *Troilus and Criseyde*," in Shoaf, ed., *Chaucer's Troilus and Criseyde*, 29–46.

29. For dating of the two Prologues, see the discussion in Explanatory Notes in the *Riverside Chaucer*, 1060; and Delany, *Naked Text: Chaucer's Legend of Good Women* (Berkeley: University of California Press, 1994), 34–43.

30. *Riverside Chaucer*, 1060.

31. Minnis, *Chaucer and Pagan Antiquity*, 69, comments that Chaucer wrote the *Legend of Good Women* "as a sequel and complement to *Troilus*."

32. Phillips, "Register, Politics."

33. Blamires, "Wife of Bath and Lollardy," 229. The Wife's commentary on "glosing" echoes similar concerns in Wycliffite discourse, as noted by Hudson, *Premature Reformation*, 393.

34. Margaret Deanesly, *The Lollard Bible and Other Medieval Biblical Versions* (Cambridge: Cambridge University Press, 1920; rpr. 1966), 442; cited in Delany, *Naked Text*, 120; see also 115–23 for a discussion of the phrase "naked text" within the Wycliffite translation project.

35. Kathryn L. Lynch, *Chaucer's Philosophical Visions* (Cambridge: D. S. Brewer, 2000), 117, 127.

36. "Quapropter multociens non secundum mentem habentes Domini passionem, ymagin[em] Christi crucifixion[is] videntes, et salutaris passionis in rememoracionem venientes, procidentes adoramus non materiam sed ymaginatum. Quaemadmodum neque euangelii materiam neque crucis materiam adoramus, sed tipum, id est, signifcacionem vel figuracionem, ab habente?" 196, trans. Derrig, 11; "ut signa venerautur, non ut res," 199, trans. Derrig, 12: *De Adoracione Ymaginum*.

37. "Vnde ipsi nullo affectu vel reuerencia mouentur ad ipsum lignum, in quantum est material ligni, vel in quantum est curiose depicta. Nichil ponderant talia, sed utuntur ymaginibus uelut recordacione, procumbentes coram ymaginibus, oblitis illis, preces emittunt ad Deum et ad sanctos eius. . . . Unde illi qui spiritualiter orare volunt, claudere solent oculum exteriorem vel auertere ab obiecto ymaginum, ne intencio vel attencio mentalis retrahatur per sensualem apprehensionem obiecti." *De Adoracione Ymaginum*, 205; trans. Derrig, 15–16.

38. Phillips, "Register, Politics," 122.

39. Edward Langley, *Master of the Game*, London BL MS cott. Vesp. B. xii, fol. 12b; cited in Caroline Spurgeon, *Five Hundred Years of Chaucer Criticism and Allusion, 1357–1900* (Cambridge: Cambridge University Press, 1925), 1:18; see also Delany, *Naked Text*, 55.

40. Peter W. Travis, "Chaucer's Heliotropes and the Poetics of Metaphor," *Speculum* 72 (1997): 415.

41. Ibid., 403.

42. Delany, *Naked Text*, 41.

43. Somerset, "Wycliffite Conceptions of the Eucharist," 128.

44. *Dives and Pauper*, 85–86.

45. For the centrality of the material body to the cult of relics, see Caroline Walker Bynum, *The Resurrection of the Body in Western Christianity, 200–1336* (New York: Columbia University Press, 1995), 59–114; see also Patterson, "Chaucer's Pardoner," 675–76.

46. Wyclif, *Sermones*, 2:165; cited in Aston, *England's Iconoclasts*, 103–4.

47. "quod reliquie sanctorum, scilicet carnes et ossa hominis mortui, non debent a populo venerari, nec de monumento fetido extrahi, nec in capsa aurea vel argentea reponi," in *Heresy Trials in the Dioceses of Norwich, 1428–31*, ed. from Westminster Diocesan Archives MS. B.2 by Norman P. Tanner, Camden Fourth Series, vol. 20 (London: Royal Historical Society, 1977), cited in Aston, *Lollards and Reformers*, 90. A Wycliffite tract also links the display of relics with the sale of pardons; see Siegfried Wenzel, "Chaucer's Pardoner and His Relics," *Studies in the Age of Chaucer* 11 (1989): 41.

48. Patterson, "Chaucer's Pardoner," 677.

49. James F. Rhodes, "The Pardoner's *Vernycle* and His *Vera Icon*," *Modern Language Studies* 13 (1983): 34–40.

50. Eugene Vance, "Chaucer's Pardoner: Relics, Discourse, and Frames of Propriety," *New Literary History* 20 (1989): 737.

51. Martin Stevens and Kathleen Falvey, "Substance, Accident, and Transformations: A Reading of the *Pardoner's Tale*," *Chaucer Review* 17 (1982): 142–58;

Kathryn L. Lynch, "The Pardoner's Digestion: Eating Images in *The Canterbury Tales*," in *Speaking Images: Essays in Honor of V. A. Kolve*, ed. R. F. Yeager and Charlotte C. Morse (Asheville, N.C.: Pegasus Press, 2001), 395; Strohm, "Chaucer's Lollard Joke," explores the graphic allusion to substance and accident in the context of reformist rhetoric about the Eucharist.

52. Karl Marx, *Selected Writings*, ed. David McLellan (Oxford: Oxford University Press, 1997), 436.

53. William Kamowski, "'Coillons,' Relics, Skepticism and Faith on Chaucer's Road to Canterbury," *English Language Notes* 28 (1991): 5.

54. Bill Brown, *A Sense of Things: The Object Matter of American Literature* (Chicago: University of Chicago Press, 2003), 29.

Chapter 4. Translating Griselda

1. "The Canterbury Interlude," in *The Canterbury Tales: Fifteenth-Century Continuations and Additions*, ed. John M. Bowers, TEAMS (Kalamazoo, Mich.: Medieval Institute Publications, 1992), 64, line 140. Hereafter lines numbers are cited in text.

2. Bowers, 57; the dating is based on the supposition that the *Canterbury Interlude* could have been written in recognition of the Canterbury Jubilee in 1420, the celebration of the 1170 death of St. Thomas that took place every fifty years.

3. "A Pilgrimage for Religion's Sake," in *The Colloquies of Erasmus*, trans. Craig R. Thompson (Chicago: University of Chicago Press, 1965), 308.

4. Ibid.

5. Daniel Knapp, "'The Relyk of a Seint': A Gloss on Chaucer's Pilgrimage," *English Literary History* 39 (1972): 1–26, esp. 5–14.

6. Donald R. Howard, *The Idea of the Canterbury Tales* (Berkeley: University of California Press, 1976), 162; or as Larry Sklute puts it in *Virtue of Necessity: Inconclusiveness and Narrative Form in Chaucer's Poetry* (Columbus: Ohio State University Press, 1984), 97, "Possibility is the central concern of the entire work and inconclusiveness is the means through which the form expresses it."

7. For Chaucer's perennial concern with language and its power to convey truth, see Robert Jordan, *Chaucer's Poetics and the Modern Reader* (Berkeley: University of California Press, 1987), 26, 119–20, 173–74.

8. On Chaucer's uses of pathos, see Jill Mann, *Geoffrey Chaucer* (New York: Harvester Wheatsheaf, 1991); Thomas Bestul, "*The Man of Law's Tale* and the Rhetorical Foundations of Chaucerian Pathos," *Chaucer Review* 9 (1975): 216–26; Robert Worth Frank Jr., "The *Canterbury Tales* III: Pathos," in *The Cambridge Chaucer Companion*, ed. Piero Boitani and Jill Mann (Cambridge: Cambridge University Press, 1986), 143–58; and Wendy Harding, "The Function of Pity in Three Canterbury Tales," *Chaucer Review* 32.2 (1997): 162–74. As Harding, 162, notes, "over the past two centuries, readers have favored Chaucer's humor and irony while finding his pathos almost an embarrassment. Recently though, interest in Chaucer's art of pathos has revived, as scholars take up the challenge of understanding texts that are quite alien to contemporary literary aesthetics." David Aers has contributed to

this historicizing challenge in his critique of the representation of piety in essays in the volume *Chaucer's Religious Tales*, ed. C. David Benson and Elizabeth Robertson (Cambridge: D. S. Brewer, 1990), esp. Linda Georgianna, "The Protestant Chaucer," 55–69, as well as Georgianna, "The Clerk's Tale and the Grammar of Assent," *Speculum* 70 (1995): 793–821; see Aers, "Faith, Ethics, and Community: Reflections on Reading Late Medieval English Writing," *Journal of Medieval and Early Modern Studies* 28 (1998): 341–69, and the elaboration of his essay in *Faith, Ethics, and Church: Writing in England, 1360–1409* (Cambridge: D. S. Brewer, 2000), 1–55.

9. Charles Zika, "Hosts, Processions and Pilgrimages: Controlling the Sacred in Fifteenth-Century Germany," *Past and Present* 118 (1988): 31; Gibson, *Theater of Devotion*, 1–18; and Sarah Beckwith, who uses the term as a chapter title, "Real Presences: The York Crucifixion as Sacramental Theater," in *Signifying God*.

10. For the absence of the Eucharist in Chaucer, see Aers, *Faith, Ethics and Church*, ch. 2; Lynn Staley, *Languages of Power in the Age of Richard II* (University Park: Pennsylvania State University Press, 2005), describes the *Canterbury Tales* as "asacral" (140).

11. David Aers, "Faith, Ethics, and Community," 358.

12. See, for instance, Michaela P. Grudin, "Chaucer's Clerk's Tale as Political Paradox," *Studies in the Age of Chaucer* 11 (1989): 63–92; Wallace, *Chaucerian Polity*; Larry Scanlon, *Narrative, Authority, and Power: The Medieval Exemplum and the Chaucerian Tradition* (Cambridge: Cambridge University Press, 1994), 175–91; and Staley, *Powers of the Holy*, 233–59.

13. Scholarship examining Chaucer's affiliations with Lollardy is extensive; for a few recent studies, see Collette, *Species, Phantasms*, 111–17; Knapp, *Chaucer and the Social Contest*, 63–76; Paul Olson, *The Canterbury Tales and the Good Society* (Princeton, N.J.: Princeton University Press, 1986), esp. 6–9 and 162–67; William Kamowski, "Chaucer and Wyclif: God's Miracles against the Clergy's Magic," *Chaucer Review* 2002 (37): 5–25; Aers, *Faith, Ethics, and Church*, 27; Delany, *Naked Text*, 45–47; and Derrick Pitard's bibliographical survey in *Lollards and Their Influence in Late Medieval England*, ed. Somerset, Havens, and Pitard, 315–16 and the electronic bibliography maintained by the Lollard Society: http://home.att.net/~lollard/. Although Chaucer was sympathetic to many points of Lollard reformism, "the belief that Chaucer was a Lollard has been out of critical favor for well over a century," Pitard comments (316).

14. Kamowski, "Chaucer and Wyclif," 11, 21.

15. Aers, "Faith, Ethics, and Community," 359.

16. "Nam in cultu et veneracione eukaristie cum cultu mortuorum corporum atque ymaginum per generacionem adulteram ecclesia est seducta," Wyclif, Sermon 22, in *Sermones*, ed. Loserth, 2:165; trans. Kamowski, "Chaucer and Wyclif," 10.

17. Aers and Staley, *Powers of the Holy*, 216.

18. Both of these sources are printed in the classic study by J. Burke Severs, *The Literary Relationships of Chaucer's Clerkes Tale* (New Haven, Conn.: Yale University Press, 1942). Petrarch's text from *Epistolae Seniles*, 17.3, is translated by Robert Dudley French, *A Chaucer Handbook*, 2nd ed. (New York: Appleton-Century-Crofts, 1947), 290–311. Most readers agree that Chaucer secularizes the pietistic narrative of his sources—though there is little consensus on the ends of this revision. As

Severs, 233, 235, reads these shifts, Chaucer heightens pathos by emphasizing Griselda's suffering. Chaucer increases "her gentleness, her meekness, her submissiveness," even as he heightens the sergeant's apparent wickedness. At the same time, however, Chaucer sharpens the active quality of her will, as witnessed, for example, in Chaucer's addition to the moment of the reunion with the children the picture of her clasping them so tightly in a swoon that her arms have to be forcibly parted. This change, Severs, 235, claims, "imparts a certain emphatic quality to her will which gives it the nature of separate existence rather than that of mere submersion in the will of her lord."

19. Petrarch's translation of Boccaccio's Griselda story is included in a 1373 letter to Boccaccio and appears in *Epistolae Seniles* 17.3; for the letter in English, see James A. Robinson, *Petrarch: The First Modern Scholar* (New York: Putnam, 1914), 195–96.

20. Elizabeth Salter, *Chaucer: The Knight's Tale and the Clerk's Tale* (London: Edward Arnold, 1962), 48–49. More recently Staley, *Powers of the Holy*, 237–40, understands Griselda as a type of radical Christ.

21. Wallace, *Chaucerian Polity*, 287.

22. *Middle English Dictionary*, s.v. *translaten*, 1.c.

23. Compare Petrarch: "velut subito transformatum, vix populus recognovit," and *Le Livre de Griseldis*: "comme soudainement transmuee et changié, a paine la recongnust le peuple," Severs, *Literary Relationships*, 264–65. *The Goodman of Paris*, however, adds humanizing detail: "Who then saw a poor girl, brown with the sun and thin from poverty, so nobly adorned and richly crowned and suddenly transformed so that people scarcely knew her, well might he marvel thereat," trans. Eileen Power (New York: Harcourt, Brace & Co., 1928), 119.

24. See G. J. C. Snoek, *Medieval Piety from Relics to the Eucharist: A Process of Mutual Interaction* (New York: Brill, 1995), 19.

25. Ibid., 252.

26. Ibid., esp. ch. 4, "The Transposition of Forms of Reverence," 227–307. On the importance of the elevation of the host in the Mass, see Rubin, *Corpus Christi*, esp. 131–34; and Duffy, *Stripping of the Altars*, 96–107.

27. John Mirk, *Instructions for Parish Priests*, ed. Gillis Kristensson (Lund: Gleerup, 1974); in Snoek, *Medieval Piety*, 59.

28. Arthur Penrhyn Stanley, *Historical Memorials of Canterbury* (New York: Anson D. F. Randolph, 1888), 269.

29. Zika, "Hosts, Processions and Pilgrimages," 30; and Beckwith, *Christ's Body*, 32.

30. Kathryn L. Lynch, "Despoiling Griselda: Chaucer's Walter and the Problem of Knowledge in *The Clerk's Tale*," *Studies in the Age of Chaucer* 10 (1988): 62. See also Robert Stepsis, "Potentia Absoluta and *The Clerk's Tale*," *Chaucer Review* 10 (1975): 129–46; David C. Steinmetz, "Late Medieval Nominalism and the *Clerk's Tale*," *Chaucer Review* 12 (1977): 38–54.

31. Zika, "Hosts, Processions and Pilgrimages," 37; on the cultural reception of optical theory in the Middle Ages, see also Collette, *Species, Phantasms*, 1–31; and on "ocular communion" see Biernoff, *Sight and Embodiment*, 140–64.

32. Beckwith, "Sacramentality and Dissent," 267 ff.

33. *De Concordia inter Ric. II et civitatem london* (London: Camden Society, 1838); see Strohm, *Hochon's Arrow,* 105–11.

34. "set scrutantibus verum videbatur non dari set pocius emi, nam non modicam pecuniam refundebat rex Anglie pro tantilla carnis porcione," *Westminster Chronicle,* 24–25; the translation of the last line is emended "to secure this tiny scrap of humanity," by Andrew Taylor in "Anne of Bohemia and the Making of Chaucer," *Studies in the Age of Chaucer* 19 (1997): 95. See also discussion in Strohm, *Hochon's Arrow,* 107; and Wallace, *Chaucerian Polity,* 361–63.

35. Taylor, "Anne of Bohemia," 95–96.

36. Teresa Tavormina, *Kindly Similitude: Marriage and Family in Piers Plowman* (Cambridge: D. W. Brewer, 1995), 223.

37. Ibid., see also Christopher N. L. Brooke, *The Medieval Idea of Marriage* (Oxford: Oxford University Press, 1989), 132; and Kimberly Keller, "For Better and Worse: Women and Marriage in *Piers Plowman,*" in *Medieval Family Roles: A Book of Essays,* ed. Cathy Jorgensen Itnyre (New York: Garland, 1996), 67–83.

38. Staley, *Languages of Power,* 285; for Philippe on marriage, see 131, 281–87.

39. "Concubinage and Marriage in Medieval Canon Law," in *Sex, Law, and Marriage in the Middle Ages* (Brookfield, Vt.: Variorum, 1993), 7; Shannon McSheffrey, *Love and Marriage in Late Medieval London,* TEAMS (Kalamazoo, Mich.: Medieval Institute, 1995), 4; and Staley, *Languages of Power,* 281n.

40. See Michael Sheehan, "The Formation and Stability of Marriage in Fourteenth-Century England: Evidence of an Ely Register," rpr. in *Marriage, Family, and Law in Medieval Europe: Collected Studies,* ed. James K. Farge (Toronto: University of Toronto Press, 1996), 40, 45; see also Henry Angstar Kelly, *Love and Marriage in the Age of Chaucer* (Ithaca, N.Y.: Cornell University Press, 1975), esp. ch. 6, "Ecclesiastical Precept and Lay Observance," 161–76.

41. McSheffrey, *Love and Marriage,* 5.

42. Ibid., 9.

43. For an argument about the instability of marriages that occurred without a church ceremony see Kathryn Jacobs, *Marriage Contracts from Chaucer to the Renaissance Stage* (Gainesville: University Press of Florida, 2001), 30.

44. Roger Dymmok, *Liber contra duodecim errors et hereses Lollardorum,* ed. H. S. Cronin (London: Wyclif Society, 1922), 130; cited in Strohm, "Chaucer's Lollard Joke," 40; see also discussion by Carolyn Dinshaw, *Getting Medieval: Sexualities and Communities, Pre- and Postmodern* (Durham, N.C.: Duke University Press, 1999), 81

45. Salter, *Chaucer: The Knight's Tale and the Clerk's Tale,* 62.

46. Compare Petrarch in Severs, *Literary Relationships,* 268: "Solam igitur in thalamum sevocatam, turbida fronte sic alloquitur"; trans. French, 299: "Therefore, he called her alone into his chamber and addressed her thus, with troubled brow."

47. Compare Petrarch in Severs, *Literary Relationships,* 270: "Letus ille responso, sed dissimulans visu mestus abscessit, et post paululum unum suorum satellitum fidessimum sibi, cuius opera gravioribus in negociis uti consueverat"; trans. French, 300: "Happy in her reply, but feigning sadness in his looks, he left her; and a little while later, he sent to her one of his underlings, a most faithful man, whose

services he was wont to use in his most weighty affairs, and whom he instructed in the task before him." Readers have frequently noted that Chaucer dramatizes the terror and the pathos of this scene.

48. Petrarch locates the moment at the point when the daughter is weaned, which suggests that Walter's motives are independent of the daughter and are even an act of hidden kindness. In Severs, *Literary Relationships*, 268.

49. Chaucer's translation is closest to the *Livre de Griseldis* here: "et toutesfoiz courage meur et ancien estoit muciez et enclos en sa virginite," vs. Petrarch, "nil molle nil tenerum cogitare didicerat, sed virilis senilisque animus virgineo latebat in pectore," in Severs, *Literary Relationships*, 260–61.

50. The English Croxton *Play of the Sacrament* survives in a single sixteenth-century manuscript, but stories of Jewish tortures and violations of the consecrated host circulated in Italy and France from the fourteenth century on; for the text of the Croxton *Play* and a summary of continental versions, see Norman Davis, ed., *Non-Cycle Plays and Fragments*, EETS (New York: Oxford University Press, 1970), lxxii–lxxiv; for a recent study see David Lawton, "Sacrilege and Theatricality: The Croxton *Play of the Sacrament*," *Journal of Medieval and Early Modern Studies* 33 (2003): 281–309. For host-desecration accusations, see Rubin, *Gentile Tales: The Narrative Assault on Late Medieval Jews* (New Haven, Conn.: Yale University Press, 1999).

51. Carolyn Dinshaw, *Chaucer's Sexual Poetics* (Madison: University of Wisconsin Press, 1989), esp. 148, 150. For an excellent article that contrasts Petrarch's and Chaucer's differing epistemological and philosophical interests in the Griselda story, see Warren Ginsberg, "Petrarch, Chaucer and the Making of the Clerk," in *The Performance of Middle English: Essays on Chaucer and the Drama in Honor of Martin Stevens*, ed. James J. Paxson, Lawrence Clopper, and Sylvia Tomasch (Cambridge: D. S. Brewer, 1998), 25–41.

52. Staley, *Powers of the Holy*, 201.

53. Wallace, *Chaucerian Polity*, 287.

54. See especially Jill Mann, *Geoffrey Chaucer*, 146–64; for a succinct review of feminist criticism and Chaucer's sexual politics, see Elaine Tuttle Hansen, "Fearing for Chaucer's Good Name," *Exemplaria* 2.1 (1990): 23–36, who argues that Chaucer "invokes the myth of female difference, through his representation of women and Woman, to resist the feminization he at once acknowledges and deplores, and to lay claim to the authority of a disembodied authorial voice" (33). See also Dinshaw, *Chaucer's Sexual Politics*, who argues that "a new hermeneutic—a way of reading, indeed, like a woman—proceeds from the Clerk's identification with the female" (137). For an opposing analysis that argues that the voice of the Clerk is embodied in Griselda, but only as an ironic voice of excessive abject obedience, see Andrew Sprung, "Coercion and Compliance in Chaucer's *Clerk's Tale*," *Exemplaria* 7.2 (1995): 345–69; and the similar argument by David Aers, *Chaucer* (Atlantic Highlands, N.J.: Humanities Press, 1986), 34, who argues that Griselda contributes to Chaucer's critique of tyranny, since "in her servile obedience to her ruler, she renounces all responsibility, moral or religious."

55. For an argument that the Clerk adorns the tale with the very kinds of rhetorical flourishes the Host asks him to leave out, see Warren Ginsberg, "'And speketh so Pleyn': The Clerk's Tale and Its Teller," *Criticism* 20 (1978): 319.

56. Wallace, *Chaucerian Polity*, 267.

57. Compare Petrarch in Severs, *Literary Relationships*, 254: "... Liguriam gurgite violentus intersecat; dehinc Emiliam atque Flaminiam Veneciamque disterminans multis ad ultimum et ingentibus hostiis in Adriacum mare descendit. Ceterum pars illa terrarum de qua primum dixi, que et grata planicie et interiectis collibus ac montibus circumflexis, aprica pariter ac iocunda est, atque ab eorum quibus subiacet pede montium nomen tenet, et civitates aliquot et opida habet egregia. Inter cetera, ad radicem Vesulli, terra Saluciarum vicis et castellis satis frequens ... ," trans. French, 291.

58. For a very different reading of this double move, see Anne Middleton, "The Clerk and His Tale: Some Literary Contexts," *Studies in the Age of Chaucer* 2 (1980): 147, who argues that the Clerk performs these two modes as an exercise of his literary/critical wit.

59. Mann, *Geoffrey Chaucer*, 146.

60. For an alternative reading, see Elaine Tuttle Hansen, *Chaucer and the Fictions of Gender* (Berkeley: University of California Press, 1992), 205: "The Clerk's humorous ending deflates rather than protects Griselda's virtue, surely, and deflects us from both the real experience and the figurative value of her suffering and endurance."

61. Derek Pearsall, *The Life of Geoffrey Chaucer: A Critical Biography* (Oxford: Blackwell, 1992), 267.

62. See, for instance, lines 484, 489, 648, 681, 725, 1065, 1071, 1081, 1093.

63. For an argument that Chaucer's revisions of Petrarch secularize, rather than sanctify, to locate the tale in a setting that is "domestic not cosmic," see Valerie Edden, "Sacred and Secular in the *Clerk's Tale*," *Chaucer Review* 26.4 (1994): 374. For a similar argument that Chaucer's changes to the tale "suggest the difficulties of faith rather than God's famous victories," see C. David Benson, "Poetic Variety in the Man of Law's and the Clerk's Tales," in *Chaucer's Religious Tales*, ed. Benson and Robertson, 140.

Chapter 5. The Clergeon's Tongue

1. Mary Douglas, *Purity and Danger: An Analysis of the Concepts of Pollution and Taboo* (London: Routledge & Kegan Paul, 1966; rpr. Boston: Ark Paperbacks, 1985), 125.

2. Julia Kristeva, *Powers of Horror: An Essay on Abjection*, trans. Leon S. Roudiez (New York: Columbia University Press, 1982), 4.

3. For these images, see Camille, *Image on the Edge*, 82–84, who also comments, 82, that marginal sculpture often pays attention to the mouth, "the site of so many different kinds of sin." For an odd legal record from 1380 about a phony tongue involved in the performance of London street theater, see Wallace, *Chaucerian Polity*, 159–60.

4. See Kerby-Fulton and Despres, *Iconography and the Professional Reader*, 100–101.

5. *Piers Plowman*, ed. Kane and Donaldson, 2.041, 5.086, 3.322.

6. Sherman Hawkins, "Chaucer's Prioress and the Sacrifice of Praise," *Journal of English and Germanic Philology* 63 (1964): 599–624.

7. See especially Bruce Holsinger, "Pedagogy, Violence, and the Subject of Music: Chaucer's *Prioress's Tale* and the Ideologies of Song," *New Medieval Literatures* 1 (1997): 157–92; and for medieval song schools, Corey J. Marvin, "I Will Thee Not Forsake: Kristevan Maternal Space in Chaucer's *Prioress's Tale* and John of Garland's *Stella Maris*," *Exemplaria* 8 (1996), 38–39.

8. Rita Copeland, "Childhood, Pedagogy, and the Literal Sense: From Late Antiquity to the Lollard Heretical Classroom," *New Medieval Literatures* 1 (1997): 156.

9. The *Middle English Dictionary* gives as its second definition for "construen," "To frame or give a translation of (a Latin passage or text), translate by way of conveying the meaning"; "construen on English" means to translate into English.

10. Rita Copeland, *Rhetoric, Hermeneutics, and Translation in the Middle Ages: Academic Traditions and Vernacular Texts* (Cambridge: Cambridge University Press, 1991), 179–80, 200; see also Nicholas Watson, "The Politics of Middle English Writing," in *The Idea of the Vernacular: An Anthology of Middle English Literary Theory, 1280–1520*, ed. Jocelyn Wogan-Browne, Nicholas Watson, Andrew Taylor, and Ruth Evans (University Park: Pennsylvania State University Press, 1999), 331–51.

11. Justice, *Writing and Rebellion*, 40–48; and Susan Crane, "The Writing Lesson of 1381," in *Chaucer's England: Literature in Historical Context* (Minneapolis: University of Minnesota Press, 1992), 201–21.

12. Copeland, "Childhood, Pedagogy," 148.

13. Aston, *Lollards and Reformers*, 207.

14. *Knighton's Chronicle*, 534–35; see Hudson, *Premature Reformation*, 76; Aston, *Lollards and Reformers*, 202; and Justice, *Writing and Rebellion*, 30–31.

15. For the consequences of Arundel's Constitutions on English literary production see Watson, "Censorship and Cultural Change"; Lynn Staley, *Margery Kempe's Dissenting Fictions* (University Park: Pennsylvania State University Press, 1994), ch. 4, "The English Nation," 127–70, esp. 131; Simpson, *Reform and Cultural Revolution*, 335, 342, 378; and the cluster "Vernacular Theology," ed. Holsinger.

16. Chaucer's insistent concerns with language and desire for linguistic transparency have been noted by many readers; see, for instance, Helen Cooper, *The Structure of the Canterbury Tales* (Athens: University of Georgia Press, 1984), 165; and Delany, *Naked Text*, esp. ch. 2, "Women, Nature and Language." Readers have also noted the Prioress's impassioned identification with the Clergeon, as Richard Rambuss puts it, "to imitate—in an idiom that is suitably exclamatory and full of childlike wonder—the linguistic innocence of the litel clergeon": "Devotion and Defilement: The Blessed Virgin Mary and the Corporeal Hagiographics of Chaucer's *Prioress's Tale*," in *Textual Bodies: Changing Boundaries of Literary Representation*, ed. Lori Hope Lefkowitz (Albany: SUNY Press, 1997), 91.

17. H. Marshall Leicester Jr., "Piety and Resistance: A Note on the Representation of Religious Feeling in *The Canterbury Tales*," in *The Endless Knot: Essays on Old and Middle English in Honor of Marie Borroff*, ed. M. Teresa Tavormina and

R. F. Yaeger (Cambridge: D. S. Brewer, 1995), 153; see also Elizabeth Robertson, "Aspects of Female Piety in the *Prioress's Tale*," in *Chaucer's Religious Tales*, 145–60; and Richard Osberg, "A Voice for the Prioress: The Context of English Devotional Prose," *Studies in the Age of Chaucer* 18 (1996): 25–54.

18. See, for instance, Louise O. Fradenburg, "Criticism, Anti-Semitism, and the Prioress's Tale," *Exemplaria* 1 (1989): 69–115; and Steven F. Kruger, "The Bodies of Jews in the Late Middle Ages," in *The Idea of Medieval Literature: New Essays on Chaucer and Medieval Culture in Honor of Donald R. Howard*, ed. James Dean and Christian Zacher (Newark: University of Delaware Press, 1992), 301–23.

19. R. J. Shoeck: "Chaucer's Prioress: Mercy and Tender Heart," *The Bridge: A Yearbook of Judaeo-Christian Studies* 2 (1956): 239–55; E. T. Donaldson, *Chaucer's Poetry* (New York: Appleton-Century-Crofts, 1958), 933–34. For a summary of these critical responses to the tale's anti-Semitism, see Albert B. Friedman, "The *Prioress's Tale* and Chaucer's Anti-Semitism," *Chaucer Review* 9 (1974): 118–29.

20. See, for instance, Richard Rex, "Wild Horses, Justice and Charity in the *Prioress's Tale*," *Papers in Language and Literature* 22.4 (1986): 339–51; Allen Kouretsky, "Dangerous Innocence: Chaucer's Prioress and Her Tale," in *Jewish Presences in English Literature*, ed. Derek Cohen and Deborah Heller (Montreal: McGill-Queen's University Press, 1990), 24.

21. Holsinger, "Pedagogy, Violence," argues that the boy's song is deeply implicated in the tale's spectacle of violence, emerging as it does from pedagogical practices in medieval song schools that were inherently equated with punitive corporal discipline.

22. Fradenburg, "Criticism, Anti-Semitism," 109. The particular target of Fradenburg's critique is Hawkins's article, "Chaucer's Prioress." Other studies arguing that anti-Semitism was such a common cultural trope that a fourteenth-century writer would have been unlikely to use it to single out its practitioner as a bigot include Florence Ridley, *The Prioress and the Critics*, University of California Publications, English Studies 30 (Berkeley: University of California Press, 1965); John C. Hirsh, "Reopening the *Prioress's Tale*," *Chaucer Review* 10 (1975): 30–45; John Archer, "The Structure of Anti-Semitism in the *Prioress's Tale*," *Chaucer Review* 19 (1984): 46–54; and more recently Sylvia Tomasch, "Postcolonial Chaucer and the Virtual Jew," in *Chaucer and the Jews: Sources, Contexts, Meanings*, ed. Sheila Delany (New York: Routledge, 2002), 69–85.

23. Lee Patterson, "Living Witnesses," 507–60.

24. "The Protestant Chaucer," in *Chaucer's Religious Tales*, ed. Benson and Robertson, 67. Other essays to explore the tale's emergence out of a culture of affective piety include Carolyn Collette, "Sense and Sensibility in the *Prioress's Tale*," *Chaucer Review* 15 (1981): 138–50 and Alfred David, "An ABC to the Style of the Prioress," in *Acts of Interpretation: The Text in its Contexts, 700–1600: Essays on Medieval and Renaissance Literature in Honor of E. Talbot Donaldson*, ed. Mary Carruthers and Elizabeth Kirk (Norman, Okla.: Pilgrim Books, 1982), 147–57; for a general discussion, see Collette, "Critical Approaches to the *Prioress's Tale* and the *Second Nun's Tale*," in *Chaucer's Religious Tales*, ed. Benson and Robertson, 95–107.

25. Aers, "Faith, Ethics, and Community," 341–69.

26. Leicester, "Piety and Resistance," 153.

27. *Middle English Dictionary*, s.v. "pite," sense 4.

28. Leicester, "Piety and Resistance," 160.

29. Barbara Nolan has noted that at the center of all four of Chaucer's rhyme-royal tales are "the speeches of the protagonists, and these speeches are always and only prayerful expressions of Christian faith and love"; "Chaucer's Religious Tales of Transcendence: Rhyme Royal and Christian Prayer in the Canterbury Tales," in *Chaucer's Religious Tales*, ed. Benson and Robertson, 36–37.

30. Tomasch, "Postcolonial Chaucer," 73. Other recent essays to grapple with the tale's anti-Semitism include Stephen Spector, "Empathy and Enmity in the *Prioress's Tale*," in *The Olde Daunce: Love, Friendship, Sex and Marriage in the Medieval World*, ed. Robert R. Edwards and Stephen Spector (Binghamton: SUNY Press, 1991), 211–28; Mary F. Godfrey, "The Fifteenth-Century Prioress's Tale and the Problem of Anti-Semitism," in *Rewriting Chaucer: Culture, Authority and the Idea of the Authentic Text: 1400–1602*, ed. Thomas A. Prendergast and Barbara Kline (Columbus: Ohio State University Press, 1999), 93–115; Philip S. Alexander, "Madame Eglantyne, Geoffrey Chaucer, and the Problem of Medieval Anti-Semitism," *Bulletin of the John Rylands Library* 74 (1992): 109–20; Emily Stark Zitter, "Anti-semitism in Chaucer's Prioress's Tale," *Chaucer Review* 25 (1990–91): 227–84; Rex, "Wild Horses, Justice and Charity," 339–51.

31. Žižek, *Sublime Object*, 126, see also 125; also Spector, "Empathy and Emnity," 222.

32. Kruger, "Bodies of Jews," 318. For the *Prioress's Tale* and eucharistic miracles involving Jews, see Denise Despres, "Cultic Anti-Judaism and Chaucer's Litel Clergeon," *Modern Philology* 91 (1994): 413–27. For eucharistic miracles and Jews, see Miri Rubin, "The Eucharist and the Construction of Medieval Identities," in *Culture and History*, 53–57, and especially her discussion of host-desecration narratives as developed throughout *Gentile Tales*; see also Kathleen Biddick, "Genders, Bodies, Borders: Technologies of the Visible," *Speculum* 68 (1993): 401–12. On the Croxton *Play of the Sacraments*, see Sarah Beckwith, "Ritual, Church and Theatre: Medieval Dramas of the Sacramental Body," in *Culture and History 1350–1600: Essays on English Communities, Identities and Writing*, ed. David Aers (Detroit: Wayne State University Press, 1992), 65–89; and Lawton, "Sacrilege and Theatricality."

33. For the absent Muslim presence implied by this opening, see Sheila Delany, "Chaucer's Prioress, the Jews, and the Muslims," in *Chaucer and the Jews*, 43–57.

34. Ibid. Archer, "The Structure of Anti-Semitism," 52, claims that both the lord and the provost are pagan authorities. Edward H. Kelly, "By Mouth of Innocentz: The Prioress Vindicated," *Papers in Language and Literature* 5.4 (1960): 368, argues that "Asia" indicates a place where both Jew and Christian are alien.

35. See Archer, "Structure of Antisemitism," 49–52, for a succinct overview of practices of usury in medieval England.

36. Iain Higgins, *Writing East: The "Travels" of Sir John Mandeville* (Philadelphia: University of Pennsylvania Press, 1997), 117; see also Linda Lomperis, "Medieval Travel Writing and the Question of Race," *Journal of Medieval and Early Modern Studies* 31 (2001): 155.

37. *Mandeville's Travels*, ed. M. C. Seymour (Oxford: Clarendon Press, 1967), 100.

38. Kathryn Lynch, "East Meets West in Chaucer's Squires and Franklin's Tales," *Speculum* 70 (1995): 532. Although Asia was a common locus for miracles of the Virgin, most of the analogues that have been identified for the *Prioress's Tale* leave the location unspecified or set in a distant country, as pointed out by Beverly Boyd, *Chaucer and the Liturgy* (Philadelphia: Dorrance, 1967), 21, and *Riverside Chaucer*, 914n. Based on Aquinas, Hirsh, "Reopening the Prioress's Tale," 40, has argued that the Asian "greet citee" is Jerusalem, and hence an archetypal locus for the working of the typologies of the narrative.

39. As Boyd, *Chaucer and the Liturgy*, 22, points out, the construction of the Jewry as a street open at either end can still be seen in European cities, indicating that "Chaucer knew what a ghetto might look like, whether or not his concept came from any of the former Jewries of England." The few remains of Prague's old Jewry that survive include six synagogues, the town hall, and the cemetery, which were spared only due to Hitler's decision that they should become an "Exotic Museum of an Extinct Race": Sadakat Kadri, *Prague* (London: Cadogan Books, 1991), 164.

40. Alfred Thomas, *Anne's Bohemia: Czech Literature and Society, 1310–1420* (Minneapolis: University of Minnnesota Press, 1998), 1.

41. Sumner Ferris, "Chaucer at Lincoln (1387): The Prioress's Tale as Political Poem," *Chaucer Review* 15 (1981): 295–321.

42. Rubin, *Gentile Tales*, 137.

43. "quia tamen hujusmodi usurarii nephas horrendum et detestabile . . . hodie nedum per populares verum etiam per magni status homines multimodis et quaesitis et fucatis coloribus, quod dolenter referimus, frequentatur, propter quod ab ipsis Iudaeis et aliis infidelibus in improperium nobis objicitur et fidelium cordibus in Dei ecclesia scandala gravantur," October 16, 1381, *Concilia pragensia, 1353–1413,* ed. C. Höfler, Prague, 1861, p. 30; trans. and cited in Rubin, *Gentile Tales*, 137.

44. For Anne in Bohemia before she came to London, see the discussion in Wallace, *Chaucerian Polity*, 357–64.

45. For a fuller development of this argument see Sarah Stanbury, "Host Desecration, Chaucer's Prioress's Tale, and Prague 1389," in *Mindful Spirit in Late Medieval Literature: Essays in Honor of Elizabeth Kirk* (New York: Palgrave, 2006), 211–24.

46. Latin versions of the story are recounted in *Passio judaeorum secundum Johannes rusticus quadratus*, ed. Paul Lehmann, *Parodistische texte, beispiele zur lateinischen parodie im mittelalter* (Munich: Drei Masken, 1923), 36–41; see Rubin, *Gentile Tales*, 135–40. For discussions of the 1389 host-desecration accusation in Prague, see also Eli Valley, *The Great Jewish Cities of Central and Eastern Europe* (Northvale, N.J.: Jason Aronson, Inc., 1999), 6–8; and David Philopson, *Old European Jewries* (Philadelphia: Jewish Publishing Society of America, 1894), 87–89.

47. "O reges, reges pudeat vos criminis huius!
Usuras capitis, quas gens maledicta lucratur,
In quo vos ipsos maledictor esse probates usuratores."
E. S. Bauer, *Frömmigkeit, Gelehrsamkeit und Zeitkritik an der Schwelle der grossen Konzilien: Johannes von Wetzlar und sein Dialogus super Magnificat* (Mainz: Selbstverlag

der Gesellschaft für mittelrheinische kirchengeschichte, 1981), 274, lines 2084–86; trans. Rubin, *Gentile Tales*, 139.

48. Elizabeth Robertson, "Aspects of Female Piety," also argues that the tale critiques "masculine adult authority" (157). See also Gail Berkeley Sherman, "Saints, Nuns, and Speech in the *Canterbury Tales*," in *Images of Sainthood in Medieval Europe*, ed. Renate Blumenfeld-Kosinski, Timea Szell, and Brigitte Cazelles (Ithaca, N.Y.: Cornell University Press, 1991), 160. For the tale as a story of the triumph of a female speaker, see Judith Ferster, "Your Praise Is Performed by Men and Children: Language and Gender in the Prioress's Prologue and Tale," *Exemplaria* 2.1 (1990): 155

49. Žižek, *Sublime Object*, 116–17.

50. Marie Padgett Hamilton, "Echoes of Childermas in the Tale of the Prioress," *Modern Language Review* 34 (1939): 1–8.

51. John Wickham Legg, ed., *The Sarum Missal* (Oxford: Oxford University Press, 1916), 32. See also Hamilton, "Echoes of Childermas," 3; and J. C. Wenk, "On the Sources of the *Prioress's Tale*," *Mediaeval Studies* 17 (1955): 214–19. The references to John (lines 579–85) and especially to the boy's mother as a "newe Rachel" also echo the Mass. The Communion text for the Holy Innocents in the Sarum rite is taken from Matthew 2:18, which recounts Herod's slaughter of the innocents and the following lamentation: "In Rama was there a voice heard, lamentation and great mourning, Rachel weeping for her children, and would not be comforted, because they are not": *The Sarum Missal*, trans. Frederick E. Warren (Milwaukee, Wis.: Young Churchman, 1913), 1:112; Hamilton, 3–4. See Boyd, *Chaucer and the Liturgy*, 68.

52. Boyd, *Chaucer and the Liturgy*, 54.

53. Duffy, *Stripping of the Altars*, 124.

54. For a description of the processions, see Mervyn James, "Ritual, Drama and the Social Body in the Late Medieval English Town," *Past and Present* 98 (1983): 5.

55. "Ad cuius translationem tam grandis conventus utriusque sexus de diversis mundi partibus convenerat, ut numquam retroactis temporibus, ut dicitur, tam magna multitudo hominum ad unum locum in Anglia coadunata fuerat": Daniel Rock, *The Church of Our Fathers, as Seen in St. Osmund's Rite for the Cathedral of Salisbury*, new edition G. W. Hart and W. H. Frere (London, J. Hodges, 1905), 3:404, cited in Snoek, *Medieval Piety*, 253.

56. Snoek, *Medieval Piety*, 153, from a compilation in Rock, *Church of Our Fathers*, 405–7, derived from accounts of translations of saints Albanus (1129) and Guthlac (1136). For a discussion of the translation processional in *St. Erkenwald*, see Boyd, *Chaucer and the Liturgy*, 6.

57. For the grain as the eucharistic wafer and a review of scholarly interpretations of "greyn," see especially Kathleen M. Oliver, "Singing Bread, Manna, and the Clergeon's 'Greyn,'" *Chaucer Review* 31 (1997): 357–64.

Chapter 6. Nicholas Love's Mirror

1. The widely influential *Meditationes*, which survives in 113 manuscripts, was probably written by Johannes de Caulibus, a Franciscan friar in San Gimignano in the mid-fourteenth century, but was long attributed to St. Bonaventure. The

Mirror survives in 56 complete manuscripts, according to the inventory in *Nicholas Love's Mirror of the Blessed Life of Jesus Christ: A Critical Edition Based on Cambridge University Library Additional MSS 5478 and 6686*, ed. Michael G. Sargent (New York: Garland, 1992), lxxii–lxxxvi. Citations from the text, by page and line number, are from this edition. For a succinct review of theories about the composition and dissemination of the *Meditations*, see "The *Meditationes Vitae Christi* and Franciscan Spirituality," in *Mirror*, ix–xx. For other general introductions to Love's *Mirror* and its textual affiliations, see Elizabeth Salter, *Nicholas Love's Myrrour of the Blessyd Lyf of Jesu Christ*, Analecta Cartusiana 10 (Salzburg: Institut für Englische Sprache und Literatur, 1974), ch. 5, "Meditation on the Sacred Humanity in Love's 'Myrrour,'" 119–78; Vincent Gillespie, "Strange Images of Death: The Passion in Later Medieval English Devotional and Mystical Writings," in *Zeit, Tod, und Ewigkeit in der Renaissance Literatur*, ed. James Hogg, Analecta Cartusiana 17 (Salzburg: Institut für Englische Sprache und Literatur, 1987), 111–59; and John V. Fleming, *An Introduction to the Franciscan Literature of the Middle Ages* (Chicago: Franciscan Herald Press, 1977), esp. ch. 6, "Franciscan Style."

2. "The Testimony of William Thorpe," in *Two Wycliffite Texts*, ed. Anne Hudson, EETS, o.s., 301 (Oxford: Oxford University Press, 1993), 56; see Rita Copeland, "William Thorpe and His Lollard Community: Intellectual Labor and the Representation of Dissent," in *Bodies and Disciplines: Intersections of Literature and History in Fifteenth-Century England* (Minneapolis: University of Minnesota Press, 1996), 199–221.

3. *Two Wycliffite Texts*, 58.

4. Sargent, *Mirror*, xlv.

5. Ibid., xlvi; and Kantik Ghosh, *The Wycliffite Heresy: Authority and the Interpretation of Texts* (Cambridge: Cambridge University Press, 2002), 148.

6. Watson, "Censorship and Cultural Change," 852–53; and Hughes, *Pastors and Visionaries*, 230–36.

7. Beadle, "'Devoute ymaginacioun' and the Dramatic Sense in Love's *Mirror* and the N-Town Plays," in *Nicholas Love at Waseda: Proceedings of the International Conference 20–22 July 1995*, ed. Shoichi Oguro, Richard Beadle, and Michael G. Sargent (Cambridge: D. S. Brewer, 1997), 9–12.

8. Ibid., 8.

9. *Middle English* Dictionary, s.v. "ded," sense 4.e.

10. *SEWW*, 85.

11. *Wycliffite Bible*, 1:34; Aston, *England's Iconoclasts*, 125.

12. The Twelve Conclusions of the Lollards are printed in *SEWW*, 24–29.

13. *Fasciculi Zizaniorum Magistri Johannis Wyclif cum Tritico*, ed. W. W. Shirley (London: Longman, Brown, Green, Longmans, and Roberts; 1858), 430, trans. Aston, *England's Iconoclasts*, 115n.

14. *A Tretise of Miraclis Pleyinge*, ed. Clifford Davidson, Early Drama, Art, and Music Monograph Series 19 (Kalamazoo, Mich.: Medieval Institute Publications, 1993), 98, 104; and see discussion in Davidson's introduction, 23–26. On theater and idolatry see Theresa Coletti, *Mary Magdalene and the Drama of Saints* (Philadelphia: University of Pennsylvania Press, 2004), 201–2.

15. Beckwith, *Christ's Body,* 70.

16. Ghosh, *Wycliffite Heresy*, 158; Simpson, *Reform and Cultural Revolution*, 436, makes a similar point: "within the vernacular, lay realm of devotional experience Love is unexpectedly liberal."

17. "Ut potes, quia incorporeus est, sed aspice eum tanquam magnum dominum, sedentem in solio exulso, vultu benigio, prio et paterno, quasi reconciliare volentem, sive reconciliatum esse, haec verbe dicentem," *Meditationes Vitae Christi*, in S. Bonaventurae Opera Omnia, ed. A. C. Peltier (Paris: Vives, 1868), 12:514b.15–20, cited in *Mirror*, 260n.

18. *De Mandatis Divinis*, 156; trans. Aston, *England's Iconoclasts*, 99.

19. *SEWW*, 27.

20. For images in monastic contemplation, see Jeffrey Hamburger, "The Visual and the Visionary: The Image in Late Medieval Monastic Devotions," *Viator* 20 (1989): 161–204.

21. See discussion of this truncation in Sargent, *Mirror*, lviii; see also Salter, *Nicholas Love's Mirror*, 178n, who notes that Love abbreviates the *Meditation*'s emphasis on the way contemplation on the sacred humanity of Christ serves in a hierarchical system of meditation.

22. *Meditations on the Life of Christ: An Illustrated Manuscript of the Fourteenth Century*, ed. Isa Ragusa and Rosalie Green (Princeton, N.J.: Princeton University Press, 1961), 279; see discussion in Hamburger, *Visual and the Visionary*, 166.

23. The *Meditations* makes it apparent that meditation on the body and events of Christ's life ought to be superseded when one passes to a higher, noncorporeal form of meditation, much like the progress invoked in a 1310 miniature illustrating a treatise known as *La Sainte Abbaye*: A Dominican nun, in one image, prays to an image of the coronation of the Virgin, then in the next prays to the Eucharist, and finally receives a vision of God in majesty (Hamburger, *Visual and the Visionary*, 174, fig. 12). Love, in contrast, claims the sufficiency of meditation on corporeal substance and action; meditation on "gostly substances" (10.34) is defined through "erþly þinges" (10.38).

24. Ghosh, *Wycliffite Heresy*, 202.

25. Pecock, *The Repressor*, 1:269–70. On Pecock and imagination see Aston, *England's Iconoclasts*, 152n.

26. *Doctrinale antiquitatum fidei ecclesiae catholicae*, ed. B. Blanciotti (Venice, 1757–59; rpr. Farnborough, Hampshire: Gregg Press, 1967), 3:937; trans. Ghosh, *Wycliffite Heresy*, 202.

27. Simpson, *Reform and Cultural Revolution*, 437; see also Watson, "Conceptions of the Word," 96, who says that Love produces "a kind of textual image, full of lush description and imagery."

28. Fleming, *Franciscan Literature*, 246; Sargent, *Mirror*, xx, 261n; Gibson, *Theater of Devotion*, 8–9, 49, 51.

29. Margaret Rickert, *Painting in Britain in the Middle Ages* (London: Penguin, 1954), 173.

30. According to Ellen Ross, wall paintings conveyed the same meanings and were images "writ large": *The Grief of God: Images of the Suffering Jesus in Late Medieval England* (New York: Oxford University Press, 1997), 53. See also Benson, *Public Piers Plowman*, ch. 5, "Public Art: Parish Wall Paintings."

31. Morgan, "Patrons and Devotional Images," 93.

32. Gibson, *Theater of Devotion*, 49.

33. Arguing that Christ's body in late medieval culture operates as both "focus and medium through which clerical control asserts itself" and also as a "focus for the democratizating lay tendencies of late medieval piety," Beckwith, *Christ's Body*, 32, 64, looks at the ways that the *Mirror* organizes Christ's body through images of "violent hierarchization" and "linguistic condescention." Through a controlled representation of Christ's body, she suggests, Love's narrative of incarnation thus becomes a means to contain the destabilizing potentials of lay affective piety, dangers that are implicit in the text's careful directives to its readers.

34. On the *Mirror's* implied female audience and manuscript ownership, see Carol M. Meale, " 'oft siþis with gete deuotion I þought what I miȝt do pleysyng to God': The Early Ownership and Readership of Love's *Mirror*, with Special Reference to its Female Audience," in *Nicholas Love at Waseda*, 19–46; and also Simpson, *Reform and Cultural Revolution*, 437.

35. Beckwith, *Christ's Body*, 45; Gibson, *Theater of Devotion*, 10, 49.

36. See Rubin, "The Eucharist," 43–63.

37. Meale, "Early Ownership," 38–43.

38. Kamerick, *Popular Piety*, 44–68.

39. *Sight and Embodiment*, 134, 140–44.

40. Camille, "Before the Gaze"; and Biernoff.

41. Margaret E. Thompson, *The Carthusian Order in England* (London: Society for Promoting Christian Knowledge, 1930), 182–84. For Love as Prior at Mount Grace, see Sargent, xxi–xxix.

42. *William Worcestre: Itineraries*, ed. John H. Harvey (Oxford: Clarendon, 1969), 271, cited in Joseph Gribbin, *Aspects of Carthusian Liturgical Practice in the Later Middle Age* (Salzburg: Institut für Anglistik und Amerikanistik, 1995), 42–43.

43. Thompson, *Carthusian Order*, 106, 266.

44. See Sargent, *Mirror*, xxv; see also David Knowles, *Religious Orders in England* (Cambridge: Cambridge University Press, 1961–62), 2:223; and Gibson, *Theater of Devotion*, 21.

Chapter 7. Arts of Self-Patronage

1. See Gibson, *Theater of Devotion,* esp. chs. 2 and 4; Duffy, *Stripping of the Altars,* 63–68, 155–60, 166–69; M. D. Anderson, *History and Imagery in British Churches* (London: John Murray, 1971), 208–21. See also Rosenthal, *Purchase of Paradise;* and Pamela Graves, "Social Space in the English Medieval Parish Church," *Economy and Society* 18 (1989): esp. 311–19.

2. Citations by chapter and line number are from *The Book of Margery Kempe,* ed. Barry Windeatt (Essex: Longman, 2000).

3. Kempe's strategic self-construction through her body, voice, and persona is the subject of several full-length studies, including Staley, *Margery Kempe's Dissenting Fictions*; and Karma Lochrie, *Margery Kempe and Translations of the Flesh* (Philadelphia: University of Pennsylvania Press, 1991). See also David Aers, *Community,*

Gender, and Individual Identity: English Writing 1360–1430 (London: Routledge, 1988), ch. 2; Sarah Beckwith, "A Very Material Mysticism: The Medieval Mysticism of Margery Kempe," in *Medieval Literature: Criticism, Ideology and History*, ed. David Aers (Sussex: Harvester, 1988), 34–57; Riddy, "Women Talking"; Sue Ellen Holbrook, "'About Her': Margery Kempe's Book of Telling and Working," in *The Idea of Medieval* Literature, ed. James Dean and Christian Zacher (Newark: University of Delaware Press, 1992), 265–84; Rosalynn Voaden, "God's Almighty Hand: Women Co-Writing the Book," in *Women, The Book and the Godly*, ed. L. Smith and J. H. M. Taylor (Cambridge: Cambridge University Press, 1995), 55–65.

4. See, for instance, Gibson, *Theater of Devotion*, ch. 3, pp. 47–65; Beckwith, *Christ's Body*, 78–111; Denise Despres, "Franciscan Spirituality: Margery Kempe and Visual Meditation," *Mystics Quarterly* 11.1 (1984): 12–18; David Lawton, "Voice, Authority, and Blasphemy in the *Book of Margery Kempe*," in *Margery Kempe: A Book of Essays* ed. Sandra J. McEntire (New York: Garland, 1992), 99; David Wallace, "Mystics and Followers in Siena and East Anglia: A Study in Taxonomy, Class and Cultural Mediation," in *The Medieval Mystical Tradition in England*, ed. Marion Glasscoe (Cambridge: D. S. Brewer, 1984), 169–91; Aers, *Community, Gender*, esp. 104–6.

5. Kamerick, *Popular Piety,* 131–54.

6. Clarissa W. Atkinson, *Mystic and Pilgrim: The Book and the World of Margery Kempe* (Ithaca, N.Y.: Cornell University Press, 1983), 92–93.

7. According to Hope Emily Allen's note, "from an inventory of Lynn priory of 1454, the 'capella' seems then to have contained the library as well as the liturgical furniture," in *The Book of Margery Kempe*, ed. Sanford Brown Meech and Hope Emily Allen, EETS (London: Oxford University Press, 1940), 324/155.

8. According to the note in *The Book of Margery Kempe*, ed. Meech and Allen, 316/131, this would have been the chapter house of the collegiate church of St. John the Evangelist, at Beverly (Beverly Minster). Although the chapter house is no longer extant, surviving chapter houses in England, such as at Salisbury, Lincoln, and Westminster, demonstrate typically elaborate sculptural programs. The entrance to the chapter house at Salisbury contains a sculptural program of the virtues and vices, and the spandrels of the arcading around the walls of the house itself show a set of carvings representing the Old Testament from the creation to the delivery of the Ten Commandments; Selby Whittingham, *Salisbury Chapter House* (London, 1974).

9. The chapel contained a representation of the nativity (which gave it its name from OF *Gesine*, childbed), according to Henry J. Hillen, *History of the Borough of King's Lynn* (Norwich: East of England Newspaper Company, 1907), 2:741–45, 814–15; see also note in Meech and Allen, *The Book of Margery Kempe*, 324; and discussion in Gibson, *Theater of Devotion*, 64.

10. For Kempe's strategic uses of place, see Virginia Chieffo Raguin, "Real and Imagined Bodies in Architectural Space: The Setting for Margery Kempe's Book," in *Women's Space: Patronage, Place, and Gender in the Medieval Church*, ed. Virginia Chieffo Raguin and Sarah Stanbury (Binghamton: State University of New York Press, 2005), 105–40.

11. For a discussion of the role played by private ownership of devotional objects in the development of art connoisseurship at the end of the Middle Ages,

see Belting, *Likeness and Presence: A History of the Image Before the Era of Art*, trans. Edmund Jephcott (Chicago: University of Chicago Press, 1994), esp. 409–57.

12. I take the term autoportrait from Louis Marin, "Topic and Figures of Enunciation: It is Myself that I Paint," in *Vision and Textuality*, ed. Stephen Melville and Bill Readings (Durham, N.C.: Duke University Press, 1995), 195–214.

13. Sixten Rinbgom, "Devotional Images and Imaginative Devotions: Notes on the Place of Art in Late Medieval Private Piety," *Gazette des Beaux-Arts* 73 (1969): 159–70. A particular example of this relationship can be seen in the story of a peasant whose sight-curing vision of St. Foy corresponded to an extant gilded statue and reliquary; see *Liber miraculorum Sancte Fideis*, ed. A. Bouillet (Paris, 1897), 9–10, as noted in Aston, *Faith and Fire*, 221.

14. See especially Hamburger, "The Visual and the Visionary"; Ringbom, "Devotional Images," 161–64, briefly discusses St. Catherine of Siena, St. Bridget, Julian of Norwich, St. Teresa of Avila, and St. Catherine of Genoa as evidence that "among fourteenth-century mystics the women seem to have been particularly responsive to images"; see also J. E. Ziegler, *Sculpture of Compassion: The Pietà and the Beguines in the Southern Low Countries, c. 1300–1600* (Brussels: Institut Historique Belge de Rome, 1992), 39–40, 117–39.

15. See, for instance, Corine Schleif, "Hands that Appoint, Anoint and Ally: Late Medieval Donor Strategies for Appropriating Approbation Through Painting," *Art History* 16.1 (March 1993): 1–32; Marks, *Stained Glass*, 1–27.

16. For donor practices and imaging in late medieval England, see Morgan, "Patrons and Devotional Images," 93–121.

17. Sidney Cockerell, *Two East Anglian Psalters at the Bodleian Library, Oxford: The Ormesby Psalter, MS Douce 366 and the Brunholm Psalter, MS Ashmole 1523* (Oxford: Roxburghe Club, 1926), fig. 1, p. 19; Lasko and Morgan, *Medieval Art in East Anglia*, 18, note that some of the numerous coats of arms throughout the manuscript represent Norfolk families.

18. Christopher Woodforde, *The Norwich School of Glass-Painting in the Fifteenth Century* (London: Oxford University Press, 1950), index, s.v. "heraldic glass."

19. For details of these brasses and also other marks of local patronage in St. Margaret's, see the website *Mapping Margery Kempe*, ed. Sarah Stanbury and Virginia Raguin, s.v. "St. Margaret's": http://www.holycross.edu/departments/visarts/projects/anglia/margaret.htm.

20. Large lettering on the north porch urges viewers to "Pray for ye sowlis of William Cloopton, Margy and Margy his wifis, and for ye sowle of Alice Clopton and for John Clopto', and for alle thooo sowlis' yt ye seyd John is bo'nde to prey for," cited in Gibson, *Theater of Devotion*, 80.

21. Ibid., 101, 105; see also Graves on patronage in East Harling: "It may be suggested that the average inhabitant of East Harling witnessed at least one act of patronage during their lifetime . . . the identity of the donor would be constantly in evidence through the repeated motifs of heraldry found throughout the fabric, to which the worshipper would be witness on every visit to church," "Social Space," 312.

22. Marks, *Stained Glass*, 12, notes that donors kneeling at the feet of saints and of Christ on the cross are common in English fourteenth-century glass. See also Schleif, "Hands that Appoint," 1.

23. Marks, *Stained Glass*, 4–5, 12, and fig. 1; the windows of the nave were glazed between 1291 and 1339 by clerical and lay donors, including members of the nobility and merchant class, which Marks notes as symptomatic of the transformation of English society to a complex structure embracing a "rich urban mercantile class" (4).

24. Ibid., 5–6; Gibson, *Theater of Devotion*, 79–96.

25. Beckwith, *Christ's Body*, 91; for Kempe's struggles with clerical control, see also Susan Dickman, "Margery Kempe and the Continental Tradition of the Pious Woman," in *The Medieval Mystical Tradition in England,* ed. Marion Glasscoe (Exeter: University of Exeter Press, 1980), 150–68.

26. On the mercantile rhetoric of Kempe's text, see Sheila Delany, "Sexual Economics: Chaucer's Wife of Bath and *The Book of Margery Kempe,*" *Minnesota Review* 5 (1975): 104–15; and Deborah Ellis, "Merchant's Wife's Tales: Language, Sex and Commerce in Margery Kempe and in Chaucer," *Exemplaria* 2 (1990): 595–626.

27. *Book of Margery Kempe*, ed. Meech and Allen, 324/155.

28. See Duffy's discussion of lay ownership of primers, *Stripping of the Altars*, 209–32. For an argument that cloistered women may have comprised the largest audience for mystical and didactic literature and may have played a central role in the development of devotional imagery, see Jeffrey F. Hamburger, *The Rothschild Canticles: Art and Mysticism in Flanders and the Rhineland Circa 1300* (New Haven, Conn.: Yale University Press, 1990), 3–5. On new possibilities for women to possess devotional images privately in the late Middle Ages, see also Ziegler, *Sculpture of Compassion*, 129, who claims that women's new access to images in fourteenth-century beguinages marked a distinct change from earlier centuries where "sacred objects had been the purview of male monastery, cloister, and cathedral, where they were used and enjoyed collectively," see also 131; Ziegler notes, however, that precise documentation of possession and use is uncertain, 139 n. 80. For a study establishing a relationship between female readers and books of hours, see Sandra Penketh, "Women and Books of Hours," in *Women and the Book: Assessing the Visual Evidence*, ed. Jane H. M. Taylor and Lesley Smith (Toronto: British Library and University of Toronto Press, 1996), 266–80. Startling images suggesting dramatically different relationships to corporeal images appear in the *Prayer Book of James IV*, Vienna, Osterreichische Nationalbibliothek, col. 1897, fols. 24v and 243r, which shows James IV in a private chapel before a painted triptich, whereas the devotion of Queen Margaret in the same manuscript depicts her kneeling before a private altar but seeing the Virgin and child in a spiritual vision; illus. in Ringbom, "Devotional Images," 167.

29. On the privileging of the high altar as a locus for expensive gifts, in particular panel painting, in East Anglia, see Christopher Norton, David Park, and Paul Binski, *Dominican Painting in East Anglia: The Thornham Parva Retable and the Musée de Cluny Frontal* (Suffolk: Boydell Press, 1987), 83; Belting, *Likeness and Presence*, 398–404, 7; Benson, *Public Piers Plowman*, 170; see also Freedberg, *The Power of Images*, 118 ff. The special status of the high altar in a Suffolk church as a site for the most beautiful images is indicated in the valuable account by Roger Martin in the 1580s or 1590s describing "The State of Melford Church and Our Ladie's Chappel at the East End, As I Did Know It." Martin gives a detailed account of the images at the Martin family chapel, the Jesus Aisle that was to the south side of the

chancel, but only after describing the clearly more elaborate Passion reredos behind the high altar and flanking gilt tabernacles housing carvings of the Trinity; see Dymond and Paine, *The Spoil of Melford Church*, 1–2.

30. Duffy, *Stripping of the Altars*, 132: "In the course of the twelfth and thirteenth centuries a demarcation of responsibility had emerged between parson and people: he was to maintain the chancel, they the nave." See also 97, 110–11. See 113–14 for a discussion of the control of nave altars by the laity, and 157–61 for the laity's experience of the high altar and the rood screen at a Sunday Mass. On lay patronage of rood screens in East Anglia, see Duffy, "Parish, Piety, and Patronage," 133–62. Monasteries also replicated the gender distinction that privileged a male clergy with access to images, since in late medieval England monasteries outnumbered nunneries 6:1, according to Roberta Gilchrist, *Gender and Material Culture: The Archaeology of Religious Women* (London: Routledge, 1994), 61; see also Norman P. Tanner, *The Church in Late Medieval Norwich, 1370–1532* (Toronto: Pontifical Institute for Mediaeval Studies, 1984), 25, who indicates that this ratio was mirrored at the local level.

31. Hillen, *History of the Borough of King's Lynn*, 168.

32. For pew ownership and maintenance see Katherine L. French, "The Seat Under Our Lady: Gender and Seating in Late Medieval English Parish Churches," in *Women's Space*, ed. Raguin and Stanbury, 141–60. Duffy, *Stripping of the Altars*, 123–26, argues instead that documented interest by the gentry in the entire life of parish ritual leveled rather than privatized ritual experience. Nevertheless, the designation of certain spaces and the images they contained as special, entailed, or even exclusive would have contributed to the mystification of structures of authority and hierarchy.

33. Graves, "Social Space," 301, 317.

34. Ibid., 319; M. Glasscoe, "Late Medieval Paintings in Ashton Church, Devon," *Journal of the British Archaeological Association* 140 (1987): 182–90.

35. The image was also popular for private ownership in the late Middle Ages, as recorded by the Datini correspondence in which the merchant of Prato was counseled by Domenico di Cambio that an *imago pietatis* is the appropriate image for the bedchamber; see Belting, *The Image and Its Public*, 232 n. 45.

36. One of the most famous of these images was the mosaic at Santa Croce in Gerusalemme in Rome, an image Bertelli argues was brought to the church in 1385–86 and there became a pilgrimage shrine; see Carlo Bertelli, "The *Image of Pity* in Santa Croce in Gerusalemme," in *Essays in the History of Art Presented to Rudolf Wittkower* (London: Phaidon, 1967), 46. As Bertelli notes, by the time the image appeared in Rome, the iconography of the Man of Sorrows was widespread in the West.

37. Schiller, *Iconography of Christian Art*, 2:197–201; Duffy, *Stripping of the Altars*, 107, 108–9; Belting, *Image and its Public*, ch. 2; Patricia de Leeuw, "Unde et Memores, Domine: Memory and the Mass of St. Gregory," in *Memory and the Middle Ages*, ed. Nancy Netzer and Virginia Reinburg (Chestnut Hill, Mass.: Boston College Museum of Art, 1995), 33–41. On liturgical uses of the altarpiece in fifteenth-century north European painting, see Barbara G. Lane, *The Altar and the Altarpiece: Sacramental Themes in Early Netherlandish Painting* (New York: Harper & Row,

1984), 8–10, 11.128–31; for the Man of Sorrows and "ocular communion," see Bier-noff, *Sight and Embodiment*, 144–49.

38. See de Leeuw, "Memory and the Mass of St. Gregory," 33–41; Schiller, *Iconography*, 2:200; Belting, *Image and Its Public*, 36–38. An *imago pietatis* forms the central drama of the Croxton Play of the Sacrament in *Non-Cycle Play and Fragments*, ed. Norman Davis, EETS (London: Oxford University Press, 1970).

39. The first appearance of the image's powers of indulgence is an inscription on a relief in Regensburg at the beginning of the fifteenth century: Bertelli, "Image of Pity," 46. See also de Leeuw, "Unde et Memores," 35; Woodforde, *Norwich School of Glass Painting*, 23; Ringbom, "Devotional Images," 165. On the history of indulgenced images in general, see Belting, *Image and Its Public*, 14–15, 64, 132–33.

40. St. Peter Mancroft, Blakeney, West Rudham, and Diggington, Hunts: see Woodforde, *Norwich School*, 23.

41. For a discussion of English representations of the Man of Sorrows, see Campbell Dodgson, "English Devotional Woodcuts of the Late Fifteenth Century, with Special Reference to Those in the Bodleian Library," *Walpole Society* 17 (1928–29): 95–108.

42. A Man of Sorrows appears in the glazing at Long Melford in close conjunction with a figure of Lady Annes Fray, perhaps the donor of the window, with the inscription below her, "pray for dame Annes Fray"; see Woodforde, *Norwich School*, 121. It is by no means certain, however, that these images were proximal in the original program of the glazing.

43. Woodforde, *Norwich School*, 117–88.

44. Bertelli, "The *Image of Pity*," 45 n. 37, also notes that the Man of Sorrows was not infrequently represented on church portals and on chapels represented in Italian Trecento paintings. For the churches Kempe visited in Rome, see the web site *Mapping Margery Kempe*, ed. Stanbury and Raguin, s.v. "Churches in Rome."

45. This image is discussed in Morgan, "Patrons and Devotional Images," 100; cat. Scott, *Later Gothic Manuscripts*, #83.

46. *Middle English Dictionary*, s.v. "stockfish." This usage is reported from c. 1475.

47. A bench end, now in the Victoria and Albert Museum, from St. Nicholas's church, the chapel-of-ease that was the Brunham family chapel, shows a carving of three dried fish, or stockfish; see Anderson, *History and Imagery in British Churches*, 217.

48. Bridget of Sweden, *The Revelations of Saint Birgitta*, ed. William Patterson Cumming, EETS 178 (London: Oxford University Press, 1929), 86.

49. *St. Katherine of Alexandria*, ed. Nevanlinna and Taavitsainen, 80, lines 446–48.

50. G. H. Cook, *Medieval Chantries and Chantry Chapels* (London: Phoenix House, 1947; rev. edition, 1963), 3–5.

51. C. M. Kauffmann, *Romanesque Manuscripts, 1016–1190*, in *A Survey of Manuscripts Illuminated in the British Isles* (London: H. Miller, 1975), vol. 3, item #78, describes the New Minster Register (Liber Vitae), London, British Library MS Stowe 922. I am grateful to Madeline Caviness for this reference.

52. Anderson, *History and Imagery in British Churches*, 95; see also Cheetham, *English Medieval Alabasters*, 296. It has been suggested that Norwich may have

been a center for alabaster carving, particularly for stone fonts, though Cheetham, *English Medieval Alabasters*, 15, considers it unlikely.

53. Cheetham, *English Medieval Alabasters*, 31.

54. This painting is described in Tristram, *English Wall Painting*, 166.

55. For discussions of Kempe's orthodoxy, see Staley, *Margery Kempe's Dissenting Fictions*, 5–11, who argues that Margery is a fictive persona created by Kempe who strategically negotiates charges of Lollardy even as she lodges a critique against orthodoxy; Beckwith, "Material Mysticism," 45–46; for Kempe's anticlericalism, see Beckwith, *Christ's Body*, "The Uses of Corpus Christi and Margery Kempe," 78–111.

56. *SEWW*, 153/97.

57. Ibid., 27.

58. Morgan, "Patrons and Devotional Images," 102.

59. Woodforde, *Norwich School*, 70–71.

60. Cheetham, *English Medieval Alabasters*, 308.

61. British Library MS Add. 29705, fol. 193v, illus. in Marks, *Stained Glass in England*, fig. 138, p. 172.

62. Marks, *Stained Glass*, 34, 252 n. 41.

63. *The Book of Margery Kempe*, ed. Meech and Allen, xxxii.

64. *Mirror*, ed. Sargent, xxii.

65. Bertelli, "The Image of Pity," 47–49; Rosemary Woolf, *The English Religious Lyric in the Middle Ages* (Oxford: Clarendon Press, 1968), 391n.

66. On the quality of liveliness, see Bernhard Ridderbos, "The Man of Sorrows: Pictorial Images and Metaphorical Statements," in *The Broken Body: Passion Devotion in Late Medieval Culture*, ed. A. A. MacDonald, H. N. B. Ridderbos, and R. M. Schlusseman (Groningen: Egbert Forsten, 1998), 167.

67. For a facsimile, see *An Illustrated Yorkshire Carthusian Religious Miscellany, British Library London Additional MS. 37049*, ed. James Hogg, Analecta Cartusiana 95, no. 3 *The Illustrations* (Salzburg: Institut für Anglistik und Amerikanistik, 1981); for a recent overview, see Douglas Gray, "London, British Library, Additional MS 37049: A Spiritual Encyclopedia," in *Text and Controversy From Wyclif to Bale: Essays in Honour of Anne Hudson*, ed. Helen Barr and Ann M. Hutchinson (Turnhout, Belgium: Brepols, 2005), 99–116. The manuscript is described as scribe illustrated by Kerby-Fulton and Despres, *Iconography and the Professional Reader*, 11; interplay between text and image is also noted by Woolf, *English Religious*, Appendix E, "History of the Imago Pietatis," 389–91.

68. For speaking gestures, see Moshe Barasch, *Giotto and Lanuage of Gesture* (Cambridge: Cambridge University Press, 1987), 8, 17, 57; and Suzanne Lewis, *Reading Images: Narrative Discourse and Reception in the Thirteenth-Century Illuminated Apocalypse* (Cambridge: Cambridge University Press, 1995), 92.

69. For the extensive rebuilding of churches in fifteenth-century East Anglia, see Tanner, *Church in Late Medieval Norwich*, 4; Gibson, *Theater of Devotion*, 26; Graves, "Social Space," 312–13; and Duffy, *Stripping of the Altars*, 132, who notes that "maybe as many as two-thirds of all English parish churches saw substantial rebuilding or alteration in the 150 years before the Reformation."

70. Hillen, *Borough of King's Lynn*, 879.

71. For these terms in the *Book*, see Despres, "Franciscan Spirituality."

Works Cited

Aers, David. *Chaucer*. Atlantic Highlands, N.J.: Humanities Press, 1986.

———. *Community, Gender, and Individual Identity: English Writing 1360–1430*. London: Routledge, 1988.

———. *Faith, Ethics, and Church: Writing in England, 1360–1409*. Cambridge: D. S. Brewer, 2000.

———. "Faith, Ethics, and Community: Reflections on Reading Late Medieval English Writing." *Journal of Medieval and Early Modern Studies* 28 (1998): 341–69.

———. *Sanctifying Signs: Making Christian Tradition in Late Medieval England*. Notre Dame, Ind.: University of Notre Dame Press, 2004.

Aers, David, and Lynn Staley. *The Powers of the Holy: Religion, Politics, and Gender in Late Medieval English Culture*. University Park: Pennsylvania State University Press, 1996.

Alexander, Jonathan. "*Labeur* and *Paresse*: Ideological Representations of Medieval Peasant Labor." *Art Bulletin* 72.3 (1990): 436–52.

Alexander, Jonathan, and Paul Binski, eds. *The Age of Chivalry: Art in Plantagenet England, 1200–1400*. London: Royal Academy of Arts, Weidenfeld and Nicolson, 1987.

Alexander, Philip S. "Madame Eglantyne, Geoffrey Chaucer, and the Problem of Medieval Anti-Semitism." *Bulletin of the John Rylands Library* 74 (1992): 109–20.

Anderson, M. D. *History and Imagery in British Churches*. London: John Murray, 1971.

Apter, Emily. "Introduction." In *Fetishism as Cultural Discourse*, edited by Emily Apter and William Pietz. Ithaca, N.Y.: Cornell University Press, 1993.

Archer, John. "The Structure of Anti-Semitism in the *Prioress's Tale*." *Chaucer Review* 19 (1984): 46–54.

Aston, Margaret. *England's Iconoclasts*: vol. 1, *Laws Against Images*. Oxford: Clarendon Press, 1988.

———. *Faith and Fire: Popular and Unpopular Religion, 1350–1600*. London: Hambledon Press, 1993.

———. *Lollards and Reformers: Images and Literacy in Late Medieval England*. London: Hambledon Press, 1984.

———. "The Use of Images." In *Gothic: Art for England 1400–1547*, edited by Richard Marks and Paul Williamson, with Eleanor Townsend. London: Victoria and Albert Publications, 2003.

Atherton, Ian. "The Dean and Chapter, Reformation to Restoration: 1541–1660."

In *A History of Ely Cathedral*, edited by Peter Meadows and Nigel Ramsay. Woodbridge, Suffolk: Boydell, 2003.

Atkinson, Clarissa W. *Mystic and Pilgrim: The Book and the World of Margery Kempe*. Ithaca, N.Y.: Cornell University Press, 1983.

Barasch, Moshe. *Giotto and Lanuage of Gesture*. Cambridge: Cambridge University Press, 1987.

Barnum, Priscilla Heath. *Dives and Pauper*. Vol. 1. EETS, 275. London: Oxford University Press, 1976.

Bartlett, Robert. "Medieval and Modern Concepts of Race and Ethnicity." *Journal of Medieval and Early Modern Studies* 31.1 (2001): 39–56.

Bauer, Ernst Stephan. *Frömmigkeit, Gelehrsamkeit und Zeitkritik an der Schwelle der grossen Konzilien: Johannes von Wetzlar und sein Dialogus super Magnificat*. Mainz: Selbstverlag der Gesellschaft für Mittelrheinische Kirchengeschichte, 1981.

Beadle, Richard. "'Devoute ymaginacioun' and the Dramatic Sense in Love's *Mirror* and the N-Town Plays." In *Nicholas Love at Waseda: Proceedings of the International Conference 20–22 July 1995*, edited by Shoichi Oguro, Richard Beadle, and MichaelG. Sargent. Cambridge: D. S. Brewer, 1997.

Beckwith, Sarah. *Christ's Body: Identity, Culture and Society in Late Medieval Writings*. New York: Routledge, 1993.

———. "Ritual, Church and Theatre: Medieval Dramas of the Sacramental Body." In *Culture and History 1350–1600: Essays on English Communities, Identities and Writing*, edited by David Aers. Detroit: Wayne State University Press, 1992.

———. "*Sacrum Signum*: Sacramentality and Dissent in York's Theatre of Corpus Christi." In *Criticism and Dissent in the Middle Ages*, edited by Rita Copeland. Cambridge: Cambridge University Press, 1996.

———. *Signifying God: Social Relation and Symbolic Act in the York Corpus Christi Plays*. Chicago: University of Chicago Press, 2001.

———. "A Very Material Mysticism: The Medieval Mysticism of Margery Kempe." In *Medieval Literature: Criticism, Ideology and History*, edited by David Aers. Sussex: Harvester, 1988.

Belting, Hans. *The Image and Its Public in the Middle Ages: Form and Function of Early Paintings of the Passion*. Translated by Mark Bartusis and Raymond Meyer. New Rochelle, N.Y.: Caratzas, 1990.

———. *Likeness and Presence: A History of the Image Before the Era of Art*. Translated by Edmund Jephcott. Chicago: University of Chicago Press, 1994.

Benjamin, Walter. "The Work of Art in the Age of Mechanical Reproduction." In *Illuminations*, edited by Hannah Arendt and translated by Harry Zohn. New York: Schocken, 1968.

Benson, C. David. "Poetic Variety in the Man of Law's and the Clerk's Tales." In *Chaucer's Religious Tales*, edited by C. David Benson and Elizabeth Robertson. Cambridge: D. S. Brewer, 1990.

———. *Public Piers Plowman: Modern Scholarship and Late Medieval Culture*. University Park: Pennsylvania State University Press, 2004.

Bertelli, Carlo. "The *Image of Pity* in Santa Croce in Gerusalemme." In *Essays in the History of Art Presented to Rudolf Wittkower*. London: Phaidon, 1967.

Besançon, Alain. *The Forbidden Image: An Intellectual History of Iconoclasm*. Translated by Jane Marie Todd. Chicago: University of Chicago Press, 2000.

Bestul, Thomas. "The *Man of Law's Tale* and the Rhetorical Foundations of Chaucerian Pathos." *Chaucer Review* 9 (1975): 216–26.

Bhabha, Homi K. "The Other Question: Difference, Discrimination and the Discourse of Colonialism." In *Out There: Marginalization and Contemporary Cultures*, edited by Russell Ferguson, Martha Gever, Trinh T. Minh-ha, and Cornel West. New York: New Museum of Contemporary Art, 1990.

Biddick, Kathleen. "Genders, Bodies, Borders: Technologies of the Visible." *Speculum* 68 (1993): 389–418.

———. "Translating the Foreskin." In *Queering the Middle Ages*, edited by Glenn Burger and Steven F. Kruger. Minneapolis: University of Minnesota Press, 2001.

Biernoff, Suzannah. *Sight and Embodiment in the Middle Ages*. New York: Palgrave, 2002.

Binski, Paul. "The English Parish Church and Its Art in the Later Middle Ages: A Review of the Problem." *Studies in Iconography* 20 (1999): 1–25.

Blamires, Alcuin. "The Wife of Bath and Lollardy." *Medium Aevum* 58 (1989): 224–42.

Bokenham, Osberg. *Legendys of Hooly Wummen*. Edited by Mary S. Serjeantson. EETS, o.s., 206. London: Oxford University Press, 1938.

Bouillet, A. *Liber miraculorum Sancte Fideis*. Paris: A. Picard, 1897.

Bowers, John M., ed. *The Canterbury Tales: Fifteenth-Century Continuations and Additions*. TEAMS. Kalamazoo, Mich.: Medieval Institute Publications, 1992.

Boyd, Beverly. *Chaucer and the Liturgy*. Philadelphia: Dorrance, 1967.

Bridget of Sweden. *The Revelations of Saint Birgitta*. Edited by William Patterson Cumming. EETS 178. London: Oxford University Press, 1929.

Brody, Saul N. "Making a Play for Criseyde: The Staging of Pandarus's House in Chaucer's *Troilus and Criseyde*." *Speculum* 73 (1998): 115–40.

Brooke, Christopher N. L. *The Medieval Idea of Marriage*. Oxford: Oxford University Press, 1989.

Brown, Bill. *A Sense of Things: The Object Matter of American Literature*. Chicago: University of Chicago Press, 2003.

———, ed. *Things*. Chicago: University of Chicago Press, 2004.

Brundage, James. *Sex, Law, and Marriage in the Middle Ages*. Brookfield, Vt.: Variorum, 1993.

Burgess, Clive, ed. *Pre-Reformation Records of All Saints', Bristol*. Part 1. Bristol Record Society 46. Stroud: Alan Sutton, 1995.

Bynum, Caroline Walker. *The Resurrection of the Body in Western Christianity, 200–1336*. New York: Columbia University Press, 1995.

Camille, Michael. "Before the Gaze: The Internal Senses and Late Medieval Practices of Seeing." In *Visuality Before and Beyond the Renaissance*, edited by Robert S. Nelson. Cambridge: Cambridge University Press, 2000.

———. *The Gothic Idol: Ideology and Image-Making in Medieval Art*. Cambridge: Cambridge University Press, 1989.

———. "The Iconoclast's Desire: Deguileville's Idolatry in France and England." In

Images, Idolatry, and Iconoclasm in Late Medieval England: Textuality and the Visual Image, edited by Jeremy Dimmick, James Simpson, and Nicolette Zeeman. Oxford: Oxford University Press, 2002.

———. "The Image and the Self: Unwriting Late Medieval Bodies." In *Framing Medieval Bodies*, edited by Sarah Kay and Miri Rubin. New York: Manchester University Press, 1994.

———. *Image on the Edge: The Margins of Medieval Art*. London: Reaktion, 1992.

Capgrave, John. *The Book of the Illustrious Henries*. Translated by Francis C. Hingeston. London: Longman, Brown, Green, Longmans, & Roberts, 1858.

———. *The Life of Saint Katherine*. Edited by Karen A. Winstead. TEAMS. Kalamazoo: Western Michigan University, 1999.

Caviness, Madeline. *The Windows of Christ Church Cathedral, Canterbury*. Corpus Vitrearum Medii Aevi, Great Britain, 2. London: Oxford University Press, 1981.

Cawley, A. C. *Everyman and Medieval Miracle Plays*. London: Dent, 1956. Reprint, 1974.

Chaucer, Geoffrey. *The Riverside Chaucer*. 3rd ed. Edited by Larry D. Benson. Boston: Houghton Mifflin, 1987.

Cheetham, Francis. *English Medieval Alabasters*. Oxford: Phaidon/Christie's, 1984.

Clark, J. P. H. "Image and Likeness in Walter Hilton." *Downside Review* 97 (1979): 204–20.

———. "Walter Hilton in Defence of the Religious Life and of the Veneration of Images." *Downside Review* 103 (1985): 1–25.

Cockerell, Sidney. *Two East Anglian Psalters at the Bodleian Library, Oxford: The Ormesby Psalter, MS Douce 366 and the Brunholm Psalter, MS Ashmole 1523*. Oxford: Roxburghe Club, 1926.

Cohen, Jeffrey Jerome. "Hybrids, Monsters, Borderlands: The Bodies of Gerald of Wales." In *The Postcolonial Middle Ages*, edited by Jeffrey Jerome Cohen. New York: St. Martin's, 2000.

Coldstream, Nicola. "Ely Cathedral: The Fourteenth-Century Work." In *Medieval Art and Architecture at Ely Cathedral*. Transactions of the British Archaeological Association 2. Leeds: Maney & Son, 1979.

Coletti, Theresa. *Mary Magdalene and the Drama of Saints: Theater, Gender, and Religion in Late Medieval England*. Philadelphia: University of Pennsylvania Press, 2004.

Collette, Carolyn. "Critical Approaches to the *Prioress's Tale* and the *Second Nun's Tale*." In *Chaucer's Religious Tales*, edited by C. David Benson and Elizabeth Robertson. Cambridge: D. S. Brewer, 1990.

———. "Sense and Sensibility in the *Prioress's Tale*." *Chaucer Review* 15 (1981): 138–50.

———. *Species, Phantasms, and Images: Vision and Medieval Psychology in "The Canterbury Tales."* Ann Arbor: University of Michigan Press, 2001.

Concilia pragensia. 1353–1413. Edited by Karl Höfler. Prague: K. Seyfried, 1862.

Cook, G. H. *Medieval Chantries and Chantry Chapels*. London: Phoenix House, 1947; rev. edition, 1963.

Cooper, Helen. *The Structure of the Canterbury Tales*. Athens: University of Georgia Press, 1984.

Copeland, Rita. "Childhood, Pedagogy, and the Literal Sense: From Late Antiquity to the Lollard Heretical Classroom." *New Medieval Literatures* 1 (1997): 125–56.

———. *Rhetoric, Hermeneutics, and Translation in the Middle Ages: Academic Traditions and Vernacular Texts*. Cambridge: Cambridge University Press, 1991.

———. "William Thorpe and His Lollard Community: Intellectual Labor and the Representation of Dissent." In *Bodies and Disciplines: Intersections of Literature and History in Fifteenth-Century England*. Minneapolis: University of Minnesota Press, 1996.

Crane, Susan. *The Performance of Self: Ritual, Clothing, and Identity During the Hundred Years War*. Philadelphia: University of Pennsylvania Press, 2002.

———. "The Writing Lesson of 1381." In *Chaucer's England: Literature in Historical Context*. Minneapolis: University of Minnesota Press, 1992.

Creighton, Gilbert, trans. *Italian Art 1400–1500: Sources and Document*. Englewood Cliffs, N.J.: Prentice-Hall, 1980.

Crone, G. R., ed. and trans. *The Voyages of Cadamosto, and other documents on Western Africa in the second half of the fifteenth century*. London: Hakluyt Society, 1937.

Dahl, Ellert. "Heavenly Images: The Statue of St. Foy of Conques and the Significance of the Medieval 'Cult-Image' in the West." *Acta ad Archeologium et Artium Historiam Pertinentia* 8 (1978): 175–91.

d'Ardenne, S.R.T.O., and E. J. Dobson, eds. *Seinte Katerine*. EETS, s.s., 7. Oxford: Oxford University Press, 1981.

David, Alfred. "An ABC to the Style of the Prioress." In *Acts of Interpretation: The Text in its Contexts, 700–1600: Essays on Medieval and Renaissance Literature in Honor of E. Talbot Donaldson*, edited by Mary Carruthers and Elizabeth Kirk. Norman, Okla.: Pilgrim Books, 1982.

Davidson, Clifford, ed. *A Tretise of Miraclis Pleyinge*. Early Drama, Art, and Music Monograph Series 19. Kalamazoo, Mich.: Medieval Institute Publications, 1993.

Davis, Norman, ed. *Non-Cycle Plays and Fragments*. EETS, s.s., 1. London: Oxford University Press, 1970.

De adoracione ymaginum. Trans. Kathleen Derrig. Typescript.

Dean, James M., ed. *Six Ecclesiastical Satires*. TEAMS. Kalamazoo, Mich.: Medieval Institute Publications, 1991.

Deanesly, Margaret. *The Lollard Bible and Other Medieval Biblical Versions*. Cambridge: Cambridge University Press, 1920. Rpr. 1966.

De Concordia inter Ric. II et civitatem London. London: Camden Society, 1838.

Delany, Sheila. "Chaucer's Prioress, the Jews, and the Muslims." In *Chaucer and the Jews: Sources, Contexts, Meanings*, edited by Sheila Delany. New York: Routledge, 2002.

———. *Naked Text: Chaucer's Legend of Good Women*. Berkeley: University of California Press, 1994.

———. "Sexual Economics: Chaucer's Wife of Bath and *The Book of Margery Kempe*." *Minnesota Review* 5 (1975): 104–15.

———. "Techniques of Alienation in *Troilus and Criseyde*." In *Chaucer's Troilus and Criseyde: "Subgit to alle Poesye": Essays in Criticism*, edited by R. A. Shoaf. Binghamton, N.Y.: Medieval & Renaissance Texts and Studies, 1992.

de Leeuw, Patricia. "Unde et Memores, Domine: Memory and the Mass of St. Gregory." In *Memory and the Middle Ages*, edited by Nancy Netzer and Virginia Reinburg. Chestnut Hill, Mass.: Boston College Museum of Art, 1995.

Derrida, Jacques. *The Gift of Death*. Translated by David Wills. Chicago: University of Chicago Press, 1995.

Despres, Denise. "Cultic Anti-Judaism and Chaucer's Litel Clergeon." *Modern Philology* 91 (1994): 413–27.

———. "Franciscan Spirituality: Margery Kempe and Visual Meditation." *Mystics Quarterly* 11.1 (1984): 12–18.

Dickman, Susan. "Margery Kempe and the Continental Tradition of the Pious Woman." In *The Medieval Mystical Tradition in England*, edited by Marion Glasscoe. Exeter: University of Exeter Press, 1980.

Diehl, Huston. *Staging Reform, Reforming the Stage: Protestantism and Popular Theater in Early Modern England*. Ithaca, N.Y.: Cornell University Press, 1997.

Dinshaw, Carolyn. *Chaucer's Sexual Poetics*. Madison: University of Wisconsin Press, 1989.

———. *Getting Medieval: Sexualities and Communities, Pre- and Postmodern*. Durham, N.C.: Duke University Press, 1999.

Dodgson, Campbell. "English Devotional Woodcuts of the Late Fifteenth Century, with Special Reference to Those in the Bodleian Library." *Walpole Society* 17 (1928–29):95–108

Donaldson, E. T. *Chaucer's Poetry*. New York: Appleton-Century-Crofts, 1958.

Douglas, Mary. *Purity and Danger: An Analysis of the Concepts of Pollution and Taboo*. London: Routledge & Kegan Paul, 1966. Rpr. Boston: Ark Paperbacks, 1985.

Duffy, Eamon. "Holy Maydens, Holy Wyfes: The Cult of Women Saints in Fifteenth and Sixteenth Century England." In *Women in the Church*, edited by W. J. Sheils and Diana Wood. Oxford: Blackwell, 1990.

———. "The Parish, Piety, and Patronage in Late Medieval East Anglia: The Evidence of Rood Screens." In *The Parish in English Life, 1400–1600*, edited by Katherine L. French, Gary G. Gibbs, and Beat Kümin. Manchester: Manchester University Press, 1997.

———. *The Stripping of the Altars: Traditional Religion in England, 1400–1580*. London: Yale University Press, 1992.

Dülmen, Richard Von. *Theatre of Horror: Crime and Punishment in Early Modern Germany*. Translated by Elisabeth Neu. Cambridge: Polity Press, 1990.

Dyer, Christopher. "The Social and Economic Background to the Rural Revolt of 1381." In *The English Rising of 1381*, edited by R. H. Hilton and T. H. Aston. Cambridge: Cambridge University Press, 1984.

Dymmok, Roger. *Liber contra duodecim errors et hereses Lollardorum*. Edited by H. S. Cronin. London: Wyclif Society, 1922.

Dymond, David, and Clive Paine. *The Spoil of Melford Church: The Reformation in a Suffolk Parish*. Ipswich: Salient Press, 1992.

Edden, Valerie. "Sacred and Secular in the *Clerk's Tale*." *Chaucer Review* 26.4 (1992): 369–76.

Ellis, Deborah. "Merchant's Wife's Tales: Language, Sex and Commerce in Margery Kempe and in Chaucer." *Exemplaria* 2 (1990): 595–626.

Erasmus, Desiderius. *The Colloquies of Erasmus*. Translated by Craig R. Thompson. Chicago: University of Chicago Press, 1965.

Evans, Joan. *English Art 1307–1361*. Oxford: Clarendon Press, 1949.

Evans, Ruth, Andrew Taylor, Nicholas Watson, and Jocelyn Wogan-Browne, eds. *The Idea of the Vernacular: An Anthology of Middle English Literary Theory, 1280–1520*. University Park: Pennsylvania State University Press, 1999.

Fasciculi Zizaniorum Magistri Johannis Wyclif cum Tritico. Edited by Walter W. Shirley London: Longman, Brown, Green, Longmans, and Roberts, 1858.

Fernie, Eric. *An Architectural History of Norwich Cathedral*. Oxford: Clarendon, 1993.

Ferris, Sumner. "Chaucer at Lincoln (1387): The Prioress's Tale as Political Poem." *Chaucer Review* 15 (1981): 295–321.

Ferster, Judith. "Your Praise Is Performed by Men and Children: Language and Gender in the Prioress's Prologue and Tale." *Exemplaria* 2.1 (1990): 149–68.

Fleming, John V. *An Introduction to the Franciscan Literature of the Middle Ages*. Chicago: Franciscan Herald Press, 1977.

Foucault, Michel. *Essential Works of Michel Foucault, 1954–84*. Vol. 1. Edited by Paul Rabinow and translated by Robert Hurley et al. New York: New Press, 1994.

Fradenburg, Louise O. "Criticism, Anti-Semitism, and the Prioress's Tale." *Exemplaria* 1 (1989): 69–115.

———. "'Our owen wo to drynke': Loss, Gender, and Chivalry in *Troilus and Criseyde*." In *Chaucer's Troilus and Criseyde: "Subgit to alle Poesye": Essays in Criticism*, edited by R. A. Shoaf. Binghamton, N.Y.: Medieval & Renaissance Texts and Studies, 1992.

Frank, Robert Worth, Jr. "The *Canterbury Tales* III: Pathos." In *The Cambridge Chaucer Companion*, edited by Piero Boitani and Jill Mann. Cambridge: Cambridge University Press, 1986.

Freedberg, David. *The Power of Images: Studies in the History and Theory of Response*. Chicago: University of Chicago Press, 1989.

French, Katherine L. "The Seat Under Our Lady: Gender and Seating in Late Medieval English Parish Churches." In *Women's Space: Patronage, Place, and Gender in the Medieval Church*, edited by Virginia Chieffo Raguin and Sarah Stanbury. Binghamton: State University of New York Press, 2005.

French, Katherine L., Gary G. Gibbs, and Beat A. Kümin, eds. *The Parish in English Life, 1400–1600*. Manchester: Manchester University Press, 1997.

French, Robert Dudley, ed. *A Chaucer Handbook*. 2nd ed. New York: Appleton-Century-Crofts, 1947.

Friedman, Albert B. "The *Prioress's Tale* and Chaucer's Anti-Semitism." *Chaucer Review* 9 (1974): 118–29.

Froissart, Jean. *The Chronicles of Froissart*. Translated by John Bourcher and edited by G. C. Macaulay. New York: Macmillan, 1895.

Gallacher, Patrick J., ed. *The Cloud of Unknowing*. TEAMS. Kalamazoo, Mich.: Medieval Institute Publications, 1997.

Geary, Patrick. "Sacred Commodities: The Circulation of Medieval Relics." In *The Social Life of Things: Commodities in Cultural Perspective*, edited by Arjun Appadurai. New York: Cambridge University Press, 1986.

Georgianna, Linda. "The Clerk's Tale and the Grammar of Assent." *Speculum* 70 (1995): 793–821.

———. "The Protestant Chaucer." In *Chaucer's Religious Tales*, edited by C. David Benson and Elizabeth Robertson. Cambridge: D. S. Brewer, 1990.

Ghosh, Kantik. *The Wycliffite Heresy: Authority and the Interpretation of Texts.* Cambridge: Cambridge University Press, 2002.

Gibson, Gail McMurray. *The Theater of Devotion: East Anglian Drama and Society in the Late Middle Ages.* Chicago: University of Chicago Press, 1989.

Gilchrist, Roberta. *Gender and Material Culture: The Archaeology of Religious Women* London: Routledge, 1994.

Gillespie, Vincent. "Strange Images of Death: The Passion in Later Medieval English Devotional and Mystical Writings." In *Zeit, Tod, und Ewigkeit in der Renaissance Literatur*, ed. James Hogg. Analecta Cartusiana 17. Salzburg: Institut für Englische sprache und Literatur, 1987.

Ginsberg, Warren. "'And Speketh so Pleyn': The Clerk's Tale and Its Teller." *Criticism* 20 (1978): 307–23.

———. "Petrarch, Chaucer and the Making of the Clerk." In *The Performance of Middle English: Essays on Chaucer and the Drama in Honor of Martin Stevens*, edited by James J. Paxson, Lawrence Clopper, and Sylvia Tomasch. Cambridge: D. S. Brewer, 1998.

Glasscoe, M. "Late Medieval Paintings in Ashton Church, Devon." *Journal of the British Archaeological Association* 140 (1987): 182–90.

Godfrey, Mary F. "The Fifteenth-Century Prioress's Tale and the Problem of Anti-Semitism." In *Rewriting Chaucer: Culture, Authority and the Idea of the Authentic Text: 1400–1602*, edited by Thomas A. Prendergast and Barbara Kline. Columbus: Ohio State University Press, 1999.

Gower, John. *The Major Latin Works of John Gower—The Voice of One Crying and the Tripartite Chronicle: An Annotated Translation into English with an Introductory Essay on the Author's Non-English Works.* Translated by Eric W. Stockton. Seattle: University of Washington Press, 1962.

Graves, Pamela. "Social Space in the English Medieval Parish Church." *Economy and Society* 18 (1989): 297–322.

Gray, Douglas. "London, British Library, Additional MS 37049: A Spiritual Encyclopedia." In *Text and Controversy From Wyclif to Bale: Essays in Honour of Anne Hudson*, edited by Helen Barr and Ann M. Hutchinson. Turnhout, Belgium: Brepols, 2005.

Gribbin, Joseph. *Aspects of Carthusian Liturgical Practice in the Later Middle Age.* Salzburg: Institut für Anglistik und Amerikanistik, 1995.

Grudin, Michaela P. "Chaucer's Clerk's Tale as Political Paradox." *Studies in the Age of Chaucer* 11 (1989): 63–92.

Hagen, Susan K. *Allegorical Remembrance: A Study of The Pilgrimage of the Life of Man as a Medieval Treatise on Seeing and Remembering.* Athens: University of Georgia Press, 1990.

Hahn, Thomas. "The Difference the Middle Ages Makes: Color and Race Before the Modern World." *Journal of Medieval and Early Modern Studies* 31.1 (2001): 1–37.

Hamburger, Jeffrey F. *The Rothschild Canticles: Art and Mysticism in Flanders and the Rhineland Circa 1300*. New Haven, Conn.: Yale University Press, 1990.

——. "The Visual and the Visionary: The Image in Late Medieval Monastic Devotions." *Viator* 20 (1989): 161–204.

Hamilton, Marie Padgett. "Echoes of Childermas in the Tale of the Prioress." *Modern Language Review* 34 (1939): 1–8.

Hansen, Elaine Tuttle. *Chaucer and the Fictions of Gender*. Berkeley: University of California Press, 1992.

——. "Fearing for Chaucer's Good Name." *Exemplaria* 2.1 (1990): 23–36.

Harding, Wendy. "The Function of Pity in Three Canterbury Tales." *Chaucer Review* 32.2 (1997): 162–74.

Harvey, John H. *William Worcestre Itineraries*: Oxford: Clarendon, 1969.

Hawkes. David. *Idols of the Marketplace: Idolatry and Commodity Fetishism in English Literature, 1580–1680*. New York: Palgrave, 2001.

Hawkins, Sherman. "Chaucer's Prioress and the Sacrifice of Praise." *Journal of English and Germanic Philology* 63 (1964): 599–624.

Hector, L. C., and Barbara F. Harvey, eds. and trans. *The Westminster Chronicle, 1381–1394*. Oxford: Clarendon Press, 1982.

Higgins. Iain. *Writing East: The "Travels" of Sir John Mandeville*. Philadelphia: University of Pennsylvania Press, 1997.

Hillen, Henry J. *History of the Borough of King's Lynn*. Norwich: East of England Newspaper Company, 1907.

Hilton, Walter. *The Scale of Perfection*. Edited by Thomas H. Bestul. TEAMS. Kalamazoo, Mich.: Medieval Institute Publications, 2000.

——. *The Scale of Perfection*. Translated by J. H. P. Clark and Rosemary Dorward. New York: Paulist Press, 1991.

——. *The Scale of Perfection*. Edited by Evelyn Underhill. London: Watkins, 1923.

——. *Walter Hilton's Latin Writings*. Edited by John P. H. Clark and Cheryl Taylor. Analecta Cartusiana 124. Salzburg: Institut für Anglistik und Amerikanistik, 1987.

Hirsh, John C. "Reopening the *Prioress's Tale*." *Chaucer Review* 10 (1975): 30–45.

Hoccleve, Thomas. *The Regiment of Princes*. Edited by Charles R. Blyth. TEAMS. Kalamazoo, Mich.: Medieval Institute Publications, 1999.

Hogg, James, ed. *An Illustrated Yorkshire Carthusian Religious Miscellany, British Library London Additional MS. 37049*. Analecta Cartusiana 95, no. 3. Salzburg: Institut für Anglistik und Amerikanistik, 1981.

Holbrook, Sue Ellen. "'About Her': Margery Kempe's Book of Telling and Working." In *The Idea of Medieval* Literature, edited by James Dean and Christian Zacher. Newark: University of Delaware Press, 1992.

Holly, Michael Ann. "Past Looking." In *Vision and Textuality*, edited by Stephen Melville andBill Readings. Durham, N.C.: Duke University Press, 1995.

Holsinger, Bruce. "Pedagogy, Violence, and the Subject of Music: Chaucer's *Prioress's Tale* and the Ideologies of Song." *New Medieval Literatures* 1 (1997): 157–92.

Holsinger, Bruce, and Elizabeth Robertson, eds. "Vernacular Theology and Medieval Studies." In *Literary History and the Religious Turn*. Special issue of *English Language Notes* 44 (2006): 77–137.

Hope, W. H. St. John, "On a Painted Table or Reredos of the Fourteenth Century, in the Cathedral Church of Norwich." *Norfolk Archaeology* 13 (1898): 292–314.

Horstmann. Carl., ed. *Altenglische Legenden, Neue Folge, mit Einleitung und Anmerkungen*. Heilbronn: Verlag Von Gebr. Henninger, 1881.

———. *The Early South English Legendary*. EETS, o.s., 87. London: Trübner, 1887.

Howard, Donald R. *The Idea of the Canterbury Tales*. Berkeley: University of California Press, 1976.

Hudson, Anne. "A Lollard Sect Vocabulary." In *Lollards and Their Books*. London: Hambledon, 1985.

———. *The Premature Reformation: Wycliffite Texts and Lollard History*. Oxford: Clarendon Press, 1988.

———, ed. *Selections from English Wycliffite Writings*. Cambridge: Cambridge University Press, 1978.

———, ed. *Two Wycliffite Texts: The Sermon of William Taylor 1406; The Testimony of William Thorpe 1407*. EETS, o.s., 301 Oxford: Oxford University Press, 1993.

Hughes, Jonathan. *Pastors and Visionaries: Religion and Secular Life in Late Medieval Yorkshire*. Woodbridge, Suffolk: Boydell, 1988.

Hugh of St. Victor. *On the Sacraments of the Christian Faith*. Translated by Roy J. Deferrari. Cambridge, Mass.: Medieval Academy of America, 1951.

Huizinga, Johan. *The Waning of the Middle Ages*. New York: St. Martin's Press, 1985

Humbert of Romans. *Beati Umberti sermones*. Venice, 1603.

Jacobs, Kathryn. *Marriage Contracts from Chaucer to the Renaissance Stage*. Gainesville: University Press of Florida, 2001.

James, M. R. *The Sculptures in the Lady Chapel at Ely*. London: D. Nutt, 1895.

James, Mervyn. "Ritual, Drama and the Social Body in the Late Medieval English Town." *Past and Present* 98 (1983): 3–29.

Jenkins, Jacqueline. "St. Katherine and Laywomen's Piety: The Middle English Prose Life in London, BL Harley MS 4012." In *St. Katherine of Alexandria: Texts and Contexts in Western Medieval Europe*, edited by Jacqueline Jenkins and Katherine J. Lewis. Turnhout, Belgium: Brepols, 2003.

Jenkins, Jacqueline, and Katherine J. Lewis, eds. *St. Katherine of Alexandria: Texts and Contexts in Western Medieval Europe*. Turnhout, Belgium: Brepols, 2003.

Jhally, Sut. *The Codes of Advertising: Fetishism and the Political Economy of Meaning in the Consumer Society*. New York: St. Martin's Press, 1987.

John of Damascus. *On the Divine Image*. First Apostasy, section 16. Translated by David Anderson. Crestwood, N.J.: St. Vladimir's Seminary, 1980.

Jones, W. R. "Lollards and Images: The Defense of Religious Art in Later Medieval England." *Journal of the History of Ideas* 34.1 (1973): 27–50.

Jordan, Robert. *Chaucer's Poetics and the Modern Reader*. Berkeley: University of California Press, 1987.

Julian of Norwich. *The Shewings of Julian of Norwich*. Edited by Georgia Ronan Crampton. TEAMS. Kalamazoo, Mich.: Medieval Institute, 1993.

Justice, Steven. *Writing and Rebellion: England in 1381*. Berkeley: University of California Press, 1994.

Kadri, Sadakat. *Prague*. London: Cadogan Books, 1991.

Kamerick, Kathleen. *Popular Piety and Art in the Late Middle Ages: Image Worship and Idolatry in England, 1350–1500*. New York: Palgrave, 2002.

Kamowski, William. "Chaucer and Wyclif: God's Miracles against the Clergy's Magic." *Chaucer Review* 2002 (37): 5–25.

———. "'Coillons,' Relics, Skepticism and Faith on Chaucer's Road to Canterbury: An Observation on the Pardoner's and the Host's Confrontation." *English Language Notes* 28 (1991): 1–8.

Kauffmann, C. M. *Romanesque Manuscripts, 1016–1190*. Vol. 3. In *A Survey of Manuscripts Illuminated in the British Isles*. London: H. Miller, 1975.

Kaye, Joel. *Economy and Nature in the Fourteenth Century: Money, Market Exchange, and the Emergence of Scientific Thought*. Cambridge: Cambridge University Press, 1998.

Keane, Webb. "Calvin in the Tropics: Objects and Subjects at the Religious Frontier." In *Border Fetishisms: Material Objects in Unstable Spaces*, edited by Patricia Spyer. New York: Routledge, 1998.

Kearney, James J. "Trinket, Idol, Fetish: Some Notes on Iconoclasm and the Language of Materiality in Reformation England." *Shakespeare Studies* 28 (2000): 257–61.

Keller, Kimberly. "For Better and Worse: Women and Marriage in *Piers Plowman*." In *Medieval Family Roles: A Book of Essays*, edited by Cathy Jorgensen Itnyre. New York: Garland, 1996.

Kelly, Edward H. "By Mouth of Innocentz: The Prioress Vindicated." *Papers in Language and Literature* 5.4 (1969): 362–74.

Kelly, Henry Angstar. *Love and Marriage in the Age of Chaucer*. Ithaca, N.Y.: Cornell University Press, 1975.

Kempe, Margery. *The Book of Margery Kempe*. Edited by Barry Windeatt. Essex: Longman, 2000.

———. *The Book of Margery Kempe*. Edited by Sanford Brown Meech and Hope Emily Allen. EETS. London: Oxford University Press, 1940.

Kennedy, Ruth, ed. *Three Alliterative Saints' Hymns: Late Middle English Stanzaic Poems*. EETS, o.s., 321. Oxford: Oxford University Press, 2003.

Kerby-Fulton, Kathryn, and Denise L. Despres. *Iconography and the Professional Reader: The Politics of Book Production in the Douce Piers Plowman*. Minneapolis: University of Minnesota Press, 1999.

Knapp, Daniel. "'The Relyk of a Seint': A Gloss on Chaucer's Pilgrimage." *English Literary History* 39 (1972): 1–26.

Knapp, Peggy. *Chaucer and the Social Contest*. New York: Routledge, 1990.

Knighton. Henry. *Knighton's Chronicle, 1337–1396*. Edited and translated by G. H. Martin. Oxford: Clarendon Press, 1995.

Knowles, David. *Religious Orders in England*. Cambridge: Cambridge University Press, 1948.

Knowles, David, and R. Neville Hadcock. *Medieval Religious Houses*. London: Longman, 1971.

Kolve, V. A. *Chaucer and the Imagery of Narrative: The First Five Canterbury Tales*. Stanford, Calif.: Stanford University Press, 1984.

Kouretsky, Allen. "Dangerous Innocence: Chaucer's Prioress and Her Tale." In

Jewish Presences in English Literature, edited by Derek Cohen and Deborah Heller. Montreal: McGill-Queen's University Press, 1990.

Kristeva, Julia. *Powers of Horror: An Essay on Abjection*. Translated by Leon S. Roudiez. New York: Columbia University Press, 1982.

Kruger, Steven F. "The Bodies of Jews in the Late Middle Ages." In *The Idea of Medieval Literature: New Essays on Chaucer and Medieval Culture in Honor of Donald R. Howard*, edited by James Dean and Christian Zacher. Newark: University of Delaware Press, 1992.

———. "Fetishism, 1927, 1614, 1461." In *The Postcolonial Middle Ages*, edited by Jeffrey Jerome Cohen. New York: St. Martin's, 2000.

Lane, Barbara G. *The Altar and the Altarpiece: Sacramental Themes in Early Netherlandish Painting*. New York: Harper & Row, 1984.

Langland, William. *Piers Plowman: The B Version*. Edited by George Kane and E. Talbot Donaldson. London: Athlone Press, 1975; rev. ed., 1988.

Lasko, P., and N. J. Morgan, eds. *Medieval Art in East Anglia 1300–1520*. Norwich: Jarrold & Sons, 1973.

Lawton, David. "Sacrilege and Theatricality in the Croxton *Play of the Sacrament*." *Journal of Medieval and Early Modern Studies* 33 (2003): 281–309.

———. "Voice, Authority, and Blasphemy in the *Book of Margery Kempe*." In *Margery Kempe: A Book of Essays*, edited by Sandra J. McEntire. New York: Garland, 1992.

Legg, John Wickham, ed. *The Sarum Missal*. Oxford: Oxford University Press, 1916.

Lehmann, Paul. *Parodistische texte, beispiele zur lateinischen parodie im mittelalter*. Munich: Drei Masken, 1923.

Leicester, H. Marshall, Jr. *The Disenchanted Self: Representing the Subject in the Canterbury Tales*. Berkeley: University of California Press, 1990.

———. "Piety and Resistance: A Note on the Representation of Religious Feeling in *The Canterbury Tales*." In *The Endless Knot: Essays on Old and Middle English in Honor of Marie Borroff*, edited by M. Teresa Tavormina and R. F. Yeager. Cambridge: D. S. Brewer, 1995.

Lerer, Seth. "'Representyd Now in Yower Syght': The Culture of Spectatorship in Late-Fifteenth-Century England." In *Bodies and Disciplines: Intersections of Literature and History in Fifteenth-Century England*, edited by Barbara A. Hanawalt and David Wallace. Minneapolis: University of Minnesota Press, 1996.

Lewis, Katherine J. *The Cult of St. Katherine of Alexandria in Late Medieval England* Woodbridge: Boydell, 2000.

Lewis, Suzanne. *Reading Images: Narrative Discourse and Reception in the Thirteenth-Century Illuminated Apocalypse*. Cambridge: Cambridge University Press, 1995.

Lochrie, Karma. *Margery Kempe and Translations of the Flesh*. Philadelphia: University of Pennsylvania Press, 1991.

The Lollard Society. Maintained by Derrick Pittard. http://lollardsociety.org/bibhome .html.

Lomperis, Linda. "Medieval Travel Writing and the Question of Race." *Journal of Medieval and Early Modern Studies* 31 (2001): 147–64.

Love, Nicholas. *Nicholas Love's Mirror of the Blessed Life of Jesus Christ: A Critical Edition Based on Cambridge University Library Additional MSS 5478 and 6686*. Edited by Michael G. Sargent. New York: Garland, 1992.

Lupton, Julia. *Afterlives of the Saint: Hagiography, Typology, and Renaissance Literature*. Stanford, Calif.: Stanford University Press, 1996.

Lydgate, John. *The Pilgrimage of the Life of Man*. Edited by F. J. Furnivall. EETS, e.s., 77. London: Kegan Paul, Trench, Trübner, 1899.

Lynch, Kathryn L. *Chaucer's Philosophical Visions*. Cambridge: D. S. Brewer, 2000.

——. "Despoiling Griselda: Chaucer's Walter and the Problem of Knowledge in *The Clerk's Tale*." *Studies in the Age of Chaucer* 10 (1988): 41–70.

——. "East Meets West in Chaucer's Squires and Franklin's Tales." *Speculum* 70 (1995): 530–51.

——. "The Pardoner's Digestion: Eating Images in *The Canterbury Tales*." In *Speaking Images: Essays in Honor of V. A. Kolve*, edited by R. F. Yeager and Charlotte C. Morse. Asheville, N.C.: Pegasus Press, 2001.

Macbain, William, ed. *Life of St. Catherine by Clemence of Barking*. Anglo-Norman Text Society 18. Oxford: Blackwell, 1964.

Machaut, Guillaume de. *Le Livre dou voir dit (The Book of the True Poem)*. Edited by Daniel Leech-Wilkinson and translated by R. Barton Palmer. New York: Garland, 1998.

Mandeville's Travels. Edited by M. C. Seymour. Oxford: Clarendon Press, 1967.

Mann, Jill. *Geoffrey Chaucer*. New York: Harvester Wheatsheaf, 1991.

Mapping Margery Kempe: A Guide to Late Medieval Material and Spiritual Life. Maintained by Sarah Stanbury and Virginia Raguin. http://www.holycross.edu /departments/visarts/projects/anglia/margaret.htm.

Marin, Louis. "Topic and Figures of Enunciation: It Is Myself That I Paint." In *Vision and Textuality*, edited by Stephen Melville and Bill Readings. Durham, N.C.: Duke University Press, 1995.

Marks, Richard. "An Age of Consumption: Art for England c. 1400–1547." In *Gothic: Art for England 1400–1547*, edited by Richard Marks and Paul Williamson, with Eleanor Townsend. London: Victoria and Albert Publications, 2003.

——. *Image and Devotion in Late Medieval England*. Phoenix Mill, Gloucestershire, U.K.: Sutton Publishing Ltd., 2004.

Martin, Geoffrey. "Knighton's Lollards." In *Lollardy and the Gentry in the Later Middle Ages*, edited by Margaret Aston and Colin Richmond. New York: St. Martin's, 1997.

Martindale, A. H. R. "Altarpiece, Scenes from the Passion, Resurrection, and Ascension of Christ Norwich? C. 1380–1400." In *Medieval Art in East Anglia 1300–1520*, edited by P. Lasko and N. J. Morgan. Norwich: Jarrold & Sons, 1973.

Marvin, Corey J. "I Will Thee Not Forsake: The Kristevan Maternal Space in Chaucer's *Prioress's Tale* and John of Garland's *Stella Maris*." *Exemplaria* 8 (1996): 35–58.

Marx, Karl. *Selected Writings*. Edited by David McLellan. Oxford: Oxford University Press, 1997.

McClintock, Anne. *Imperial Leather: Race, Gender and Sexuality in the Colonial Contest*. New York: Routledge, 1995.

McFarlane, K. B. *Lancastrian Kings and Lollard Knights*. Oxford: Clarendon, 1971.

McSheffrey, Shannon. *Love and Marriage in Late Medieval London*. TEAMS. Kalamazoo, Mich.: Medieval Institute, 1995.

Meale, Carol. M. "'oft siþis with gete deuotion I þought what I miȝt do pleysyng to God': The Early Ownership and Readership of Love's *Mirror*, with Special Reference to its Female Audience." In *Nicholas Love at Waseda: Proceedings of the International Conference 20–22 July 1995*, edited by Shoichi Oguro, Richard Beadle, and Michael G. Sargent. Cambridge: D. S. Brewer, 1997.

Mellinkoff, Ruth. *Outcasts: Signs of Otherness in Northern European Art of the Late Middle Ages*. Berkeley: University of California Press, 1993.

Merback, Mitchell B. *The Thief, the Cross and the Wheel: Pain and the Spectacle of Punishment in Medieval and Renaissance Europe*. London: Reaktion, 1999.

Metcalfe, W. M., ed. *Legends of the Saints in the Scottish Dialect of the Fourteenth Century*. Scottish Text Society 25. London: Blackwood, 1896.

Middleton, Anne. "The Clerk and His Tale: Some Literary Contexts." *Studies in the Age of Chaucer* 2 (1980): 121–50.

Minnis, A. J. *Chaucer and Pagan Antiquity*. Cambridge: D. S. Brewer, 1982.

Mirk, John. *Instructions for Parish Priests*. Edited by Gillis Kristensson. Lund: Gleerup, 1974.

Morgan, Nigel. "Patrons and Devotional Images in English Art of the International Gothic c. 1350–1450." In *Reading Texts and Images: Essays on Medieval and Renaissance Art and Patronage in Honour of Margaret M. Manion*, edited by Bernard J. Muir. Exeter: University of Exeter Press, 2002.

Netter, Thomas. *Doctrinale antiquitatum Fidei ecclesiae catholicae*. Vol. 3. Edited by B. Blanciotti. Venice, 1757–59. Rpr. Farnborough, Hampshire: Gregg Press, 1967.

Nevanlinna, Saara, and Irma Taavitsainen. *St. Katherine of Alexandria: The Late Middle English Prose Legend in Southwell Minster MS 7*. Cambridge: D. S. Brewer, 1993.

Nolan, Barbara. "Chaucer's Religious Tales of Transcendence: Rhyme Royal and Christian Prayer in the Canterbury Tales." In *Chaucer's Religious Tales*, edited by C. David Benson and Elizabeth Robertson. Cambridge: D. S. Brewer, 1990.

Norton, Christopher, David Park, and Paul Binski. *Dominican Painting in East Anglia: The Thornham Parva Retable and the Musée de Cluny Frontal*. Suffolk: Boydell Press, 1987.

O'Connell, Michael. *The Idolatrous Eye: Iconoclasm and Theater in Early-Modern England*. New York: Oxford University Press, 2000.

Oliver, Kathleen M. "Singing Bread, Manna, and the Clergeon's 'Greyn.'" *Chaucer Review* 31 (1997): 357–64.

Olson, Paul. *The Canterbury Tales and the Good Society*. Princeton, N.J.: Princeton University Press, 1986.

Osberg, Richard. "A Voice for the Prioress: The Context of English Devotional Prose." *Studies in the Age of Chaucer* 18 (1996): 25–54.

Panofsky, Erwin. *Early Netherlandish Painting, Its Origins and Character*. Vol. 1. Cambridge, Mass.: Harvard University Press, 1953; New York: Icon, 1971.

Patterson, Lee. *Chaucer and the Subject of History*. Madison: University of Wisconsin Press, 1991.

———. "Chaucer's Pardoner on the Couch: Psyche and Clio in Medieval Literary Studies." *Speculum* 76 (2001): 638–80.

———. "'The Living Witnesses of our Redemption': Martyrdom and Imitation in Chaucer's *Prioress's Tale*." *Journal of Medieval and Early Modern Studies* 31 (2001): 507–60.

Pearsall, Derek. "Hoccleve's *Regement of Princes*: The Poetics of Royal Self-Representation." *Speculum* 69 (1994): 386–410.

———. *The Life of Geoffrey Chaucer: A Critical Biography*. Oxford: Blackwell, 1992.

Pecock, Reginald. *Repressor of Overmuch Blaming of the Clergy*. Vol.1. Edited by Churchill Babington. London: Longman,1860.

Pels, Peter. "The Spirit of Matter: On Fetish, Rarity, Fact, and Fancy." In *Border Fetishisms: Material Objects in Unstable Spaces*, edited by Patricia Spyer. New York: Routledge, 1998.

Peltier, A. C., ed. *Meditationes Vitae Christi*. In *S. Bonaventurae Opera Omnia*. Paris: Vives, 1868.

Penketh, Sandra. "Women and Books of Hours." In *Women and the Book: Assessing the Visual Evidence*, edited by Jane H. M. Taylor and Lesley Smith. Toronto: British Library and University of Toronto Press, 1996.

Philipson, David. *Old European Jewries*. Philadelphia: Jewish Publication Society of America, 1894.

Phillips, Helen. "Register, Politics, and the *Legend of Good Women*." *Chaucer Review* 37.2 (2002): 101–28.

Pietz, William. "Fetishism and Materialism: The Limits of Theory in Marx." In *Fetishism as Cultural Discourse*, edited by Emily Apter and William Pietz. Ithaca, N.Y.: Cornell University Press, 1993.

———. "The Problem of the Fetish, I." *Res* 9 (Spring 1985): 5–17.

———. "The Problem of the Fetish, II: The Origin of the Fetish." *Res* 13 (Spring 1987): 23–45.

Powell, Edgar. *The Rising in East Anglia in 1381*. Cambridge: Cambridge University Press, 1896.

Power, Eileen, trans. *The Goodman of Paris*. New York: Harcourt, Brace & Co., 1928.

Puppi, Lionello. *Torment in Art: Pain, Violence, Martyrdom*. New York: Rizzoli, 1991.

Quennell, C. H. B. *The Cathedral Church of Norwich*. London: G. Bell & Sons, 1898.

Raguin, Virginia Chieffo. "Real and Imagined Bodies in Architectural Space: The Setting for Margery Kempe's Book." In *Women's Space: Patronage, Place, and Gender inthe Medieval Church*, edited by Virginia Chieffo Raguin and Sarah Stanbury. Binghamton: State University of New York Press, 2005.

Ragusa, Isa, and Rosalie B. Green. *Meditations on the Life of Christ: An Illustrated Manuscript of the Fourteenth Century*. Princeton, N.J.: Princeton University Press, 1961.

Rambuss, Richard. "Devotion and Defilement: The Blessed Virgin Mary and the Corporeal Hagiographics of Chaucer's *Prioress's Tale*." In *Textual Bodies: Changing Boundaries of Literary Representation*, edited by Lori Hope Lefkowitz. Albany: SUNY Press, 1997.

Ramsay, Nigel. "The Dean and Chapter, Reformation to Restoration: 1541–1660." In *A History of Ely Cathedral*, edited by Peter Meadows and Nigel Ramsay. Woodbridge, Suffolk: Boydell, 2003.

Rex, Richard. "Wild Horses, Justice and Charity in the *Prioress's Tale*." *Papers in Language and Literature* 22.4 (1986): 339–51.

Rhodes, James F. "The Pardoner's *Vernycle* and His *Vera Icon*." *Modern Language Studies* 13 (1983): 34–40.

Rickert, Margaret. *Painting in Britain in the Middle Ages*. London: Penguin, 1954.

Ridderbos, Bernhard. "The Man of Sorrows: Pictorial Images and Metaphorical Statements." In *The Broken Body: Passion Devotion in Late Medieval Culture*, edited by A. A. MacDonald, H. N. B. Ridderbos, and R. M. Schlusseman. Groningen: Egbert Forsten, 1998.

Ridley, Florence. *The Prioress and the Critics*. University of California Publications, English Studies 30. Berkeley: University of California Press, 1965.

Riehle, Wolfgang. *The Middle English Mystics*. Translated by Bernard Standring. London: Routledge and Kegan Paul, 1981.

Rinbgom, Sixten. "Devotional Images and Imaginative Devotions: Notes on the Place of Art in Late Medieval Private Piety." *Gazette des Beaux-Arts* 73 (1969): 159–70.

Robertson, D. W., Jr. *A Preface to Chaucer: Studies in Medieval Perspectives*. Princeton, N.J.: Princeton University Press, 1962.

Robertson, Elizabeth. "Aspects of Female Piety in the *Prioress's Tales*." In *Chaucer's Religious Tales*, edited by C. David Benson and Elizabeth Robertson. Woodbridge, Suffolk: D. S. Brewer, 1990.

Robinson, James A. *Petrarch: The First Modern Scholar*. New York: Putnam, 1914.

Rock, Daniel. *The Church of Our Fathers, as Seen in St. Osmund's Rite for the Cathedral of Salisbury*. Vol. 3. Edited by G. W. Hart and W. H. Frere. London: J. Hodges, 1905.

Rosenthal, Joel. *The Purchase of Paradise: Gift Giving and the Aristocracy, 1307–1485*. London: Routledge & Kegan Paul, 1972.

Ross, Ellen. *The Grief of God: Images of the Suffering Jesus in Late Medieval England*. New York: Oxford University Press, 1997.

Rubin, Miri. *Corpus Christi: The Eucharist in Late Medieval Culture*. Cambridge: Cambridge University Press, 1991.

———. "The Eucharist and the Construction of Medieval Identities." In *Culture and History 1350–1600: Essays on English Communities, Identities and Writing*, edited by David Aers. Detroit: Wayne State University Press, 1992.

———. *Gentile Tales: The Narrative Assault on Late Medieval Jews*. New Haven, Conn.: Yale University Press, 1999.

Russell-Smith, Joy M. "Walter Hilton and a Tract in Defence of the Veneration of Images." *Dominican Studies* 7 (1954): 180–214.

Salter, Elizabeth. *Chaucer: The Knight's Tale and the Clerk's Tale*. London: Edward Arnold, 1962.

———. *Nicholas Love's Myrrour of the Blessyd Lyf of Jesu Christ*. Analecta Cartusiana 10. Salzburg: Institut für Englische Sprache und Literatur, 1974.

Sandler, Lucy Freeman. *Gothic Manuscripts 1285–1385*. London: H. Miller, 1986.

Saul, Nigel. *Richard II*. New Haven, Conn.: Yale University Press, 1997.

Scanlon, Larry. *Narrative, Authority, and Power: The Medieval Exemplum and the Chaucerian Tradition*. Cambridge: Cambridge University Press, 1994.

Schillebeeckx, Edward. *Christ: The Sacrament of the Encounter with God*. New York: Sheed and Ward, 1963.

Schiller, Gertrud, *Iconography of Christian Art*. Translated by Janet Seligman. Greenwich, Conn.: New York Graphic Society, 1971.

Schleif, Corine. "Hands that Appoint, Anoint and Ally: Late Medieval Donor Strategies for Appropriating Approbation Through Painting." *Art History* 16.1 (1993): 1–32.

Schneider, Norbert. *Art of the Portrait*. Cologne: Taschen, 1994.

Scott, Kathleen L. *Later Gothic Manuscripts 1390–1490*. London: Harvey Miller, 1996.

Sermons of Thomas Brinton. Edited by Sister Mary Aquinas Devlin. Camden Third Series. London: Royal Historical Society, 1954.

Severs, J. Burke. *The Literary Relationships of Chaucer's Clerkes Tale*. New Haven, Conn.: Yale University Press, 1942.

Sheehan, Michael. "The Formation and Stability of Marriage in Fourteenth-Century England: Evidence of an Ely Register." In *Marriage, Family, and Law in Medieval Europe: Collected Studies*, edited by James K. Farge. Toronto: University of Toronto Press, 1996.

Sherman, Gail Berkeley. "Saints, Nuns, and Speech in the *Canterbury Tales*." In *Images of Sainthood in Medieval Europe*, edited by Renate Blumenfeld-Kosinski, Timea Szell, and Brigitte Cazelles. Ithaca, N.Y.: Cornell University Press, 1991.

Shoeck, R. J. "Chaucer's Prioress: Mercy and Tender Heart." *The Bridge: A Yearbook of Judaeo-Christian Studies* 2 (1956): 239–55.

Sklute, Larry. *Virtue of Necessity: Inconclusiveness and Narrative Form in Chaucer's Poetry*. Columbus: Ohio State University Press, 1984.

Smyser, H. M. "The Domestic Background of *Troilus and Criseyde*." *Speculum* 31 (1956): 297–315.

Snoek, G. J. C. *Medieval Piety from Relics to the Eucharist: A Process of Mutual Interaction*. New York: Brill, 1995.

Snowdon, Frank M., Jr. *Before Color Prejudice: The Ancient View of Blacks*. Cambridge, Mass.: Harvard University Press, 1983.

Somerset, Fiona. "Here, There, and Everywhere? Wycliffite Conceptions of the Eucharist and Chaucer's 'Other' Lollard Joke." In *Lollards and Their Influence in Late Medieval England*, edited by Fiona Somerset, Jill C. Havens, and Derrick G. Pitard. Woodbridge, Suffolk: Boydell Press, 2003.

Somerset, Fiona, Jill C. Havens, and Derrick G. Pitard. *Lollards and Their Influence in Late Medieval England*. Woodbridge, Suffolk: Boydell Press, 2003.

Spector, Stephen, "Empathy and Enmity in the *Prioress's Tale*." In *The Olde Daunce: Love, Friendship, Sex and Marriage in the Medieval World*, edited by Robert R. Edwards and Stephen Spector. Binghamton: SUNY Press, 1991.

Spierenburg, Pieter. *The Spectacle of Suffering: Executions and the Evolution of Repression*. Cambridge: Cambridge University Press, 1984.

Sprung, Andrew. "Coercion and Compliance in Chaucer's *Clerk's Tale*." *Exemplaria* 7.2 (1995): 345–69.

Spurgeon, Caroline. *Five Hundred Years of Chaucer Criticism and Allusion, 1357–1900*. Cambridge: Cambridge University Press, 1925.

Staley, Lynn. *Languages of Power in the Age of Richard II*. University Park: Pennsylvania State University Press, 2005.

——. *Margery Kempe's Dissenting Fictions*. University Park: Pennsylvania State University Press, 1994.

Stanbury, Sarah. "Host Desecration, Chaucer's *Prioress's Tale*, and Prague 1389." In *Mindful Spirit in Late Medieval Literature: Essays in Honor of Elizabeth Kirk*. New York, Palgrave, 2006.

——. "The Lover's Gaze in *Troilus and Criseyde*." In *Chaucer's Troilus and Criseyde*: *"Subgit to alle Poesye": Essays in Criticism*, edited by R. A. Shoaf. Binghamton, N.Y.: Medieval & Renaissance Texts and Studies, 1992.

——. "Regimes of the Visual in Premodern England: Gaze, Body, and Chaucer's *Clerk's Tale*." *New Literary History* 28 (1997): 261–90.

——. "The Voyeur and the Private Life in *Troilus and Criseyde*." *Studies in the Age of Chaucer* 13 (1991): 141–58.

Stanley, Arthur Penrhyn. *Historical Memorials of Canterbury*. New York: Anson D. F. Randolph, 1888.

Steinmetz, David C. "Late Medieval Nominalism and the *Clerk's Tale*." *Chaucer Review* 12 (1977): 38–54.

Stepsis, Robert. "Potentia Absoluta and *The Clerk's Tale*." *Chaucer Review* 10 (1975): 129–46.

Stevens, Martin, and Kathleen Falvey. "Substance, Accident, and Transformations: A Reading of the *Pardoner's Tale*." *Chaucer Review* 17 (1982): 142–58.

Stewart, D. J. *On the Architectural History of Ely Cathedral*. London: VanVoorst, 1868.

Stoller, Robert J. *Observing the Erotic Imagination*. New Haven, Conn.: Yale University Press, 1985.

Strohm, Paul. "Chaucer's Lollard Joke: History and the Textual Unconscious." *Studies in the Age of Chaucer* 17 (1995): 23–42.

——. *England's Empty Throne: Usurpation and the Language of Legitimation, 1399–1422*. New Haven, Conn.: Yale University Press, 1998.

——. *Hochon's Arrow: The Social Imagination of Fourteenth-Century Texts*. Princeton, N.J.: Princeton University Press, 1992.

——. *Social Chaucer*. Cambridge, Mass.: Harvard University Press, 1989.

Stubbs, Charles William. *Historical Memorials of Ely Cathedral*. New York: Scribners, 1897.

Swinburn, Lilian M., ed. *The Lanterne of Liȝt*. EETS, o.s., 151. London: Kegan Paul, Trench, Trübner & Co., 1917.

Tanner, Norman P. *The Church in Late Medieval Norwich, 1370–1532*. Toronto: Pontifical Institute for Mediaeval Studies, 1984.

——, ed. *Heresy Trials in the Dioceses of Norwich, 1428–31*. Camden Fourth Series 20. London: Royal Historical Society, 1977.

Tavormina, Teresa. *Kindly Similitude: Marriage and Family in Piers Plowman*. Cambridge: D. W. Brewer, 1995.

Taylor, Andrew. "Anne of Bohemia and the Making of Chaucer." *Studies in the Age of Chaucer* 19 (1997): 95–119.

Thomas, Alfred. *Anne's Bohemia: Czech Literature and Society, 1310–1420*. Minneapolis: University of Minnnesota Press, 1998.

Thompson, Margaret E. *The Carthusian Order in England*. London: Society for Promoting Christian Knowledge, 1930.

Tomasch, Sylvia. "Postcolonial Chaucer and the Virtual Jew." In *Chaucer and the Jews: Sources, Contexts, Meanings*, edited by Sheila Delany. New York: Routledge, 2002.

Travis, Peter W. "Chaucer's Heliotropes and the Poetics of Metaphor." *Speculum* 72 (1997): 399–427.

Trialogus. Edited by G. Lechler. Oxford: Clarendon Press, 1869.

Tristram, E. W. *English Wall Painting of the Fourteenth Century*. London: Routledge & Kegan Paul, 1955.

Tuck, J. A. "Nobles, Commons and the Great Revolt of 1381." In *The English Rising of 1381*, edited by R. H. Hilton and T. H. Aston. Cambridge: Cambridge University Press, 1984.

Valley, Eli. *The Great Jewish Cities of Central and Eastern Europe*. Northvale, N.J.: Jason Aronson, Inc., 1999.

Vance, Eugene. "Chaucer's Pardoner: Relics, Discourse, and Frames of Propriety." *New Literary History* 20 (1989): 723–45.

Vincent Gillespie. "Strange Images of Death: The Passion in Later Medieval English Devotional and Mystical Writings." In *Zeit, Tod, und Ewigkeit in der RenaissanceLiteratur*. Edited by James Hogg. Analecta Cartusiana 17. Salzburg: Institut für Englische Sprache und Literatur, 1987.

Virgoe, Roger. "The Crown and Local Government: East Anglia under Richard II." In *The Reign of Richard II: Essays in Honor of May McKisack*, edited by F. R. H. DuBoulay and Caroline Barron. London: Athlone, 1971.

Voaden, Rosalynn. "God's Almighty Hand: Women Co-Writing the Book." In *Women, The Book and the Godly*. Edited by L. Smith and J. H. M. Taylor. Cambridge: Cambridge University Press, 1995.

Wallace, David. *Chaucerian Polity: Absolutist Lineages and Associational Forms in England and Italy*. Stanford, Calif.: Stanford University Press, 1997.

——. "Mystics and Followers in Siena and East Anglia: A Study in Taxonomy, Class and Cultural Mediation." In *The Medieval Mystical Tradition in England*, edited by Marion Glasscoe. Cambridge: D. S. Brewer, 1984.

Walsingham, Thomas. *The Chronica Maiora of Thomas Walsingham, 1376–1422*. Translated by David Preest. Woodbridge: Boydell, 2005.

[Walsingham, Thomas.] *Chronicon Angliae, ab anno domini 1323 usque ad annum 1388*. Edited by Edward Maunde Thompson, Rolls Series 64. London: Longman, 1874.

Warren, Frederick E., trans. *The Sarum Missal*. Milwaukee, Wis.: Young Churchman, 1913.

Watson, Nicholas. "Censorship and Cultural Change in Late-Medieval England: Vernacular Theology, the Oxford Translation Debate, and Arundel's Constitutions of 1409." *Speculum* 70 (1995): 822–64.

——. "The Composition of Julian of Norwich's *Revelation of Love*." *Speculum* 68 (1993): 636–83.

——. "'Et que est huius ydoli materia? Tuipse': Idols and Images in Walter Hilton." In *Images, Idolatry, and Iconoclasm in Late Medieval England: Textuality and the Visual Image*, edited by Jeremy Dimmick, James Simpson, and Nicolette Zeeman. Oxford: Oxford University Press, 2002.

——. "The Politics of Middle English Writing." In *The Idea of the Vernacular: An Anthology of Middle English Literary Theory, 1280–1520*, edited by Jocelyn Wogan-Browne, Nicholas Watson, Andrew Taylor, and Ruth Evans. University Park: Pennsylvania State University Press, 1999.

Way, Albert, Esq. "Notice of a Painting of the Fourteenth Century, Part of the Decorations of an Altar: Discovered in Norwich Cathedral." In *Memoirs Illustrative of the History and Antiquities of Norfolk and the City of Norwich*. Proceedings of the Archaeological Institute 1847. London: Archaeological Institute, 1851.

Wenk, J. C. "On the Sources of the *Prioress's Tale.*" *Mediaeval Studies* 17 (1955): 214–19.

Wenzel, Siegfried. "Chaucer's Pardoner and His Relics." *Studies in the Age of Chaucer* 11 (1989): 37–41.

Whittingham, Selby. *Salisbury Chapter House*. London, 1974.

Winstead, Karen A. *Virgin Martyrs: Legends of Sainthood in Late Medieval England*. Ithaca, N.Y.: Cornell University Press, 1997.

——, ed. and trans. *Chaste Passions: Medieval English Virgin Martyr Legends*. Ithaca, N.Y.: Cornell University Press, 2000.

Wogan-Browne, Jocelyn, and Glyn S. Burgess. *Virgin Lives and Holy Deaths: Two Exemplary Biographies for Anglo-Norman Women*. London: Dent, 1996.

Woodall, Joanna. *Portraiture: Facing the Subject*. Manchester: Manchester University Press, 1997.

Woodforde, Christopher. *The Norwich School of Glass-Painting in the Fifteenth Century*. London: Oxford University Press, 1950.

Woolf, Rosemary. *The English Religious Lyric in the Middle Ages*. Oxford: Clarendon Press, 1968.

Wrong, George M. *The Crusade of 1383, Known as That of the Bishop of Norwich*. London: James Parker & Co., 1892.

Wyclif, John. *Select English Works of John Wyclif*. Edited by Thomas Arnold. 3 volumes. Oxford: Clarendon Press, 1871.

——. *Tractatus de Mandatis Divinis*. Edited by Johann Loserth and F. D. Matthew. Wyclif Society. London: C. K. Paul, 1922.

Ziegler, J. E. *Sculpture of Compassion: The Pietà and the Beguines in the Southern Low Countries, c. 1300–1600*. Brussels: Institut Historique Belge de Rome, 1992.

Zika, Charles. "Hosts, Processions and Pilgrimages: Controlling the Sacred in Fifteenth-Century Germany." *Past and Present* 118 (1988): 25–64.

Zitter, Emily Stark. "Antisemitism in Chaucer's Prioress's Tale." *Chaucer Review* 25 (1990–91): 227–84.

Žižek, Slavoj. *The Sublime Object of Ideology*. New York: Verso, 1989.

Index

Note: Page numbers in italics refer to illustrations.

Adam, 57
adventus (procession), 131–32
Aers, David, 13, 128, 161, 239–40n.8, 243n.54
affective piety, 5–7, 101, 109, 161–62, 183, 252n.33
Agnes, Saint, 74
alabaster carvings, 26–27, 176, 211, *212*, 257–58n.52
Alexander, Jonathan, 82, 233n.22
Alice in Wonderland (Carroll), 198
Alien films, 55
allegory, 74–75
Allen, Hope Emily, 201, 253n.7
All Saints (Leicester), 194
All Saint's Church (Bristol), 30
altarpieces, 27–28, 211. *See also* Despenser Retable
Anne of Bohemia, 135–36, 165, 166, 242 n.34
anti-Semitism, 88, 160, 161, 162, 246n.22
Apter, Emily, 29
Arbus, Diane, 101
Archer, John, 246n.22, 247n.34
art, 104–5, 173–74, 232n.10
Arundel, Archbishop: Constitutions, 13, 159, 194; vs. the Lollards, 172–73; *The Testimony of William Thorpe*, 21, 172-73
Ashton church (Devon), 202
Asia, 164, 165, 168, 248n.38
Aston, Margaret, 7, 25, 47, 220n.15, 226n.14
Augustine, Saint, bishop of Hippo, 21, 220n.13; *De Trinitate*, 53
Avicenna, 220n.13

Bacon, Roger, 220n.13
Barbara, Saint, 68
Baret, John, 196
Barnum, Priscilla Heath, 8
Bartholomeus Anglicus, 236n.4
Baudrillard, Jean, 120
Beadle, Richard, 173

Beatis, Antonio de, 60
Becket, Thomas, Saint, 132–33, 170
Beckwith, Sarah, 127, 133, 175, 182–83, 252n.33
benefactor lists, 191, 192. See also *The Book of Margery Kempe*
Benjamin, Walter, 79
Berry, duc de, 82
Bertelli, Carlo, 256n.36, 257n.44
Beverly Chapterhouse, 194, 253n.8
Biddick, Kathleen, 225n.97
Biernoff, Susannah, 188, 220 n.13
Binski, Paul, 5, 80, 224n.86
Blackfriar's Council, 159
The Blob, 55
body: of Christ, 133, 182–83, 198, 252n.33; formulae for describing, 103; vs. image, 38, 43, 46; Jew's, fetish of, 163; sanctified, and relics, 135
Bohemia, 165–67
Bokenham, Osbern, *Legendys of Hooly Wummen*, 34
Book of Hours, 50, *51*, 202
The Book of Margery Kempe (Kempe): as autobiography/spiritual memoir, 193, 195; Carthusian imagery in, 215; on Christ as living person, 16; Christ's body in, identification with, 198; desires represented in, 214–15; dialogue with Christ in, 195, 198, 200, 203, 205, 207–8; eucharistic imagery in, 207; on images, 193–94, 195, 201–2; interviews with ecclesiastics in, 195; and Lollard accusations against Margery, 16, 211, 214, 216, 218, 258n.55; and Lollard prosecutions, 194–95; Man of Sorrows image in, 203, 215–16; Margery as donor in, 181, 193, 195, 203, 205, 209–15, 218; Margery prays for end to sexual relations with husband, 194–95; on Margery's

excessive weeping, 200, 201; and *The Mirror of the Blessed Life of Jesus Christ*, 193, 215–16, 218; name dropping/self-aggrandizement in, 195, 211–12, 218; narrative style of, 194; organization of, 214; pictorial Trinity/Book of Life visions in, 208–12, 214–15; public space claimed by, 193, 195, 201, 207–8, 214, 218; sites named in, 194, 253n.8; St. Katherine in, 209; on St. Margaret's chapel-of-ease, 218; survival of, 215; travels mapped in, 193; visions in, 193–94, 195, 198

Book of Numquam, 60

The Book of the Duchess (Chaucer), 101, 105–6

Book of Wisdom, 26

Boston Museum of Fine Arts, 211, *212*

Boston Symphony Orchestra, 192

boundary violations, 55, 229n.59

Boyd, Beverly, 169, 248nn.38–39

Braunche, Letitia, 196

Braunche, Margaret, 196

Braunche, Robert, 196

Bridget, Saint, 209, 254n.14

Brinton, Thomas, 7

Brosses, Charles de, 18

Brown, Bill, 30, 120

Brundage, James, 137

Brunham family, 257n.47

Burghard, John, 202

Butler, Judith, 48

Bynum, Caroline Walker, 231n.81

Cadamosto, Alvise, 22, 223n.58

Cambio, Domenico di, 256n.35

Camille, Michael, 5, 11, 57, 93, 220n.14, 236n.4

The Canterbury Interlude, 122–24, 239n.2

Canterbury Jubilee (1420), 239n.2

Canterbury ritual, 122–24

The Canterbury Tales (Chaucer), 122, 124–25, 158, 163, 168, 239n.6, 240n.10. *See also specific tales*

Capgrave, John, 89–92, 234n.38. *See also The Life of Saint Katherine*

Carmelite Missal, 214

Carroll, Lewis, *Alice in Wonderland*, 198

Carthusian Miscellany, 215–16, *217*

Carthusians, 189, 215

Catherine of Genoa, Saint, 254n.14

Catherine of Siena, Saint, 254n.14

Caulibus, Johannes de, *Meditationes Vitae Christi*, 172, 175–79, 182, 249n.1, 251n.21, 251n.23

Cecilia, Saint, 45, 184

censorship, 13

chantry altars, 5

charities, posthumous, 47–48

Chaucer, Geoffrey: death of, 114; Hoccleve's portrait of, 97; Wyclif's influence on, 128

Chaucer, Geoffrey, images, 95–121; familiarity with/participation in the debate, 98–99, 111, 115, 120–21, 128; overview of, 15; writing vs. images, 114–15

Chaucer, Geoffrey, writings: *The Book of the Duchess*, 101, 105–6; *The Canterbury Tales*, 122, 124–25, 158, 163, 168, 239n.6, 240n.10 (*see also specific tales*); Christian prayer in, 247n.29; daisy as devotional object in, 112–13, 114–15, 120–21; descriptive practice in, 100–101; devotional images in, 129; ekphrasis in, 100, 103–4, 105, 237n.23; eucharistic controversy in, 98, 119; eyewitnesses in, 102–3; gaze in, 101, 102, 105–6, 108–10, 116, 134, 237n.23; *The House of Fame*, 102; influences on, 115; *The Knight's Tale*, 101, 102–5, 106, 125, 237n.23; *The Legend of Good Women*, 15, 101–2, 106, 110–16, 128, 129, 152, 237n.31; literary production of, 111; Lollard influence on, 111–12, 116, 128–29; *Man of Law's Tale*, 43; *The Merchant's Tale*, 121, 137; *The Miller's Tale*, 101; optics in, 109; *The Pardoner's Tale*, 15, 16, 98, 117–21, 128–29; pathos in, 126, 239–40n.8; *The Physician's Tale*, 99; pleasure/playfulness in, 115–16; portraiture in, 101; private will vs. public performances in, 15, 125; *The Second Nun's Tale*, 99, 107; self-commentary in, 111–12; *The Squire's Tale*, 101, 105; *Tale of Saint Cecilia*, 15, 125; textual authority in, 111–12, 113; *Troilus and Criseyde*, 98, 101, 106–10, 111, 116, 237n.31; vernacular in, 112, 116, 142–43. See also *The Clerk's Tale*

Cheetham, Francis, 28, 257–58n.52

Chester, Alice, 30

Chichester Psalter, 83, *84*

chivalry, 104, 110, 125, 237n.23

Christ: ascension of, 85, *86*; clerical control via body of, 133, 182–83, 198, 252n.33; as dynamic image, overview of, 15–16; flagellation of, *81*, 82–83, *84*, 85; hair of, 85; imagining his life in action, 16, 172, 177–82, 251n.21, 251n.23; at last supper, 85, *87*, 179; meditation on humanity of, 172, 251n.23 (see also *The Mirror of the Blessed Life of Jesus Christ*); mystical marriage to St. Katherine, 35, 40, 209. See also *The Book of Margery Kempe*; Man of Sorrows; Passion; Trinity

Christ Church Cathedral (Oxford), *67*, 67–68

Christopher, Saint, 34

Chronicle (Knighton): on body vs. image, 38, 43, 46; chronology in, 38; and cult/legend of Katherine, 36, 38, 40, 41, 44, 46, 52; decapitating/burning of Katherine statue in, 33, 34, 38, 41–42, 43, 107; on early life (*vita*) of Katherine, 35; as historicizing, 36; on iconophobia, 42; on the Katherine wheel, 36; on the martyrdom of Katherine, 36, 39, 41; on Maxentius's/philosophers' debate with Katherine, 35–36, 38, 39; misogynist violence in, 40, 41, 43; name-calling in, 43–44; object vs. fetish in, 38, 40; overview of, 14–15; on passion (*passio*) of Katherine, 35–36, 38, 39; place in, 33–34; on seductions of images, 39–40; sexual/scatological metaphors in, 41, 227nn.21–22; on Smith, 33, 38–43, 47, 50, 52, 159; on statue used for cooking fuel, 41; on torture of Katherine, 36; translation of, 227n.22; vernacular used in, 43; on Waytestathe, 33, 38–43, 47, 159; witchcraft accusations in, 44

Church of St. Helen (Ranworth), 71, *73*

Church of the Assumption of the Blessed Virgin Mary (Attleborough), 214

church rebuilding, 26, 218, 258n.69

Circle of the Master of the Martyrdom of the Apostles, 60

Clark, J. P. H., 53, 229n.57

class: in the Despenser Retable, *81*, 82, 83, 85–91; and devotional images, 19, 26, 31, 46–47; and image access/ownership, 201–2, 256n.32

Cleanness, 174

Clemence of Barking, 34, 231n.79

The Clerk's Tale (Chaucer), 125–52; center of consciousness in, 130; and contemporary

discourses on piety, 128; ending, 149–50, 244n.60; ethical accountability in, 147–48; feminist critique of, 243n.54; gaze in, 134; Griselda's translation from peasant to queen/sacred site in, 125, 130–34, 135–36, 139; language/speech acts/voice in, 141–52, 243n.54, 244n.60; marriage and private will in, 126, 134–39; narrator in, 125, 146–47; overview of, 15; pathos in, 147–48, 150, 241n.18; on Petrarch, 141, 142, 144–46, 148–51; piety in, 125–27, 150; vs. *The Prioress's Tale*, 156; and private will vs. public spectacle, 15, 125; Prologue, 144–50, 244n.58; queen as spectacle in, 5; resolution of, 130, 151–52; sacramental ritual in, 125–29, 133–34, 135, 138; the sacred vs. the secular in, 244n.63; sources for, 129, 133, 240–41n.18; vernacular used for, 142–43, 147–48, 151–52, 244n.58; Walter orchestrates privacy/secrecy in, 139–40, 243n.47; Walter's testing of Griselda, 137–38, 140–41

Clopton, John, 196, 204–5

Clopton, William, *197*

Clopton family, 30, 198, 254n.20

Cloud of Unknowing, 53, 54, 228n.50, 230n.61

coats of arms, 196, 254n.17. *See also under* Despenser Retable

Coldstream, Nicola, 3

Collette, Carolyn, 99

commemoration, 29–31. *See also* images, devotional, donor

Constitutions (Arundel), 13, 159, 194

"construe," meaning of, 157–58, 159, 245n.9

Copeland, Rita, 157, 158

Corpus Christi Day, 169–70

Costas, King, 35

Courtenay, Archbishop, 38

Crane, Susan, 158

The Creation, and the Fall of Lucifer (York), 55

Cromwell, Thomas, 2

crucifixes, 12, 21–22, 28, 99–100, 113

crusade (Flanders, 1383), 89, 234n.35, 235n.48

daisy, as devotional object, 112–13, 114–15, 120–21

Dante Alighieri, 106

Danvers, Anne, 198

Datini, Francesco di Marco, 74
David, King, 154
"dead," meanings of, 174
De adoracione ymaginum (Hilton), 21, 54, 113–14, 229n.57
death, 45, 47–49
Debord, Guy, *Society of the Spectacle*, 5
Decalogue, 26
Decius, 68
"declare," meaning of, 159
"De heretico comburendo" (1401), 9, 13
Delany, Sheila, 116, 164
Derrida, Jacques, 48
Deschamps, Eustache, 115
desire, visual, 6–7, 220n.13
Despenser, Henry, 78, 89–92, 232n.14, 234n.35, 234n.38, 235n.48
Despenser Retable (Norwich Cathedral), 5, 76, 76–94, 202; ascension/resurrection panels of, 85–87, 86, 89, 94, 180; audience for, 78–80, 94; bodies managed in, 87–88; class in, 81, 82, 83, 85–91; coats of arms/banners on, 15, 78–80, 88–89, 93, 94, 192–93, 196; critical history of, 77–78, 232nn.6–7; dating of, 78; discovery of, 76, 231n.1; discussions of, 89, 231–32n.3; flagellation panel of, 81, 82–83, 85, 180; frame of, 15, 77–80, 88–89, 93–94; Hope on, 77, 232n.7; panels of, generally, 79–80; Passion narrative of, 15, 79, 80–89, 81, 93–94; peasants/scourges in, 81, 82, 83, 85; Pilate in, 81, 83, 85; race in, 81, 88; before reconstruction, 78, 79; spectators of, 180; stylistic origins of, 77, 79, 232nn.6–7; as thank-you gift for suppressing 1381 rebellion, 15, 78–79, 89, 90, 93–94; Tudor-Craig on, 77, 79, 83; use as a table, 76–77; Way on, 76, 77
De Trinitate (Augustine), 53
De ymagine peccati (Hilton), 52
Diana, 102, 105
Diehl, Huston, 42
Dinshaw, Carolyn, 142
Dives and Pauper, 8–9, 25–26, 57, 59, 66, 71, 74, 116
Dominici, Cardinal, 34
Donaldson, D. Talbot, 160
donor images, 16, 24–25, 29–31, 37, 181, 214, 224n.86
donor portraits, 197

Dorothy, Saint, 74
Douglas, Mary, 153
Duffy, Eamon, 3, 28, 29–30, 226n.9, 256n.32, 258n.69
dulia (reverence for God's creation), 7, 21, 186–87
Dyer, Christopher, 235n.52
Dymmok, Roger, 138

East Harling, 196–97, 254n.21
Edward I, king of England, 132
Edward the Confessor, 132
ekphrasis, 15, 100, 103–4, 105, 237n.23
Ely Cathedral, 1–3, 1–3, 6–7
Ely Register, 137
Erasmus, 138; *A Pilgrimage for Religion's Sake*, 123–24
Eucharist, 6, 220n.14; Christ's incarnation in, 20–22; controversy over, 98; Love's *Mirror* on, 182, 183, 187; and relics, 132; Wyclif on, 128–29. *See also* transubstantiation
Eve: sins of, 57; as virago, 43, 44, 46
exoticism, 165, 233n.33
"expounde"/"expositio," meaning of, 156, 158, 159
extramission, 220n.13

Faversham Church (Kent), 28
Ferris, Sumner, 166
fetish/fetishism: vs. allegory, 74; characterization/meanings of, 14, 17, 18–19, 22, 74, 119–20; commodity, 18, 19, 120; and faith vs. matter, 31; genealogy of, 18, 22, 119–20, 225n.97; and longing and mystified value, 29; publicity, 120; and relative value of objects, 22–23, 31, 223n.58; sexual, 120; as speech act, 18. See also *Chronicle*; Despenser Retable; *The Life of Saint Katherine*; *Scale of Perfection*
Fitzralph, Richard, 47
Fitzwarin Psalter, 83
Flanders crusade (1383), 89, 234n.35, 235n.48
fonts, stone, 257–58n.52
Foucault, Michel, 48
Fradenburg, Louise, 161, 162, 246n.22
Franciscan visual meditation, 172
Fray, Annes, 257n.42
Fray, Elizabeth, 198
Fray, Margaret, 198

Freud, Sigmund, 120
Froissart, Jean, 92, 115, 235n.48

Gabriel, 178–79
Gambia, 22, 223n.58
gargoyle, 154
gaze: in Chaucer, 101, 102, 105–6, 108–10, 116, 134, 237n.23; in Chaucer's *Prioress's Tale*, 156; lover's, 108–9; of spectators, 180; and visual desire, 6; as witnessing, 6; in works of art, 232n.10
Geary, Patrick, 222n.47
Genet, Jean, 153
Georgianna, Linda, 138, 161
Germanus I, 21
Gernon family, 78–79
Ghosh, Kantik, 175, 177
Gibson, Gail McMurray, 47–48, 127, 182, 196
gifts, 47–48
Giovanni da Lignano, 149
glass painting, 196
glazing, patronage in, 197
God, 53, 127. *See also* Trinity
The Goodman of Paris, 241n.23
Goodrich, Bishop, 219n.2
Gorleston Psalter, 196, 254n.17
Gosford, John, 92
gothic survival, 2–3, 4
Gower, John, *Vox Clamantis*, 99
Graves, Pamela, 202–3, 254n.21
Gregory, Saint, 203
Griselda story, 127, 129, 136, 241n.23. See also *The Clerk's Tale*; Petrarch, Griselda story of
Guinea, 22

Hahn, Thomas, 233–34n.33
hair fashions, 85
Hales, Sir Stephen, 78, 91
Hamilton, Marie, 169
Hansen, Elaine Tuttle, 243n.54
Harding, Wendy, 239n.8
Harling, Ann, 196–97
Hawkins, Sherman, 155, 246n.22
Henry VIII, king of England and Ireland, 189
Hereford, Nicholas de, 159
heresy: and female sexuality, 55; Lollardy as, 13, 159, 172–73

heretics: burning of, 9, 13; persecution of, 229n.55; and the power of images, 42
Herod, 249n.51
Higgins, Iain, 165
high altar, as locus of expensive gifts, 202, 255–56n.29
Hillen, Henry, 202
Hilton, Walter, 8; *De adoracione ymaginum*, 21, 54, 113–14, 229n.57; death of, 54, 229n.55; *De ymagine peccati*, 52; "image"/ "idol" in writings of, 54; on images, 54, 229n.56; influence/popularity of, 53; vs. the Lollards, 54, 229nn.56–57; and persecution of heretics, 229n.55. See also *Scale of Perfection*
Hirsh, John C., 246n.22
historical periodization, 31, 225n.97
Hitler, Adolf, 248n.39
Hoccleve, Thomas, *Regiment of Princes*, 97
Holly, Michael Ann, 232n.10
Holsinger, Bruce, 246n.21
Holy Innocents Day, 169
Holy Trinity Church (Long Melford): donor images at, 30, 198, *199*; Lady Chapel, 196, *197*, 254n.20; Man of Sorrows images at, 203–4, *204*, 257n.42; Roger Martin on holdings of, 100; Trinity images at, 210, *210*
Holy Trinity Goodramgate, 214
Hope, W. H. St. John, 77, 232n.7
hospital chapels, 225n.2
Hours of the Virgin, 48, *49*
The House of Fame (Chaucer), 102
Howard, Donald, 124
Howard family, 78–79
Hudson, Anne, 93, 211, 234n.35
Hugh of St. Victor, 20
Huizinga, Johan, 233n.22
Humbert of Romans, 20–21

iconoclasm: and fear of female saints, 42; vs. misogynistic violence, rhetoric of, 42–43; Protestant, 42; Reformation, 2–3, 4, 7, 43, 219n.2. See also *Chronicle*; Lollards
iconophobia, 42, 63
idolatry: devotional images as, 7–11, *10–11*, 14, 56–57; and heresy, 57; images as (*see under* images, devotional); pilgrimages

as, 7; relic worship as, 117–18; as self-worship, 40; sexual deviance of idols, 57–58

image culture, 5, 16–17. *See also* images, devotional

images, devotional: and affective piety, 5–7; animation of, 99–100; *The Book of Margery Kempe* on, 193–94, 195, 201–2; burning of, 9, 30 (see also *Chronicle*); Byzantine arguments about, 21; and capital/privilege, 12, 120; of Christ, 15–16 (see also *The Book of Margery Kempe*; *The Mirror of the Blessed Life of Jesus Christ*); and Christ's incarnation, 21–22; and commodities, 14; crucifixes, 12, 21–22, 28, 99–100, 113; dead, 25–27, 31, 101, 106–7, 115, 174; debate about, overview of, 7–11, *10–11*, 14–17, 31–32, 38; *Dives and Pauper* on, 8–9, 25, 26, 57; donor, 16, 24–25, 29–31, 37, 181, 214, 224n.86; ekphrastic accounts of, 100; functions of, 28; honoring of/gifts to, 28–29; iconoclastic destruction of, 2–3, 4, 7, 219n.2; of John the Baptist, 28; *Lanterne of Lizt* on, 26–27; Lollard attacks on, 7–8, 9, 12, 19, 22, 25–26, 31–32, 46 (see also *Chronicle*; *and other specific texts*); male clergy's access to, 256n.30; market for, 23–24, 26, 27–28, 31, 37; and materiality, 14, 26, 30, 31, 37, 47; mental/material, elision of, 195, 254n.13; and money/class, 19, 26, 31, 46–47; overview of, 5; Passion scenes, 6, 7; physicality of, 19–20, 21–22; *Pierce the Plowman's Crede* on, 24–25, 30–31; and power, 16; power of, 19, 26, 42, 46, 47; proliferation of, 26, 46; and relics, 20, 222n.47; richly decorated, 23–25, 26, 29, 31, 37, 46–47; of saints, 3, 5, 9, 14, 21–24, 28, 113; and sexuality (*see* fetish/fetishism); "Tretyse of Ymagis" on, 19–20, 23–24, 25–26, 29, 75, 174; of the Trinity, 5, 28; veneration of, 220n.15; of the Virgin Mary, 28. *See also* image culture; saints, images of; *Scale of Perfection*

imago dei, 53

imago pietatis, 215, 256n.35

incarnational aesthetic, 127

indulgences, 16, 203, 257n.39

Instructions for Parish Priests (Mirk), 132

International Gothic, 214

intromission, 220n.13

Italian painting, 180, 257n.44

Jean, duc de Berry: *Petites Heures*, 83; *Très Riches Heures*, 82

Jesus. *See* Christ

Jews: anti-Semitism toward, 160, 161, 162, 246n.22; vs. Christians, 160–65, 168; host-desecration accusations against, 140, 166–67, *167*, 243n.50; as martyrs, 161; otherness of, 88, 164–65; in Prague, 165–67, 248n.39; stereotypes of, 162–63; usury by, 164–68

Jhally, Sut, 18

John, Saint, 74

John 19:1, 83

John of Damascus, 21

John of Jenstein, 167

John the Baptist, 28

Jones, W. R., 7, 46, 47

Joseph of Arimathea, 185

Judas's lips, 21, 22

Julian of Norwich, 13, 254n.14; *The Shewings of Julian of Norwich*, 6, 99–100

Justice, Steven, 158

Kamerick, Kathleen, 63, 193

Kamowski, William, 120

Kara, Avigdor, 166

Katherine Group, 34

Katherine of Alexandria, Saint: Auchinleck manuscript *passio* of, 34, 39, 40, 41, 44, 231n.79; blood of transformed into milk, 36, 41, 45; and capital, 52; corporeality of, 46; and death, resistance to, 45, 48–49; incarnation defended by, 44–45; legend/popularity of, 34–35, 36, 40, 44–46, 50, 52, 226n.9; library/study built for, 35, 226n.14; martyrdom of, 45, 135–36; and Maxentius/philosophers' debate with Katherine, 35–36, 38, 39, 40; mystical marriage to Christ, 35, 40, 209; person vs. image, 46; philosophy associated with, 50; representations/symbols of, 48, 49, 50, *51*; and St. Margaret, 48, *49*; tomb of, 40; Trinity defended by, 44–45; witchcraft accusations surrounding, 44, 227–28n.32. See also *Chronicle*; *The Life of Saint Katherine*; *Scale of Perfection*

Katherine wheel: Capgrave on, 14–15, 58–
  60, 61, 66; images of, 61, *62, 67*, 67–68, *69*;
  on jewelry, 74; Knighton on, 36; as a
  token, 74
Kempe, Margery. See *The Book of Margery
  Kempe*
Kerby-Fulton, Kathryn, 100
Kerdeston family, 78–79
Kirk, Elizabeth, 160
Knighton, Henry. See *Chronicle*
The Knight's Tale (Chaucer), 101, 102–5, 106,
  125, 237n.23
Kristeva, Julia, 153
Kruger, Steven F., 163, 225n.97

Lady Chapel (Ely Cathedral), 1–3, *1–3*, 6–7
Lady Chapel (Holy Trinity Church, Long
  Melford), 196, *197*, 254n.20
Lady of Pity, 203–5, *204*
laity's role in church ritual/maintenance,
  29–30. *See also* donor images; patronage
Lange, John, 167
Langland, William, 13; *Piers Plowman*, 25,
  30, 100, 136
language: in Chaucer's *Clerk's Tale*, 141–52,
  243n.54, 244n.60; in Chaucer's *Prioress's
  Tale*, 126–27; and tongue, 154–55. *See also*
  vernacular
Lanterne of Lizt, 26–27, 75
Lasko, Peter, 254n.17
latria (honor due to God alone), 7, 21,
  186–87
Lawrence, Saint, 68, *70*, 70–71, *72–73*
Lazarus, 179
The Legend of a Good Woman (Chaucer), 15,
  101–2, 106, 110–16, 128, 129, 152, 237n.31
Legendys of Hooly Wummen (Bokenham), 34
Leicester, H. Marshall, Jr., 104, 160, 162,
  237n.23
Lewis, Katherine, 50, 74
The Life of Saint Katherine (Capgrave), 37;
  agency in, 61–62, 64, 66; images/idols in,
  61–66; on the Katherine wheel, 14–15,
  59–60, 61, 63, 66; length of, 34, 64; on
  Maxentius's dispute with Katherine over
  idols, 36, 63–65; on vivacity of matter, 65;
  on witchcraft accusations, 44
Limbourg brothers, 82
Lister, Jack, 89, 90, 91–92
literacy, access to, 158–59. *See also* vernacular

Little Hours of the Virgin, 169
Little Office of the Blessed Virgin Mary, 169
Livre de Griseldis, 129, 147, 241n.23
Livre de la vertu du sacrament de marriage
  (Mézières), 136
Lollard Knights, 98
Lollards: allegory in texts of, 75; attacks on
  devotional images, 7–8, 9, 12, 19, 22, 25–
  26, 31–32, 46 (see also *Chronicle*; *and other
  specific texts*); Chaucer influenced by, 111–
  12, 116, 128–29; on Despenser, 234n.35; as
  heretics, 13, 159, 172–73; vs. Hilton, 54,
  229nn.56–57; iconmachy identified with,
  38, 42; iconophobia among, 42, 63;
  Love's *Mirror* on, 173, 175–76, 182,
  251n.16; manuscript illumination
  impoverished by, 12–13; outlawing of
  Lollard schools, 159; on plays, 174–75;
  scriptural translation by, 158–59; "stocks
  and stones" phrase used by, 107;
  suppression of, 13; on the Trinity, 176,
  211; Twelve Conclusions, 20, 138, 174,
  211, 222n.47
London, 165–67
Long Melford church. *See* Holy Trinity
  Church
Louis, Saint, 132
love, 108–9, 110
Love, Nicholas. *See The Mirror of the Blessed
  Life of Jesus Christ*
Lovell Lectionary, 166, *167*
luminous darkness, 53
Lupton, Julia, 45, 68
Luttrell Psalter, 82
Lydgate, John, 107; *The Pilgrimage of the
  Life of Man*, 9–11, *10–11*
Lynch, Kathryn, 112, 134, 165
Lynn, 90, 193, 196, 202
Lynn priory, 194, 253n.7
Lytlington missal, 180

Machaut, Guillaume de, 115; *Voir Dit*,
  95–98, *96*, 108
Maidstone, Richard, 135–36
Mandeville's Travels, 165, 174
Mann, Jill, 148
Man of Law's Tale (Chaucer), 43
Man of Sorrows, 16, 203–8, *204, 206*, 215–16,
  217, 256nn.35–36, 257n.39, 257n.42,
  257n.44

manuscript illumination, *10–11*, 11, 12–13, 93, 196

manuscript paintings, 180

Margaret, Saint, 47, 48, *49*, 68

marguerite poems, 115

Marks, Richard, 3, 5, 28, 197, 254–55nn.22–23

marriage: contractual arrangements of, 137–38; as public sign vs. private sacrament, 136–37, 150–51; sanctity of, 137, 138–39; as a yoke, 144

Mars, 102, 105

Martin, Geoffrey, 227n.22

Martin, Roger, 100, 255–56n.29

Martindale, Andrew, 77, 231–32n.3

martyrdom: in Chaucer's *Prioress's Tale*, 155, 156, 171; of Jews, 161; of St. Katherine, 36, 39, 41, 45, 135–36. *See also* virgin martyrs

Marx, Karl, 18, 119–20

Mary Magdelene, Saint, 68

Mary of Lincoln, Saint, 43–44, 46, 47

Mary of Walsingham, Saint, 43–44, 46, 47

Mass: elevation of eucharistic body of Christ during, 133; elevation of host during, 134; familiarity of, 169; for the Holy Innocents, 169, 249n.51; images of, 85, *86–87*; spectacles of suffering in, 127

materiality: and devotional images, 14, 26, 30, 31, 37, 47; of relics, and resurrection, 231n.81

Matthew 2:18, 249n.51

Matthew 26:8, 83

Maxentius, Emperor, 35–36, 38, 39, 40, *69*

McClintock, Anne, 23

McSheffrey, Shannon, 137

meditation, 172, 251n.23

Meditationes Vitae Christi (Caulibus), 172, 175–79, 182, 249n.1, 251n.21, 251n.23

Mellinkoff, Ruth, 83, 85, 88

The Merchant's Tale (Chaucer), 121, 137

The Merchant's Tale of Beryn, 122, 138, 239n.2

"merk ymage." See *Scale of Perfection*

Metcalfe, W. M., 227n.32

Methley, Richard, 189

Mézières, Philippe de, *Livre de la vertu du sacrament de marriage*, 136

Middle Ages vs. modernity, periodization of, 225n.97

Middleton, Anne, 244n.58

The Miller's Tale (Chaucer), 101

Minnis, A. J., 237n.31

miracle plays, 174–75

Mirk, John, *Instructions for Parish Priests*, 132

The Mirror of the Blessed Life of Jesus Christ (Love), 6, 172–90; on the annunciation, 178; audience for, 173, 176–77, 179–84; and *The Book of Margery Kempe*, 193, 215–16, 218; on Christ's incarnation, 183, 252n.33; on Christ's life in action, 16, 172, 177–82, 215, 251n.21, 251n.23; community orchestrated by, 182–90; in context of debate over image worship, 172–73; devotional images legitimized by, 179–82; devout posture in, 181; on the Eucharist, 182, 183, 187; ideal gaze in, 16, 181; on images, 175–76, 187, 189–90; influence of, 179–80; on the Last Supper, 179; on the Lollards, 173, 175–76, 182, 251n.16; on Lollardy, 16; mirror metaphor in, 187; on the Passion, 178, 184, 188; Passion scene in, 135; popularity of, 172, 188; public witnessing/veneration in, 132; on sacramental miracles, 186–87; sources for, 172, 175–76, 251n.21; survival of, 249–50n.1; textual dissolve in, 177–78, 251n.27; vs. *Tretise on Miraclis Pleyinge*, 174–75; on the Trinity, 175–76, 189; vocative used in, 178, 187–88; "ymaginacion"/"ymagining" (visual imagining) in, 172, 173, 177, 189–90

monasteries vs. nunneries, 256n.30

moneylending, 166

monstrosity, 233n.33

Montagu, Sir John, 50, 98–99

Morgan, Nigel, 214, 254n.17

Morieux, Sir Thomas, 78, 232n.13

Morley, Thomas de, 89–90, 92

Mount Grace (Yorkshire), 189, 215

mouths, 244n.3

Mueller, Janel, 229n.56

Muslims, 163, 164

Mylde, Catherine, 198

mystical discourse and political/theological debates, 13

naked text. *See* vernacular

naves, 5, 202, 256n.30

Netter, Thomas, 177

Nicodemus, 185

Nolan, Barbara, 247n.29

nominalism, 134

Norfolk, 91, 218
Norton, John, 189
Norwich, 90, 193, 257–58n.52
Norwich Cathedral, 3, 4, 79, 94, 232–33n.17.
    See also Despenser Retable
Notre Dame, 154
Nottinghamshire, 28
nunneries vs. monasteries, 256n.30

Ocle, Robert, 232n.7
O'Connell, Michael, 2
ocular communion, 188
optics, 6, 109, 220n.13
Opus arduum, 234n.35
orate pro (pray for) inscription, 29, 30–31, 71,
    218
outsiders, 229n.58

Panofsky, Erwin, 50, 233n.22
The Pardoner's Tale (Chaucer), 15, 16, 98,
    117–21, 128–29
parishes, 16, 17, 180, 192, 258n.69. See also
    specific churches
parsons' responsibilities, 256n.30
Passion: binding of Christ by his torturers,
    170; and class, 88; Love's Mirror on, 178,
    184, 188; Mary's swoon in scenes of, 169;
    physiognomic/raciaized difference in
    iconography of, 83, 84; and visual desire,
    6, 7; in wall paintings, 180
patronage, 181, 191–93, 196–97, 197. See also
    donor images; women, as patrons
Patterson, Lee, 104, 118, 161, 162, 237n.23
Paul, Saint, 74
Pearl, 6
Pearsall, Derek, 97, 150
peasants, representations of, 81, 82
Peasants' Revolt (1381), 78, 82, 89–93, 158,
    232n.13, 235n.52
Pecock, Reginald, 26, 34–35, 177; Repressor of
    Over Much Blaming of the Clergy, 63
pedagogy, literal sense vs. symbolic
    interpretation in, 157
periodization, historical, 31, 225n.97
Peter, Saint, 74
Petites Heures (Berry), 83
Petrarch: Chaucer's Clerk's Tale on, 141,
    142, 144–46, 148–51; Griselda story of,
    129, 131, 136, 139, 147, 241n.23, 242–
    43nn.46–48

philanthropy, 28–29
Phillips, Helen, 111, 114
The Physician's Tale (Chaucer), 99
Pierce the Plowman's Crede, 24–25, 30–31, 181
Piers Plowman (Langland), 25, 30, 100, 136
pietà, 203–4
piety: in Chaucer's Clerk's Tale, 125–27, 150;
    in Chaucer's Prioress's Tale, 155–62, 171,
    246n.21; contemporary discourses on,
    128; emotional, 189; vernacular, 155–62,
    171, 181. See also affective piety
Pietz, William, 18, 22–23, 31, 225n.97
Pilate, 81, 83
A Pilgrimage for Religion's Sake (Erasmus),
    123–24
The Pilgrimage of the Life of Man (Lydgate),
    9–11, 10–11
pilgrimages: to Canterbury, 122–24, 132–33;
    as idolatry, 7; signs of sacred bodies
    during, 134. See also The Canterbury
    Interlude
"pite," meanings of, 161–62
Play of the Sacrament (Croxton), 140, 163,
    243n.50
poll tax, 91
pollution taboos, 153, 162
Porphyry, 36
portraiture, 95–97, 96, 101, 236n.4
Prague, 165–67, 248n.39
Prayer Book of Humphrey Duke of Gloucester,
    205, 206
Prayer Book of James IV, 255n.28
prayers, posthumous, 47–48
The Prioress's Tale (Chaucer), 153–71; abbot's
    role in child's death in, 153–55, 169; "Alma
    Redemptoris" in, 156–57, 159, 160, 162,
    171, 246n.21; anti-Semitism of, 160, 161,
    162, 246n.22; bodily violation in, 153–55;
    children vs. adult communities in, 168,
    249n.48; vs. The Clerk's Tale, 156; and
    contemporary discourses on piety, 128;
    critiques of, 160–61, 168, 249n.48; dating
    of, 159; ethnic communities/geographic
    proximities in, 163–65, 247n.34, 248n.39;
    fetish of the Jew's body in, 163; gaze in,
    156; Jews' role in child's death in, 155, 157,
    159, 160, 169; Litel Clergeon in, 45; Litel
    Clergeon's tongue in, 153–54; liturgical
    drama of, 169–71; martyrdom in, 155, 156,
    171; narrator in, 125; opening of, 163–64,

166, 167, 168; overview of, 15; pathos in, 171; pilgrimage in, 168, 171; pious language in, 126–27; "pite" in, 161–62; Prague as locale for, 165–68, 248n.38; and private will vs. public spectacle, 15, 125; as protest against institutions, 160, 162; sacramental ritual in, 125–26, 129; sources for, 169, 249n.51; translation/ interpretation/linguistic transparency in, 157–58, 159–60, 245n.9, 245n.16; typological patterns in, 155; vernacular piety in, 155–62, 171; violence vs. piety in, 160–61, 162, 246n.21; vivacity vs. sanctity in, 155–56
Protestants' feminization/sexualization of saints' images, 42
Psalm 8:2–3, 169
Psalm 38, 154
Psalm 115, 26
Pseudo-Dionysius, 53
purgatory, 48
purity vs. pollution, 162

Quennell, C. H. B., 231n.1

race: in the Despenser Retable, 81, 88; in flagellation scenes, 83, 84; as otherness, 88; physiognomy/skin color, as markers of, 88, 233–34n.33; and pollution vs. purity, 162
Rambuss, Richard, 245n.16
Ramsay, Nigel, 219n.2
reason and faith, 161
Regiment of Princes (Hoccleve), 97
Reims, 154
relics: in Chaucer's Pardoner's Tale, 117–21, 128–29; and devotional images, 20, 222n.47; and the Eucharist, 132; false, as illustrating ecclesiastical corruption, 16; false, proliferation of, 120; idolatry of worshiping, 117–18; materiality of, and resurrection, 231n.81; and pardons, sale of, 238n.47; pilgrims' encounter with, at Canterbury, 122–24, 132–33; and sanctified body, 135; Wyclif on, 117
Repressor of Over Much Blaming of the Clergy (Pecock), 63
rhetoric manuals, 103
Richard II, king of England, 91, 135–36, 166, 234n.35

Richmond, Colin, 226n.14
Ridley, Florence, 246n.22
Ringland, 214
Robertson, Elizabeth, 160, 249n.48
rood screens, 29–30, 224n.86, 256n.30
Rosenthal, Joel, 28–29
Ross, Ellen, 251n.30
Royal Injunctions (1538), 3
Rubin, Miri, 166, 220n.14

sacramental kiss, 20
sacramental theater, 127
sacrum signum, 134
La Sainte Abbaye, 251n.23
saints: attributes/signs of, 68, 69–70, 70–71, 72–73, 74–75; images of, 3, 5, 9, 14, 21–24, 28, 113. See also specific saints
Saints Felix, Regula, and Exuperantius Broken on the Wheel, 60
Sale, Sir Robert, 92
Salisbury chapter house, 253n.8
Salter, Elizabeth, 130, 138–39
Santa Croce mosaic (Gerusalemme, Rome), 205, 256n.36
Sargent, Michael, 175, 186
Sarum rite, 249n.51
Scale of Perfection (Hilton): boundaries in, 55; Cloud of Unknowing's influence on, 53, 54, 228n.50, 230n.61; dating of, 54; female audience for, 55; imago dei in, 53; influence/ popularity of, 53; "merk ymage" (dark image) in, 8, 36–37, 52–58, 230n.61; "nought" in, 55–56; popularity of, 37; sources for, 53–54; "ymage" as self-love in, 54
Scott, Kathleen, 12–13
Scott, Ridley, 55
screens, 5. See also rood screens
sculpture, English, 181
The Second Nun's Tale (Chaucer), 99, 107
seeing. See gaze; visual desire
self-commemoration, 29–31. See also images, devotional, donor
self-exhibition, impulse toward, 195–96
self-portraiture, 193
Seven Sacraments Font (Norwich Cathedral), 3, 4
Severs, J. Burke, 240–41n.18, 242–43nn.46–47
Sheehan, Michael, 137

Sherborne missal, 180

The Shewings of Julian of Norwich (Julian of Norwich), 6, 99–100

Shoeck, R. J., 160

Simpson, James, 13, 63, 177, 251n.16, 251n.27

sin, 52–53, 55–56, 57

Sklute, Larry, 239n.6

slavery, 225n.97

Smith, William, 33, 38–43, 47, 50, 52, 159

Snoek, G. J. C., 132, 133, 170

Snowden, Frank M., Jr., 233–34n.33

soap, 23

Society of the Spectacle (Debord), 5

Somerset, Fiona, 98, 116

South English Legendary, 34, 61, 131, 227–28n.32

spaces, in churches, 13–14, 17

Spaldyng, Richard, 34

species, 6

spectacle, 5, 15, 125

Spierenburg, Pieter, 230n.69

The Squire's Tale (Chaucer), 101, 105

stained glass, devotional, 180, 181, 197–98, 254–55nn.22–23

Staley, Lynn, 13, 90–91, 129, 136, 240n.10, 258n.55

Stanley, Arthur, 132

St. Anne chantry chapel (St. Peter and St. Paul, East Harling), 197

St. Chapelle (Paris), 6–7

St. Cuthbert's Shrine (Durham Cathedral), 132

St. John hospital chapel (Leicester), 33, 225n.2

St. Margaret's Church (Lynn), 194, 196, 200, 201, 202, 218

St. Nicholas's Church, 218, 257n.47

stockfish, 207, 257n.47

Stoller, Robert, 74

St. Peter and St. Paul's Church (East Harling), 196–97

St. Stephen's Church (Norwich), 194

Strohm, Paul, 22, 98

Suffolk, 218

symbols, disguised, 50

Symonds, Joanna, 232n.3

Talbot, Elizabeth, 198, *199*

Tale of Saint Cecilia (Chaucer), 15, 125

Tavormina, Teresa, 136

Taylor, Andrew, 136, 242n.34

Ten Commandment commentaries, 8–9

Teresa of Avila, Saint, 254n.14

thing theory, 30

Thomas, Alfred, 165

Thomas, Saint, 122, 239n.2

Thorpe, William, 21, 172–73

Throne of Mercy, 203, 211, *212*

Thurgarton Priory, 229n.55

Tilney, Elizabeth, 198, *199*

Tomasch, Sylvia, 162, 246n.22

tongues, 154, 244n.3

touch, pleasure of, 68

Toute Bele image. See *Voir Dit*

translation: meanings of, 131–32, 170; politicization of, 158 (*see also* vernacular); Wyclif's association with, 142–43

transubstantiation, 22, 41, 98, 186. *See also* Eucharist

Travis, Peter, 115

Très Riches Heures, 82

Tretise on Miraclis Pleyinge, 174–75

"Tretyse of Ymagis," 19–20, 23–24, 25–26, 29, 75, 174

Trinity: alabaster carvings of, 176, 211, *212*; with donors, 211, *213*; images of, 5, 28; literalizations of, 176; Love's *Mirror* on, 175–76, 189; name dropping in images of, 211–12, 214; St. Katherine's defense of, 44–45; Throne of Mercy, 203, 211, *212*; types of images of, *210*, 210–11; Wyclif on, 176, 211

Troilus and Criseyde (Chaucer), 98, 101, 106–10, 111, 116, 237n.31

Tuck, A. J., 90

Tudor-Craig, Pamela, 77, 79, 83

Tunnoc, Richard, 197–98

Twelve Conclusions, 20, 138, 174, 211, 222n.47

Tyler's Rebellion. *See* Peasants' Revolt

Urban VI, Pope, 234n.35

usury, 164–65, 166, 167–68, 171

value: cult, 79–80; exhibition, 79–80; relative, 22–23, 31, 223n.58

Venus, 102–4, 120–21, 237n.23

vernacular: Bible translated into, 112, 158–59, 173; in Chaucer, 112, 116, 142–43; and the politics of translating, 158; uses of, 13, 43, 111

vernacular piety, 181
veronicas, 118
viewing communities, 182
virgin martyrs: Mass for, 169, 249n.51;
    misogyny/idolatry in lives of, 36, 40; and
    sexual deviance of idols, 57
Virgin Mary, 28, 135–36, 178–79
vision, 6–7, 13–14, 220n.13
visions, 193–94, 195, 198, 208–12, 214–15
visual desire, 6–7, 220n.13
visual rays, 6, 109, 188
visual theophany, 127, 131, 133, 138
Vodoklys, Edward, 227nn.22–23
Voir Dit (Machaut), 95–98, 96, 108
voluntary insubordination, 48
Vox Clamantis (Gower), 99

Walker, John, 214
Wallace, David, 131, 142–45
wall paintings, devotional, 180–81, 251n.30
Walsingham, Thomas, 50, 90, 91–92, 98
Walsoken, Adam de, 196
Watson, Nicholas, 13, 38, 54, 173, 228n.50,
    229n.57, 230n.61
Waytestathe, Richard, 33, 38, 39, 40, 41–43,
    47, 159
Wenceslas IV, king of Bohemia, 166, 167
Westminster Chronicle, 82, 136
wheel (punishment device), 60–61, 230n.70.
    See also Katherine wheel
White, William, 117–18
William of Worcester, 189
William of York, Saint, 132, 197–98
Willis, Professor, 231n.1
wills, gifts in, 47–48
Winstead, Karen, 44, 50, 63

witnessing, 6, 102–3, 132
women: cloistered, 255n.28; devotional
    practices of, 195, 254n.14; images owned
    by, 201–2, 255n.28; as mystics, 254n.14
    (see also The Book of Margery Kempe);
    as patrons, 192, 196–97, 198 (see also
    The Book of Margery Kempe); public
    endowments of, 192; public roles for,
    191–92; worshipped as idols, 101. See also
    virgin martyrs
Woodford, William, 220n.15
Woodforde, Christopher, 196, 204–5
wool trade, 26
Wrong, George M., 234n.38
Wyatt, Digby, 77, 78, 79, 232n.6
Wyclif, John: on clerical corruption/
    absolutism, 128; on the Eucharist, 128–29;
    on idolatry, 57; on image burning, 30;
    outlawing of writings by, 13, 38, 159; on
    relics, 117; role in Peasants' Revolt, 93;
    translating associated with, 142–43; on
    transubstantiation, 98; on the Trinity,
    176, 211; on uses of devotional images,
    7–8
Wycliffites. See Lollards

York, 193
York, Edward Langley, duke of, 114–15
York church, 197, 254–55nn.22–23
York Minster, 71, 72

Ziegler, J. E., 255n.28
Zika, Charles, 127, 133
Žižek, Slavoj: on desire, 168; on images as
    sublime objects of ideology, 12; on Jewish
    stereotypes, 162–63; on outsiders, 229n.59

Acknowledgments

If this book can be said to have a founding moment, it would be in a research trip I took with my colleague Virginia Raguin to East Anglia to photograph the material world of Margery Kempe. We were recording the furnishings of fifteenth-century parishes in an effort to document the visual culture of those churches as a woman of Kempe's time would have known it. I owe Virginia very special thanks for friendship and collegiality as well as for wonderful photographs, reproduced in this book, which she took on that trip.

I have incurred many debts of gratitude for help on this project along the way. Thanks are due to C. David Benson, Theresa Coletti, Jim Kee, Kathryn Lynch, Virginia Raguin, Lynn Staley, and Nicholas Watson, who read parts of the book and offered astute advice. Thanks are due as well to the College of the Holy Cross for generous support for travel and research leave that made it possible to finish the book. An O'Leary Faculty Recognition Award, which came at a particularly timely moment, helped defray costs of photo permissions. Help also appeared when needed from other quarters—from Jesse Anderson with assistance on digital images, from Holy Cross student Kyle Koerber with his eye for careful fact checking, and from student Katie Derrig for her translation of a fourteenth-century treatise on devotional images. I am especially grateful to Ruth Mazo Karras and Jerry Singerman at the University of Pennsylvania Press for shepherding this project and also, in more general ways, for their leadership and vision as editors of medieval scholarship.

Parts of this book have appeared in previous publications, and I gratefully acknowledge permission to reprint. Parts of Chapter 1 appeared in *Images, Idolatry, and Iconoclasm*, edited by Jeremy Dimmick, James Simpson, and Nicolette Zeeman (Oxford: Oxford University Press, 2002); parts of Chapter 3 appeared in *A Companion to Chaucer*, edited by Peter Brown (London: Blackwell, 2000); and a version of Chapter 7 appeared in *Women's Space: Patronage, Place, and Gender in the Medieval Church*, edited by Virginia Chieffo Raguin and Sarah Stanbury (Binghamton: SUNY, 2005).